Critics and historians have interpreted the closure of the theatres in 1642 as the end of drama and theatre in England until the return of Charles II in 1660. *Drama and Politics* challenges this assumption. Arguing against the critical perception of this period as a gap between the two 'national' dramas of the Renaissance and Restoration it focusses on the generic diversity produced in the period in question – polemical pamphlets, news dramas, operas, civic shows, tragicomedies. These plays and playlets were produced by writers of different political perspectives; drama was not, as has been assumed, solely the property of royalists. In analysing the drama produced by unknown writers and well-known writers such as Margaret Cavendish, William Davenant and James Shirley, this book aims to reinterpret the dramatic evidence from the 1640s and 1650s to make one argument about plays and politics framed by another about literary history.

DRAMA AND POLITICS IN
THE ENGLISH CIVIL WAR

DRAMA AND POLITICS IN THE ENGLISH CIVIL WAR

SUSAN WISEMAN

CAMBRIDGE
UNIVERSITY PRESS

PUBLISHED BY THE PRESS SYNDICATE OF THE UNIVERSITY OF CAMBRIDGE
The Pitt Building, Trumpington Street, Cambridge CB2 1RP, United Kingdom

CAMBRIDGE UNIVERSITY PRESS
The Edinburgh Building, Cambridge CB2 2RU, United Kingdom
40 West 20th Street, New York, NY 10011–4211, USA
10 Stamford Road, Oakleigh, Melbourne 3166, Australia

First published 1998

Printed in the United Kingdom at the University Press, Cambridge

Typeset in New Baskerville 11/12½ pt   [SE]

A catalogue record for this book is available from the British Library

Library of Congress cataloguing in publication data
Wiseman, Susan
Drama and Politics in the English Civil War / Susan Wiseman
p.   cm.
Includes bibliographical references and index.
ISBN 0 521 47221 0 (hardback)
1. English drama – 17th century – History and criticism.   2. Great
Britain – History – Puritan Revolution, 1642–1660 – Literature and the
Revolution.   3. Great Britain – History – Civil War, 1642–1649
– Literature and the war.   4. Politics and literature – Great Britain –
Britain – History – 17th century.   6. Political plays, English-
History and criticism.   7. Literary Form.   I. Title.
PR680.W57   1988
822'.409358–dc21   97-6745 CIP

ISBN 0 521 47221 0 hardback

For my parents, Jeanne and Jack Wiseman

To the Reader

*I shall only say . . . I wish it you upon better terms than
Twenty Years Banishment.*

Thomas Killigrew, Comedies and Tragedies *(1664)*

Contents

ix

Illustrations

A note on texts

Twentieth-century editions are used where available. Seventeenth-century spelling and punctuation is retained except when quoting from a modern edition. Errors in the printing process are signalled.

Issues of attribution not discussed in the text are usually signalled in the bibliography.

The year is assumed to change in January rather than in March, but old-style dating is retained.

Abbreviations
CE   *Cahiers Elisabethains*
CSP   *Calendar of State Papers*
EHR   *English Historical Review*
ELH   *English Literary History*
ELR   *English Literary Renaissance*
HMC   *Historical Manuscript Commission*
MP   *Modern Philology*
NLH   *New Literary History*
NQ   *Notes and Queries*
NTQ   *New Theatre Quarterly*
PMLA   *Papers of the Modern Language Association*
PP   *Past and Present*
PRO   Public Record Office
SP   *Studies in Philology*
SR   *The Siege of Rhodes*
Thomason Thomason Tracts
TLS   *Times Literary Supplement*

Acknowledgements

I have incurred many debts in writing this book. The Society for Theatre Research made a grant in aid of research, for which I am grateful. Caroline Dickinson sponsored the start of the project, as did Jeanne and Jack Wiseman.

I must thank the staff of the British Library, especially the staff of the North Library desk on whose generosity, patience and sense of humour I have relied throughout. I must also thank the university libraries of Exeter, Canterbury Christchurch (New Zealand), Kent at Canterbury, London (Birkbeck and Senate House), Sheffield, Warwick; the Bodleian Library, the library of Worcester College, Oxford (particularly Lesley LeClaire); the Brotherton Library, Leeds; Folger Shakespeare Library. For permission to reprint part of chapter 4 I thank B. T. Batsford, and I am grateful to Cambridge University Press for permission to reprint a small part of chapter 6.

Versions of this study were read by the following: Tim Armstrong, Martin Butler, Warren Chernaik, David Norbrook, (who also shared research), Lois Potter, and an anonymous reader. Smaller sections were read by Erica Fudge, Isobel Grundy, Helen Hackett, Tom Healy, James Holstun, Derek Hughes, Tim Langley, Julie Sanders. I am very grateful indeed for their help but they are not responsible for the errors which remain. David Bond more than generously shared his research, as did Sarah Barber, Jonathan Barry, Janet Clare, Jonathan Rogers, Sophie Tomlinson and Nigel Smith. Bridget Bennett, Nicola Bowne, Claire Buck, Jane Collier, John Dodgson, Rod Edmond, Lyn Innes, Annie Janowitz, Kate Lilley, Jan Montefiore, Michelle O'Callahan, Barbara Rosenbaum, Jonathan Sawday, Catherine Sharrock, Erica Sheen, the late Mark Thirkell all helped greatly, in different ways. I am grateful, too, to fellow participants in the library and London

Renaissance Seminar including Margaret Healy, Alan Stewart, Alison Thorne. At Cambridge University Press Margaret Berrill and Teresa Sheppard were both in different ways meticulous and kind. Victoria Cooper was generous with time and advice, and Sarah Stanton was patient.

However, without Tim Armstrong it would never have been finished. No thanks are adequate.

Preface

Why do almost all the books on 'Renaissance drama' stop in 1642 with the comment that at this point 'the Puritans closed the theatres', and why do nearly all books on 'Restoration drama' open in 1660, when 'Charles II set up two new theatre companies'? That is the question I began with.

What follows is a response, rather than an answer, to that question. It takes the form of three interdependent arguments. One argument is that the critical construction of the Civil War as a dramatic lacuna is both inaccurate and serves specific accounts of cultural value. The second argument is that when read in relationship to the particular circumstances of its production the drama of 1642–60 – still, despite some recent scholarly attention, off all cultural maps – is generically diverse and enunciates equally diverse political positions. In analysing this drama it is necessary to enlarge rather than restrict our understanding of what constitutes a dramatic text. Thirdly, therefore, this study challenges some understandings of the relationship between dramatic culture and politics in the period. Assumptions that drama in the period was solely royalist, coterie or 'closet' remain influential despite extensive critical re-readings of the 1640s (by Butler, Norbrook, Smith, Zwicker and others) and the introduction examines traditions which generated and maintain these ideas.

Even as it argues for changes in the status of the 'key' dates of 1642 and 1660 this study works largely within this traditional periodisation. It does so in order to offer a detailed analytical account of the dynamic relationships between dramatic genres and politics in the Civil Wars, tracing patterns of cultural, generic and political transformation as the issues and genres of the 1640s give way to those of the Protectorate and Restoration. It is not a taxonomy or survey, but investigates specific discursive contexts.[1] The first part examines the pamphlet drama of the 1640s, including the use of drama in radical discourses. The second part proposes a recontextualisation of the dramatic productions of the 1650s including London shows, the uses of opera by James Shirley, Sir William Davenant and Richard Flecknoe; and the plays of Margaret Cavendish.

How did the Civil War and Protectorate come to be understood as simply a gap in theatrical and dramatic history? The introduction that follows offers an account of the critical, historical and historiographical interests which have shaped the imagined place – or absence – of drama in the English Civil War. It situates the drama in critical context by offering an archaeology of dominant attitudes and assumptions which continue to shape scholarly responses to these texts. In doing so it examines the literary and historical understandings of the period and the question of censorship, starting with a discussion of the edict that closed the theatres in 1642.

Introduction: how the drama disappeared

'STAGE PLAYES' AND 1642

Whereas the distress and Estate of Ireland, steeped in her own Blood, and the distracted Estate of England, threatened with a Cloud of Blood by a Civill War, call for all possible Means to appease and avert the Wrath of God, appearing in these Judgements; among which, Fasting and Prayer have been tried to be very effectual . . . and are still enjoyned; and whereas Publike Sports do not well agree with Publike Calamities, nor Publike Stage-plays with the Seasons of Humiliation, this being an Exercise of sad and pious solemnity, and the other being Spectacles of Pleasure, too commonly expressing lascivious Mirth, and Levitie it is therefore thought fit, and Ordained, by the Lords and Commons in this Parliament Assembled, that while these sad Causes and set times of Humiliation doe continue, publike Stage-playes shall cease and be forborne, instead of which are recommended to the People of this land the profitable and seasonable considerations of Repentance, Reconciliation and Peace with God, which probably may produce outward Peace and Prosperity, and bring again Times of Joy and Gladness to these Nations.[1]

This is the order which closed the playhouses on 2 September 1642. In an investigation of the relationship between drama and its political situations during the period 1642–1660, when the London theatres were – for the most part – closed, much depends on how we decide to interpret this document.

In the complex cultural history of British theatre this text is taken to mark the end of a period considered to be Renaissance drama.[2] It is usually found serving the purposes of periodicity in theatre history, which characterises 1642 to 1660 as a gap between two 'national' dramas.[3] Often in studies of Renaissance and Restoration drama and theatre it *replaces* discussion of the period, standing by synecdoche for eighteen years of largely unacknowledged and uninvestigated but immensely diverse dramatic, and some theatrical, activity. Habitually, it is used to remind scholars,

1

students and general readers that the drama of the Civil War is not
worthy of study or, as Alfred Harbage put it in his analysis of 'cavalier' drama, it is 'a body of literature which Time has justly sub-
merged'.[4]

The interdisciplinary critical revisions which have reconfigured
the canon of mid-seventeenth-century poetry and prose have, until
relatively recently, eschewed engagement with the drama of the
1640s and 1650s, and the text which closed the theatres continues
to have a ready-made meaning in cultural history: it signals the
inauguration of a gap. Nevertheless, as I shall suggest, the idea of
the eighteen empty years is invented and maintained by a particular reading of literary history and dramatic genre.

The very language of the ordinance makes it surprising that it
has been allowed to stand in place of much investigation of the discursive developments of the theatre from 1642 to 1660. The
wording makes clear that the context of the closure is immediate,
urgent, and political as well as spiritual. It emphasises that
appropriate manners at a time when the country was sliding into
Civil War – indeed when war had just begun – could not include
'Publike Sports', nor 'lascivious Mirth': as an emergency measure,
it strikes the note of moral reform, but additionally suggests a time
of political crisis (the theatres were closed on 2 September and on
9 September Essex set off to join the parliamentary army). It calls
for stage plays to be 'forborne' because of the 'sad Causes', but in
its mode of address it assumes in its readers a corresponding sense
of urgency and apprehension of the danger of the times. The producers of theatre but also the London 'public' in the very guise the
authorities found most unruly – the theatre-going crowd – are
'enjoyned' that plays should be 'forborne' in a turning to prayer
which might, ultimately, produce not only private but 'outward'
peace and prosperity.[5]

The order of 1642 is unusual among the edicts against the stage
throughout the 1640s. The order of the House of Lords of 16
October 1647 contrastingly emphasises suppression and punishment, giving the sheriffs and justices of Westminster, London,
Surrey and Middlesex jurisdiction to arrest anyone proved 'to have
acted or played in such Playhouses or Places abovesaid; and all
Person and Persons so offending to commit to any common Gaol
or Prison; there to remain until the next General Sessions of the
Peace . . . there to be punished as Rogues, according to law'.[6] This

demonstrates the imbrication of theatre in shifting political contexts. The earlier order presents the ban on theatre as a rapid
response to a dangerous situation, rather than the fruition of a
long parliamentary campaign against the theatres, as the latter
appears to be.

Indeed, London in 1641–2 was in political turmoil in and out of
parliament. As Anthony Fletcher tells us, after the Irish rising
began in 1641 the coastal areas of England were rife with rumours
of invasion.[7] Christmas of 1641 was punctuated by riots in
Whitehall and the breakdown of links between the king and
London. Scurrilous political polemic was constantly printed, and
both episcopacy and Ireland were topics of pamphlet controversy.
On 10 January, after his attempt to impeach the five members of
the Commons, the king left London – but the five members
returned amid celebrations in the City and Westminster. The City
was claiming political rights and a political voice, and so was the
grouping around Pym in parliament. Escalating demands led to
Sir John Hotham taking control of the garrison at Hull. All may
have hoped for peace, but there was clearly an atmosphere of crisis
and a political agitation which existed in the Commons and Lords
and also in private houses, in public gatherings such as the theatre
and, as the demonstrations prove, in the streets. The timing of the
edict suppressing playhouses reinforces the sense of public dis-
turbances echoing parliamentary crisis. Placed at the intersection
of print and the cultural sphere of political discussion and the
activities of the Commons, its emphasis on the need to fast and
pray suggests common cause and feeling between public and parliament even as parliament attempts to regulate the demonstration of such feelings.[8]

As a locus for the articulation of popular issues the theatre of the
1630s and the early 1640s, though it contrasts with that of the
1620s, is far from evidencing the 'decline' claimed by some critics.
Several incidents suggest that theatrical production and governmental responses to it were part of a larger pattern of social, political and religious conflict and controversy. In May 1639 a play
called *The Cardinall's Conspiracie* played at the Fortune, satirising
the bishops and church ritual, and a news report tells of the arrest
of the actors.[9] Martin Butler's suggestion that throughout 1641–2
short scurrilous afterpieces may have been acted is borne out by
these incidents and by the survival of many short satires on the

episcopate such as *Canterbury His Change of Diot, The Bishops Potion* and *Lambeth Fair*, which might be by Richard Overton.[10] In another incident in 1639 the players at the Red Bull had been reprimanded for slurs on aldermen and attacking proctors.[11] And William Davenant had been put in charge of the Cockpit (or Phoenix) when William Beeston was removed after one of the productions had glanced at the king's journey into Scotland.[12] The policing of political satire in the theatres suggests that drama and theatre participated in constructing a popular political discourse.[13]

Seen in the context of the interaction of City and Commons at a particular moment, the document closing the theatres seems to be in part an attempt to suppress controversy but also an appeal to public support in a time of crisis rather than a faction enforcing 'Puritan' measures against the stage.[14] Just as the ultimatum constituted by the *Nineteen Propositions* in June and Henry Parker's theorisation of parliamentary sovereignty, *Observations Upon Some of His Majesties Late Answers and Expresses* in July appealed to a sense of the political power of parliament, so the document closing the theatres suggests the vital interrelationship of City and Commons at this moment.[15]

The ideological impetus which asserts the propriety of praying rather than playing in September 1642 is evidently part of a programme which involves the reform of values, as David Underdown has admirably shown in his study of county loyalties in the Civil War.[16] However, the text does not suggest that at this point the closure of the theatres was a primary objective in the pursuit of such a policy: it appears to be contingent 'while these sad Causes and set times of Humiliation doe continue' and to an extent local in being addressed to London's institutionalised playhouses. At a time when, Fletcher tells us, it would be hard for contemporaries to imagine a war which would last for four years, can we think that anyone would have anticipated that these playhouses would be mostly closed for eighteen?

However, once the playhouses were closed the function of the edict against stage plays seems to have changed, and strictures against the stage recur at moments of political crisis throughout the Civil War and Commonwealth. The order which banned the theatre inevitably simultaneously foregrounded the role of theatre and drama as participating in constructing popular political debate. As the studies which follow this introduction demonstrate, the closure of the theatres served to intensify the politicised status of dramatic discourse: Civil War drama was sharply aware of its politicisation as a genre and of a political readership.

Government intervention offers evidence of repeated attempts to forestall institutional theatrical production throughout the 1640s, and the nature of the strictures can be seen to change in response to circumstances. Dramatic performances continued – as at the Oxford court's Christmas in 1643 and in regiments.[17] There were raids on playhouses, like those recorded in October 1643 and April 1645. Theatre became a central metaphor for vying political regimes; metaphors of tragedy and play-acting were two of the dominant ways in which contemporaries spoke of the war.[18] While the satirical plays which Butler thinks were staged in the early 1640s implied popular support for Pym's anti-episcopal policies and criticism of the king's advisers, the measures again suppressing plays in 1647, 1648 and the attacks on players in 1649 all suggest that the government both continued to fear large gatherings and (as the popularity of successive governments waned) anticipated that such plays might well now satirise themselves. As soon as each order for closure expired, playing began again.[19]

This evidence suggests, then, that the edict of 1642 *turned into* a campaign as the wars went on. Thus, after complaints to parliament in October 1647 measures were taken to prosecute offending actors.[20] As Hotson notes, when these expired and there was no current set of penalties players began playing again, continuing even as the Commons drafted their new ordinance. The government responded with an order for the pulling-down of stages.[21] These harsh measures were reinforced in July, but despite all this playing went on.[22] Francis Bethan was put in charge of raids on theatres and on illegal publishing (which confirms that these were seen as linked cultural–political forces). In November 1648 the Commons demanded a progress report; and that winter newsbooks recorded raids on theatres. However, the theatres were not actually destroyed until seven years after the issuing of the edict usually taken as suppressing the stage: in March 1649 the Fortune, Cockpit and Salisbury Court lost their interiors.[23] At this point the controversy was so great that a clever parodist published *Mr William Prynn His Defence of Stage-Plays*, pretending that the great opponent of the pre-war theatre had now changed his mind.[24]

Drolls – short playlets – continued at the Red Bull, as did illegal and private performances such as that of Thomas Killigrew's *Claricilla*, and pamphlets suggest that less formal street theatre also took place. On 1 January 1649, as Charles I was accused of treason, soldiers sported with the theatrical crown that had been used by players caught in the act.[25] However, that the republic was seen as potentially offering a new beginning for the reformed stage is indicated by the fact that at some point during the republic, perhaps in 1650 when debates about reform took place in and out of parliament, those 'heretofore the Actors and Black-friers and the Cock-Pit' petitioned parliament to be allowed to act 'onely such morall and harmless representations, as shall no way be distastefull to the Commonwealth or good manners'.[26] The later 1650s brought the renewed possibility of performances of both shows and plays, and with this came debate about the ethics of a potentially reformed stage for the new nation. General Monck ordered them to be closed yet again in April 1659.

Thus, in the 1640s and 1650s drama was understood as a genre crucial to political debate. But what does the term 'politics' imply in this context? Politics cannot be simply understood as political theory. Cultural politics and agency appear in the discussion of power relations in pamphlet drama, in the generic changes of Davenant's Interregnum operas, in the changed circumstances which enabled a woman to begin writing plays. As David Bevington suggests, politics needs to be considered widely and in relation to form, and his understanding of politics can be expanded to include, for example, gender relations.[27] For the purposes of this study 'politics' involves both what literary texts register in terms of the political sphere and specific circumstances, and how they intervene in debate in terms of polemic, genre, gender, trope, topos, intertextuality.

This wide definition of politics enables us to see that, although the battles of the wars were fought on binary lines, there were many, changing, divisions. Puritanism was diverse rather than monolithic and was not necessarily hostile to plays – though many Puritans were. The closure of the theatres in 1642 cannot be read as the takeover of a fanatical Puritan minority. Although many theatre historians continue to see it as exactly this, they do so by ignoring historical work on Puritanism.

Recent debate on Puritanism in England has been particularly interested in the twin radical and conservative potentials of Puritan ideology. Unhappy with Michael Walzer's model of the 'revolution of the saints', Patrick Collinson has argued cogently for a kind of mainstream Puritanism which emphasised obedience and in which the upholding of civic and church authority was inter-woven.[28] However, as Collinson notes, 'the disposition of Calvinist magistrates and ministers to obedience carried a latent potential for disobedience. The desire to preserve the world as it was did not exclude the capacity to change it.'[29] As David Underdown suggests in his study of Puritan elites in the provinces, during the 1640s and 1650s the potential of a Puritan way of life both to inaugurate radical change (as it did in the army) and produce very conserva-tive government (as it did in London) was realised.[30] There can be no singular 'Puritan' politics of theatre, and no pairing of Puritan and antitheatrical in contrast with royalist and pro-theatre. The ordinance of closure seems to be inhabited by competing dis-courses of contingency, ethical reform, politics: it cannot be read as totalitarian or as self-evidently effective. Like other texts from these wars it was open to dispute even as it occurred. What it did do, immediately, was to make drama self-consciously politicised. As will become clear, it has been the coincidence of historians' neglect of culture with literary critical assumptions that has trans-formed this complex situation into a twenty-year gap.

SEPARATE SPHERES? 'HISTORY', 'CULTURE', AND THE ENGLISH CIVIL WAR

Peter Lake and Kevin Sharpe have noted that 'recent develop-ments in the historical and literary scholarship on [the English Civil War] have rendered both "politics" and "culture" problem-atic categories'.[31] Historians have concentrated firstly on the vigor-ously disputed question of political motivation in the Civil War (a highly politicised debate about historical method), and secondly on the question of the nature of evidence, where revisionists tend to prize manuscript sources rather than print. The controversial – even adversarial – relationship between historians who do and do not work on cultural and print sources is an indication of the central importance of the 1640s and 1650s as disputed methodological and political terrain. The debates Sharpe and Lake outline seem to draw boundaries between kinds of evidence

– print versus manuscript, 'factual' versus 'imaginative' – that at times seem as strange as the literary critical compulsion to end-lessly reread the same canon of texts.

In terms of political agency, revisionist histories of the period rejected the claim that fundamental differences were explicit and theorised during the Civil War.[32] J. C. D. Clark has even asserted that we should use the term 'rebellion' rather than 'revolution' to describe what happened in the mid-seventeenth-century crisis, in order 'to disengage ourselves from the assumption that revolu-tions are always "forward-looking", that they embody the pro-gressive aspirations of "rising" social classes to speed up developments being impeded by "the forces of reaction". Rebellion is a concept more evidently devoid of such implications; it helps our appreciation that many conflicts (like the Civil War or 1688) can better be described as reactions against innovations.'[33] This is the beginning of Clark's attack on Marxist historiography, also taken up in a more detailed way by J. C. Davis.[34] Without wishing to sponsor a progressivist model of the 1640s, it does seem clear that Clark's desire to replace the signifier 'revolution' with 'rebellion' is not the replacement of a resonant, Marxist term with a neutral one: rebellion is not a term 'devoid of . . . implications'. On the contrary, the use of the term rebellion puts the initiative – and implicitly the controlling power – entirely with the aristocratic elite and within that specifically with the king in the Civil War, and sees popular protest as basically conservative.[35]

Thus, revisionist historians like Clark reject the progressive account of the seventeenth century offered by the huge feat of 'intellectual engineering' that constituted S. R. Gardiner's history of the seventeenth century in terms of the growth of political and religious tolerance.[36] However, Clark's term 'rebellion' cannot sat-isfactorily account for the single document closing the theatres, let alone the theorisation of parliament's position in documents like Parker's *Observations* and popular printed debate in 1640–2. In this study of the crisis of the mid-seventeenth-century, a central assumption is that values and situations were mutually shaping and that the political events moulded the forms as well as the promul-gated 'values' of different plays and playlets. It further assumes that, reciprocally, the way the issues and values were disputed in the drama (mainly printed but also performed) registered and therefore influenced political events.

Views such as Clark's have been challenged. In a cogent rethinking of the historiography of the Civil War period Richard Cust and Ann Hughes acknowledge revisionist insights into the multiplicity of political positions at the outbreak of Civil War. Moreover, they agree that a simple binary model of early Stuart society in which 'opposition' is set against 'government', or 'court' simplistically opposed to 'country', does not adequately describe the nuanced positions of various groups. But they rightly assert that the 'potential for conflict' did exist in early (pre-war) seventeenth-century society and they note the importance of issues of principle and value when they say that 'early Stuart England' was 'seriously divided over entwined, fundamental questions of religion and politics'.[37] The position adopted by Cust and Hughes is that divisions in mid-seventeenth-century English society were multiple though nonetheless serious, changing during the twenty-year period, and these differences were a motivational force for contemporaries. Their rejection of binary models, but contrasting maintenance of a sense of political agency and multiple spheres of political activity, provide a productive context for work in the literary as well as the historical field.

The second historiographical controversy affecting this study is the fraught question of the status of culture in the shaping and interpretation of politics, events and structures of feeling. Recent historians, revisionist and otherwise, have largely neglected the cultural aspects of the 1640s – by which I mean not only literary texts but also celebrations, shows, ceremonies.[38] With their emphasis on manuscript sources and records, most revisionist historians have paid virtually no attention to the cultural sphere, and when they do so they tend to assume that it was royalist. For example, Anthony Fletcher's immensely valuable detailed reassessment of 1642 is an instance of the revisionist rejection of the relationship between and importance of agency and the socio-cultural sphere. Accordingly, his study is masterly and illuminating in its attention to detail yet neglects the symbolic aspects of culture. In *The Outbreak of the English Civil War* Fletcher notes that in 1641–2 the streets of London were full of libels, but does not link this to any extended political consciousness, describing anti-episcopal London rioters of 27–9 December 1641 as obviously ignorant and panic-stricken.[39] Nor does he connect it to contemporary arguments conducted in the literary–cultural sphere.

Fletcher's assumption that there was no socially widespread understanding of or argument about political issues in late Caroline England is not borne out by activity in the literary sphere; from court masques to polemical afterpieces on the public stage and from scurrilous dialogues to poems on the war, literary texts were imbued with political significances. Furthermore, the reactions of the courts to satire on the bishops (the case of *The Cardinall's Conspiracie* was tried by the 'high Commission Court' leading to fines and imprisonment) reinforce my assumption that the theatre was shaping and disseminating ideas central to the crisis of 1642. The evidence suggests that the theatre at this moment, far from being morally or aesthetically bankrupt, participated in some of the debates which in the official political sphere led to such potentially radical reforms as the Root and Branch bill, which would have redistributed church power to parliament and crown.[40]

For many historians symbolic networks and representation remains, apparently, highly problematic evidence. However, recent work bridging the separation of social and political history of the Civil War has also paid attention to the cultural spheres occupied by the elites and the middling sort. Amongst others Cust, Hill, Hughes and Lake bring together analyses of politics and cultural forms. Johann Sommerville, too, has argued for the importance of the pamphlet debate in the Civil War, reading it as evidence of a critical public sphere in which, I would argue, dramatic texts also participate.[41] Kevin Sharpe, too, has written extensively on the politics of court culture in the 1630s. If the borders between social and political history are increasingly permeable, so, too, are the imagined borders between 'culture' and 'evidence'.

'WHICH TIME HAS JUSTLY SUBMERGED': POLITICS, AESTHETICS, LITERARY CRITICISM

If many historians remain chary about discussing the politics of culture and revisionist historians have denied the wide circulation of political debate in the 1640s and 1650s, historians nevertheless recognise that 'few periods in English history deserve the label "discordant" more than the seventeenth century'. The historical debate over the seventeenth century has remained controversial because understood as pertinent.[42] Literary criticism, though, has until recently produced a contrastingly monolithic account of the period, habitually associating most Civil War cultural production with royalism. Since the Restoration, in a triumph of winner's history, Civil War drama particularly has been consistently understood as either totally suppressed in 1642 or repeatedly naturalised as a self-evidently royalist mode.[43] Restoration claims have set the terms of subsequent accounts, such as James Wright's assertion that 'when the Stage was put down and the Rebellion raised' most players 'went into the King's Army and like good Men and true, serv'd their Old Master'. Such assertions from the post-war era have been taken as truth by many subsequent theatre historians.[44]

Until very recently the only theatre historian to discuss the theatrical production of the period at length was Leslie Hotson who traces theatrical legislation and performance throughout the period.[45] Hotson's brilliantly researched study is shifted away from engagement with the politics of the theatrical genre in the Interregnum by his assumption, shared with many other critics, that 'we are not to think of Parliament's first ordinance against stage plays . . . as a blight which suddenly struck a flower in full bloom', suggesting that the theatres were already weakened by repeated closure in the face of plague.[46] In making this suggestion he follows a well-established critical line which saw the closure of the theatres in 1642 as in some way a product of 'declining' theatrical conditions intrinsic to English stage culture in the 1630s.[47]

Such arguments have been countered by Martin Butler but, as we shall see, the twin ideas that the closure of 1642 was a Puritan plot and that it was an inevitable result of decline have determined the nature of critical debate on Civil War theatre and drama.[48] Theatre critics continue to assume that the closure of the theatres meant that either there were no dramatic and theatrical texts between 1642 and the Restoration, or that such texts tell us nothing significant about the culture and society of the times, being either the productions of a 'coterie' or 'closet drama'.[49]

What is the investment of literary criticism, and theatre criticism in particular, in constructing the 1640s as a gap? It is easy to see why James Wright in the Restoration wrote that the stage was royalist, but the extent to which twentieth-century criticism has so wholeheartedly endorsed royalist readings is extraordinary. David Norbrook points to the early and mid-twentieth century notion shared by Eliot and Leavis that 'the poet's true function was to transcend politics', rightly associating this with the explicit rejection and marginalisation of 'the explicitly public forms of epic and political allegory'.[50] This depoliticised way of reading, endorsed by generic preferences and underpinned by the presentation of 'great' literature as transcending politics, has allowed the politics to be read out of some plays kept in the canon, and led to the neglect of more obviously 'public' or politicised texts. The drama of the Interregnum has disappeared almost completely.

Thus the title of Alfred Harbage's book on a tradition which links the pre- and post-war stages underscores the status of the 'Interregnum' plays as small anti-Puritan punctuations in a void: it is called, *Cavalier Drama: An Historical and Critical Supplement to the Study of the Elizabethan and Restoration Stage*, indicating that he considers drama as self-evidently royalist. Moreover, writing in the 1930s, the drama which Harbage traces through the 1650s is that of courtly gentlemen and aspirant courtiers who he sees as producing a tradition which survived the Civil War and which had courtliness (implicitly and explicitly royalist, for Harbage) as its central value. Harbage's argument relies on placing Davenant and Killigrew in the same category as 'royalist', which is problematic, as chapter 6 indicates. Even more questionable is his assertion that 'cavalier drama' is the only tradition to survive the Civil War: he justifies ignoring what he calls the 'popular stage' on the grounds that the gentry and aristocratic writers had usurped the innovative positions and those 'active in the Caroline court and on the Royal side in the Civil Wars' were the ones who were producing 'serious' drama. This assertion is maintained by a refusal to consider precisely those genres which were heirs of a non-aristocratic stage and which came to prominence as polemical pamphlet drama in the 1640s and 1650s.[51] Harbage maintains a rigidly pre-war definition of what drama or theatre must be, and follows the course of particular aristocratic or aspirant-aristocratic authors. This is the drama of the Interregnum as he sees it:

The same class of authors who gave us our Cavalier lyrics wrote also a number of plays, and these plays, although long banished into the realm of half-forgotten things, form an important link in the chain of dramatic history . . . That neither 1642 nor 1660 is selected as a terminal date will also seem natural. Each was a year of political more than of literary change, and each affected the public performance of plays rather than the English love of plays and inherited aptitude for creating particular kinds. Elizabethan drama did not foresee that at such and such a time, a Parliamentary resolution would close the theatres, and was not willing to cease evolving after the days of Shakespeare, or the days of Fletcher, merely surviving with diminishing pulse ready to expire when that resolution came. By the same token, Restoration drama did not cast its nativity or assume a parcel of self determined qualities on the day when young Charles debarked from the Naseby . . . The wellsprings of drama lie deep in the national culture, a factor more powerful in the end than the spectacular edicts of new political administrations.[52]

Although he is right to see continuity in the drama, he sees only one thread – an aristocratic drama. Harbage's attitude to the relationship between politics and drama remains unspecific: what he is sure about is that it is not directly affected by political change. Indeed the opposition he suggests between drama and politics is akin to that between nature and culture: drama is associated with nature – 'wellsprings', 'nativity', 'pulse', 'evolution', are all attributed to theatre – whereas political change is effected by 'resolutions' and 'edicts'. Harbage points towards a complex relationship between drama and politics, but this remains unelucidated, being governed by the assumption that the dramatists of the Interregnum were uniformly 'cavaliers'. Although he does not characterise the period between 1642 and 1660 as a gap, and insists on a continuity of tradition between the two periods, in confining this tradition to 'cavalier drama', imagined as sustaining the concerns of the Stuart court, he neglects the political and generic changes that did take place.

Harbage's insistence on the 'natural' status of drama, and its association with a concept of 'national culture' which transcends the political, is not unusual. Many critics discuss the 'English love of plays' and they connect this with the Renaissance (signified by 'Elizabethan' drama, Shakespeare and Fletcher) and the Restoration (signalled by mention of Charles II). Thus, a less sophisticated version of a very similar argument is given by Montague Summers who long ago wrote of the 'thread' of Civil War drama:

although not infrequently strained to breaking point and seemingly upon the very event of rupture and disjunction, fortuitously was never snapped and sundered: There was a coherence; there was a succession; and in spite of the desire and intention of the sour despots who had snatched and tightly clung to the reins of government, for ever and finally to annihilate and extinguish the English stage, when at the King's return public playhouses were again reopened, favoured, and patronized, the old traditions were found to have been by no means lost . . . a very real conservation and relationship trilled, and although the stream was slender the waters were clear from their source.[53]

Summers emphasises the continuity between two national theatres, both implicitly royalist. The 1640s and 1650s feature as a
period of anti-theatrical fanaticism; to be on the side of the theatre
is to be allied with justice, royalty, Englishness. Summers's language mixes the regal with the natural: there is a 'succession' of
dramatists (as of kings) and Restoration drama is naturalised as a
spring of water from the English landscape.

These associations are maintained by some more recent critics.
The seasonal metaphor which structures Dale Randall's study,
Winter Fruit: English Drama 1642–1660, continues the naturalisa-
tion of drama as royalist with chapter titles like 'The Sun
Declining', 'The Rising Sun', explicitly basing themselves on royalist discourses where, for example, Charles II is called 'the rising
royal son'.[54] Moreover, a typical textbook discussing the theatre
audience of the Elizabethan and Jacobean theatre describes the
'natural enthusiasm of most Englishmen' for drama:

> The Puritan factions might fulminate, but the drama flourished under
> the direct or indirect patronage of the court which saw to it that, though
> some might be too 'virtuous', Sir Toby [Belch] and his thousands of
> fellow souls had their 'cakes and ale'. The Puritans, of course, finally
> achieved their goal when Parliament closed the theatres in 1642 for a
> period of about eighteen years.[55]

Once again England (here 'Englishmen'), royalty and the theatre
are allied and the theatre is associated with a euphoric vision of
feudal 'cakes and ale', exemplified by Sir Toby Belch. Such
accounts are not the responsibility of maverick critics, but follow
established scholarly tradition in moving directly from
Elizabethan and Puritan critics of the theatre (such as Stephen
Gosson, Phillip Stubbes) to its closure over forty years later.[56] Such
accounts repeatedly condense a set of signifiers so that virtue
resides with theatre, England, royalty. The three almost always
crop up together in relation to either the closure of the theatres
or their restoration – and elements of such assumptions even find
their way into reference works.[57]

The emphasis that revisionist historians placed on the central
power of aristocratic networks finds resonance in the insistence of
theatre historians and critics on the association of theatre and
monarchy. If theatre history has characterised the 1640s and
1650s as a gap in royal drama, we might expect the avowedly politically aware criticism of the new historicists to be particularly inter-

ested in the cultural production of the Civil War. This is not the case. In fact, these critics have concentrated on the earlier Renaissance dramatists and tend to rework canonical texts. Although it is important that such texts be reconsidered, it initially seems puzzling that, working with the insights of Michel Foucault, Clifford Geertz, Victor Turner, they have found little to interest them in a period of great social change.[58] Rather, they have looked to the canonical texts of the Renaissance stage as culturally symbolic of Tudor and Jacobean society.[59]

This concentration on canonical and courtly texts of the Elizabethan and Jacobean period has produced readings which tend to see the text as always at the service of the king, and conceptualise the early modern subject as unable to think outside models of power produced by monarchist discourse. Therefore such criticism has difficulty in responding to conscious and articulate linguistic challenge to authority.[60] Such critics do not question accepted accounts of the closure of the theatres.[61] As David Norbrook has rightly argued, some new historicist criticism is ambivalent about the politicisation of writing, assuming that 'as soon as resistance becomes codified into the conscious political agenda of a group or class . . . it will become potentially totalitarian'.[62] Such criticism is inevitably sceptical of the radical, rather than totalitarian, potential of political agency in the Civil War period.[63]

The place of drama and theatre as an index of cultural political debate in the mid-century struggles is only beginning to be recognised, as is the potentially democratising effects of public performance and print culture[64] With regard to drama and 1642, much criticism operates with virtually the same understanding of censorship and periodicity as Hotson, Summers and others; as for the earlier theatre historians, the 1640s and 1650s remain a cultural wasteland.

Most critics, therefore, use a single model of censorship with regard to 1642. They assume, first, that those who issued the edict wanted the stage closed permanently, secondly, that they more or less achieved this and, finally, therefore, they assume that censorship operates by stopping meaning. Christopher Hill wrote of censorship's central role in the 1630s as the 'point at which religion and culture met'.[65] Hill's account of the 1630s, anticipating always the 'revolution' of the 1640s, has not gone unchallenged and

some aspects of it are discussed in the next chapter.[66] Contemporaries seem to share a sense that the fall of Star Chamber
was important in 1641 when the mechanisms for regulating
publication collapsed.[67]

Censorship, though, does not produce an absence of meaning
but changes, even transforms, the discursive field. Although some
regimes of censorship are 'harsher' than others, it is problematic
to envisage a free realm of speech or writing wholly without encod-
ing or encryption.[68] As Lucasta Miller puts it, 'ultimately, it is
censorship that underpins language itself'.[69]

Rather than use the prism of censorship whereby drama disappears in 1642, the case studies which follow aim to examine the
relationship between drama and context and to restore to the
drama of the 1640s and 1650s 'the specific history of groupings of
discursive practices'.[70] The circumstances of 1642, whereby printing was easier than ever before but performed drama was forbidden, produced a situation in which producers and readers of
dramatic and semi-dramatic texts were, as chapter 1 suggests,
intensely aware of the relationship between dramatic discourse
and political situations.

Printed plays and their readings were part of what historians
including Hill, Russell and others have seen as constituting a
'popular' language of politics.[71] As recent critics like Nigel Smith
and Lois Potter have recognised, the institution of theatre and the
dramatic text was at the centre of debates around the meaning of
culture in the 1640s and 1650s, a centrality which made it the
terrain of dispute.[72] The outbreak of war and the ban on theatre
in 1642 were the product of something infinitely more complicated than the seizure of power by a group of fanatics who were
the parliamentary embodiment of anti-theatrical polemicists.

PART I

1642–1649: Cases in politics and drama

CHAPTER 1

New news for a new world? Genre, politics and the news dialogues of the 1640s

What news in Fraunce?
None that I can tell, still warre, warre.
. . .
Is there no good news?   (1593)[1]

PAMPHLETS AND THE 1640S: POLITICS AND GENRE

In 1640 one reader wrote, 'I hate these following railing rimes, yet keepe them for the president of the times.' He recorded this in his news diary where he stored diverse items – verses, dialogues, the whole text of the arraignment of Strafford. In 1643 William Walwyn addressed his levelling tract, *The Power of Love*, 'To Every Reader . . . for there is no respect of persons with God'.[2] In 1648 the East Anglia royalist Thomas Knyvett wrote to Sir John Hobart, describing two pamphlets. On the first, 'a declaration in the King's name', he comments 'sure a counterfeit would never have had the power over my passion that this had'. The authenticity of voice he attributes to the 'royal' pamphlet is contrasted with the bastardised parliamentarian product (as he sees it), published by the republican and father of illegitimate children, Henry Marten:

I have read it, and shall say no more but that I look upon it not only as the spurious issue of his brain, but as the sense of the saint-like house: yet brave Harry hath the better on't, to beget the bastard, and make the honourable state to father it; else, sure, it durst never have peeped abroad.[3]

Politics and scandal are bound together in Knyvett's different responses; he interprets the pamphlets according to assumed political categories beyond the texts themselves. In each case private reading complements, or is held in tension with, public

19

politics. The genre under consideration here, the Civil War dialogue, exists in and addresses this tension.

Like Walwyn's claim on 'Every Reader', Rous's and Knyvett's
ambivalent consumption of opinion and their participation in the
exchange of news and political writing indicate that there was a
sophisticated pamphlet market in the 1640s. Clearly, potential
readers would be likely to assess a pamphlet in terms of its yield of
news, polemic, pleasure, truth, godliness, but were also prey to the
seductions of style or scandal. We can detect in Walwyn's address
a religio-political polemic which also simultaneously tries to
embrace the largest number of possible consumers. The idea of a
reader free under God is part of a sales strategy which indicates the
importance and self-consciousness of the market in political ideas
in the early 1640s, part of the subject of this chapter.

Just as Walwyn invites the reader to make an imaginative leap
and to envision an ideal state realised – heaven – so contemporary
dialogue pamphlets aim to persuade their reader to 'buy into' a
text which promises to enhance political knowledge and agency.
Readers, also consumers, were addressed as individuals and
invited to participate in public debate. The genealogy of what must
be called the pamphlet dialogue (sometimes the pamphlet
playlet) in the market of news and its possible performance contexts suggests that it offered an invitation – issued from a variety of
political perspectives – to rethink public roles. The dialogic and
rhetorical nature of the form located even the private, individu-
ated, purchaser and reader as participating in public events and
ideas.[4] So the pamphlet market is important because it marks an
ambiguous border between private and public politics.

This is one reason why, in the wake of Christopher Hill's argument that the end of censorship brought an explosion of political
writing, print culture and the pamphlet and news market in the
1640s has been the focus for much debate among cultural and
literary historians.[5] From Gardiner's and Hill's use of polemical
pamphlets and newsbooks to J. C. Davis's reinterpretation of the
nature of satirical ephemera (as offering scandalous rather than
literal images of Civil War sects) pamphlet evidence is crucial. In
each case, the interpretation of pamphlet genres and a judgement
about their place in the booktrade and political economy of the
1640s is central to the historical account given.[6]

Like other genres, dialogic texts – from dialogues proper to playlet texts – were transformed in the 1640s. Generically hybrid pamphlet playlets and dialogues were produced as theatre and print regulation impacted upon one another in the 1640s. The interrelationships of genre and specifically political circumstance do not indicate a simple generic continuity of the pre-war drama into the pamphlet texts and dialogues of the wars, but indicate responses to – and attempts to shape – political events.

Bakhtin, emphasising the complex dynamic of enunciation, offers a way to illuminate the particular interrelationships of 'private' reading and 'public' politics and print in the 1640s. He argues that 'each sphere in which language is used develops its own *relatively stable types* of utterances', which he calls '*speech genres*'. The very specific changes of 1640–2 suggest that Bakhtin's rather general theory can be historicised to offer an understanding of genre as a circumstantially determined style of address; it enables us to consider styles and markets of pamphlet genres.[7] Bakhtin's sense of genre as always already hybridised and containing other genres also allows style and genre to be set against circumstances – such as the fall of Star Chamber and the closure of the theatres – and enables us to keep in mind the fluid social contexts of populist genres.[8]

PAMPHLET DIALOGUES OF THE 1640s: A GENERIC GENEALOGY?

If, as I argue, the dialogue pamphlet emerged as a sub-genre – apparently marketed within the broad category of 'news' – in 1640–2, what were the political and market conditions of its emergence?

A genealogy of the pamphlet playlet can be produced, tracing the genre's relations to the circumstances of 1641–2, and finding its genesis in the politicised culture of the 1620s and 1630s. For in the first half of the seventeenth century, perhaps most visibly during the parliaments of the 1620s, print, politics and economics emerge as instrumental in producing the conditions of printed polemic and publication. Discourse on corruption in office and the emergent discourses of political theory in the period 1620–40 are important. So is the dialogue form as constituted in the English Renaissance. We also need to consider the conditions and regulation of London theatrical production in the 1630s, and the unifying factor of the emergence of a market in printed news in the period 1620–40. Finally, it seems likely that the closure of the theatres in 1642, as one effect of changed circumstances, was the catalyst which produced the pamphlet dialogue as a particular market commodity and an important way to 'stage' politics.

First, the dialogue. This is rarely addressed in accounts of Civil War dramatic discourse, but crucial. Situated between political theory and news, the dialogue was a very flexible form which might stage political or other conflicts; it is also a form whose social history is only beginning to be elucidated. In comparison to the transformations in political genres in the period 1600–49 the dialogue seems stable, perhaps because, as Virginia Cox has argued, it is a genre which responds in nuanced and decisive ways to circumstances.[9] In England, as in most of Europe, the Lucianic dialogue (where any figure may address any other) dominated and this was taken up in the pamphlet trade of the 1640s. During the sixteenth century, as Peter Burke implies, the Renaissance dialogue in England was turned to governmental or political ends – from translations of *The Courtier* to dialogues by Thomas More, Thomas Elyot, Thomas Starkey, yet the dialogue also sometimes bordered upon the playscript.[10] The closure of the theatres, combined with the emergence of a trade in news and a print trade that was affected by changes in market and censorship, impacted upon the fictional dialogue: potentially political and in some manifestations mimicking theatre, the form was an obvious candidate for shortening and reworking in the wars of truth.

Second, accusations of 'corruption' played a part in fostering a shared political discourse. During the first half of the seventeenth century, as Linda Levy-Peck argues, 'the boundaries between legitimate and corrupt transactions were redrawn'. In the parliamentary sessions of 1621, 1625, 1626 and 1628, bills proposed increasingly precise definitions of bribery; from the 1620s onwards high-profile officers were impeached. Peck traces the simultaneous emergence of a discourse on corruption and evil counsellors.[11] This concern with corruption can be found in individual legal cases from Coke to Strafford or the attack on the ship-money judges in Richard Brathwaite's playlet *Mercurius Britannicus*; the critique of corrupt counsellors came to have the lineaments of pragmatic political theory. By 1640 political discourses inhabited populist as much as elite genres. If, as Peck has convincingly argued, Pym and Strafford shared a political language in 1641, it was a language developed through the corruption trials.[12]

Theatre, the third category, was primarily a staged medium, though also printed. The question of 'opposition' and censorship in theatre in the 1620s and 1630s has been canvassed by Heinemann, Butler, Clare, Burt and Sharpe. Plays and masques of the 1620s (Middleton's *A Game at Chess*, the tragedies of tyranny published, if not staged, by Thomas May) and even of the 1630s (plays by Massinger, Brome, even Shirley) debated contemporary controversies and used parodically allusive stage business. Indeed, as war broke out, parliament caused a translation of George Buchanan's *Baptistes Sive Calumnia* to be published; it saw the political potential of the printed play. The regulator of the stage, the Master of the Revels, was a crown appointee tied to the patronage network; his place and work were distinct from that of the Stationers' Company who regulated print (with a little help from the crown), and qualitatively different from Star Chamber. Theatre and print had different modes of organisation. These distinctions have been neglected by recent work on regulation: some accounts homologise all cultural production, others link playing to maypoles and other kinds of 'sports', with different, often rural, contexts and different modes of control.[13] Assuming, then, that print and theatre were regulated differently before the war, there were further changes to come in 1641–2.

The Master of the Revels oversaw dramatic script and theatre performance, and Sir Henry Herbert's office in the 1630s licensed provincial playing and garnered other fees. The 1620s and 1630s saw theatrical events censored for various issues, including politics and religious questions. In 1641, for example, Sir Henry Herbert took objection to the script of a particular play, and in May 1639 the players at the Fortune were fined £1,000 for deliberately parodying Laudian ceremonies. But an attempt to isolate a category of the 'political' is inevitably problematic when dealing with alterations to scripts. Sir Henry regarded it as impossible to continue in the crisis of August 1642 and closed his office book. Soon, the order closing the stage appeared and theatrical conditions were transformed.

Which brings us to the fourth variable: news and the news market. The 1620s saw the circulation of newsletters and the coranto of foreign news, often news of Protestant Europe which might have implications for domestic politics.[14] Marketing of news relied on the pleasure of communities of readers in particular events. Communities were also markets. As Richard Cust has noted, news was distributed around the shires in a variety of forms: written and printed newsletters, 'separates', pamphlets. Some news was sensational in itself – Cust records London scriveners undercutting each other in selling transcripts of Justice Croke's ship-money judgement – but other kinds needed to be shaped for an audience. The regularisation of newspaper publication in the 1640s generated a weekly momentum in the manufacture of news – and offered readers a way to assess domestic politics.[15]

Increasingly, the news trade came under crown scrutiny. On 1 February 1629 the Stationers' Company was reminded that the sale of unlicensed news was banned, and in 1632 Charles wrote himself complaining at the continued trade in corantos and pamphlets. In October 1632 the printing and sale of news from abroad was banned (as a newswriter reported). The decree of 1637 seemed to tighten up loopholes, and made licences obligatory for pamphlets and ballads – some of the material we are dealing with here.[16]

News generated responses; letters and diaries in which readers noted their reactions suggest a dynamic between private meditation and public events.[17] The evidence of Chartier and others suggests an active reading public and a lively connection between printed and verbal cultures.[18] News might be read by anyone – merchants, traders, farmers, gentlemen, women – and it seems that its spread linked local and national politics.[19] News, as Cust suggests, broke down distinctions between 'popular' and 'elite' spheres or readers and helped to shape and at times to polarise opinion. Arguably, historians of political history have inappropriately isolated these interwoven strands of culture and politics by their insistent separation of cultural production and political process, whereas all the evidence of the 1620s and 1630s points to a distribution of politicised discourse through a ranges of genres. By 1640, when parliament's sitting began to be printed as news, 'news' could be many things – politics, critique of corruption, information, commentary, 'literary' genres – and an eager reading public were already in place when the events precipitating war took place.

Another key event in the formation of the Civil War dynamic between print and plays was the fall of Star Chamber in 1641. In comparison to their effective dismantling of the major London theatres, parliament's subsequent attempts to enforce print censorship were a failure. Outrageous pamphlets were read aloud to the assembled house, as Sir Simon D'Ewes records, and printers were repeatedly to be 'questioned', 'punished' or, as in the case of John Streater, tried.[20] So from 1641 onwards not only was the news of parliament being printed regularly but the mechanisms for licensing the press disappeared. A few months later the stage was silenced.

Thus, where the strictures of 1642 made the dramatic form implicitly political, the fall of Star Chamber made the printing of pamphlets, the critique of corruption and the elaboration of political theory easily available to a large audience. Indeed, *The Actors Remonstrance* (1643) specifically claimed that playwrights were reduced to writing pamphlets.[21] Dramatic texts, previously the record of theatrical performances, had their context transformed and politicised by the closure and national events. They, like the dialogue, now offered a sequence of positions from which a topic could be debated, reframed scandalously, or satirised; and in compressed forms (reminiscent of the shortened romances of the chapbook) they could be marketed as news. Accordingly, drama and dialogue (as part of 'news') were pressed by specific circumstances into closer association in 1640–2; the market in printed news was flourishing in the metropolis and the pamphlet playlet emerged from these converging events.

To summarise, the fall of Star Chamber initiated an increased potential for publication. The sharper definition of a market for news, with the publication of parliamentary proceedings and then newspapers, produced new kinds of printed commodities. On the other hand the critical theatrical production of the 1630s and early 1640s was brought to a halt. At the moment of 1642, when theatre was caught up in national crisis, playing became a metaphor for political transgression, and plays were implicitly politicised. It seems that, unsurprisingly, the news-oriented relationship of publishers to print impacted on literary production. It initiated a hybridisation of genres in which, for example, genres from newspaper to dialogue and playscript mimic one another.

HYBRIDITY: NEWS AND THE PAMPHLET DIALOGUE

A friend of mine to me than did repaire,
Desiring me, to pen this famous *Fayr*,
Which I have done, and have it here to sell;
Come buy the *Fayre* of me, and so farewell.[22]

So Richard Overton's pamphlet of 1642 proposed itself as commodity, pleasure and politics. How did such a dialogue attempt to sell itself in the news-obsessed market of the 1640s? Circumstances meant that the 'dialogue' and the 'playlet' occupied similar positions as genres articulating and attempting to influence the political ferment; more, the contrasting crises in the regulation of print and theatre facilitated the fusion of their techniques. Printed playlets, dialogues and dialogic news invented the reader as a consumer invited to 'buy' (in a dual sense) critical opinions on all aspects of the crisis in government.

The events of the 1640s produced pamphlet dialogues hybrid between several genres and existing on a discursive continuum from philosophical dialogue to scurrilous script for street theatre. Dialogue, play and newspaper formed the defining borders of the pamphlet plays, which also mimic these adjacent genres. Some, like *A Briefe Dialogue Between A Creditor and a Prisoner* (1653) use the model of abstract political dialogue, but others aspire to be performance pieces or offer the pleasures of more 'popular' genres. Genres including news report, parody, ghostly speeches, tragicomedies, the vomiting up of ills, last-wills-and-testaments, bull baitings are dialogised and sometimes dramatised to articulate political positions. The variety of kinds of literature drawn on by pamphlet playlets is indicated by the fact that the Lucianic *Dialogue betwixt an Excise-Man and Death* uses motifs from folk-tale with dramatic *mise en scène*, while contrastingly the playlet pamphleteer Samuel Sheppard (discussed in the next chapter) recycles set scenes which were the building-blocks of pre-war city comedy. Each is turned to the purpose of persuasion.

These generic hybrids dramatised figures from the government: Lord Keeper Finch and Windebank in *Time's Alteration*; Noy and Strafford in the Lucianic dialogue *A Description of the Passage of Thomas Late Earle of Strafford, over the River of Styx.* In 1643 Strafford returned in *Strafford's Ghost* to act as a warning to other over-ambitious men. They dramatised conflicts (as in *The Lofty Bishop*,

A Dialogue betwixt an EXCISE-MAN and DEATH.

Upon a time when *Titans* Steeds were driven,
To drench themselves beneath the Western Heaven;
And sable *Morpheus* had his Curtains spread,
And silent Night had laid the World to bed :
'Mongst other Night-Birds which did seeke for Prey :
A blunt *Excise-man*, which abhor'd the Day,
Was rambling forth to seeke himselfe a Booty,
'Mongst *Merchants* Goods which had not paid the Duty :
But walking all alone Death chanc'd to meet him,
And in this manner did begin to greet him.

Death. Stand, who comes here ? what means this Knave to
And sculke a broad, when honest men should sleepe ? (peepe
Speake, what's thy name ? and quickly tell me this,
Whither thou goest, and what thy bus'ness is ?

Excise-man. What'ere my bus'nes is, thou foule-mouth'd
J'de have you know, I scorn to be controul'd   (scould
By any Man that lives, much less by thou
Who blurtest out thou knowst not what, nor how,
I goe about my lawful bus'ness :   And
Jle make you smart for bidding of mee stand.

Death. Jmperious Cox-combe ! Is your stomack vext ?
Pray slack your rage; and harken what comes next :
I have a Writt to take you up ;   Therefore
To chafe your blood I bid you, stand, once more.

Excis. A Writt to take me up ! Excuse mee, Sir,
You doe mistake, I am an Officer,
In Publick Service, for my private Wealth,
My bus'ness is if any seeke by stealth,
To undermine the *States*, I doe discover
Their falshood; therefore, hold your hand : give over.

Death. Nay, faire and soft ! Tis not so quickly done
As you conceive it is : I am not gone
A jott the sooner for your hastie Chat,
Nor braging Language : For I tell you flat
Tis more then so; though Fortune seeme to thwart us,
Such easie terms I don't intend shall part us ?
With this impartial Arme, Ile make you feele
My fingers first, and with this Shaft of Steele,
Jle peck thy bones ? *As thou alive, wert hated,*
So dead, to Doggs thou shall be Segregated.

Excis. J'de laugh at that; I would thou didst but dare,
To lay thy fingers on me : J'd not spare
To hack thy Carkass till my Sword was broken :
J'de make thee eat the words which thou hast spoken :
All men should warning take by thy transgression,
How they molested men of my Profession.

My Service to the *Sates*, is so well known,
That should I but Complaine, they'd quickly own
My publcke grievances; and give mee right
To cut your eares before to morrow night.

Death. Well said indeed : But bootelesse all; For I
Am well aquainted with thy Villianie;
I know thy Office, and thy Trade is such,
Thy Service little; and thy Gaines are much :
Thy braggs are many; But tis vaine to Swagger,
And thinke to fright me with thy guilded Dagger :
    As I abhor thy Person; Place, and Threat,
    So now Jle bring thee to the Judgement Seate.

Excis. The Judgement Seate ! I must confess that word
Doth cut my heart, like any sharpned Sword :
What ! Come t'account ! methinks the dreadfull sound
Of every word, doth make a mortal wound,
Which sticks not only in my outward skin,
But penetrates my very soule within.
Twas least of all my thoughts that ever *Death*,
Would once attempt to stop *Excise-mens* breath.
But since tis so; that now I doe perceive
You are in earnest : then I must relieve
My self another way. Come, wee'l be Friends,
If I have wronged thee, Ile make th'Amends :
Let's joyne together; Jle passe my word, this night
Shall yeeld us Grub, before the morning light;
Or, otherwise (to mittigate my sorrow)
Stay here, Jle bring you Gold enough to morrow.

Death. To morrows Gold I will not have; And thou
Shalt have no Gold upon to morrow : Now
My final Writt shall to'th execution have thee;
All earthly Treasure cannot help or save thee.

Excis. Then woe is me ! Ah ! how was I besool'd !
I thought that Gold (which answereth althings) could
Have stood my friend at any time, to Baile mee !
But griefe growes great, and now my trust doth fail mee :
    Oh ! that my conscience were but clear within;
Which now is racked with my former sin :
With horror I behold my secret Stealing .
My Bribes, Oppression, and my gracelesse Dealing;
My Office-sins which I had clean forgotten,
Will Gnaw my soul, when all my bones are rotten :
I must confess it, very grief doth force mee,
Dead, or alive, both God and Man doth Curse mee.
    Let All Excise-men *hereby warning take,*
    To shun their Practice for their Conscience sake.

FINIS.

LONDON, Printed by *I. C.* 1659.   *July 2.*

1 *A Dialogue betwixt an Excise-Man and Death* (1659). A short dialogue as found
in the 1640s and late 1650s.

the Lazy Brownist, and the Loyall Author), and attacked the Catholics (for example *Newes Newly Discovered*). Laud was reviled – using the common figure of purging in *The Bishop's Potion* and in *Canterbury His Change of Diot*, probably by Richard Overton. History was also used by pamphlets as a commentary on the present, as in the reprinting of the poem *Leicester's Ghost*. There were a number of recognisable sub-genres, for example, ghostly dialogues are sometimes signalled by illustration – as in that for the anti-Straffordian *The Earle of Strafford's Ghost*. And, in the first phase of conflict, 1641–3, as the titles suggest, they seem to have been a form popular amongst those critical of Caroline rule. Many of these hybrid texts make use of genres from the pre-war stage to facilitate their persuasion of the reader. Whole modes of writing were, at this moment, hybridised and foreshortened to be reformulated as items saleable as news.

The dialogue, both pleasurable in its overt rhetoricity and having genealogical claims to seriousness, occupied a special place in the writing of persuasion. *The Organs Funerall* (1642), for example, delineates the arguments about Laudian ceremony, asking whether the organ is 'a decent and comely thing in the Church'.[23] Many similar pamphlet dialogues and playlets circulated debate on the main issues of the war, as often serious as satirical in their setting of positions, and sometimes offering a serious exploration of the position ultimately to be defeated. At the start of war the question of whether king or parliament had the right to raise an army was vexing for many. *A Discourse or Dialogue Between The Two Now Potent Enemies: Lord Generall Militia and his Illegal Opposite, Commission of Array* (collected by Thomason in October 1642) intervened in heated public debate and attempted to provide the purchaser with arguments. Commissions of Array, organised by Charles, invited loyalty to the crown at county level, whereas the militia ordinance – opposed unsuccessfully by the Lord Mayor of London, Sir Richard Gurney – was masterminded by Pym and finally passed by both Commons and Lords on 15 March 1642.[24] As all could see, the ordinance was a constitutional means to organise the defence of parliament, but without the signature of the king. The theoretical relationship of 'King and Parliament' to 'Gentry and Cavaliers freely engaging themselves' is presented in dialogue which interweaves relatively abstract ideas (as in the abstract *A Dialogue Arguing that Arch-Bishops, Bishops etc.,*

Are to Be Cut Off By Law of God, whose author would probably have been horrified to think his work might be compared, even distantly, with a playscript) and more pleasurable irony and dramatisation to characterise topical political and religious situations.[25]

The opening sets out in very simple terms the parliamentary argument for the legality of the militia, answering objections which might be made by supporters of the Commission of Array:

MILITIA: There hath been much discourse about you and I, that is, about the Commission of Array and the Militia, and you have by the Parliament been formerly judged illegal and unlawfull.

ARRAY: Can that be unlawfull which is undertaken for the defence of the King? to whom should the military strength of the Kingdome be subject if not the King.

MILITIA: I allow this, and my desire as well as yours is, to sacrifice my bloud in maintaining the Kings right, against all such as would have him invade the privilidges of the Subject, and such as seek the dissolution of the Parliament. In a word, I stand for the King and the Parliament, you only for the King as he is carried away by the evil counsell of Malignants. (p. 3)

The debate presents positions which were already becoming familiar to readers in such a way as to persuade them of parliament's right. It intervenes at the level at which it imagines public debate to be taking place, attempting to present (or mimic?) and defeat positions which might be enunciated in spoken debate. As the frontispiece suggests by picturing both Charles's seal and parliament, it seeks to address all readers, but also to persuade them to value the parliamentary cause over that of the king in isolation (reinforced by the placement of the parliament over the king's emblem on the title-page).

As this indicates, dialogues and dramatic playlets operate at an important border – that between printed and spoken discussion. The dialogue between Militia and Array intervenes in an implicitly spoken debate, ventriloquising 'private' opinions in print in order to work on 'private' opinions – what we think of as 'public opinion' – in the field of spoken argument. In such cases 'news', operating between written and spoken genres, and dialogue, a form imitating conversation, are combined. For instance, *The Last News in London* (published just after the first closure of the theatres in October 1642) presents a 'discourse' between a citizen and a country gentleman which takes place on the road, at a meeting-place of private and public. Its title, imitating those of forensic news reports, represents the process whereby news is exchanged, thematising the making of a community of political debate even as it intervenes in that debate.

The playlet registers the creation of newly powerful social groupings in the City of London (now run by the radical Pennington as lord mayor) and calls attention to the creation of new social spheres, classes and mores, as well as the immediate 'news' of preparations for war at the Guildhall.[26]

CITIZEN: . . . did you not heare of the Guild-hall night worke?

COUNTRY: What was that I pray, do they work in the night?

CITIZEN: Noe, noe, they playd all night.

COUNTRY: Why, I thought that Plays and playhouses had beene put downe:

CITIZEN: Yes, so they were in the Suburbes, but they were set up in the City, and Guild-hall is made a Play-house.

COUNTRY: But I pray? what play was it that was Acted?

CITIZEN: Some say it was called *A King or No King, or King Careo*, but they say that *Skippon* was so frighted at the sight of him, that he left his seat; what would he have done think you, if he had seene the king indeed:

COUNTRY: Truely it was a strange play, did not they whisper Treason on it? On my word we Country folks dare not be so bold as to make sport at Kings, the very name of King (meethinks) carries such a Magestick sound with it, as that it makes the Auditors amazed to heare it, and dare your Citizens be so bold?

The conveying of news of events in the capital to places outside is represented by the Citizen recounting the changes in City government and preparations for war to the shocked Countryman whose amazed response underlines the importance of the challenge the City had mounted to the king, reinforced by the metaphor of playing. The Citizen concludes with a sentence which makes citizens and actors equivalent: 'What dare they not doe: Citizens and Players may doe anything.' The implied reversal is, of course, that now the theatres are closed, in which rebellion used to be acted or 'played', life is imitating drama and rebellion is in the City. The familiar trope of *theatrum mundi* calls attention to the way the roles actors had personated on the public stage have now emerged, not wholly scripted, into the public sphere.

This dialogue – mixing what Burke called 'catechism' and 'conversation' – aims to structure political debate and to deliver an account of events. The ending is paradoxical in its ambivalence about reformation and the ills of Stuart government. The dramatic analogy is used to focus feeling against the City government (although it is also implicitly critical of Charles I). It appeals to the country as the repository of 'ancient' values and practices forgotten by the City, reformulating the 'country' critique thematised in the theatre in the 1630s – especially in Brome's *A Jovial Crew*, Shirley's *Beggar's Bush*.[27] The ending combines a call for reformation with an assertion of 'loyalty' in an unresolved ideological clash: Citizen and Countryman agree that the church needs reformation, but that Charles should do it concluding with Countryman's assertion that 'the whole Kingdome would joyne together to Petition His Sacred Majestie, and the high and honourable Court of Parliament, to Reforme the abuses that are amongst us' (p.6).

The playlet's large demands for change within the ultimately conservative frame of the petition to royalty (a form with a long tradition in folk-tale and theatre, as well as in political bargaining between king and parliament) indicates that the new news-oriented play pamphlets played a significant – and self-conscious – part in the 'immensely educative function of the popular press in forming a new language for talking about politics'.[28] Such playlets take up the position of the 'ordinary man', assuming the voice of the reasonable citizen as their political mean. They combine 'reasonable' debate with a reworking of the dramatic convention whereby grievance is resolved by royal mediation. *The Wishing Common-wealths man* illustrates this dual emphasis on criticism and loyalty.[29] Wish-well explains how he would govern if he were king:

WISH: I would establish all the good old Laws, and (to suppress all late invented and daily acted crimes) I would enact new Edicts . . . I would not set greater taxes on the people then were necessary for them and the kingdom's safety . . . my hand should never be empty, but always open to the scholer and the soldier, as the two pillers of a free state . . . I would suppresse all factions as well as one another. (p. 5)

Wish-well's programme combines repressing factions with reinstating ancient laws, and can be seen as a plan of moderate reformation. Yet such pamphlets are not conservative in any simplistic sense. As Stuart Hall has noted, a backward-looking impulse can be linked to struggle and resistance; bound up with the values that they characterise as 'good' or 'traditional' is an imagined ideal government.[30] These dialogues reactivate and reshape old genres to occupy the cultural ground between political theory and conversation, imitating public political speech in an attempt to create and influence opinion. In the reconciliatory endings of both *The Last News* and *The Wishing Common-wealths Man* we can see the pamphlet assuming (or rather inventing) 'the voice of the people' in 1641–2: never hostile to the king but desiring reform. This critique – for critique of a sort it is – is saturated with obedience and bound to a vision of ancient social structures. The future is imagined, sometimes radically transformed, in terms of a vision of the ideal past – a mode shared with radical political theory which opposed government in terms of the 'Norman yoke'.

Even relatively simple playlets like *The Last News* or *The Wishing Common-wealths Man* self-consciously present themselves as circulating possible opinions and positions. From *The Wicked Resolution of the Cavaliers* (1642), in which cavaliers give away their evil intentions, to the attack on popish 'ambition' in the mock-trial *Times Changeling, Arraigned For Inconstancy at the Barre of Opportunity* (1643), the dialogues and playlets are aware that in reporting events they are formulating the way people think and speak.[31] Some 'educate' readers in prejudice and maintain political groupings by explaining how to 'recognise' an enemy. These divisions seem to have permeated every aspect of social life: the war brought the appearance of 'roundhead' and 'cavalier' as insults in local quarrels. As Underdown notes, such terms, disseminated by print, 'reflected and may well have strengthened people's perception that their communities were politically divided'.[32]

The techniques used to influence a reader are worth examining. One example is self-disclosure, where a pamphlet eavesdrops on an enemy apparently revealing his inmost thoughts. In *The Souldiers Language* (1644) two royalist soldiers, Nicholas and Jeffrey, meet, one coming from Bristol and one from York.[33] The context is the severe defeat of parliament at Lostwithiel in Cornwall on 2 September 1644 – regarded by royalists as compensation for the decisive defeat of Charles at Marston Moor.[34] When Nicholas says 'God damne me, but Ile run my Rapier thorow thee, if thou stand vexing me thus, and I am in haste', Jeffrey recognises him as a true royalist – profane, violent, high handed (A1r). The reader is an eavesdropper.

Jeffrey's language here presents what Bakhtin calls an 'internally dialogised' image; Jeffrey is simultaneously understandable and implicitly judged by the reader as cowardly. The satire uses this technique to present the royalist army as reassuringly ill-led and Jeffrey offers a satirical remedy: Charles should 'put none into any great office, or place, of trust, but such as were absolute Papists' (A2r). Ultimately the soldiers agree that the roundheads are 'like to prevail' and Nicholas proves himself a hypocrite when he says 'I will cut off my locks, and be as zealous as any of them all' (B4v). The dynamic whereby the reader overhears 'truth' revealed serves to mobilise hatred, underline differences and foreground myths about the opposing party.

As this text suggests, dialogues are often simultaneously fairly complex in their technique and simple in their effects. Where *The Souldiers Language* unabashedly invites the reader to take sides and supplies ways to 'recognise' the 'enemy', *The Reformed Malignants* positions itself somewhere between the fostering of enmity and a persuasive appeal to community by showing a process of change effected by rational political debate.[35] A cavalier is converted to the other side, coming to agree that Popery is 'too much favoured' – and goes off to convert others.[36] In showing the process of conversion the pamphlet parallels its own function at the level of narrative, in a sense, telling the story of the success of its own 'reasonable' methods.

Thus, the dialogue form can have a complex structure while nevertheless allowing the reader to experience the debate as simple and obvious. The relationship between the figures in the dialogue is always framed by that between the author or newsmaker and the reader, and pamphlets work to produce an 'obvious' place for the reader's sympathies. However, as *The Arraignment of Superstition* (1642) shows, this was not always a process of caricature. This verse dialogue engages seriously with issues of custom, tradition, propriety, religion and economics, while nevertheless producing a 'correct' position for the reader.[37] Actually set in a church, and structured as an argument rather than a small drama, this dialogue shows 'the good minde of the Protestant, the Indifference of the Glasier, and the puritie and zeale of the Separatist'. The point of contention is the stained glass in a church:

SEPARATIST: Come honist Glasier, we must crave your ayde
            To helpe us pull these popish windows downe,
            And set new glasse for which you shall be payd,
            For sure the Lord on us for them does frowne
            And truely brethren should we let them stand,
            I feare 'twill bring a terrour to this land.
GLASIER: I hope not so Sir, these are ancient things
            That long have stood in former ages past
            Since Churches were, at least, since Christian Kings
            Had government, they still in Churches last,
            Least by mishap some cracks or peeces shatter'd,
            But now it seemes they all must downe be battered.

                                                        (p. 1)

The Glasier offers pragmatic and logical arguments against knock-
ing out the glass, including the suggestion that as the church itself
was built under Roman Catholicism, it too should be pulled down;
and that if the wind should turn the returning Roman Catholics
would be furious at the ruin of their windows. The Separatist
argues for the breaking up of the windows 'into peeces small'
whereas the Glasier offers to keep them, 'Were you a Glasier it
would vex your minde, / To see such curious windowes broken
heere' (p. 3). The Protestant appears to be persuaded by the
Separatist, but a glass portrait of Queen Elizabeth proves to be a
turning-point in the argument. The Separatist is in favour of
keeping this icon, but the Protestant insists that an icon of Christ
in a church is more suitable 'then a pictured Queene' (p. 5).
Ultimately, the Glasier and the Protestant form a successful
alliance against the Separatist. The pamphlet takes the points of
view that it opposes very seriously, entertaining some of the opposition's better lines of argument rather than caricaturing them.
The impulse to isolate and persuade the reader, on the one hand,
and to influence collective opinion on the other, is evident.

   These playlets, then, inhabited a market where what Elizabeth
Skerpan identifies as the dominant genres of 1642 – 'petitions,
public declarations, and parliamentary speeches' – were all, also,
regenericised as 'news' and virtually anything could be sold under
the general marketing of 'news'.[38] Indeed, playlets' titles mimic
news reports, calling attention to their part in creating and disseminating news – as in *Mercurius Britannicus* (1641) and *Mercurius
Honestus or Newes from Westminster* (1648). *Mercurius Britannicus, or the
English Intelligencer: a Tragi-Comedy at Paris* (1641) may have been

performed at Paris, but the published version presents itself as news.[39]

Such 'news' in dialogic form is obviously not remote from political theory. Indeed, a decade after most of our examples, the republican theorist James Harrington attempted to theorise the dialogue. In 1659 he made a bid to produce an accessible plan for government: in dialogue form. *Valerius and Publicola,* arguing that England could now only be a commonwealth, was published ten days after the Rump was broken up by the army.[40] The place of the dialogue in fostering the movement between private and public is acknowledged in his address 'To the Reader':

The way of dialogue, being not faithfully managed, is of all other the most fraudulent; but being faithfully managed is the clearest and most effectual for the conveying a man's sense unto the understanding of his reader. There is nothing in this world, next to the favour of God, I so much desire as to be familiarly understood . . .[41]

The form, as Harrington belatedly saw, can popularise debate and can attempt to shape a reader's assent while, apparently, leaving the outcome open.

It is the operation of these twin axes of faithfulness and persuasion that characterises the dialogue as a populist form in the 1640s: short and cheap for the news market, it persuades the reader while still presenting two views. Such texts invited circulation and commentary and aimed to influence private and public debate. Indeed, when in 1666 John Bunyan disavowed his earlier reading – 'a Ballad, a News-book, *George* on Horseback or *Bevis of Southampton'* – we can imagine not only the apparently apolitical chapbook literature described by Margaret Spufford, but also the continuum of politicised and dramatised dialogues we have been discussing.[42]

Playlets carve out an economic and intellectual position for themselves by mimicking other printed genres, especially news, in such a way as to 'be' both these things and a dialogue or playlet – even, possibly, performed either in a private house or in the street. Thus the playlets (like other pamphlets but with the added dimension of dialogue and mimicry and therefore with a greater yield of pleasure to the reader) come into a new relation to the state, participating in creating the sphere of 'civil society' precisely separated from the state. The space these playlets inhabit is neither state nor private but a place between the two spheres from which they comment critically on the relation of the citizen to the demands of the state.

'IMPRINTED WITH THE LIBERTY': PRINT, PLAYING AND THE PUBLIC DOMAIN

B: What did the Rump at home during this time?
A: . . . Also they pulled down the late King's statue in the Exchange, and in the niche where it stood, caused to be written these words: *Exit tyrannus, Regum ultimus*, etc.
B: What good did that do them, and why did they not pull down the statues of all the rest of the Kings?[43]

Hobbes's Restoration text, *Behemoth*, ironised the events of the Commonwealth by producing 'B' as an innocent educated by 'A'. His use of dialogue to do so indicates the continued importance of this form in populist political rhetoric.[44] Indeed, it is in this period that Habermas notes the social importance of the dialogue in making a 'political public sphere', commenting that 'the dialogue form attested to their proximity to the spoken word. One and the same discussion transposed into a different medium was continued in order to re-enter, via reading, the original conversational medium.'[45]

This chapter had concentrated on the dynamics of reading, but what was the size and nature of the market in which these texts existed? One indication is George Thomason's collection of printed items.[46] In 1642 Thomason collected 2,134 pieces and in 1648 2,036; throughout the 1640s figures were around 1,500. In 1649 he collected 1,346 but this *halved* to 770 in 1650 and figures remained under 1,000 to 1653.[47] Whatever the reasons for this (the shock of the regicide to royalist publishing endeavours seems to be one of them), the pamphlet dialogues and playlets appear at times of greatest ferment – the 1640s to 1648, and again in the crisis of the late 1650s.

Distribution of pamphlets seems to have been via a widespread shop, stall and street trade. Contemporary play pamphlets claim to carry news 'into the Country' for country readers as well as 'others that live in the City' who would buy pamphlets and news, 'to make themselves merry at home'.[48] It has been argued that 500 copies would be a small run for an isolated pamphlet, but enough for a single issue of a weekly newsbook (in a more crowded market).[49]

A reader, and especially a reader of cheap pamphlets, is not a reader of 'high' or 'low' culture only, but consumes a mixed diet; readers of news would also have been readers of pamphlet plays, just as more elite texts may well have found a more popular audience, depending upon their price. As Chartier's use of the term 'appropriation' suggests, texts must have been read in different ways by different readers.[50] In the 1640s reading involved an active search for political meanings. Moreover the plays themselves signal their intention to perform an educative function in their popular deployment of political arguments. Some tracts, as David Norbrook argues – *Areopagitica* is one of the most obvious – were highly conscious that in the new circumstances of the Civil War 'truth emerges in dialogue'.[51] Many seem designed to appeal to as wide an audience as possible, or to have what Natalie Zemon Davis calls multiple publics.[52]

Historians agree that literacy was rising in the period and perhaps because print *did* reach people, as did playing, social control and print were interwoven in the 1640s and 1650s.[53] The House of Commons tried to keep track of printing as well as theatrical performance. Early in 1642 parliament had atttempted to suppress newsbooks.[54] That the policing of pamphlets and plays was seen by contemporaries as linked is a further indication that both were perceived as disseminating political ideas in popular forms: in October 1647 the pro-parliamentary *Mercurius Melancholicus* condemned the legislation against printing, saying 'My Conscience tells me, 'tis a libertie . . . the Common Inns of sin, and Blasphemy, the Play-houses begin to be custom'd again, and to act filthinesse and villany to the life . . . why should Play-houses be cry'd up and pamphlets be cry'd down: are they bawdy houses too?'[55] At times pamphlets, ballad-singing and performed drama seem to have been interchangeable in government policies – in September 1648 the Commons appointed Francis Bethan to 'apprehend and surprise . . . all Persons as sell, sing or publish, Ballads or Books, scandalous to the Parliament . . . and to suppress Playhouses, and apprehend the Players'.[56]

Theatrical performance and pamphlets provided the occasion for political discussion and, as I shall show in chapter 2, various forms of critique and conflict were circulated in this form. Offensive pamphlets, some dramatic, were constantly being discussed by the Commons. In 1642 the order was passed that the name of any printer or author should be registered, but in June 1643 parliament passed the ordinance to 'prevent and suppress the licence of printing' (Milton argued against this in his – unlicensed – *Areopagitica*). The Commons frequently sent their own officers after offenders and on 3 February 1647 the Commons issued an exasperated order:

that the Lord Mayor of London, the Justices of the Peace of Westminster and liberties, Middlesex and Surrey, near unto the City, be hereby required and enjoined forthwith, and from time to time, to suppress the Publishing and Vending by Ballad-singers and such loose Persons, all libels, and all libellous Pamphlets and Ballads . . . And the House doth expect, that this order be put in due Execution, and a good account given thereof.[57]

The flourishing – or at least confused – state of the publishing industry thus remained a source of anxiety for those in power. But how 'oppositional' exactly was this print culture? Pamphlet playlets and dialogues can be seen as responding to the dominant situation and attempting to sway a readership to particular points of view. However, the objects of anger changed during the 1640s from the king to parliament and the army grandees. As David Underdown comments, 'a striking feature of the English Revolution is the complete reversal of popular sympathies that it entailed'. Without necessarily being 'radical' in terms of putting forward any political programme, playlets engaged with whatever policy was in operation, producing many kinds of 'popular' 'opposition'.[58] What the plays shared was medium, marketplace and, above all, the persuasive possibilities of the flexible politico-dramatic–serious–scurrilous genre.[59]

Thus, the dialogic and dramatic or semi-dramatic pamphlet texts of the 1640s suggest that the matrix of cultural production inhabited by news, opinion and the stage was reconfigured in the 1640s. Readers in the 1640s, like John Rous and Thomas Knyvett, discussed at the opening of this chapter, were both seduced by the point of view of the pamphlet and responded vociferously. Henry Marten, the 'brave Harry' whose pamphlet was attacked by Knyvett as 'spurious issue', 'bastard', was the object of continued scandal – for atheism, his republicanism and (continuously) for living with a woman out of wedlock. Not surprisingly, given the heat of the attacks, Marten had his own thoughts about opinions. Amongst his papers is a draft title-page to a pamphlet response to criticism,

'Opinions offered for examination by H.M.', including an emphatic rejection of licensing – 'at London by A.B. for C.D. . . . Imprinted with liberty'. Although he only composed the dedicatory epistle and two largely scored-out lines – on 'God' – he did leave a list of contents:

God
Religion
Love
{Fear
Hope
Grief
Anger
Jealousy}
Honour
Death
Sinne
{Stage playes
Opinion}

It is useful to have contemporary evidence that some people – one classical republican, at least – thought of stage and commentary (Opinion) together.[60]

CHAPTER 2

'With the agreement of the people in their hands' transformations of 'radical' drama in the 1640s

INTRODUCTION: RADICAL TALKING

Sinne
{Stage playes
Opinion}

It is a pity that Henry Marten, as a republican, never delivered himself of his Opinions on stage plays. In part this chapter attempts to use the available evidence to reconstruct the positions of tolerationist radicalism and other critical discourses of the 1640s with regard to stage plays and dramatic form. In registering events, as the last chapter argued, pamphlet plays were reciprocally influencing and influenced by contemporary 'public' debate. By tracing the playlets offering political critique in the 1640s into the 1650s we can see that some playlets which have been regarded as simply 'royalist' have links to the demands and protests in the radical writing of the 1640s: royalist and radical positions in popular polemic were not always diametrically opposed, but drew on some similar strands of popular discontent. Thus, radicalism in popular pamphlets combines at points with popular royalism and, in the 1650s, even with Quaker fervour.[1]

Another reason to return to these texts is that in contemporary literary and historical debate 'radicalism' is itself a disputed term. Whilst some critics see early modern radicalism as their object of study, others, including Conal Condren, challenge the term and associated concepts.[2] Condren is obviously right to argue that not only 'radical', 'left', 'right', but other apparently less loaded terms such as 'citizen', 'community', 'court', 'country', have resonances for us which inevitably permeate our use of them. However, his proposed solution (a return to seventeenth-century vocabulary) is impossible because of the same conditions that render it, for him, desirable – the changing connotations of language which affect *all* language. The term 'radicalism', therefore, is retained in this chapter as part of the critical discourse *on* rather than *of* the period. It is used to designate not a single specific political position – as the chapter suggests these shift significantly in the period 1640 to 1660 – but to indicate that some of the texts discussed offer a root-and-branch critique of social systems and situations. Not all texts discussed here are radical in this sense, and for this chapter a significant distinction between the critical playlets of Overton and Sheppard is the extent to which they imply not only criticism but a vision of other possibilities for social organisation.

The term 'radical' requires such careful definition because, as Ann Hughes puts it, the 'civil war . . . still matters to us' and often has partly acknowledged allegorical status in historical and literary critical writing.[3] Historians challenging the liberal-left consensus under which historians including A. L. Morton, Walzer, Stone and Hill could be grouped, revised the paradigms of the conflict (*did the Civil War have long-term causes?*) and challenged earlier methods of historical research.[4] It could be argued that their refusal of long-term trends, their turn to management structures, personalities and the elites rather than the 'people' of A. L. Morton's title, produced a civil war which complemented, sometimes supported, the dominant economic and political modes of thought in Britain and America of the 1980s. At such a time, in such a history, to write of 'radicalism' indeed seemed to foist on the past a cluster of ideas apparently redundant in the present. The aim of this chapter is to offer a case study which should demonstrate – as a limit case in my argument – that some radical and many critical stances were, indeed, compatible with and expressed in the dramatic structures usually seen as the property of 'royalists'.

POPULAR PLAYLETS AND CHANGING POLEMIC
OVERTON, SHEPPARD AND OTHERS

In a number of dramatic and semi-dramatic pamphlets of the 1640s Richard Overton appointed himself the radical, tolerationist heir to the Elizabethan polemicist Martin Marprelat:

Martin Mar-Prelat was a bonny lad
His brave adventures made the Prelats mad:
Though he be dead yet he hath left behind
A generation of the Martin kind.[5]

Overton's target was church government. His first critique of the religio-political nation was *Vox Borealis or the Northern Discovery* (1641), and he was an active pamphleteer throughout the 1640s, sharply aware of the potential of the circulation of opinions to effect radical change. In two signed pieces from 1642, *Articles of High Treason Exhibited Against Cheap-side Cross* and *New Lambeth Faye,* and the well-known attack on Archbishop Laud, *Canterbury His Change of Diet,* he opposed what he regarded as tyrannical state religion. As Martin Mar-Prelat he wrote in favour of religious toleration, mobilising the tendentious potential of pamphlet playlets and humanistic praise of folly to these ends.[6]

His tracts contrast with some later playlets and with other polemic because they are not only satirical but begin to develop a political programme in a popular form. The forty-five-page semi-dramatic pamphlet *The Arraignment of Mr Persecution* (1645) is an example of the union of the populist persuasive powers of semi-dramatic discourse and abstract, radical political polemic.[7] The playlet castigates the persecutory designs of 'Sir Simon Synod and Sir John Presbyter'. Overton objected to the directives of the Westminster assembly, the commission of divines who were attempting to formulate religious policy. He objected to the threat of Presbyterianism and, above all, sought liberty of conscience for all. The pamphlet puts religious intolerance on trial, using the shape of a court-room drama in which lengthy and carefully argued speeches alternate with witticisms and parodies of tortuous religious justifications for persecution. The debate draws on both abstract argumentation and the techniques of scurrilous satire. Overton uses the pamphlet genre as a self-consciously invented hybrid of abstract argument and popular satire employing personification to make abstract ideas accessible. For instance, Mr Power-in-Parliament uses a colloquial, secular nationalist argument for liberty of conscience:

Persecution for Conscience is inconsistent with the Soveraignty of the Kingdomes, for it divideth their powers one against another, and in themselves occasioneth murmerings, grutchings and repinings, which in time break forth into Conspiracies, Rebellions, Insurrections and c. as well to the prejudice of soveraignty as to the ruine of the Subject: and which is more, the tendency and operation of Persecution, is to reduce the power of Kingdomes and Parliaments from themselves into the hands and disposall of the Pontificall Clergie. (p. 4)

The pamphlet's insistence on the issue of religious choice being private and secular concerns being the province of government goes beyond the familiar territory of politico-religious debate, exceeding and contradicting such demands for parliamentary sovereignty as Henry Parker's *Observations Upon Some of His Majesties Late Answers and Expresses* (1642).[8] Whereas Parker asserts that the parliamentary body represents the nation, Overton sees the possibility of universal amity and toleration achieved through accepted diversity of religious opinion and united secular interests.

This position is made available to the reader through the story of Persecution, who had been roaming in Protean fashion in 'the briery thickets of Rhetoricall Glosses, Sophistications and scholastick Interpretations'. Whenever he was about to be caught 'the cunning Hocus Pocus vanish'd out of their sight' (pp. 1–2). The text's attack on the 'briery thickets' of 'scholastic glosses' contrasts with his own ludic readability – Overton's pamphlet requires a familiarity with politico-religious debates that were affecting everyone but it puts the controversy firmly in the semi-colloquial language of the public sphere. Thus, when Persecution is eventually caught his trial has a personified cast ranging from Mr Unity-of-Kingdomes through to Mr Nationall-Strength, Mr Sealed-Peace, Mr Humane-Society, Mr Nationall-Wealth, Mr Civill-Government, Mr Domesticke-Misery. The jury which agree that Persecution should be indicted as an enemy to God are, implicitly and explicitly, expressions of secular and national interest. Liberty-of-Conscience is prevented from speaking in the first part of the trial because Persecution begs for Sir Symon Synod to be brought in, and Synod attempts to pack the jury with his supporters:

to wit, Mr *Satan*, Mr *Antichrist*, Mr *Spanish-Inquisition*, Mr *Councell-of-Trent*, Mr *High-Commission*, Mr *Assembly-of-Divines*, Mr *Rude-Multitude*, Sir *John-Presbyter*, mine only son. Mr *Scotch-Government*, Mr *False-Prophets*, Mr *Ecclesiasticall-Supremacy*, Mr *Pontificall-Revenue*: These never failed the designs of the Clergy. (p. 7)

The incorporation of '*Rude-Multitude*' in a list which also includes Satan is an indication that even as these pamphlets attempt to reach a wide audience they maintain a distance from the 'mob', constructing their reader in opposition to it. The figure 'King's Servant' is used to illuminate the congruence of interest between church and king when he speaks in favour of Symon Synod's proposed jurors, saying that 'there be divers of these whom *Royall Prerogative* hath called in to his Assistance' (p. 7). Thus theological and political abstractions are transformed into a drama of opinions in which the reader experiences the combined pleasures of lucid argument and narrative interest.

This playlet might be seen as a relatively fixed point in a political continuum. It can stand as a 'radical' text in its advocacy of liberty of conscience, an idea alien to many of its potential readers. It promulgates a decisive – even utopian – view of potential reforms, made acceptable to a reader by the playlet's comedic shape whereby 'liberty' wins and Synod, Presbyter and Persecution are defeated. But the ideas are nonetheless highly polemic for a mid-seventeenth-century audience: when Liberty-of-Conscience is finally allowed to speak he argues for the biblical basis for toleration of 'Turks, Jewes, Pagans and Infidells' (p. 22). Persecution is sentenced to be tortured day and night for ever and Sir John Presbyter is sent 'to the uncleane, filthy, impious, and worldly *Dungeon*, called Jure Humano . . . to be bound with *Magesteriall Chaines* of humaine Lawes, Ordinances, Edicts etc.' (p. 44). Martin Mar-Prelat ends with a postscript insisting that he is entirely in favour of 'Civill league' between England and Scotland.

Thus, the tract dramatises the interconnection between liberty of conscience and all other liberties using narrative anticipation (what will happen to Persecution?) and satirical wordplay to create a comedy with a complex structure that interweaves dramatic tension and political polemic. It brilliantly positions the reader as disenfranchised by anti-tolerationists and therefore likely to be in agreement with the pamphlet's programme, admirably illustrating McKenzie's contention that this ephemeral literature of the Civil War is often characterised by 'political sophistication'. This playlet uses scepticism and mockery to crystallise a painful image of the coercion implicit in an intolerant, state church.

Overton repeated his tolerationist argument in *Martin's Echo*

(1645, collected by Thomason in June). Once again we note the secular, embracing rhetoric of the Leveller address:

I beseech you *friends*, consider what you doe, consider the fruit of your bodies, unto what slavery you are fit to enthrall them, I know you would be loath your children after you should be deprived of trading or living in the kingdom, though they should differ a little in opinion from others. I could wish we might lay down this controversy about opinions, and not thus devour, rend and tear one another about them . . .[9]

Not all pamphlet playlets attempted so powerfully to convince a reader of something as alien as toleration. Leveller arguments for toleration persisted and developed into an attack on parliament, finding its best known statement in the constitutional document *The Agreement of the People* (1647). From 1645 onwards Overton joined his voice with John Lilburne and William Walwyn against Presbyterianism and what they saw as parliamentary tyranny. Their writings suggest a change in popular feeling, in which the focus of attack shifts from Charles and Presbyterianism to parliament, and later to the army grandees during 1647–9. As David Underdown notes, the new regimes were disliked in the towns and villages, even those which had been strongholds of reforming activity. The Levellers translated this mounting dissent from the activities and apparatus of the new order into political polemic and theory in such documents as the *Petition to the House of Commons* (September 1648) which indicates their discontent with the tardiness of reform. Lilburne articulates disillusionment in *Legall Fundamental Liberties* (1649) when he says of king and parliament, 'it was our interest to keep up one tyrant to balance another, till we certainly knew what that tyrant that pretended fairest would give us as our freedoms'.[10]

Although Overton's attacks on hierarchy are the only ones amongst the Leveller tracts to take dramatic form, Walwyn used monologue, and the rhetorical flourishes of Lilburne found theatrical expression in the strange drama of his trial, at which long sections of his pamphlet writings had to be read out, 'Which pleased the people as well as if they had acted before them one of *Ben Jonson's* plays, for their excellency'.[11] The trial itself became a kind of public theatre in which the judges were constantly careful to preserve themselves from the charge of denying Lilburne his rights, and contemporary accounts convey the theatricality of

Lilburne's proceedings in both 1649 and 1653. On trial for his life because of his writings, Lilburne's success in persuading the jury to acquit him can be seen as an example of the intimacy of political persuasion and popular theatre during the period. The writings of this group were influential in some pamphlets of the later 1640s and 1650s which both addressed their positions and selectively adopted and adapted their polemic and ideas.

The changes in political perspectives and the feelings of the audience for pamphlet playlets (as well as those of the authors) from the end of the first war onwards can be traced in popular events and in print. Playlets addressed and fostered the mounting political tension over the problem of what to do with the king, and satire came to be increasingly at the expense of parliament. By 1647 the City, so active in the first years of Civil War, had become a force behind the conservative bid for Presbyterianism on the Scottish model and, like parliament, the City wanted the army disbanded, and feared the alliance of City radicals and soldiers.[12] Parliament's bid to disband the army in 1647 brought about the alliance between Agitators elected by army regiments and the Levellers. Political theory and popular protest came together in *The Agreement of the People*, presented to the Army Council in October 1647 and published in November. It saw the war in terms of the freedom of the people (and army) who:

Having by our late labours and hazards made it appeare to the world at how high a rate wee value our just freedome . . . do now hold ourselves bound in mutual duty to each other, to take the best care we can for the future, to avoid both the danger of returning to a slavish condition, and the chargeable remedy of another war . . . (p. 238)

The intersection of political and dramatic discourse in the formation of public opinion of the Civil War, and their shared audience, is demonstrated by the speed with which this document was recycled in a dramatic satire highly critical of the Levellers. *The Levellers Levell'd* (1647) blamed the king's flight to the Isle of Wight on their attempt to murder him.[13] Mercurius Pragmaticus introduces himself in the first person, as an actor in state affairs – 'I that have lasht base Traytors to the bone, / Have whipt ambition, pride, and spared none' (A1v). After beginning as a masque with England's Genius made so afraid by Rebellion that it runs off to a cave to hide, the playlet attacks rebellion using the model of Jonson's

Catiline, the five conspiring Levellers swear by an effigy of Catiline preserved as a 'sacred relique', promising:

By the fam'd memorie of this brave spirit, that once made Rome to tremble at his nod, who took the horrid Sacrament in blood to levell her proud battlements, sweare not to lay downe armes till King Charles be sent to the invisible land, till all Lawes are repealed and abrogated, *meum* and *tuum* on pain of death not mentioned. (1.ii)

The power of Leveller polemic is itself suggested by this playlet's demonising presentation of the Levellers and Agitators as plotting against the king (flown to the dubious safety of the Isle of Wight) and threatening property. The prologue describes the Agitators as 'a Remora', and the Levellers are called 'Conspiracie', 'Democracie', 'Apostasie', 'Treachery' and 'Impiety'; the play also includes the figure 'Regicide'. When the play quotes *The Agreement of the People* against itself – using the voice of Democracie demanding 'some rare unwonted liberty which we declare to be our native Rights' (11.ii, p. 220–1) – we can see that the playlet anticipated that its readers would know the political material it was using. Moreover, the journalistic accuracy shown in situating part of the play at the great gathering of the army at Ware indicates that the playlets were also 'news'.

Nedham, to whom the pamphlet was attributed, but who denied authorship, attacked Leveller ideas in *The Case of the Commonwealth of England Stated* (1650), though he later emerged from prison to become a journalistic mainstay of the Commonwealth and foremost republican theorist.[14] The way individuals such as Overton and Nedham switch between the forms of political disputation and dialogue, and even include political tracts in plays, indicates the heat of the debate over the nature of the Commonwealth in popular pamphlet genres.

During the renewed crisis of government in 1647–9 political debate took place in an overlapping combination of theoretic and popular discourse. The political situation following the capture of the king was a critical moment, initiating change in political sentiments registered in pamphlets and counter pamphlets. For example, the danger of an alliance with the Scots was attacked in the playlet *The Scotch Politike Presbyter* (1647). The frenzied pamphleteering of 1647 to 1649, and the part played by both Leveller and royalist playlets, suggests once again that political debate was not confined to high, abstract discourses. Moreover, criticism and satire were not by any means always clearly 'royalist' or 'Leveller', but took on a new political hybridity and ambivalence as it became increasingly clear that parliament was unable to answer the nation's woes, and at the time of Pride's Purge the Levellers feared a new parliamentary tyranny. A new political position, sympathetic to the radical cause but opposed to the purged parliament, begins to be articulated in pamphlets.

An example of this more ambivalent political discourse is the playlet *A New Bull-Bayting* (1649).[15] The Levellers Overton, Lilburne and Prince (now imprisoned in the Tower) appear goading 'the Town Bull of Ely' – 'Enter Noll drawne to the stake by the four Bear-wards; his hornes all bloudy and a garland on his head.' The pamphlet attacks the excise, taxes, the regicide, Bradshaw as the president of the court which tried Charles, and other abuses, prophesying that the Irish will finish Cromwell. It ends with that favourite pamphlet structure, 'Noll's Last Will and Testament.' This pamphlet clearly has a sense of the way Leveller positions have changed, a sensitivity to political history shared by *The Picture of a New Courtier* discussed below. It calls attention to the history of Leveller positions, and the irony that they began as supporters of Cromwell. When the figure representing Thomas Prince reminds Overton of this he replies, 'I profess I did; but he has (by swerving from his first principles) deceived me and thousands more' (p. 8). This playlet offers a commentary on the history of Leveller radicalism versus negotiation, satirises Cromwell, and indicates the emergence of political positions which refused to favour Charles, parliament or the army grandees. Critics tend to gloss such plays as either radical, possibly Leveller, polemic or royalist; in fact the swiftly shifting political situation generated more ambivalent and blended criticisms. It is only in the twentieth century, because of our old habit of thinking of the Civil War as a binary struggle, that such positions appear to be 'confused'. Of course, contemporary events were confusing and unclear and contradictory polemic is bound up with this. Indeed radical and royalist protest coexist with attacks on obvious, pragmatic, targets such as taxes. Some plays satirise the army grandees and their aspirant wives – such as *The Cuckoos-Nest at Westminster, Cromwell's Conspiracy, The Famous Tragedie of Charles I*. But not all critical playlets fit easily into a 'royalist' paradigm. A play sometimes attributed to Overton himself, which appeared in 1649, is the two-part *New-Market Fayre, or Mrs Parliaments New Figgaries*. The first play takes its cue from the sale of Charles I's goods by the army grandees and represents them as inheriting the king's lands and goods and then, on hearing of the destruction of the navy, as killing themselves. Mysteriously revived in the second play, Cromwell and Fairfax are again centre-stage and again destroyed.

The plays are examples of a new position emerging in popular rhetoric whereby the post-regicidal grandees become the target of popular opposition. *New-Market Fayre*, as Wolfe notes, refers sympathetically to the 'people', to *The Agreement of the People*, and to the widow of the radical commander Rainsborough (she is contrasted with the lecherous Mrs Cromwell and Lady Fairfax) but it also mentions Charles Stuart the Younger as the possible bringer of peace.[16] In the second part of *New-Market Fayre* Hugh Peter appears as a necromancer who has unnaturally renewed the life in the bodies of Cromwell and Fairfax, dead at the end of the first play but now 'possessed with Devils'. In what reads like a parody of the choice speech in Marlowe's *Doctor Faustus*, Hugh Peter says, 'Preaching is too tedious for me; Ile leave that to Owen, and to Goodwin – Have I not done a Miracle to repossesse these Bodies with Spirits, that were before meer Skellitons, and stinking Carkasses?'(ii.iii).

The Sherriff and others had gone to Fairfax 'with the *Agreement of the People* in their hands' (v.x). Finally, after a huge fight involving Lady Fairfax and Mrs Cromwell, and the murder of Ireton, Pride and others as witches, the play ends with the 'People' shouting angrily 'Lets Petition our King home, we shall never be happy else' (v).

Thus, the 'People' appear taking political action which embraces advocating *The Agreement of the People* and popular royalism. As the editor notes, *New-Market Fayre*'s attack on the army grandees draws on royalist news-sheets for May and June 1649.[17] But it is also ambivalent towards the radical Leveller programme: both popular royalism and *The Agreement of the People* are put forward as possible solutions, opposed by Cromwell and Fairfax. Thus, Fairfax rushes away from a crowd saying, 'The Devil stop your mouths; will nothing serve you but *The Agreement of the People, The Agreement of the People*! Are not the Parliament the People's Representatives' (v.x). Fairfax's terror is that the demands for reform exceed the borders of the discussion of representation in parliament and self-interest. He falls asleep but awakes from violent dreams to the entry of 'Sheriffs and others with the *Agreement of the People* in their hands' (v.x). They drag Fairfax away to die while he shouts, ambiguously, 'Who builds his Hopes upon a *Common Rout* / Thus must he fall.' Further evidence in the Leveller programme is suggested in the next scene when Constantius and Fidelius opine that 'if *Overton* speaks true; the Bull's designed for the slaughter next', referring to Cromwell. The final scene shows Cromwell and the rest to be corpses reanimated by Jesuit charms and the People decide to recall the king.

This play can hardly be said to be straightfowardly royalist and bears testimony to the fact that although the Levellers were in the Tower they were a powerful voice in popular politics. Their demands haunt Fairfax, and Overton's pamphlets are referred to familiarly, suggesting that the play's attack on the grandees is mediated through some of the hopes of reformation which had found their expression in *The Agreement of the People*. As Cromwell prepared to go to Ireland, opposition continued and in this play and elsewhere we can find an interweaving of Leveller demands for constitutional reform, hatred of the present regime, and a vision of Charles II as an imagined solution.

What happened to the popular aspect of Leveller demands after the regicide? The ambivalence of *New-Market Fayre* is one indication. More evidence for a new kind of populist polemic and critique can be found in the complicated nexus of royalist–populist–Leveller aspirations in a playlet recently brought to our attention by Lois Potter, *The Terrible, Horrible Monster Out of the West* (1651), a playlet attacking parliament.[18] However, it presents Carolina (a shepherd of Charles I?) as helpless, led by Rusticus, who seems to be another figure for the people, albeit in a gentler, agrarian aspect.[19] Like *New-Market Fayre* this pamphlet employs a discourse approximating to royalism in its presentation of the king as powerless, but also deploys familiar Leveller attacks on the army grandees, tithes, tyranny. The play opens with an attack on the parliament and the abuses they have generated, before Toby Tel-Troth clears the stage for the demonstration of a monster whose stomach is as hard as a camel's knees, after devouring everything in the kingdom. Elements which run counter to a possible reading of the play as a Leveller document are the items included in the lists of things the parliament-monster has swallowed – which include the king's stock of arms and bishops. But it has also devoured the Man in the Moon's critical printing press (also mentioned in *A New Bull-Bayting*, above). And it has found Lilburne impossible to swallow.

The Terrible, Horrible Monster is a politically ambiguous document. At the very least it is evidence of the continuity of the combination of abstract and scatalogical language characteristic of some Leveller satire, indicating its survival after the regicide. Obviously, it points to the continuation of Lilburne as a popular hero. The largest claim that could be made for the play as a Leveller document rests on the mentions of tithes and Lilburne: nonetheless it does seem to constitute a continuation of popular debate around Leveller ideas, but in a new form and combined with a nostalgic royalism. It is also an index of the transformation of popular radical opposition, which is now firmly against parliament. It seems likely that *New-Market Fayre* and *The Terrible, Horrible Monster* would be recognised as drawing on Leveller threads because Lilburne was a popular hero and Leveller pamphlets were thoroughly distributed, at least throughout the army. The efficiency of Leveller distribution networks is attested by one of their critics, Richard Baxter, who commented, 'a great part of the mischief they did among the soldiers was by pamphlets which they abundantly dispersed; such as R. Overton's *Martin Mar-Priest*, and more of his, and some of J. Lilburne's'.[20]

There were other strands of critique of the government using other modes, not offering a radical programme but certainly deploying intense criticism of parliament. Amongst printed pamphlets produced in the general alienation from parliament in the late 1640s, for example, Samuel Sheppard stands out as a pamphleteer who not only represents the turn of opinion against parliament, but whose plays also use for polemical ends the devices, scenes and comic plotting supplied by Jacobean city comedy. Sheppard had been a supporter of the army and had written a prose paean to Fairfax's generalship in 1646 but later attacked both sectaries and Ranters.

Indeed, Sheppard's views on government are an instance of the transformation of popular opinion in the later 1640s. In 1646 he wrote in support of Fairfax and Cromwell in *The Yeare of Jubilee; or,*

England's Releasment (London, 1646). In the same year he satirised religious faction in *The Times Displayed in Six Sestyads* (London, 1646) a theme he returned to after the regicide with the playlet *The Joviall Crew or, the Devill Turn'd Ranter* (London, 1651). In 1646 he also attacked John Lilburne, supporting the House of Lords in *The Famer Fam'd* (London, 1646) and *Animadversions Upon John Lilburnes Last Two Books . . . London's Liberty in Chaines Discovered, the other Anatomy of the Lords Cruelty* (London, 1646). However, in 1647 he wrote the two-part *The Committee-Man Curried* (1647), indicating a shift against parliament and City government.

In 1646 he replied to Overton's defence of the imprisoned Lilburne in *The False Alarum.*[21] In *The Famer Fam'd* Sheppard had defended the Peers in their condemnation of Lilburne, but not in royalist terms: '. . . many Peers have done worthy deedes for the good of the people, but ye have exceeded them all *undergoing the frowne of Majestie, which who looks on sees a Basilkisk, and seldom escapeth Death*' (A2r–v). So not only was Sheppard not a royalist (in 1646) but involved in actively supporting parliament against the Levellers. His position seems to be slightly different by 1647. Sheppard's use of a rhetoric of character rather than symbolic representation combined with his attack on the bureaucratic small fry of London's government make his two *Committee* plays very different from Overton's radical, abstract personification. However, their political analysis is by no means simply royalist.

The semi-dramatic *Grand Plutoe's Progresse* (1647) presents London as in chaotic rebellion: as he approaches London Pluto is delighted to hear a 'loud and clamorous noise', of people calling 'we will not be subject/ Unto our betters'. The government and taxing of London by committees, and disputes between Presbyterians and sectaries, is similarly a focus of Sheppard's play *The Committee-Man Curried.* It was acquired by Thomason on 16 July 1647, the same day on which the House of Commons drew up a new order for the more effective suppression of 'Plays and Playhouses, and all Dancings on the Ropes'.[22] The play claims that it discovers 'the corruption of Committee-men, and Excise-men . . . the unjust sufferings of the Royall party, the divellish hypocrisie of some Roundheads, the revolt for gaine of some Ministers' and begins with a prologue on the relationship of plays to stages, and of satirical political pamphlets to censorship:

Since it is held a crime, that on the Stage
Wit should present it selfe (since that the Age)
Degenerates so farre, that nothing may
Be countenanc't, that shew but like a Play:
How shall these Scaenes scape free (ye wiser few)
That are not retrograded with the crew
O'the reforming ones, since tis enacted
That nought but fiery Faction shall be acted;

. . .

Fooles onely speake *Cum Privilegio*
We in obedience, so as we can,
Have given words to the Committee-man. (A1v)

The Volponesque opening scene presents Suck-Dry, 'a Committee man', who wants to 'pocket up the Commons Coyn today', waking up and beating his clerk Sneake. The next scene presents a cavalier, Loyalty, bewailing with apparent self-interest the lot of the king 'like a huge Pyramid' who, 'in his fall / Hath crusht his props to nothing'. In consequence Loyalty is forced to go to the house of his Uncle:

A warm furred sir, one that leanes on
His bags as on his staffe, and commits Sodomy
With Mammon; – he hath pretended zeale
For Church and State, hath set out horse and man
Against his Soveraigne (A3r)

Loyalty knocks at the door only to be read a lecture and refused money. Sheppard's way of presenting the new prosperous London classes is drawn from pre-war plays which explored the interconnection of family, economic motives and politics. Although we have no record that it was staged, this is one of the plays from the period that – as stage directions, references to curtains and props, fast and breathless comic speech and action all indicate – is stageworthy. The dramatic structures and tricks are reminiscent of city comedies such as Middleton's *Trick to Catch the Old One* and *A Mad World My Masters*, or Massinger's *A New Way to Pay Old Debts* (they might also point forward to Behn's anti-City characterisation of City types in plays like *The City Heiress*). Here, however, it is not only status, ethos and wealth which are contrasted. The split between the wealthy and the poverty-stricken found in the plays of Middleton is exacerbated in a more sharply opposed characterisation of City–sectarian–wealthy and royalist–poor. The morality of royalists is split between 'Loyalty' and Ruffian, a 'Dammee', but in Sheppard's play the Uncle is unredeemably a parliamentarian and a City type – closer perhaps to Massinger's Overreach than Middleton's uncles. The play also presents the taking of sides in the Civil War as making explicit deep divisions in family, generation, religious and class interests.

After the royalist, Loyalty, leaves England for France the play plunges into a biting satire on the mismanagement of London under the reforming ascendancy of corrupt and popularly loathed Committee-men and Excise-men. During the tavern scene in Act III Rebellion and Time-server (a trimming priest) come to the Sun tavern in Aldgate where Common-curse and Suck-dry are drowning their sorrows. Common-curse and Suck-dry are discovered at the drawing of a curtain 'taking Tobacco, Wine before them'. When he arrives at the tavern Rebellion protests, 'What Circe hath with murmuring charmes, thus Metamorphos'd seeming civil men to beastly swine, O Mr Time-server – with what weeping eyes behold these sinnes here Acted, for which a nation mournes.' In the next scene however, Rebellion and Time-server expose themselves as drunken hypocrites.

The presentation of scenes involving the cavalier 'Dammee' a 'Ruffian', qualify the play's loyalism, even as they present the Dammee's revenge: the final act presents Dammee, the lover of Lightheele, wife to citizen Horne. Lightheele is dallying with her other lover, Suck-dry the Committee-man, who has been reading his dire verses in her honour: 'Eyes are seducing Lights, that the good Women know / And hang out these, a neerer way to show', when Ruffian arrives to interrupt. Ruffian, in himself no catch as a lover, is nevertheless the vehicle for the exposure of the awful Suck-dry: Ruffian breaks down the bedroom door and chases him and his mistress out on to the stage 'naked', before beating him severely.

In the sequel to _The Committee-Man Curried_ (14 August 1647) the farce continues.[23] Rebellion is tricked out of his money in a short-hand version of a gulling scene reminiscent of Middleton's London comedies; in Act IV Loyalty persuades Rebellion to pay his creditors on the ground that he is dying. Loyalty, masquerading as one about to die, arranges a show of a young man dead, revived by the arrival of money. Once more this echoes the prodigal mirth of earlier plays such as *Knight of the Burning Pestle*, but it is also used to underline Rebellion's literary and interpretative obtuseness – he does not understand the entertainment as an allegory of his own situation. Horne, the citizen who rents out his wife, is defeated too. She runs off, leaving him to close the play, 'Come then, and since I've lost my citie wife, / Ile for the future lead a Countrey life.' The deceptions of the City are (albeit ambiguously) contrasted to the country, but Horne's progress into Warwickshire does not indicate a political or religious change of heart.

The City jokes are all against the hated tax-collectors but, although J. C. Davis emphasises that Sheppard wrote for royalist newsbooks in both the later 1640s and the 1650s, some of the royalists of *The Committee-Man Curried* entirely lack morality (compare *The Famous Tragedie of Charles I*, chapter 3), and we are invited to read the play as a condemnation of government rather than a plea for the restoration of Charles; Loyalty is only one figure among many bemoaning his lot, fighting for survival in the City and using deception to gain his ends.[24] Certainly, the *Committee-Man* playlets carry the implication of popular resentment of any kind of governmental power, whether one that imposed monopolies or committees.

Inevitably, their criticism of the current regime in London and attacks on corruption replicate the attacks on abuses in pamphlet plays from the very early 1640s, analysed above and in chapter 1. Indeed, as the Levellers and Sheppard both realise, parliament in the mid- to late 1640s found itself forced to act in a high-handed and arguably unconstitutional way to raise funds – just as Charles had. On the other hand, by late 1649 Cromwell was emerging as a conservative figure and reforms were not sweeping away the injustices of the old order. The pamphlet plays of Overton and Sheppard illuminate the diversity of critical politics in the mid-to-late 1640s and demonstrate the gradual shift of protest from attacks on monarchy to attacks on parliament, Cromwell and the army grandees. Moreover, in a literary arena where one scholar can attribute *New-Market Fayre* to Richard Overton and another to a royalist it is evident that political satire and polemic to some extent shared a common language, a sharing which reinforces my point that Civil War and Protectorate dramatic polemic criticised the government of the moment from a range of perspectives but shared genres and rhetoric. Analysis of playlets from these years demonstrates once again the active part played by dramatic discourse in the public political sphere – in registering and shaping opinions. It underscores the necessity of reconceptualising the significance of dramatic discourse during the later 1640s, and provides evidence against any binary model of the conflict.

In the world of political events Pride's Purge did decisively polarise opinion about parliament. During the period after the bitter second civil war popular resentment of the Commons had intensified: David Underdown notes the increased loathing of the reformers and 'Godly sort' who were trying to suppress ancient festivities, and Hirst notes petitions to return to the old ways of government.[25] Justifications of the new government included Anthony Ascham's *A Discourse Wherein is Examined What is Particularly Lawful During the Confusion and Revolutions of Government* (1648) and John Goodwin's defence of Pride's Purge, *Right and Might Well Met* (1648), in which he argues that the purged members 'were strangely struck with a political frenzy', and therefore it was legal for parliament to 'wrest a sword out of the hand of a madman'.[26] However, Pride's Purge marks a watershed in parliament's career leading up to the regicide, and much popular drama at this point turned decisively against the new government.

Dialogues such as *The Hampton Court Conspiracy* attacked Levellers and Agitators in the post-war debates about the army. Often these anti-parliamentarian satires abuse particular great men or personify parliament: dramatic and semi-dramatic satires on Pride's Purge brought the government itself on to the stage as the source of misery and madness in plays like the partially dramatic *The Cuckoos-Nest at Westminster*. *Stop Your Noses or England at her Easement* is a scatalogical satire indicating that, as a solution other than regicide failed to appear, a popular hatred for parliament grew in royalists, 'moderates', and those who could not imagine killing a king. *England at Her Easement* mobilises these feelings, dramatising England's need to get rid of the 'clods' which 'almost strangled her', in an inversion of Pride's Purge. One particular target is the regicide Henry Marten (who returned to parliament on 7 December, after Pride's Purge) and whose secular, libertarian, republicanism provoked vitriolic attacks:

TIME: Once more shit freely, O the man of sinne
  Who's this whose bones do rattle in his skin.

ENGLAND: Tis Harry Martin; the treacherous Saint, who esteems no
sinne so veniall as Adultery, this is one of the principall firebrands
hath burnt downe many of my townes and villages, and hath placed
his chief felicity, in destroying the Kings Loyall Subjects.[27]

In the end England has expelled all – 'the Committee-man, a sooty
sinner', Fairfax and Lambert (pp. 5–6). Such playlets present
England as at a moral and political nadir in 1648–9, and the idea
of 'purging' was reiterated in *The Disease of the House* (1649), an
attack on the remnants of government after the death of the king.
The body of parliament, sick and headless, is abused in various
violent and grotesque ways in the name of political medicine, but,
as the name 'mountebanck' implies, nothing is to be done and
John Capon leaves, saying 'Farewell dull Commons, for evermore
farewel,/ I cannot stay; these have made England Hell.' Like the
Mar-Prelat tracts it uses a vernacular language to formulate a
polemic, unlike them it offers no reforming or political possibilities.

Overton's career as a writer seems to have ended with *The
Bayting of the Great Bull of Bashan* in July 1649.[28] His radical pamphlets were one strand in a complex market of popular polemic.
As I have shown, strands of radical polemic survived in the 1650s
in an alliance, or engagement, with populist royalism, and the historical circumstances which produced these critical playlets suggests that particularly after 1649 any criticism attempting to
generalise a binary split between radical and royalist needs qualification. Perhaps we need to think of the powerful critical thinking of the 1640s as being transformed and reshaped by shifting
issues and circumstances, rather than 'dying' or 'surviving'.

The radical Leveller programme of the 1640s blended with a
popular royalism after 1647 when disaffection with parliament
became intense. The appearance of both Leveller demands and
nostalgic royalism in some pamphlets serves to recontextualise any
sense of royalism as a *purely* conservative position: in the 1650s it
was also the most obvious route for popular critique of contemporary government. By 1649, which brought the regicide and the
establishment of the republic, the objects of criticism had changed
decisively. Popular royalism seems to have grown in the 1650s
though some aspects of Leveller critique were preserved well into
the 1650s in Quaker polemic. If the popular drama of the 1640s
and Commonwealth (1649–53) engages with the possibility of

radically rethinking the nation (see chapters 3 and 8), the Protectorate brought new circumstances again. As Waller wrote, Cromwell gave 'hope again that well-born men may shine'. Waller was not unjustified in his hope that the old hierarchy would begin to be in part reinstated under Cromwell and in London a social life resembling the pre-war ways began to be re-established.

For many, Cromwell becoming Protector and the fear that he might become king represented a defeat in some ways bigger than the return of the Stuarts. This sense of betrayal was particularly strong amongst the radical sects, Fifth Monarchists and Quakers, and the measures against interrupting preaching in 1655 intensified this sense of betrayal. At this point Quakers, religious radicals, Presbyterians – many of whom would themselves have been vehemently opposed to theatrical performance, theatres, or the playing of parts – might use the dialogue form. An example is the pamphlet dialogue *An Honest Discourse Between Three Neighbours, touching the Present Government in these Three Nations* published in 1655, when George Fox was in prison, also the year in which John Lilburne was touched by Quakerism in Dover gaol. It supports Christopher Hill's contention that Quakerism took on the radical mantle of the Levellers; moreover, they would be less likely to use plays or semi-dramatic forms as modes of communication, and Presbyterians promoted the 'reform' of manners which helped to keep the theatre closed.[29]

Among the political playlets and dialogues organised for print consumption, *The Picture of a New Courtier Drawn in a Conference between Mr Timeserver and Mr Plain-heart* illuminates both the continuities of secular radical critique into the 1650s, and the different circumstances it addressed.[30] This playlet may be by the radical and republican publisher John Streater; certainly, it addresses the key concerns of classical republicans and presents the image of Cromwell familiar from Leveller polemic, discovering the 'horrid Hypocrisies of the Usurper and his timeserving Parasites'. It returns to the question of licensing, describing itself as 'Printed in the year of *England's* great trouble and slavery, and . . . to be found at the signe of the people's Liberties, right opposite to the Usurpers Court'. One issue which forced together royalist and other critique in the mid-1650s was the centrality of Cromwell here (in 1656) characterised as a king opposed to 'Brother *Sincerity*, and all the rest of those good souls, which

endeavoured *England's* freedome ... to secure the liberties of
English men; and root out Monarchy, root and branch' (p. 2).
These words are spoken by Timeserver as he recalls his true-
hearted radical past before his care became 'to comply with great
men's actions, be they good or bad' and to be employed 'by his
Talnesse to ensnare the Plain-hearted' (pp. 2, 3). Notably, then,
Timeserver has allowed the turning of the political tide to defeat
his republican aspirations:

TIMES: Sir, I am at present a Courtier, and dwell at White-hall.
PLAINHEART: Indeed ... I was banisht from thence, on the first erect-
     ing of the new Court: for none of my name ... could abide there
     any longer, without making Ship-wrack of Faith and a good
     Conscience, in conniving at the great mans wickedness which is
     grown to such a magnitude, that it may be descerned without any
     Spectacles. (p. 3)

The pamphlet's configuration of old and new political structures
is complex; Cromwell is new but worse than the old monarchy
('the King chastised with Whips, but Cromwell chastiseth with
Scorpions' (p. 4)) and republicanism is figured a powerful discourse with access to truth, sidelined by the reappearance of
monarchy. Thus, political critique survives, reconfigured, and with
a sense of the history of the circumstances determining its current
position. Radical claims both continued and were reconfigured,
and when the situation changed again with Cromwell's death
radical polemic and playlets reappeared. At this point the republican Henry Neville's *Shuffling, Cutting and Dealing* (1659) offers a
more cynical view of the fragmentation of radicalism and republicanism since the 1640s: the 'Papist' has the final word – 'If you all
complain, I hope I shall win at last.'[31]

THE 1640S: 'RADICALISM'?

Pamphlet drama of the 1640s offered both radical and pragmatic
criticism of the status quo, sometimes (as in the Leveller texts)
articulating alternative programmes of government. Although
Quakers, Baptists and Presbyterians would be unlikely to turn to
dramatic forms, secular, tolerationist and some independent
writers clearly saw the potential influence of dramatic form.

It is evident, from the texts that I have cited and the pattern
traced, that certain forms of radicalism were readily articulated

within printed dramatic forms. The Protestant ethic of debate and persuasion finds expression in such forms as well as the classical tradition in the dialogue discussed in chapter 1. Moreover, the diversity of critical positions and the way they change characterises polemical pamphlet drama of the 1640s, and some offer a radical critique of the status quo. In the 1640s this critique is sometimes coupled with a vision of another, possible world, a vision which fades and, at times, blends into the strange Leveller–royalist critique of some 1650s playlets and dialogues. It is significant that we can trace polemical opposition to the status quo in Leveller, royalist, Quaker and – on the verge of the Restoration – secular republican playlets. The evidence presented here suggests that not only were drama and certain kinds of radicalism entirely compatible, but also that dramatic pamphlets played a part in circulating and debating radical positions.

Some critics, such as Jonathan Dollimore, look to the drama of the pre-war seventeenth century for an articulation of the issues which were to bring about the conflict of the Civil War, noting that the plays of the pre-war era often simultaneously embody the ideologies he sees them as challenging.[32] Leonard Tennenhouse, Jonathan Dollimore and others link the radical potential they find in Jacobean tragedy to the crisis of the Civil War. Tennenhouse, however, sees pre-war culture as serving almost exclusively the holders of aristocratic power.[33] Dollimore's contrastingly nuanced account traces in Jacobean tragedy a twin radicalism in genre and moments of radical critique. He sees the court settings of these plays as offering a 'historically specific focus for a contemporary critique of power relations' and understands tragedies such as *The Duchess of Malfi* and *Bussy D'Ambois* as also formally radical.[34]

Drama obviously was a crucible for social and political discontents through the 1630s and early 1640s. Given the politicisation of the genre by the ban of 1642, it would be surprising indeed if radical critique and drama had, as many accounts suggest, suddenly parted company in the 1640s. Yet, undoubtedly, the significance of dramatic genres did change in 1642. The 'radicalism' of the plays discussed here is not so much a moment of formal radicalism disrupting or changing a dramatic genre, but part of a network of discourses found in and out of dramatic texts. The radical and critical playlets emerge from explicit political programmes as well as wider discursive frameworks. Secondly, the radicalism of form found in the plays discussed here is not the avant-garde anti-realism which Dollimore located in the earlier plays but responds to the exigencies of publication in the 1640s.

It is possible to trace some continuities but only within the framework of a transformation of the generic, ideological and political conditions. 1642 cannot be invoked as a magic year in which the ideological contradictions of Jacobean and Caroline drama are somehow resolved in a revolutionary moment, but the critical potential of drama was confirmed by the ban of 1642. Thus, Harold Love's comment that 'the idea of the dramatist being a fit person to comment at will on domestic politics, or a theatre audience a fit body to receive such comment, was very much a Restoration discovery' is qualified by the evidence presented here which also suggests an emerging sphere of printed dramatic debate of which the Restoration audience would also have been aware.[35]

It is clear from the printed and performed circulation of political plays that drama (and theatre), in terms of both material and audience for printed and perhaps performed texts, was highly politicised during the 1640s and 1650s. Some playlets and semi-dramatic pamphlets, analysed here, advocated radical reforms. Secular and tolerationist radicalism used these forms. The period from 1645 to 1650 sees the development of positions which combine the continuation of demands for reform with a swing towards heavy criticism of the new part played by the Commons and the army grandees. These positions are complex and, as I have argued, cannot be accommodated by a binary model of the divisions of the Civil War – certainly not by the taxonomy of 'royalist' versus 'parliamentarian', though, obviously, those divisions were crucial in setting the wars going. Rather, this period sees the circulation of an increasingly complex set of political polemics inhabiting similar genres and drawing on the continuing and changing political debate.

CHAPTER 3

Royalist versus republican ethics and aesthetics The Famous Tragedie of Charles I *and* The Tragedy of the Famous Orator Marcus Tullius Cicero

INTRODUCTION: POLITICAL AESTHETICS

This chapter investigates the way two plays printed in the republic intervened in the aesthetic–political debates of the moment. Little or nothing remained of the 'golden age' of the Caroline court by 1649. A myth of halcyon days survived beside militaristic royalism, but after the regicide all royalist myths were in competition with the actuality of the new republic. That government itself needed to establish a cultural rhetoric, and lacked a rich repository of images. What transformation into a republic meant was not clear; nor was it evident how the republic was to assert its status in opposition to all the centuries of royal iconography. Accordingly, claims to aesthetic value were densely politicised, whether the royalist claim to wit and aesthetic pleasure or the austere ethic of the early republic.[1] It is in the debate between texts such as *The Famous Tragedie of Charles I* (1649) and *The Tragedy of the Famous Orator Marcus Tullius Cicero* (1651) that the politicised aesthetics of royalist and republican were brought into being under the new republic.[2] The debate is in part between royalism and classical republicanism, but it is also about how politics can be represented and symbolised.

CLAIMING THE HIGH GROUND: DRAMA AND POLITICAL DISCOURSES

The Famous Tragedie calls upon divine right, future opinion and cultural capital to underwrite its analysis of events. It presents the closing moments of royalist struggle in 1648, particularly the siege

62

of Colchester (presented initially as Troy). Satirical detail is shaped to demonstrate the escalating evil of the parliamentary army and the terrible nature of regicide placing the deaths of the royalist generals Lucas and Lisle on 28 August 1648 and the regicide, in the same historical typology – a schema reused in *Cromwell's Conspiracy* (1660). Interweaving the siege of Colchester with Cromwell's plotting, the play juxtaposes Cromwell and Peters planning the king's death with Fairfax, Ireton and Rainsborough besieging Sir Charles Lucas, Sir George Lisle, Lord Capel and Lord Goring at Colchester.

Historically, the siege became a focus for dispute about each army's ethics and codes of practice when the surrendering royalist generals, Lucas and Lisle, were shot by the parliamentary commanders. Capel was tried and beheaded on 6 March 1649.[3] Therefore, three aspects of the play's attempt to mythologise royalism are of particular interest: its context in the journalistic and political debates on the siege of Colchester; its presentation of royalist ethics and aesthetics as a claim to cultural inheritance; its representation of Cromwell and Hugh Peters as Machiavellian rhetoricians and producers of 'eare-deceiving paradox' (1, p. 1).

The strategies of representation used for Cromwell and Hugh Peters in *The Famous Tragedie* draw on the familiar satirical discourses of this period, and the representation of the scenes at Colchester draw on news reports, suggesting that the author may have been a journalist. Thomason collected the play on 26 May 1649, four months after Charles's execution, so May is the latest possible date for composition. As Joseph Frank notes, the censorship of the press during the spring and summer of 1649 varied; it was tightened after May, gradually eliminating most of the royalist newsbooks.[4] The Council of State was attempting to suppress memorialisation of the king's death, as the campaign against *Eikon Basilike* indicates.

The play's anonymous appearance in the context of post-regicidal censorship makes it hard to locate an author. However, shock at the regicide was widely shared, even amongst those who sought reform. At that moment several newswriters seem to have held views consonant with those expressed in the play, including the dramatist, Samuel Sheppard.[5]

Writers of news and pamphlets were under serious pressure in 1649. Although it is unlikely that he wrote this play, Marchmont

Nedham's publications in 1646–50 illustrate the exigencies of a political journalist's career. He began as a republican writer with *Mercurius Britanicus,* but since 1646 he had been editing the royalist journal *Mercurius Pragmaticus,* the name under which *The Levellers Levell'd* was published, though not necessarily written by him.[6] He did not cover the trial of the king but did publish *A Plea for the King and Kingdome* in November 1648, *Digitus Dei,* an attack on the Duke of Hamilton (who had led a Scots army into England) in April 1649, and a parody of Hugh Peters.[7] In the spring and summer Nedham was also publishing *Mercurius Pragmaticus (for King Charles II).* He was arrested in June and remained in Newgate until November, when he signed the Engagement. In May 1650 Nedham published *The Case of the Commonwealth of England Stated,* and appeared as a republican when the first issue of the Commonwealth's newsbook *Mercurius Politicus* was published.[8]

As the example of Nedham's eventful life indicates, the period during which *The Famous Tragedie* must have been written, January to May 1649, was one of deep ideological crisis and transformation. It was not only royalists that found the regicide disturbing; the difficulty contemporaries had in interpreting regicide is indicated (as Lois Potter suggests) by the fact that *The Famous Tragedie* is unusual in dramatising it.[9] Although the king was rapidly transformed into a martyr, royalist rhetoric was left without an immediate focus.[10] The 'meaning' of the Civil War itself was bitterly contested and the siege of Colchester and the regicide were two occasions whose meanings were disputed by a press which intervened on both sides.[11]

In a sense, then, *The Famous Tragedie* was 'authored' by one of its print contexts: a series of 'Colchester' pamphlets, news reports, dispatches, elegies and funeral sermons for Generals Lucas and Lisle. Various newspapers reported on the siege; following the defeat of the army in the north, Fairfax's siege of Colchester occupied the news throughout July and August of 1648.[12] As hopes faded for the relief of the garrison the siege's strategic importance became clear and it began to occupy a central place in the press. Initially the royalist commanders, Norwich, Capel and Lucas, 'rejected, and scornfully retorted' Fairfax's offer of terms which, according to a parliamentarian report, made Fairfax except these three from the promised conditions. An anti-royalist publication –

purporting to be neutral – told of Lucas's and Lisle's cruelty to the town. In early August *The Colchester Spie* appeared to redress the misrepresentations of 'State-Pamphleteers' who 'indeavour to persuade the people that Colchester is in a very wretched and miserable condition, thereby deluding some and disheartening others'.

The manner of the generals' deaths was hotly disputed. A parliamentarian report tells us that George Lisle 'exprest a desire of speedy execution, more desperate than Romane'. Copies of Sir Charles Lucas's final speech were sold like relics (though sometimes with an additional reply from a parliamentarian soldier on the topic of Lucas's own unfairness), and Lucas in particular was much elegised as a royalist hero. The royalist hagiography of Lucas focussed on his bravery and his death for the king's cause. Lionel Gatford, 'the true but sequestered Rector of Dinnington' (Suffolk), began the celebration of Lucas's martyrdom in *Englands Complaint* (31 August), and another biblical analogue appeared, *The Cruell Tragedy Or Inhumane Butchery, of Hamar and Shechem*, 'Lately revived and reacted heere in England by Fairfax and Ireton, upon the persons of Sir Charles Lucas and Sir George Lisle, Colchester, the 28 August'.[13]

Perhaps the most famous part of this debate to have survived is Milton's Sonnet x v 'On the Lord General Fairfax at the Siege of Colchester', which was probably written in early August.[14] Milton praises Fairfax as a general whose victories 'daunt remotest kings' (line 4), but concludes by looking to the future and the reformation of the Presbyterian parliament:

> O yet a nobler task awaits thy hand;
> For what can war but endless war still breed,
> Till truth and right from violence freed,
> And public faith cleared from the shameful brand
> Of public fraud? In vain doth valour bleed
> While avarice and rapine share the land.   (lines 9–14)

Although this was not printed at the time it reinforces the sense that the battle of Colchester was seen as decisive in the events and public understanding of the 'meaning' of the Civil War. It also confirms the sense that victory over the royalists would clear the way for peace and a political settlement less accommodating to the king than parliament was hoping for. For Milton the events at Colchester reinforced the righteousness of the independent and army cause and showed potential for a radical transformation of the nation.

Enunciating a very different position from Milton, *The Famous Tragedie* attempts to produce a royalist representation of Colchester and the regicide. If the war is to be holy then posterity must endorse the royal cause. As the 'Prologue to the Gentry' indicates, the play anxiously attempts to control future historical interpretation:

> No marvell, they lap bloud as milk and glory
> To be recorded, villaines, upon Story.
> 'For having kill'd their King, where will they stay
> 'That thorow God and Majestie, made way,
> 'Throwing the Nobles, and the gentry downe,
> 'Levelling, all distinctions, to the Crown.   (A4v)

This verse suggests that regicide is only the beginning of the rebels' all-embracing disrespect for social order. By bringing history's judgement forward (in the use of quotation marks to indicate words taken as if from a future 'story' or history) the play attempts to co-opt the agreement of the future. This prologue also attempts to co-opt *past* cultural icons for royalism:

> Though *Johnson, Shakespeare, Goffe,* and *Davenant,*
> *Brome, Sucklin, Beaumont, Fletcher, Shirley,* want
> The life of action, and their learned lines
> Are loathed by the Monsters of the times:
> Yet your refined Soules can penetrate
> Their depth of merit . . .   (A4r)

Jacobean and Caroline playwrights are used here as markers for the continuing cultural importance of the aesthetics of Charles I's court. The prologue makes the typical royalist move of appropriating all cultural icons – a determined enlisting of the arts in the cause of the king which sometimes finds a rather unquestioning echo in twentieth-century criticism. The prologue's bid for history is reinforced in the play itself when Sir Charles Lucas, envisaging the memorialising of the noble acts of the cavaliers, imagines the royalists' 'heroic acts' will 'provide us fame when we are dead that the next Age, when they shall read the story of this unnaturall, uncivill, Warre' (II, p. 14).

The play repeats this claiming of past and future as a literary–royalist genealogy when the deaths of Lucas and Lisle become, in the final act, tributary martyrdoms augmenting the tragedy of Charles I's suffering. Battle between cavaliers and parliamentary generals is represented as a crisis of ethos and of rhetoric. This is displayed in the parley before Colchester (Act II) in which the two sides fling typical insults at each other:

LISLE: Know, Fellow, I have been victorious even against a multitude, have trod the thorny paths of cragged Warre, my Body naked and my feet unshod, have view'd those horrors of a purple Field untroubled and untouch'd, which but to heare summ'd up would fright thy Coward-soule from forth her dirty Dog-hole.

RAINSBOR: Why spend time in Dialogue with these Miscreants, these Cautiffe Elves, who fight for Yoakes and Fetters, with as much zeale as halfe-starv'd Wretches beg a boone to sate their hungers, and wish profusely for to spend their blouds to please a Tyrants lust.

CAPEL: Away, mechanick Slave, what sawcy Devill prompts thee to prate when to the meanest here thou ought'st to stoop with all obsequious duty? thou sordid Groom, whom of a Skippers Boy the Westminster Rebels made their Admiral . . . (II, p. 10)

This exchange takes place in the popular language of royal versus *salus populi* politics. Rainsborough's levelling arguments present a version of regicidal thought, echoing Protestant tyrannicidal ideology such as Milton's *The Tenure of Kings and Magistrates*.[15] Lisle's adherence to a code of honour contrasts with Rainsborough's attack on the royalists as beasts 'who fight for Yoakes'. The violent language of this exchange indicates that, post-recigide, status (founded on land, wealth and titles) no longer translated uninterruptedly into public recognition.

The play's representation of royalist ritual also illustrates this crisis of confidence in the rhetoric of royalism. The royalist toast in Act II is used to emphasise the play's loyal royalism in a positive representation of loyal ritual contrasted with the image of the wild, drunken Dammee.[16] As the siege rages about them: 'All kneele, they drinke the Health round while the Chambers are shot, and Trumpets perpetually sound' (II, p. 17). Sir Charles Lucas's speech during the revels ends with a strident insistence that to act against kings is to act against gods, asserting: 'Kings are Earth's Gods, and those that menace them / (Were't in their power) would share his Diadem' (II, p. 13). His emphatic invocation of what Mary Douglas calls 'all the powers of the universe' to protect the king, also, of course, suggests the powerlessness of post-regicidal royalist rhetoric: the only threat remaining was supernatural intervention.[17] Such unambiguous identification of royal and godly emerges most strongly in Civil War rhetoric at this point.

Only the presentation of Fairfax troubles the play's relentless polarisation of royalist and parliamentarian. Fairfax, contrasted sharply with Rainsborough, speaks twice in favour of mercy, first in Act I and later about the fate of the surrendering generals. He insists that 'the law of arms' will not allow the murder of the generals who 'yield themselves on Quarter, and for the Peers (I mean Goring and Capel) our power doth not extend to question them' (III.ii, p. 24). By the time the play was published the king was dead and Fairfax had refused to attend the trial, which may be why he is identified as moderate and, significantly, a professional general.

Apart from Fairfax, the play's reinforcing of cavalier stereotypes of honour, loyalty and bravery contrasts with its presentation of Cromwell and Peters as lascivious plotters and Machiavellian rhetoricians. Once again, the play uses the prevailing terms of contemporary satire such as *Craftie Cromwell* by Mercurius Melancholicus, the name of one of the four newsbooks launched by royalists in September 1647.[18] *Craftie Cromwell*, amongst the best-known dialogues from 1648, attacks Cromwell in a parody of panegyric, 'Shall Cromwell not be famous made / Unto the after-times / . . . / Shall not his Nose Dominicall, / In Verse be celebrated?'[19] Equally scurrilous in their representation of the army grandees is the debate between the two potential 'queens', Mrs Cromwell and Mrs Fairfax, in *The Cuckoos-Nest at Westminster*, and the final moments of the anti-purge grotesque of parliament, *Stop Your Noses, or England at her Easement*, 'evacuating those clods at Westminster'. In each case the violence of the attack on parliament and army means that the plays speak only to those already hostile to the parliament, without even the degree of religio-political analysis present in the politically knowing *The Levellers Levell'd* from the previous year. *The Famous Tragedie* participates in this harsh polemic characterised by the use of satire directed against physical attributes and sexual transgressions: satire which registers 'the increasing hopelessness of the royalist position'.[20]

However, whilst attacking Cromwell and Peters the play returns to them repeatedly, apparently unable to resist emphasising the stature of Cromwell, who appears to have such infinite foresight that his schemes always turn out well. Cromwell is described as invincible: 'Nature hath given him an iron soule, able and active limbs, a politique brain' (I, p. 7). Like other contemporary texts, *The Famous Tragedie* makes Cromwell a focus for consideration of the complexities of Machiavellian thought, embodying the tension between the technical and ethical aspects of the use of rhetoric.[21] Strangely admirable in his ability to twist reason and ethics, Cromwell images his thoughts as 'smooth and deep Rivers glide as silent as the Night' (III, p. 19). Even as it sneers at him, the play's characterisation of Cromwell as an unavoidable force is reminiscent of Marvell's description: 'So much one man can do, / That does both act and know.' [22]

Cromwell and Peters's reliance on manipulative rhetoric may be immoral but involves a linguistic and mental dexterity that would make them the centre of any performance of the play – Cromwell's brain is presented as 'a store-house of politique stratagems' (I, p. 7), and he expects Peters to compose 'a pithie formall Speech against the essence and the Power of Kings' (I, p. 1). The passage acknowledges the power of Peters's rhetoric; as Cromwell says, 'I know that Nectar hangs upon thy Lippes, and that the most absurd Syllogisme, or eare-deceiving paradox, maintained by thee, shall seem oraculous, more dangerous to question than the Sacred Writ' (I, p. 1–2). Peters knows the power of language to mislead, suggesting 'Our Language should be like the Lawes we meane to give, awfull and to be wonder'd at' (I, pp. 3–4) while in private 'Venus . . . challenge[s] our utmost faculties' (I, p. 4).

We can trace in the play the crisis of political rhetoric at this pivotal moment. The very terms in which *The Famous Tragedie* elaborates a royalist iconography at the crisis of 1649 indicates the fragility of that rhetoric. The issues elaborated in *The Famous Tragedie* continued to be central under the republic and Protectorate, and it is rewritten as a documentary drama of the 1650s. But just as *The Famous Tragedie* used the scene of Troy, the 1650s – especially the early 1650s and the republic – were read by contemporaries in terms of biblical and historical analogues. History, both biblical and Roman, was understood during the Civil War in terms of motivating precedents; Hobbes was probably not alone in understanding the reading of Greek and Roman books of policy – 'Aristotle and Cicero' – as creating the Civil War.[23] The tradition of anti-tyrannical thinking had access to classical republican thought, to Machiavelli and to the influential Protestant tradition of debate about the killing of tyrants; as Markku Peltonen has indicated, Ciceronian ideals had some influence in the Caroline period, and humanist thought offered a repository of ideas about commonwealth.[24]

As early as 1643 popular forms had been used by parliament to support the critique of the king framed in terms of evil counsellors. They ordered the republication of *Tyrannicall Government Anatomized* (1643), a translation of *Baptistes Sive Calumnia* by George Buchanan, instrumental in the Scottish reformation and regarded as part of the Protestant anti-monarchical inheritance. This was specially licensed by the Commons. The topic of the play is John the Baptist's encounter with Herod: presumably the message was that Charles, like Herod, was a tyrant despite his good intentions. Herod allows the counsellor–priest Malchas (a figure analagous to Laud) completely free rein. He is also willing to contravene the law – as the Chorus comment, 'the only mirror of a wicked life: Slaughter with violence, fraud, theft and rapine, are thy chief exercise' (Pt 5, p. 26).[25]

The play's subtitle, 'Discourse Concerning Evil Counsellors', indicates its uses and echoes the terms used in 1643 to oppose Charles I. As with other texts of the early 1640s, it is hard to tell how conscious a contemporary reader would be to the slight disjunction between the title condemning evil counsel and the culpability of Herod himself. In relation to the other plays published in the early 1640s which were not printed at the order of the government, this play is unusual in the way it makes an alliance with a Protestant tradition of tyrannicide found in the writings of Buchanan and others.

A play making an alliance with Roman, as opposed to biblical, history and printed under the Commonwealth in 1651 (probably published between the battles of Dunbar and Worcester), was *The Tragedy of Marcus Tullius Cicero*. In Senecan form familiar from pamphlet playlets, the play opens with Julius Caesar's ghost prophesying, 'The dayes of Sylla shall return', taking up the theme of the Commonwealth and its attackers. One of the first things Cicero says is, 'I have condemned the swords of *Catiline*' (1.i); Catiline was the clearest instance of rebellion from Roman history and the widely used analogy for Cromwell suggests the power it held for contemporaries.

Rome, where *The Tragedy of Marcus Tullius Cicero* is set, was an important cultural signifier during the whole period under discussion: Graham Parry shows how Fanshawe used Roman history to prophesy the Restoration, and, as Annabel Patterson has noted, Cromwell attempted to redeploy the Virgilian eclogue.[26] Consideration of classical republicanism did not begin with the Civil War. It was always implicitly part of the education of a gentleman in that it appeared in classical texts used for educative purposes. Long before the Civil War, in 1632, a pamphlet called *Augustus, or an Essay of those Measures and Counsels, Whereby the Commonwealth of Rome was Altered and Reduced into a Monarchy* – sometimes attributed to the Laudian Peter Heylyn – was published.[27] The essay traces the history of Rome from Superbus to the end of Octavius Caesar's reign – 'a narration of the greatest change that ever happened in the Common-wealth and state of Rome' (A3v). Although it concludes with praise of Augustus, he is portrayed ambiguously throughout. At the height of the republic the commonwealth is described as 'poised': 'But as in the naturall body, there can be noe exact and arithmeticall proportion of the humours and elements, without some predominancie: so in the body politique, can there be no equall mixture of Plebians and Patricans, without the supremacy of one or the other' (p. 18). Thus, Augustus (and monarchy) are by no means obvious choices for the best kind of government, but Aristotelian political anatomy was disseminated by classical education in the 1630s. As a champion of both republicanism and natural law it might be anticipated that Cicero would become a hero of the republican and anti-monarchist writers of the 1640s.

Blair Worden has investigated the group of classical republicans, in and out of parliament, some of whom (like Algernon Sidney) certainly were readers of Cicero. The influence of the group – Sidney, Thomas Chaloner, Henry Neville, Henry Marten and Marchmont Nedham – reached its zenith between 1650 and the dissolution of the Long Parliament in 1653.[28] 'Classical republicanism' is the imprecise grouping given to the views of these figures, imprecise because, as Jonathan Scott notes, it suggests a remote theorising when, in fact, they were interested in the application of historical precedents and theories – both those of the Roman republic and, in a complex tension with Christian belief – Machiavellian insights.[29] This group's interest in Roman

history as practical, theoretical or ethical precedent was, in the
1640s, remote from the Leveller demands articulated in the
popular playlets discussed in the last chapter.[30] Yet the issues they
raised were not solely the property of the elite or the province of
the treatise: while Sidney's highly critical 'Court Maxims' circulated in manuscript, under Nedham's editorship the weekly
Mercurius Politicus aimed 'to undeceive the people'.[31]

The Rump was far from united. Yet the winter of 1650–1 saw the
passing of a toleration act, and Worden detects a shift from apoc-
alyptic radicalism to a more worldly – secular – rhetoric, a shift he
associates with the republican group.[32] Not only *Mercurius Politicus*
but a range of pamphlets extolled the virtues of a republic – naval,
economic, agrarian and commercial.[33] But how was the republic
to present itself symbolically?

There is an anecdote that (probably in 1651) Henry Marten
dressed George Wither 'in the Royal Habilments' – taken from a
chest – who 'with a thousand Apish and Ridiculous actions
exposed these Sacred Ornaments to contempt and laughter'.
Royalty could be symbolically denigrated, but the republic needed
to propose systems of meaning to replace that rhetoric.[34] The regicide spotlighted the fact that everything in the Commonwealth
needed to be rethought under the republic. By 1651 classical
republican thinking and tyrannicide coincided more fully; where
Tyrannical Government Anatomized situated itself in biblical history,
Marcus Tullius Cicero took part in the deployment of classical learning and history in the mid-century struggle. Above all, it offered a
significant *narrative* of Cicero's life at the moment when classical
republican theory was highly influential, in 1651. As a play *Marcus
Tullius Cicero* gives a literary, pleasurable, exploration of classical
republicanism, generically distinct from news and political theory.
Lois Potter's thesis that it was designed for school performance
would reinforce this argument that it reshapes history as dramat-
ically pleasurable, educating pupils or readers in the virtues
characteristic of the new republic.[35]

As might be expected, Cicero was a favoured figure to epitomise the good republican. One index of his importance was that the
meaning of his political theory for the government of the
Commonwealth was actively contested by Thomas Hobbes and the
republican James Harrington. As Tuck rightly suggests, Hobbes
loathed Cicero's rationalist insistence on the citizen's liberty. In

1651, the year *Marcus Tullius Cicero* was published, Hobbes wrote of Cicero as one of those who deduced a commonwealth not from first principles but from mere experience:

... we are made to receive our opinions concerning the Institution, and Rights of Commonwealths, from *Aristotle* and *Cicero*, and other men, Greeks and Romanes, that living under Popular States, derived those Rights, not from the Principles of Nature, but transcribed them into their books out of the Practice of their own Common-wealths, which were Popular; as the Grammarians describe the Rules of Language, out of the Practise of the time; or the Rules of Poetry, out of the Poems of *Homer* and *Virgil*.[36]

Hobbes finds Cicero a republican from contingency and practice, not from first principles. Harrington responds to this as follows:

... *he* [Hobbes] *saith of* Aristotle *and of* Cicero, *of the* Greeks *and of the* Romans, *who lived under popular States, that they derived those rights not from the principles of Nature, but transcribed them into their books, out of the practice of their own Common-Wealths, as Grammarians describe the rules of Language out of Poets.* Which is as if a man should tell famous *Hervey*, that he transcribed his famous *Circulation* of the bloud not out of the *Principles of Nature*, but out of the *Anatomy* of this or that body.[37]

Harrington fuses argument from experience and principle using Harvey's discovery of the circulation of the blood as an example. But it does not entirely answer Hobbes's claim. Most important for us here is Hobbes's attempt to downgrade classical republican theory as merely ignorant of other modes of government.

Thus, Cicero held an important position in the genealogy of English republican thought. Indeed, just as sacralising discourses and the idea of the 'naturalness' of monarchical hierarchy (as opposed to the artificiality of republicanism) reinforce the 'truth' of royalist thought in *The Famous Tragedie*, the figure of Cicero is used to validate republican thought. Cicero was particularly useful to republican projects because his writings on natural law gave a conservative underpinning to his status as a republican and suggested some kind of quasi-Christian understanding of the state. Cicero wrote of a higher law, 'absorbed and imbibed from nature herself'. In *De Re Publica* he defined what he meant by 'natural' or 'higher' law:

There is in fact a true law – namely, right reason – which is in accordance with nature, applies to all men, and is unchangeable and eternal. By its commands this law summons men to the performance of their duties; by its prohibitions it restrains them from doing wrong . . . to annul it is wholly impossible . . . there will be one law, eternal and unchangeable, binding at all times upon all peoples; and there will be, as it were, one common master and ruler over men, namely God, who is the author of this law and its sponsor. [38]

Thus 'reason' and 'natural law' are seen as potentially Christian *and* as the basis for a politics of resistance. What the natural law had to say about kingly or republican government was one of the heated issues in the struggle after the second civil war. All sides claimed natural law as theirs, or that the other side had broken it while they themselves were endeavouring to bring about its restoration. Here Cicero represents a neo-Christian conservatism and a potentially tyrannicidal stance under the catch-all clause of right reason.

Marcus Tullius Cicero draws on models of Senecan tragedy and earlier English dramatisations of political issues. It is (perhaps inevitably) implicated in a politicised rereading of Jonson's tragic drama, especially *Catiline.* The play opens as a Senecan drama with the return of Julius Caesar's ghost who prophesies the torments of Rome under the triumvirate:

> But I was too mild; a heavier hand
> Shall make thee stoop to Soveraign command,
> And kisse the yoak, though sullied first and died
> In thine own gore; a scourge shall check thy pride,
> The days of Sylla shall return, and bloud
> Swim down thy streets . . .   (I, B1r)

It is tempting to follow this clue and read the play as drawing on Jonson and his deployment of the classics, and therefore as offering a commentary on the present. This might produce a reading in which Caesar corresponded, roughly, to Charles I and the danger of the return of Sylla would lie in the threat of Cromwell's power within the Council of State. Whether or not such specific allegory is appropriate, the play takes Cicero as a defender of the republic and central focus – like a sequel to *Catiline.* We follow Cicero's crises as he and the senators attempt to preserve the republic from rule by tyrants. The city of Rome is at the mercy of Anthony and Octavius and when these become allies, Cicero, although he has fostered Octavius, is to burn his writings against Anthony, or die.

It is clear from the start, and emphasised in the speeches them-selves, that republicanism offers a clear and honest way of running a state. As the quotation above suggests, when Caesar appears prophesying revenge to Rome that revenge is to come in the form of a king. His speech is immediately followed by Cicero praising the virtues of the Roman state:

> That now at length the Fathers of the Publick
> With free unforced judgments dare lay open
> The sick distempers which deform and trouble
> The body Politique? me thinks in this
> I see some gleame of liberty break forth,   (I.i, B1v)

Terms such as 'liberty' can hardly fail to remind readers to see the text in terms of the current struggle, and the term is positively associated with Cicero who praises good republican government.

The text is also at pains to contextualise Cicero as a believer in the right sort of 'liberty': no mere rebel, but a tragic hero. The play points up the differences between Cicero as a good republican and Catiline, foregrounding Cicero's role as defender of liberty against the attempt of Catiline to usurp power. The text heavily emphasises the difference between Cicero and kings, but also between Cicero and Catiline. Catiline becomes a usurper; and by establishing a binary opposition between Cicero and Catiline the text recuperates Cicero as both a republican and a preserver of the staus quo. Cicero is troubled by the rumour that he, like Catiline, plans 'T'usurp the Fasces' as Tyro his freedman and the chronicler of events tells him. Cicero defends himself to the Tribune Publius Apuleius, replying:

> CICERO: Sure thou art deceiv'd,
>   'Tis meant some Ambitious thief, or sword-player,
>   Or some new minted *Catiline*.
> TYR.: No my Lord;
>   You are the man.
> MAR.: O Heavens that I who ruin'd
>   The Counsells of base *Catilline*, should now
>   Turne *Catiline* my selfe! is any man
>   So lost, so wicked as to raise this of me?
>   So rash, so furious to beleeve it! Heavens!
>
> *Enter PUBLIUS APULEIUS*
>
> Alas good Tribune, how is *Cicero* wrong'd?
> APUL.: I know you are, and therefore . . .
>   Before the people have I urg'd your innocence,
>   And partly choakt the rumour. I propos'd

> All your endeavours for the Publick State
> Before their censures, and the whole Assembly
> Pronounc't they never yet could find you guilty
> So much as of a thought against the welfare
> Of the Republick: but what noise is this?   (II, CIV)

Cicero is horrified to be associated with Catiline. Importantly, this
rumour is quelled not by Cicero himself but by a Tribune: a chosen
representative of the people defending Cicero to them. The political connotations of this defence in 1651 are not only, as Potter
suggests, to differentiate Cicero from Catiline but also to recast the
people of England and their government as preservers of a valuable status quo, exemplifying a republican conservatism.[39] In
investing Cicero with the role of republican philosopher–statesman attempting to preserve the state, the play seeks to mobilise
classical precedent to the defence of the present republic. Cicero
as a signifier generates a complex of political meanings, both
republican and moderate, and the play uses him to establish the
purity of republican ethics.

The play is also at pains to emphasise the intrinsic brutality of
kingly power. The emphasis on the royal cruelty of Cicero's
murder verges on bathos in the scene in which we are shown the
dismembered parts of the orator's body:

> Enter *POPILUS LAENAS with MARCUS TULLIUS*
> *CICEROS head and hands*

> A princely gift, by *Jove*; *Popilus Laenas*,
> Thou hast now play'd the royal butcher, on;
> And let *Antonius* blesse his longing eyes
> With sight of such a welcome present.   (V, E3v)

Popilus Laenas goes on to flap Cicero's hands saying, 'are these /
Those hands which whilome thumpt our *Rostra* so?' (V E3v). Such
bathetic effects accumulate not to satirical ends but to reinforce
the audience's sense of the awful punishment exacted of Cicero
for exercising his rights as a citizen.

Where *The Famous Tragedie* mobilises Charles I to confirm royalist ethics and ritual, *Marcus Tullius Cicero* presents the death of the
republican philosopher–statesman in such a way as to emphasise
his virtues. The text may be using Plutarch as the source of the
philosopher's death, a point of dispute because some historians
had represented Cicero as vacillating and afraid of death.

Historians alive at the time gave differing versions of his death. Seneca the Elder says that Asinius Pollio gave an account of the life of Cicero which ended with his fear of death in the words 'and for my part I should not regard even his ending as pitiable, if he himself had not thought death so sad a thing'. Seneca notes that Pollio also suggested that Cicero agreed to burn his speeches. However, Livy and other historians represent Cicero's death as noble.[40] The play represents death as fully and unequivocally Cicero's preferred option to burning his *Philippics* – his political writing. Thus Cicero is maintained as a figure of public and private integrity.

The sympathetic representation of Cicero as a full republican (unlike Catiline), and one who rejected personal good for that of the commonwealth, represents a breakthrough in the staging of secular and anti-monarchical politics in drama. As republican rather than rebellious he is used to produce an understanding of the state as ultimately in the possession of the just citizen. Rulers are presented as coercive, but Cicero acts according to the higher law. Cicero in this play – and elsewhere – during the mid-century years was a positive figure of secular republicanism. The educative purpose of the political pamphlets is echoed in the long, histori-cally instructive speeches in this play bidding for the political alle-giance of the reader.

However, the mobilisation of Cicero as part of a republican text is only a fragment of the debate over the potentially republican implications of the classical tradition. The debates continued to be fierce, and it is possible to trace the contestation of the classics beyond the Civil War period into the Restoration, a continuity which underlines the importance of classical learning and repub-lican models as a site of political and literary struggle during the seventeenth century. For example, in 1668 *Cicero's Prince* was pub-lished advocating 'Moderation in Government and use of Reason in Princes'. The writer tells us that:

This Piece was once a Jewel (wrapt up in Latine) in the Cabinet of the Renowned Prince *Henry*, and composed by an excellent Artist out of the rich Mines of that famous Statesman and Orator *M. Tullius Cicero*. It hath in it Maximes, which void of all stains and Flaws of *Machiavellian* intent, are raised only upon Principles of Honour and Vertue, which best become a Prince. In the discourse they are directed to a Soveraign, but may be of no less use to any great person . . . [41]

The title of the book echoes Machiavelli's *Prince*, translated by Edward Dacres in 1640 and reprinted in 1661 and again in 1663 with his translation of the *Discourses*. However, the statist alliance made in the title is both reinforced and to an extent subverted by the assertion in the dedication – to Charles II's illegitimate son, James Duke of Monmouth, who some counsellors were already putting forward as a potential heir – that Cicero's ideas are 'void of all stains and Flaws of Machiavellian intent'.[42] Once again Cicero is a disputed signifier. The title *Cicero's Prince* simultaneously invokes Machiavellian versions of republicanism in relation to Cicero, and repudiates them. Moreover, Cicero's advice is initially represented as good for Princes but then redeployed as useful to any 'great person' such as the dedicatee. The associations here are not ambiguous but represent oppositional connotations held together in a political discourse mediated through a discussion of Cicero. It is not that Cicero can be read here as a figure mediating between monarchism and republicanism, but that the signifier Cicero represents a source, a 'rich mine' from which two, distinct, political discourses can be drawn and even – momentarily – held in juxtaposition. The function of 'Cicero' as the nominative source of these discourses is explicitly in relation to his classical status.

Cicero continued to be disputed. For instance, Christopher Wase's *Electra* (1649) had moralised Sophocles as a royalist dramatist, using annotation to school the reader into a royalist interpretation. He saw clearly the stake of political dispute in the classics, and when he translated Cicero in 1671 we find the text once again annotated. *Cicero Against Catiline in IV Invective Orations* were translations of four orations of Cicero against Catiline.[43] Wase does not moralise Cicero as he had Sophocles, but his annotations frequently echo the terminology of the Civil War. Translating this classical text he sees it as illuminating recent struggles, describing someone being 'made Dictator, or Protector, and Captaine General' (p. 6) and noting: 'Much of the divisions in the popular State of *Rome* was about Levelling the State, in such sort that the over-Wealthiness of some Grandees, and extreme indigence of the Generality, might be taken away' (p. 4). Like *Marcus Tullius Cicero* Wase's annotation makes classical narrative practical in shaping it to the present. However, in 1651, *Marcus Tullius Cicero* was part of an emergent rhetoric of the republic which was mobilising these narratives for the service of immediate and more abstract political ends – it was part of the attempt to provide the republic with a mythic vocabulary.

In *The Tenure of Kings and Magistrates* (1649) Milton wrote in defence of tyrannicide, initiating his argument with the assertion that 'indeed none can love freedom heartilie but good men; the rest love not freedom but licence'. Milton's defence of the court which tried Charles (also approved by Harrington but repudiated by the Levellers for its illegality) indicates starkly the way in which the republic needed to improvise its new power: classical precedent and analogies with the ancient Roman republic could act as underpinning to justify the way it dealt with urgent contingencies. *The Tenure of Kings and Magistrates* seeks to turn the tables on the Presbyterians (now objecting to Charles I's trial) and attacks the 'falsifi'd names of Loyalty and Obedience' which colour the 'base compliances' of some subjects' (p. 2).

Milton's attempt to control and remake political discourse after the regicide is similar to those of *The Famous Tragedie* and *Marcus Tullius Cicero*. The years from 1649 to 1651 saw a crisis in political rhetoric experienced by all parties.[44] The republic urgently needed to underpin political claims with a social and cultural vocabulary, yet this task was made problematic by the cultural asceticism implied by the Rump. As Nigel Smith notes, Milton's regicide tracts also initiate an aesthetic programme; in terms of drama they mark 'his attempt to create a new theatre for the republic, [in which] classical drama becomes the site of civic liberation' – Seneca, not Shakespeare.[45]

Where *The Famous Tragedie* makes aesthetic claims, recuperating Shakespeare and Jonson (a figure strongly claimed by both texts) as royalist, and attacks the rhetorical strategies and sexual mores of Cromwell and Peters, it also attempts to define 'true' royalism. Similarly, *Marcus Tullius Cicero* attempts to claim a historical aesthetic of republicanism for the new republic of 1651 using the figure of Cicero to propose historical precedent. Moreover, by contrasting Cicero with Catiline, apparently here both the historical Catiline and Jonson's, the play produces a conservative civic republicanism in which the true citizen takes responsibility for collective good. Austere and strange as it is, using the archaic conventions of Senecan drama made familiar again by the pamphlet plays of the Civil War, *Marcus Tullius Cicero* does produce a new use of history for a new age. But what that new age could become depended, in part, on naturalising such an aesthetic–political vocabulary.

Republican thinking did not disappear with the arrival of the Protectorate. Indeed, there is an anecdote that in 1656 Algernon Sidney had a play 'of publicke affront to him' acted before the Protector. It is said that the play was *Julius Caesar* but it could just as well have been *Marcus Tullius Cicero*: the coded meanings and imaginings of republican representation continued long after the unsatisfactory English experimental republic was defeated by Cromwell.[46]

Interchapter. 'The life of action': playing, action and discourse on performance in the 1640s

How can we think of theatrical performance and the contexts of such performance in the 1640s? In September 1647 *Mercurius Pragmaticus* wrote of Hugh Peters: '*Sam Rowley* and he were a *Plyades*, and *Orestes*, when he played a womans part at the Curtaine Play-house, which is the reason his garbe is so emphaticall in the Pulpit.'[1] As Hotson notes, Peters was accused of everything. This charge makes the connection once again between the style of Puritan preaching and a role-playing which this newspaper associates not only with acting but with that focus of obsessive concern – the playing of a woman's part on stage. This turns against Puritans the usual ammunition of Prynne's pre-war critique of theatre as 'not sufferable in any well-ordered Christian Republike'.[2] However, cohabiting with such criticism of Puritan or sectarian behaviour as actorly, inauthentic and role-playing is another discourse punning on 'acting' and taking 'action'.

Peters is *both* hypocritical and effective as a preacher. Such an accusation was facilitated in the 1640s because the contemporary discourse on acting and performance relied heavily on distinctions between related words like 'acting' and 'action', differences which enabled puns on shades of meaning or slippages between the two. Such nuanced differentiations – as between 'action' and 'acting' – play into a conceptual network which distinguishes meanings but which, in the vey act of distinguishing them, invites cross-connections. Indeed, at times we do not have to decide which is the more important of the chains of association because, as Alice Rayner puts it, in a play rather than a courtroom, 'the freedom of the fiction allows the complexity of [the] situation to rest as complexity'. [3] Through puns and associative links and, of course, because of the politicisation of theatre by the bans, discourse on acting in the 1640s and 1650s overlaps with discourse on political and military action. Plays from the 1640s are nothing if not sharply aware of the interrelationship, and politics, of the connections between text, action and performance for a public.

Thus, *The Famous Tragedie* introduces acting in a pun on military action: the great playwrights like Jonson, Shakespeare, Shirley 'want / The life of action'. The theatrical 'life of action' is punningly claimed here as part of the royalist cultural arsenal. This is just one instance of the relationship between acting and action or playing and performing. The two languages of theatre and politics are interwoven in texts which may have been performed at the time, producing a language of politicised playing played out in theatrical performance – a kind of seamless mutual referentiality of the theatrical–political. The question is not whether the political or the theatrical is the primary term but how the two inhabit each other.[4] Thus, Sir Humphry Mildmay records seeing a punning 'play of Warre' in 1643 – possibly *The Cruell Warre*, the pamphlet play discussed in chapter 5.[5]

While some politicised playlet pamphlets and dialogues are clearly related to print genres and abstract debate, others make political points within the framework of performance scripts. Printed dramatic and dialogic texts are cast on a continuum from those clearly aimed at reading to performance script, but the only clear differentiation between reading aloud and acting out is commercial.[6] Although the closure of the theatres inevitably significantly altered the relationship between playtext and performance, it did not preclude performance; many of these short plays could have been performed and, in some cases, the printed script may record performance. Martin Butler has argued convincingly that satirical playlets of 1641–2 such as *The Bishop's Potion* and *Canterbury His Change of Diot* were probably performed on London stages in the moments leading up to the war; as he argues, some of these pieces use performance devices.[7] Writers found the metaphor of *theatrum mundi* inexhaustibly appropriate to figure Civil War, but playing in or of pamphlets may have had more than metaphorical valency in the 1640s.[8] That playing may have had local context is suggested, too, by Adam Fox's research on the creation and reading of manuscript scandals. He finds such scandals being read to – or performed before – '"an hundred severall persons"'.[9]

Certainly, full-length plays were performed at the theatres

before their interiors were damaged, and activities on the periphery of playing seem to have continued, such as satirical puppetry at Bartholomew Fair. Rural traditions may have continued too – there is a nineteenth-century record of a 'Cromwell' in a mumming play in Ireland: 'Beelzebub . . . at last running away with the bold usurper whom he tweaked by his gilded nose'. Presumably the 1640s is a likely moment for the incorporation of such a diabolic figure, especially in the light of the emphasis on Cromwell's nose – a caricature which would have made more sense when watchers had access to a popular visual rhetoric for Cromwell.[10]

Some playlets might have been acted after a longer or full-length piece. Some, by virtue of their brevity, might have been performed informally like the short drolls of the 1650s.[11] 'Short' plays such as *The Committee-Man Curried* (discussed in chapter 2), are long enough to make a show on their own; such topical playlets registering the concerns of London residents might well have been acted. Moreover, actually staging a play or playlet would have had an obvious politicised *frisson* for players and audience precisely because of the continuing ban – a staged playlet would be political action of a (punning) kind. It seems possible that some of the surviving printed evidence is versions of pieces acted at festivals, markets, fairs and even, mimicking news, in the street. *The Arraignment, Conviction and Imprisonment of Christmas* (January 1646) has a scripted structure as a hue and cry and makes references to contemporary performances, calling the Queen's Christmas 'a theater exceeding all the playes of the Red Bull, the Fortune, or the Cockpit', all playhouses that were active during the 1640s.[12] It does seem that during the 1640s the Christmas period was one of theatrical activity; James Wright said that acting took place at the Red Bull 'At Christmas and Bartholomew fair', and possibly political skits of this kind were acted.[13]

It may be significant that several of the pamphlet dramas are connected with fairs and at least one, *A Bartholomew Fairing* (1649), suggests a possible performance of this kind, perhaps at a fair, in its prologue and epilogue:

Prologue

A Pedlar in haste with an Horn.
Stand off, make roome, give way, for I come Post,

My Fairings do run wilde from the Irish Coast;
Poore Cram a Cree untrouz'd O bone! O bone!
Hath lost his cows, his sheep, his Bagh, all's gone:
All is transported hither, view it, view,
Patrick is to be sold at Bartholomew. [14]

The end of the play is signalled by 'Roger left behind', who gives
a moral. Although details of performance for this and other plays
remain conjectural, the pamphlet suggests that there could have
been both a read and performed context for at least some of these
pamphlet plays. The playlet on current events might be read or
acted, and then copies sold in the way that ballads were.

The *Dialogue Between Dick of Kent and Wat the Welch-man* suggests
that pamphlets might be sold at the same time as the play was
improvised in the street – a method of distribution like that for
news pamphlets. *Dick . . . and Wat* opens with a figure, Dick of Kent,
selling news:

Come, who buys my new merry Books?
Here's new Newes, and true Newes
From all the world over . . .[15]

A source of evidence that is potentially richer, though difficult
to interpret because of its alertness to theatre as a metaphor, is
offered by a political skit and pamphlet play called *A New Fiction,
or As Wee Were*, printed in 1661 and utilising the network of associations that hold together (and apart, as puns) acting and action,
playing and performing.[16] It tends to support the connections
between news and playing made so far, but also uses 'playing' to
discuss the costumes of the bishops (from 1641), Cromwell, *and*,
apparently, the presentation of plays. The scene is 'White-hall',
and the dramatis personae are a mixture of personifications of the
topical issues who had been acting on the political stage since
1642 (Protestation, Common-Prayer, Allegiance, Sir Solemn
League and Covenant, Engagement, Instrument) and the forces
of law and order within the City – 'Constables, Beadles'. It also
thematises illicit playing. Allegiance, Protestation and Common
Prayer enter 'as at two doors', Allegiance commenting 'let this be
diurnall'd', that is, recorded as news. Joined by Sir Solemn and
Engagement, they dispute until Instrument (who is Cromwell)
appears:

ENGAGE: But what! Here comes our last!

Enter INSTRUMENT
See, what a Nose he has! I the worst has past.
SOLEMN: H'as smelt us out.
PROTEST: Smelt we so strong of Bloud!   (p. 3)

The joke about Cromwell's 'instrument' of government and 'nose' sets the scene for metadramatic puns on 'play' and players and the political 'theatre'. The pun of the government being interrupted during its 'action' is mapped on to what seems to be a record of players being interrupted. The dramatis personae begin to argue, but are interrupted by the entrance of 'Constables, Beadles and c.':

1 CONST: What? Had they done?
2 CONST: They've gone. I thought we should make thee House too hot
    for'mt
1 CONST: What house?
2 CONST: This, this same paltry Play-house of theirs. Your poyets (as
    they call um) why they will make you a House of anything and
    anything of an House, to serve their turn. These players (I have
    heard our Minister say) are in plain Greek such very Hypocrits.
    (p. 5)

In this way the play presents the characters of the Interregnum – also the characters of the pamphlet plays of the 1640s and 1650s – as a play interrupted by the forces of order. The players, like the Rump and the earlier bishops, have gone in such haste that they have left their props behind, including a fake nose for the figure of Instrument/Cromwell:

1 BEADLE: Whoop Holliday! What have we here? George o' Horse-back!
    Upon the Post there: Don't you see?
2 BEADLE: For Gods sake; How does he kill the Dragon?
1 BEADLE: E'en as it please the painter, I'le warrant.
2 BEADLE: Ho! Whats this?
1 CONST: An old Bishops square Cap. Is't not?
1 BEADLE: And here's another like it.
2 CONST: A Judges, this; it should be. Let's see. We han't lost our labour
    yet.
1 CONST: I believe, they had not quite done, they've gone in such hast.
2 CONST: The fools ne'r left their bawbles behind them, if they had not
    been frighted. What? a Vizzard too? Who was this for trow? what a
    Nose it has. (p. 6)

The 'George o'Horseback' can be used to convey the several levels on which this play is operating. At the level of political allegory it suggests George Monck, now (in 1661) Master of the Horse, who several Rump ballads characterised as St George. Secondly, this George would appear to suggest an inn sign repainted either during the Commonwealth or at the Restoration.[17] Thirdly, the image points us back towards the theatre, in this case towards the mummers' play of St George which first appeared in 1596 but which was still being performed during the Interregnum.[18]

The jokes about old bishop's clothing echo pamphlets such as Overton's *New Lambeth Fayre,* which used clothing in anti-episcopal satire at the beginning of the war. Finally a neighbour comes on and asks, 'What has been the businesse?' and all the Constables and Beadles go off with him to tell him, the whole piece ending with a 'Chorus of By-Standers' and an explanation in French. The play operates twice: once as a history of the Protectorate and Rump surprised into flight by the Restoration. Secondly, the emblematic figures, as well as representing the events of the past twenty years, also stand for the dramatis personae familiar from populist satire. The play which is interrupted is both the 'play' of the history of the Protectorate and an epitome of the performances of the political satires and short pieces of the time, which had been interrupted by Constables and Beadles, or by soldiers. From this we can extrapolate a context for performance for some of the pamphlet plays of the period, particularly the many political satires. Not only was the metaphor of playing central to Civil War conceptions of politics, but also it was a multivalent metaphor used by plays to refer to their own status as theatre as well as to the political stage. Obviously some scripts could have been staged and, as *A New Fiction* indicates, systematically played on the conceptual relationship of 'action' and 'acting'.

The period's acute self-consciousness about playing and politics and their interrelationships, both as concepts and in practice, is indicated by a parliamentarian colonel's reconfiguration of Mayday celebrations. He ordered the troops to perform a play of the battles that they were themselves involved in fighting. Something similar is found in one of the City shows, but the account of this May festivity suggests the knowing centrality of the discourse of performance at the start of the wars, a self-consciousness which allowed the wars to be reproduced as re-enactment even as they were going on.

Colonel Blunt set up a May-day entertainment in which he ordered 'two Regiments of his foot Souldiers to appear the last May-day . . . at Blackheath' and act out the Civil War:[19]

The Roundheads they carried it on with care and love, temperance and order, and as much gravity as might be, every one party carefull in his action, which was so well performed that it was much commended.

But the Cavaliers, they minded drinking and roaring and disorder, and would bee still playing with the women, and compasse them in, and quarrell, and were exceedingly disorderly.

Apparently the 'Countrey people' enjoyed it. But Blunt's use of his soldiers to play themselves and to play the enemy suggests not only the extreme stability of stereotype produced by the Civil Wars (discussed in chapter 1), but a simultaneously operating extreme instability, or sensed arbitrariness, about the role members of each army might perform.

PART II

The 1650s: Protectorate, politics and performance

CHAPTER 4

Gender and status in dramatic discourse
Margaret Cavendish, Duchess of Newcastle

INTRODUCTION

How did women writing during the Civil War and Protectorate use dramatic discourses, and how were women positioned by these discourses? The 1650s saw the writing of plays by at least one female dramatist, Margaret Cavendish, Duchess of Newcastle, and this chapter investigates her relationship with theatre and politics. In doing so, it concentrates on the ideas of female performance in her plays, and Civil War challenges to social hierarchy.

In one of the many preambles to her first volume of plays – written in the 1650s and published, after delays, in 1662 – she wrote:

I cannot chuse but mention an erroneous opinion got into this our Modern time and men, which is, that it should be thought a crime, or debasement for the nobler sort to Act Playes, especially on publick Theatres . . . for certainly there is no place, wayes or meanes, so edifying to Youth as publick Theatres, not only to be spectators but Actors; for it learns them gracefull behaviours . . . [1]

Significantly, she includes public theatres in her claim for theatre as the cultural capital of the nobility. The emphasis on the moral power of theatre is in accord with the general thinking of her circle, which included Thomas Hobbes and William Davenant. We see clearly her concern with status, and her desire to claim the theatre for the nobility.

But what about the relationship between gender and theatre? The issues of status and gender in Cavendish's plays can be read as shaped by the values dominant in their dramatic, theatrical and social contexts.[2] However, by the 1630s a number of different ideologies about female dramatic writing and performance seem to have been in play.[3] *The Tragedy of Miriam* (1613) by Elizabeth Cary,

91

Lady Falkland, is a rare example of a published play by a woman from before the war, but the 1650s and 1660s saw a marked increase in the number of plays published by women, and eventually in 1660 the arrival of actresses on the public stage, closely followed by plays written by women; the dramatists of the Restoration included Katherine Philips, Frances Boothby, Elizabeth Polwhele and Aphra Behn. Moreover, evidence – including the emergence of the actress on the *public* stage in 1660 – suggests that ideologies around female performance were shifting significantly in the Civil War period. The anonymous author of *Mr William Prynne His Defence of Stage Playes* (1649) responds to critics of boys playing by writing: 'if this be all, it is a fault may easily be amended; and we may do in *England*, as they do in *France, Italy, Spain* and other places, where those which play women's parts are women indeed'.[4] Some of the changes in kinds of performance brought about by the Civil War and Restoration may have facilitated the passage of women into the profession. One such change is from the distinctly demarcated 'private' dramas (performed before invited audiences) and the 'public' theatres of the 1630s and early 1640s, to the blending of courtly and public performance after the Restoration, with the increased presence of the court at the public theatre.

Douglas Grant comments, 'The disadvantage of writing plays during the interregnum was the impossibility of their being produced.'[5] But for a woman writing plays we could also see the Civil War bans on drama as in some ways inaugurating a new and temporary equality in the status of plays by men and women since neither sex was likely to have plays staged. Moreover, a comparison of her plays with other contemporary plays (particularly those by the marginalised aristocrats of the 1650s such as Thomas Killigrew), makes her writing practice appear much less eccentric.[6] Ten-act plays were not unheard of in the explosion of dramatic genres in the 1640s and 1650s; Killigrew wrote them, and pamphlet plays were also published in two parts (one was *The Committee-Man Curried* discussed in chapter 2).

In her own writing, however, Cavendish desired to be considered 'singular', and for someone reading her prodigious and various output, it is often difficult to avoid replicating her own version of herself as completely self-invented.[7] Her contemporaries regarded her as 'singular' in a different way – eccentric – and found her behaviour anti-social and repugnant. Pepys's well-known comments address themselves to issues the Duchess of Newcastle was herself much concerned with in her plays: theatre and display. However, for Pepys, it is the Duchess herself who is displayed and observed.[8] Dorothy Osborne heaped scorn on Cavendish, and a closer acquaintance, Mary Evelyn, disapproved of her dress and conversation.[9] In 1667 Charles North wrote of her, 'The Dutchess Newcastle is all ye pageant now discoursed on: Her breasts all laid out to view at a playhouse with scarlett trimd nipples. Her intrado was incognito else a triumphale chariott with 12 horses.'[10] This neatly pinpoints the contrast between Cavendish's idea of the uses of theatre as a locus for the staging of an ideal self and the way she was perceived by at least one contemporary. Although women might enter theatrical discourse as the generators of texts, their activities continued to be specularised and to give scandalous pleasure to observers.

Twentieth-century critics have tended to accommodate Cavendish's 'singularity' by regarding her writing as 'women's autobiography'.[11] As Sara Heller Mendelson and Catherine Gallagher note, such scholars use Margaret Cavendish's writing as part of an attempt 'to establish a pedigree for modern feminism' – an approach which Cavendish's texts both encourage and resist. However, as I shall argue, Cavendish's writing about gender and hierarchy is complex and contradictory, and her paradoxical attitudes are clearly connected to her circumstances during the Civil War and Interregnum, indicating that, as Natalie Zemon Davis asserts, gender needs to be studied as a part of the overall 'cultural network'. Davis rightly argues that 'we should be interested in the history of both women and men, that we should not be working only on the subjected sex any more than an historian of class can focus exclusively on peasants'.[12] If one is attempting, as I am here, to trace discursive changes in relation to some sense of literary and cultural context, Davis's remark offers a way of focussing an argument on the contradictions in Cavendish's plays. The relationship between status and gender, which concerns Davis, is an issue of central importance in Cavendish's plays and related to the contestation of status fought out in the English Civil War and Protectorate.

Cavendish was writing during the 1650s; her plays and circumstances serve to illuminate the fractures and disjunctures of power and gender ideologies. Although she was in exile with her husband, his daughters remained in England. They too wrote plays, and may even have staged their entertainments at home. Private performances inevitably dramatised the political and social concerns of those who wrote and performed them. An obvious example is the series of politicised entertainments written by Mildmay Fane for private performance at Apthorpe during the 1640s: in 1641 'the youth and Servants' acted 'Tymes Trick upon the Cards'.[13] The new emphasis thrown perforce on private or family performance in which women participated during the Civil War and Protectorate may have contributed to altering attitudes to women's public performance. Equally, such performances might in the 1630s and 1640s have drawn on assumptions about female performance at Henrietta Maria's court. At any rate, by the time Charles II returned masques could not be performed at court because no-one 'could make a tolerable entry'.[14]

Newcastle's daughters apparently wrote their two plays with their father in mind, addressing passages directly to the Duke.[15] The Duke's own first plays, co-written by Shirley, were published in 1649 and his daughters' plays seem to belong to the 1640s.[16] The Duke wrote plays with assistance from real dramatists both before and after the war. So a significant part of Margaret Cavendish's specific context as a writer is her membership of a family who wrote plays or in various ways participated in playmaking. Although they did not live together, and the dates of composition are different, there seem to be some similarities between the unpublished plays of the Duke of Newcastle's daughters and those of his wife, who, like his daughters, addresses him in dedicatory verses.

The main plot of the play by Newcastle's daughters, 'The Concealed Fansyes', dramatises the courtship between Lucenay and Tattyney and their suitors Courtley and Praesumption, alongside the affair between their father Monsieur Calsindow and Lady Tranquillity. Written at some point after the Duke left for the continent following his defeat at Marston Moor (and remaining in manuscript form until 1931) the topic of courtship negotiations and gender roles in aristocratic marriages bears an obvious relation to the circumstances of the two young women, though the Civil War context is suggested mainly in the language of siege and military discourse. The circumstances of a civil war which enforced the retirement of the two young women and which saw them besieged at Welbeck by parliamentary forces is more explicitly present in the entertainment composed by the two sisters called 'A Pastorall', which is part of the manuscript book containing poems to various relatives. One poem, 'On hir most sacred Majestie', suggests an intimate identification of these young women with the royal cause through Henrietta Maria's heroism which can tame 'Armyes of Rebells': 'Your Eye if looke, it doth an Army pay / And soe, as Generall, you doe lead the way' (fol. 9).

Pastoral, here, refers only ironically to rural retreat but dramatises wartime issues with direct bearing on the situation of the two women – isolation, loneliness and depression. It moves from the representation of the forces of darkness – witches – in the first antimasque to the country people bewailing their losses by plunder in the second antimasque. It suggests the impact of Civil War on the countryside as two country wives and Goodman Rye and Goodman Hay discuss the strange beasts called satyrs who have come into the country, 'halfe Men, halfe Beasts' – presumably cavaliers. When Henn, one of the country figures, asks, 'what will they plunder', Hay replies, 'Noe they understand not that phrase; Plunder', and Rye explains,'But I will tell you, they are very loving people.' The part of the play dealing with the poor but resourceful peasants dramatises a war in which the country people suffer, and the second antimasque ends with a song about how all the farm animals have been stolen.

However, war is presented rather differently in relation to the ladies. The five witches in the first antimasque had announced their intention to 'metamorphose everybody' and declared their preference for 'making Ladyes Captives', and 'Seeinge howe prittily they can looke wise', 'And speake witt soe against us'. The Duke's influence is suggested by the emphasis on 'wit' which is represented as both the most desirable quality of a suitor (alongside military courage) and a weapon in the armoury of the aristocratic female captive: in this play the aristocratic lady's war is metamorphosed into witty linguistic combat.

Most of the pastoral focusses on a group of melancholy shepherdesses living far from their friends in 'a sad Shee Hermetts

Cave'. One of the shepherdesses, Chastity, declares that she is
'resolved to live a Country life/Since from my friends I cannot
heare/I'm smothered in sighes, torter, feare' (fol. 12). 'A
Pastorall' links the concern of 'The Concealed Fansyes' with courtship to an exploration of the immediate circumstances of the war:
the two camps (witches and satyrs, parliamentarians and royalists),
the sieges, and above all the solitude, autonomy and dangerous
position of the young women left unprotected on captured estates.
Even more than 'The Concealed Fansyes' the pastoral is a
response to the circumstances of the war in which soldiers were a
danger even to remote country houses. As Christopher Nicolson
wrote to Christopher Dudley from Newcastle in 1651, troops were
dangerous and destructive unless bribed, 'You are to blame if you
keep not at Yanwith. There is a briggade of horse coming downe
which way I know not, but at such tymes you should make meanes
to procure an officer to save that destructive waste that troupers
make.'[17]

Although these plays could have been performed there is no
record of performances, and they give little more than a glimpse
of the ideologies of gender in relation to private theatre at a specific moment in the seventeenth century. They cannot alone be
the basis for a full argument about women's acting even during the
1640s and 1650s. However, the 'Pastorall' seems to be influenced
by the pastoral court drama, like Walter Montagu's *Shepherds
Paradise* in which Henrietta Maria and her ladies danced. This
picture of women's participation in court drama suggests that
Henrietta Maria's time at court had greatly changed the ethos of
aristocratic female acting from a generation earlier. A contrasting
picture of women's relationship to amateur courtly drama is given
by the cast-list of the recently rediscovered *Cupid's Banishment*
(1617), a masque put on by Ladies Hall, an academy for daughters of the elite, for the patron Lucy, Countess of Bedford and in
homage to Anne of Denmark.[18] In it the girls took small parts, but
nearly all the major roles were played by men, including Richard
Brown as Diana.

The Newcastle family's plays can be considered as a nucleus of
dramatic writing, most of it by aristocratic women, which is imbri-
cated with the circumstances of the Civil War and which uses (and
in the case of Margaret Cavendish, transforms) pre-war dramatic
genres. Moreover, other dramatic entertainments, possibly by

women, exist such as the apparently later manuscript 'Christmas Entertainment' employing a familiar Civil War thematics of retirement, melancholy and courtship (as well as same-sex desire).[19] Charity speaks the prologue explaining the play's combination of comic romance with military drama as 'a confus'd Chaos of womens brains'. Where these texts invite analysis of the meanings and contexts of female performance, Margaret Cavendish's writing could be said to elaborate a theory or theories of such performance.

ACTING, THEATRE AND THE READER

In Margaret Cavendish's writing, contradictions emerge around the issues of the court, power, gender, sexual desire and representation as they converge on the signifier 'theatre'. Her dramatic and non-dramatic writing plays with and redefines the marginalised position of women in relation to the 'theatre' of public affairs, on the one hand, and the theatre of representation on the other.[20] Cavendish's *The Female Academy* (*Playes*, 1662) explores the women's negotiation of both these forbidden 'theatres' by the female protagonists. The connotations of 'theatre' within the plays work to relocate and redefine the relationship between femininity and the public sphere. Interchangeable meanings of 'theatre' as public affairs or the stage make transformations possible for the figured female, especially the nobility.

Although Cavendish herself describes her brain as the only stage on which her plays/fantasies are acted, her plays are not, as has been asserted, completely without a sense of the stage. In fact, the 'theatre', both literal and metaphorical, is important to all her writing. Moreover, Cavendish is alert to the role of the reader in engaging with the texts and animating the action. The instruction she gives for the reading aloud of the plays is that they are not to be read as narrative, but as if staged, requiring a kind of mental acting from the reader: 'Playes must be read to the nature of those several humours or passions, as are expresst by Writing: for they must not read a Scene as they would a Chapter; for Scenes must be read as if they were spoke or Acted' (*Playes*, 1662, A6v). She writes of herself that 'For all the time my Playes a making were, / My brain the Stage, my thoughts were acting there' (A2r), and the reader is to re-enact them.[21] She suggests that the plays, for her, are the manifestations of her 'contemplations' and seems to be aware of the reader as engaging her or his own fantasy. Her analysis constitutes, if not a full theory of performance, a commentary on the dramatic structure of the plays and on theatre as a realm of fantasy for a reader to fulfil wishes.[22]

The signifier 'theatre' corresponds to several related signifieds in Cavendish's writing and functions in a number of symbolic ways. Sexuality, gender, courts and politics are, for Cavendish, inextricably intertwined; her writing returns repeatedly to the paradoxical relationship of acting on the stage and acting in the theatre of the world. On the one hand she offers her plays as fantasies acted on the stage of her imagination. But simultaneously the political triumphs of women (disguised as pages becoming generals to win their lovers) is woven into an analysis of and commentary on the contemporary situation through the use of the idea of theatre. Cavendish's theatre may then be (merely?) the theatre of the imagination and the triumphs of her heroines imaginary triumphs (imagined by both the play and its 'Noble Reader'). But any sharp opposition between a 'real' world and an 'imaginary world' (in which noble women triumph) is problematised by the extension of the idea of 'theatre' to embrace both. Within the play the acting out of a role in an imaginary world and the acting of that role interpenetrate.

An example of this interconnection, and what Denise Riley calls Cavendish's 'scholastic flamboyance', is *The Female Academy*, published in the 1662 volume of plays.[23] It approaches the relationship between femininity, fantasy, linguistic and intellectual pursuits in what is for Cavendish a tautly structured five-act play exploring the ideas of education and rhetoric for girls and women. The play combines the secluded all-female academic locus with eroticised educational/dramatic display. The academy's scholars are all members of the female nobility which Cavendish represents as unjustly constrained: they are 'of antient Descent, as also rich' (First Lady, i.i, p. 653). Their learning 'to speak wittily and rationally, and to behave themselves handsomely, and to live virtuously' is achieved through 'discoursing' (First Lady, i.i, p. 653). Each lady is given a topic on which she speaks in public. Although nobody is allowed to enter the academy, men and women are allowed to stand on the other side of a grille to hear the young ladies talking.

This situation is similar to that depicted in the frontispiece to Cavendish's *Poems, or Several Fancies*, in which the figure of the author sits looking at the viewer who is separated from the female figure by a railing in the foreground of the picture.[24] In the play, the listening men are allowed to watch the women orate upon the public stage but they are silenced onlookers at the discourses which turn increasingly to the twin topics of language and love. Here, as elsewhere in Cavendish's plays, the women represented as sexually exciting to men (indeed these young women are represented as overwhelmingly exciting to the male viewers) are women displaying themselves within a masculine preserve. Other examples are the women dressed as pages, or as generals; all are women in control of positions usually held by men.[25] Cavendish's plays act out scenarios in which women are on display, desired but also triumphant, and offer the reader, particularly the female reader, material for elaboration as fantasy.

The topics given to the speakers in the female academy include 'whether women are capable to have as much Wit or Wisdom as men' (I.ii, p. 654) – a question which the speaker regards as complicated by differentials in access to education, eventually concluding that women have wit, but not wisdom (I.ii, p. 655). The topic of discourse is itself proposed twice. The first speaker says, 'there are two sorts of discourses . . . as there is discoursing within the mind, and a discourse with words' (I.iv, p. 657); the second speaker makes a similar distinction but adds a third kind – 'discoursing by signs, which is actions or acting' (I.xvi, p. 666).

Actions and acting turn out to facilitate imaginative movement between the theatre and the world when the Lady Speaker talks about theatre:

A Theatre is a publick place for publick Actions, Orations, Disputations, Presentations, whereunto is a publick resort; but there are two Theatres, which are the chief, and the most frequented; the one of War, the other of Peace; the Theatre of Warr is the field, and the battels they fight, are the Plays they Act, and the Souldiers are the Tragedians, and the theatre of Peace is the stage, and the Plays there Acted are the Humours, Manners, Dispositions, Natures, Customes of men thereon described and acted, whereby the Theatres are as Schools to teach Youth good Principles . . . the designer of the rough Plays of Warr is a General or Councel; the designer of the smooth Plays of Peace is a Poet, or a Chief Magistrate. (IV.xxi, pp. 669–70)

Here the two kinds of 'theatre' are indistinguishable – the play of peace can be staged by either a poet or a chief magistrate making the theatre of the world and the theatre of the stage interchangeable. The theatre and war both offer training in public roles and duties. This substitutable relation between representation and reality is echoed in the poem 'A Dialogue Between Peace and War' in *Poems or Several Fancies* (1668). Warre gets the last word:

> A School am I, where all Men may grow Wise:
> For Prudent Wisdom, in Experience lies.
> A Theatre, where noble minds do stand:
> A Mint of Honour, Coyn'd for Valour's Hand.
> I am a Throne, which is for Valour fit;
> And a great Court, where Royal Fame may sit:
> A Field, in which ambition much doth run:
> Courage still seeks me; Cowards do me shun.[26]

Cavendish is again connecting theatre, education, the court and public action, pursuing the analogy between action and performance. Turning on the dual meaning of the 'theatre', her texts manage to expand the category so that all human action becomes representation (and implicitly vice versa). The court is, of course, the stage of exemplary and corrupt human action in peace-time just as the battlefield is the theatre of war and the playhouse the school of manners. Here the manners of the world are represented and the young men are educated (as by the orations of the young ladies in *The Female Academy*) in the right ways of thinking about the world.

The idea of the theatre serves to connect several significant topics: education, the army, the public theatre, government and court. Furthermore, it offers the reader scenes of domination to elaborate. The notion of acting is synonymous with action: through representation a woman 'acting' the part of a general may take public 'action'. The slippage between the theatre and the world and the theatre of the world serves very specific purposes in *The Female Academy* and other Cavendish plays, including *The Convent of Pleasure*. The imagined acting woman slips through the plurisemic signifier 'theatre' into a world of action.

Cavendish writes of the 'female actor' she booked rooms to see on the Mountebank's stage in Antwerp:

Upon this Profess'd Mountebank's Stage, there were two Handsom Women Actors, both Sisters, the one of them was the Mountebank's, th'other the Fool's Wife . . . his Wife was far the Handsomer, and better Actor, and danc'd better than the other; indeed she was the Best Female Actor that ever I saw; and her Acting a Man's Part, she did it so Naturally as if she had been of that Sex, and yet she was of a Neat, Slender Shape: but being in her Dublet and Breeches, and a Sword hanging by her side, one would believe she had never worn a Petticoat, and had been more used to Handle a sword than a Distaff; and when she Danced in a Masculine Habit, she would Caper Higher, and Oftener than any of the Men . . . [27]

Acting styles and disguise in the commercial theatre are shown here as releasing the female protagonists from the characteristics of gender. The spectator is presented as being in the same position as the male viewers in *The Female Academy*. As Sophie Tomlinson's discussion of this incident indicates, Cavendish reports on her own viewing, and the reader watches her watching; she went 'to see them act upon the Stage, as I caused a room to be hired in the next House to the stage, and went every day to See them, not to Hear what they said for I did not Understand their Language' (p. 407). The experience of watching the theatrical spectacle is such that when the pleasure is withdrawn (owing, we are told, to Magistrates fearing the plague), she says 'my Fancy set up a stage in my brain and the Incorporeal Thoughts were the several Actors, and my Wit play'd the Jack Fool', until 'the Magistrates of the Mind' chase her imaginary theatre away.

Thus the theatre for Cavendish represents a locus of multiple possibilities. In her analysis of the 'female actor' it erases the signs of gender, and liberates the 'incorporeal' imagination into making fictions. The multiple idea of theatre operates most obviously, but yet again differently, in relation to the heroines of her texts. Here sexual politics is closely entwined with the theatre of war. For example, in *Love's Adventures* (which follows patterns drawn from romance), the Lady Orphant has been promised by her now dead father to Lord Singular. He has vowed never to marry; she disguises herself as a man and joins the army as his page. Unlike Viola in *Twelfth Night*, the Lady Orphant establishes an impeccable army record: she makes an excellent man, defends herself against false accusations and persuades her Lord to allow her to fight alongside him, distinguishing herself first in the field and then in the council of war. Lord Singular's role is to be astonished and impressed by

Orphant/Affectionata's wisdom and courage (a scenario played out also in Cavendish's *Bell in Campo*). Eventually the scene returns to England, where her guardians are about to be tried for murder because of the disappearance of their charge. At the trial she reveals all – that is, her gender: 'Most Reverend Judges, and Grave Jury, sentence me not with censure, nor condemn me to scandals, for waiting as a Man, and serving as a Page; For though I dissembled in my outward habit and behaviour, yet I was alwaies chaste and modest in my nature' (Pt 2. v.xxxvi, p. 75). In a courtroom scene reminiscent of her prose fiction, 'The Contract', Affectionata is reinserted into the social order at an appropriate level.[28] She and Singular declare a mutual passion and leave the stage with her reputation, chastity, honour, money and, above all, obedience to her father still intact.

For the female actor, and for the disguised Affectionata, acting transformed visible gender. But in this case the restitution of female status is crucial to the plot. Thus, disguise in Cavendish's plays is in an ambiguous relationship to theatrical cross-dressing (in which men played women) on the one hand and the gender-disguises of prose romance (in which men and women were disguised) on the other. In *The Convent of Pleasure* we find a man disguised as a woman disguised as a man (see IV.i, p. 32 and v.i, p. 47) in a way which echoes romance and contemporary comedic pastoral in its destabilising of desire and gender identities. Indeed, it could be argued that in that play the only stable term in attraction between the same or different genders is status. A complex debate about the issue of sexuality and cross-dressing in seventeenth-century theatre has developed in recent critical writing, but these plays, written without a stage context but for imaginative reading, add a new twist to these arguments.[29]

In this respect, *The Convent of Pleasure* seems to be a very different case from *Love's Adventures* and the role of cross-dressing and disguise would appear to change according to acting ethos (private or public?) and the way in which each material instance discursively reworks codes already present. How can we think of 'women' or female parts in plays of the 1650s but published in the early 1660s? It seems likely that during the 1650s the shifts that were taking place in the ethos and political implications of acting made these plurisemic disguises even more unstable. But while the meanings generated by women on stage were transformed by the arrival of the actress at the Restoration, there was in the read texts of this period the possibility of complete congruity of gender between part and actor; the 'women' in Cavendish's plays, as read, can be imagined as if acted by a woman – as opposed to signifying as alternately masculine and feminine.

The choices would be with the reader, too, and would probably be influenced by that reader's knowledge of both theatrical and literary genres. These dramatic texts, published as women actors first began to appear on the public stage, draw on codes of both public and private, aristocratic and commercial theatre. In the pre-war theatres these two codes of theatrical representation configured gender slightly differently, especially because of the masque tradition which troped feminine dramatis personae, played by women, as representations of society's ideal values. The 1650s brought together these two codes in William Davenant's public but masque-like productions such as *The Cruelty of the Spaniards in Peru* (see chapter 6), and that fusing implied a shift in theatrical uses of gender. Cavendish's plays seem to place an imaginary woman's body on stage but also use disguise in a way very similar to pre-war plays. One might contrast *The Female Academy*, where gender distinctions appear to be stable, and *Love's Adventures*. The latter, a text drawing on codes of romance, locates the erotic power of femininity in the relationship between femininity and public action combined with the erotic, attractive, power implied in disguise and potential discovery.

For several reasons – the reiterated idea of the two kinds of theatre, the analysis of the female actor liberated into a 'natural' masculinity, and the triumphant heroines of the plays acting out masculine roles in the theatre of war – the idea of the theatre generates repeated scenes of the transformation of power and gender. The plays by Cavendish discussed here rely on a version of the 'vital if ill-defined connection between the theatre and the world'.[30] The theatre functions as a place where problems of gender become superable for the heroine. The multiple signifieds of 'theatre' serve to link power, fantasy and gender in ways which figure the transcendence of the cultural meanings of femininity for the heroines (and possibly for the reader). It is perhaps the very absence of an actual playhouse, a circumstance particular to the 1650s, which permits such an intimate, flexible and highly connotative link between all the world and the stage of the imagination.

Some of Cavendish's female protagonists appear on stage in the same manner that a woman is on display at a court, performing what Ann-Rosalind Jones calls the court lady's spectacular function, a 'generalised erotic function directly opposed to the silent fidelity demanded of the private woman'.[31] Display is combined with an emphasis on the chastity of the noble heroine like that of a *femme forte*. However, the heroine's assumption of masculine roles and prerogatives constitutes a representation of a society radically transformed in terms of gender relations. As I shall suggest, the nobility of the heroine is central in such a transformation. In order to begin to do so I shall first examine the way in which Cavendish's writing speaks to royalism and patriarchal discourse.

ROYALISM AND REPRESENTATION

Sherry Ortner has argued that 'the sex/gender system . . . can be best understood in relation to the workings of the "prestige system", the system within which personal status is ascribed, achieved, advanced and lost'.[32] Writing, and especially dramatic writing, offers Cavendish an opportunity to renegotiate the place of women in the prestige system, momentarily. Pre-war seventeenth-century English society regarded the aristocratic hierarchy as (ideally, if not actually) the custodians of the society's encompassing ideals. This is made literal in the language of patronage. Cavendish, writing in the 1650s, wants to preserve this threatened role. On the other hand, the system relied implicitly on the continued use and exchange of women as bearers of value (including some of pre-war England's 'ideal' values). Some, at least, of the developments of the 1650s suggested that some women were amongst those who would benefit from the fall of the old hierarchy and values, which Cavendish in the main wished to preserve. The theatre provides a metaphor which can resolve, in writing, such intractable contradictions, at least for the noble protagonist.

A closer focus on the intersection of gender and nobility in Cavendish's plays and writings on theatre alerts the reader to a whole set of further slippages that take place within Cavendish's texts around royalist ideologies and the status of women.

Obviously, there is no reason to expect the texts to be either ideologically coherent or 'feminist'. To do so would be to take no account of the cross-currents of status and gender in Cavendish's texts, to dehistoricise 'feminist' issues within the plays by demanding that texts conform to a contemporary agenda.[33] Cavendish was, as her endless prefaces declare, a woman writing (whatever that means). She was also the wife of a peer who enters the writing market at the level of buying authors to write plays for him. While making demands for certain kinds of women in certain situations, she predicates her work on masculine authority and permission which she simultaneously undermines. Her writings produce a circuit of associations and disjunctions between the claims of gender and hierarchy, not a sequence of arguments.

Patriarchal political thinking was powerful but, as Margaret Ezell suggests, it is more difficult to map the relationship between political discourse and its implication for individuals and the material decisions of daily life.[34] That is not to say that patriarchal discourse was nothing more powerful than a disposable meta-language. However, the Civil War did expose the self-interest of the social elite. As Brian Manning notes, 'stripped of the trappings of government, the monarchy was seen to rest, not upon the love of the people, but upon the interests of a class'.[35] Clarendon said of Newcastle that he 'loved monarchy, as it was the foundation and support of his own greatness'.[36] The same could, perhaps, be said of his wife. Thus Cavendish's negotiations of questions of gender and status can best be read in relation to the discourses which supported monarchy, but which also syncretically supported the structure of the family; the same metaphorical thinking held the king in place as head of the state and the father as head of the family.

Cavendish argues on the one hand that women are unjustifiably marginalised, and on the other, for the primacy of the monarch. Her arguments circle the same central issues – conversation, public display and action, marriage and remarriage (see *Bell in Campo, Playes*, 1662) – issues which concerned all women, but which she usually presents through the predicament of a particular noble figure. Even as she rails against it, her heroines (such as the Lady Sanspareille) endorse the division of the world into binary opposites based on the masculine right to authority. Cavendish attempts to claim status as a writer not by repudiation of gender hierarchies but by a process of negotiation which holds together opposing positions in 'subtle appropriations and reshufflings of the prevailing notions of feminine virtue'.[37]

In her prose writing on the topic of gender relations and the rights of women, Cavendish is highly contradictory, suggesting that marriage is undesirable, and approaches positions which assert female autonomy, only to back away. She combines a conception of the wife's role in marriage which might have been taken from the educationalist Jean Luis Vives with a telling critique of the power relations between the sexes. She follows the gendered ascription of qualities and its implications for women's engagement with the world and particularly the public sphere: 'The minde and the body', we read, 'must be married together; but so as the minde must be the husband; to govern, and command, and the wife to obey, and reason which is the judge of the minde must keepe the senses in awe.'[38] Cavendish is not the only woman entering discourse in support of monarchy and the family. In 1649 Elizabeth Poole wrote of Charles I that, although he had broken his side of the patriarchal contract, the country (as wife) was still subject to his authority. 'And although this bond be broken on his part; You never heard that a Wife might put away her husband, as he is head of her body.'[39] Here, too, we can see a woman writing within the paradigms offered by patriarchal familial–political theory, and in support of preserving the life of the referent – the king himself. But at the same time as Cavendish and Poole are subjects in patriarchal discourse, the operation of this in terms of familial and political authority is precisely the object of their discourse. Thus, Cavendish's writings inevitably occupy a double position, in some carefully selected areas – primarily the scope of the noble woman – negotiating norms, in other areas invoking and enforcing social hierarchy.

The play *Youths Glory and Deaths Banquet* lets us map these contradictory relationships more clearly here. The Lady Sanspareille comments on political questions: the area which Cavendish believed closed to women's action. Delivering a commentary on 'justice' she declares that 'humane Justice [belongs] to Monarchical Princes . . . For which Justice Gods and Princes are both feared and loved.' Through this analogy monarchy becomes inseparable from justice (Pt 2, I.i, p. 155). Earlier she has commented in a Hobbesian way that the 'Marshall Law' is 'the

Supream Authority, placing and displacing, and is the Monarchical Power, that doth not only protect all other Laws, but commands them with threats' (Pt 1, v.xv, p. 150). For Cavendish and her heroines the supreme authority is royal and the monarchical duty is the protection of the peace of the commonwealth through martial justice and 'without which', she writes, 'there could be no peace kept'. Thus justice and military power simultaneously constitute monarchy and are validated by it. Lady Sanspareille addresses a female monarch as follows:

SANSP: most glorious Princess, you and your Subjects are like the Sun, and the rest of the Planets, moving perpetually, keeping their proper Sphere, they moving in civiler loyalty about you, to receive the light of your Authority . . . (Pt 2, I.i, p. 156)

As Catherine Gallagher notes, Cavendish's insistence on hierarchical order can only coincide with the recognition of the rights of women to power at the very top of the hierarchy.[40] Thus, Cavendish's prose writing contains a range of contradictory opinions about politics, ranging from the orthodox to the eccentric.[41] Often, the writing slides from one position to the other. An example of such slippage and reorganisation can be seen in *The World's Olio*, where she comments 'Womens Tongues are like Stings of Bees; and what man could endure our effeminate monarchy to swarm about their ears?' She implicitly links the bid for authority by a female with a danger – a 'swarm' – and goes on to link that bid for authority with speech. The 'effeminate monarchy' is attempting to seize power through speech. She continues:

True it is, our Sex make great complaints, that men from their first Creation usurped a Supremacy to themselves, although we were made equal by Nature, which Tyrannical Government they have kept ever since, so that we never could come to be free, but rather more and more enslaved, using us either like Children, Fools, or Subjects, that is to flatter or threaten us, to allure or force us to obey, and will not let us divide the World equally with them, as to Govern and Command, to direct and Dispose as they do; which Slavery hath dejected our Spirits, as we are become so stupid that Beasts are but a Degree below us . . . (A4r)

A slippage takes place here, as the views initially attributed to her complaining sex in general then seem to become absorbed into the text as its own complaint. From condemning 'effeminate monarchy' it moves rapidly to apparently sponsoring a feminist position. Cavendish seems on the one hand to subscribe to an ideology of contempt for female rule as a kind of tyranny, on the other to evade or escape her marginal or actively transgressive status as literary producer. The first attribution of the 'complaints' to loci external to the text produces an aporia between the official, unified 'I' as in agreement with the anti-feminist position, and allows an ambiguous, unowned, intervention of other views. In short, assertions of a feminist kind rest uneasily in Cavendish's texts because these rely on a conceptualisation of authority wholly derived from the male, ruling, speaking figure.

Yet Cavendish returns again and again to the theme of female wisdom and women's ability to make laws and to organise military campaigns and to orate. Again and again her heroines, like Lady Contemplation, Lady Sanspareille and Lady Orphant, take on male roles and are respected, so that these heroines are allowed to answer the case against female rule and government. The Lady Sanspareille in *Youths Glory* is quickly sketched in as a paragon of wit and learning; granted a proper education by an esteemed father, she goes on to astonish the world with a series of orations on all subjects from politics through marriage to the theatre. She is so impressive that one surprised 'gentleman' comments that he could wish for 'that I never wisht before' – to be a woman, 'but such a woman as the Lady Sanspareille' (Pt 1, IV.xiii, p. 145).

One of the most prolonged explorations of these contradictions between power and femininity comes in another of the earlier plays, *Bell in Campo*.[42] Here too the only resolution of the problem of femininity versus authority is the coincidence of these qualities through a woman raised to the top of the hierarchy: in this case a female general. This play also reflects Cavendish's engagement with the Civil War: the triumphal entry may well be a reading of Henrietta Maria's triumphal entry into Oxford in 1643.[43] *Bell in Campo* tells the story of the war between 'this Kingdom of Reformation' and 'the Kingdome of Faction' (Pt 1, I.i, p. 579) contrasting the sad fortunes of women left behind by war-going husbands with the successful career of the Lady Victoria who is elected to be head of a female army made up of 'women of all sorts' (I.ix, p. 587). Part of the play is given over to the wise law-giving of the Lady Victoria, but most of Acts III, IV and Part 2, Acts II, III and IV interweave the reported successes of the Female Army with the sad fates of war widows. The successes bring the Masculine and

Female armies closer together, and the second part ends with the plan for Lady Victoria's triumph:

1 GENT: . . . the Lady Victoria shall be brought through the city in triumph, which is a great honour, for never any makes triumphs in a Monarchy but the King himself; then that there shall be a blank for the Female Army to write their desires and demands; also there is an Armour of gold and a Sword a making, the hilt being set with Diamonds, and Chariot all gilt and imbroidered to be presented to the Lady Victoria, and the city is making great preparation against her arrival.

2 GENT: Certainly she is a Lady that deserves as much as can be given from Kings, States, or Poets. (Pt 2, IV.xviii, p. 627)

This passage and the juxtaposed list of female demands serves to focus the contradictions between monarchist ideology and rhetoric on the one hand and the claims Cavendish also articulates for noble, aristocratic, women on the other. Again a heroine – 'liberated' by theatre from the restraints of gender – outdoes the men in fields traditionally barred to her. The list of demands returns the play from celebration of heroinism to analysis of women in their domestic relations, as they articulate demands for domestic autonomy which seem petty in comparison to the great triumphs of the Lady Victoria. The demands of the women include:

First, That all women shall hereafter in this Kingdome be Mistris in their own Houses and Families.

Secondly, They shall sit at the upper end of the Table above their Husbands.

Thirdly, that they shall keep the Purse.

. . .

Tenthly, They shall go to Playes, Masks, Balls, Churchings, Christenings, Preachings, whensoever they will, and as fine and bravely attired as they will.

Lastly, That they shall be of their Husbands Counsel. (Pt 2, v.xx, p. 625 (mispaginated))

The women warriors cheer the victory won for them by the prowess of the aristocratic heroine in the theatre of war. When the play shifts from a single aristocratic woman to women in general, it shifts its discursive field from the fantasised triumphs of war to the issues of the battle of the sexes fought out in comic drama, conduct books and in the antifeminist tracts of the earlier seventeenth century. The right to power, for women in Cavendish's writing, is a privilege attendant upon birth and status; her plays dramatise the differences between noble women warfarers and other women, especially citizen women.

GENDER, STATUS AND MOBILITY
THE CIVIL WAR CONTEXT

These texts adopt positions about gender which remain contradictory even taking into account that some are spoken by Cavendish in an authorial persona, and others by fictitious characters often taken by commentators to be, unproblematically, 'Margaret'. The contradictions have perplexed a range of writers on Cavendish. Treating her life and writing as one text, a recent biographer says of her 'disapproval' of the roles some women found during the Civil Wars and after: 'Why such an insistent advocate of greater freedom for women should condemn those who exercise such freedom is difficult to assess.'[44]

While Cavendish does not seem to be exactly 'an insistent advocate of freedom for women', the movement between critique and valorisation of patriarchal institutions means that her criticisms of sexual inequality, while in no way the unconscious of the texts, are formed within the discourses of power and informed by her social investments in those discourses. The relationships between Cavendish's pleasure in hierarchy and critique of the familial bounds of the noble woman are figured in her image of the noble female 'actor' with all attendant puns. This can be set against something to which critics of Cavendish's plays have paid little attention but which is implicit in the Civil War and Protectorate context in which the plays were written – the representation of gender in relation to social mobility.

In William Cavendish's plays, women of the lower orders are represented as sexually interested and available. In the plays by his daughters, such women are limited to the parts of servants or farm women. Although they are presented sympathetically, they are called by farm names such as 'Henn' in 'A Pastorall'. Margaret Cavendish's representation of citizen women, maids and servants insists on their desire for social mobility. For example, the citizen women who appear momentarily in *The Female Academy* are angry at being excluded from the academy orations or discourses which are held exclusively for a noble audience. Their recourse is to the men's academy: the men, they say, will not turn them away but make them welcome (*Female Academy*, 11.xi, p. 662).

One of the most detailed treatments of social aspiration and femininity occurs in a plot developed autonomously through Part 1 of the play *The Matrimonial Trouble* (*Playes*, 1662). In this plot, Bridget Greasy, a 'Cook-maid', is accused of stealing by Thirsty the steward, who berates her, initially for her unskilful making of 'pudding in guts':

. . . you are a Slut, and did not take all the dung out of them, nor wash, nor scrape nor cleanse them as they should have been, but you order the guts as you do the dishes, the one is dungy, the other greasie; besides, my Master complains, that his Fowl tastes rank, and his Brawn tastes strong, and his Beef tastes musty, and that's because you are so lazy, as not to shift your Brawn into fresh Sousing drink, nor make the brine strong enough in the powdering-tub, nor thrust your fingers far enough into the Fowls rumps to draw them clean . . . besides, your sluttery is such, as you will poyson all the House: for in one place I find a piece of butter, and a greasie comb, full of nitty hairs lying by it; and in another place flour and old worn stockings, the feet being rotted off with sweat; and in a third place, a dish of cold meat cover'd with a foul smock . . . [45]

At this point the master, Sir John Dotard, comes in; the rest of this plot traces Bridget Greasy's rise through the ranks to become his wife. Much of her progress is reported disapprovingly by other servants who comment on her hypocrisy and thieving. While Cavendish defends the entry of noble (fictional) ladies into the theatre of the world, Bridget is represented as disgusting and 'naturally' low. As Sara Mendelson comments, 'class interests are certainly more obvious than gender solidarity among seventeenth-century women'.[46] This formulation is only suggestive with regard to the interrelationship of class and gender in Cavendish's plays and in her writing generally. Cavendish's multiple 'theatres' are open only to the noble female. Her emphasis on the sexual attractiveness and power of the noble female is underpinned by a commitment to a hierarchical structure in which the femininity of the lower orders must be kept under control. The sexual desirability and desires of women of the lower orders endanger the security of the noble woman and are constructed as disgusting and transgressive. The same is true of their actions in the world; Cavendish speaks approvingly of the breaking-up of a conventicle of 'preaching sisters' which she had nevertheless gone to see.

The theatre preserves the heroines and noble ladies as beautiful and chaste while elevating them to masculine roles; it allots to lower-class women (and sexually desirous courtiers in *The Presence*) all the many negative attributes of femininity as constructed in seventeenth-century society.[47] Socially mobile women – particularly in the plays in the 1662 volume – connote danger and chaos. Citizens' wives remain the focus of animosity throughout Cavendish's plays. Sometimes they act as foils to deserving or vulnerable women. An example is the citizen's wife in the play within a play in *The Convent of Pleasure*, who goes looking for her husband in the tavern and agrees to stay there to drink with the men.

What is at stake throughout Cavendish's writing is the intransigent interrelationship between patriarchal or monarchist ideals and the desire to disrupt gender ideology. I began this chapter with Cavendish's own analysis and valorisation of the potential of the theatre as an educator of the nobility. Writing about the exclusivity of social spheres, Peter Stallybrass writes that the class aspirant shares with the members of the elite the desire to preserve 'social closure' yet contradictorily needs the structure to be sufficiently flexible to accommodate him or her.[48] A model which unites aspiration to elite values and a desire to be accommodated by those values, though – contradictorily – as a woman, is, I am suggesting, helpful in thinking about the relationship betwen status and gender suggested in Cavendish's plays from the Protectorate. As a royalist woman, Cavendish wishes to support the ideal class order, but to challenge some of the attendant gender ideologies. As the last chapter suggested, and as S. D. Amussen argues persuasively, in the 1650s gender and familial hierarchy was seen as stable while 'the criteria for determining status, the conception of the moral superiority of the wealthy and the inferiority of the poor were also called into question'.[49] Moreover, the 1650s, when Cavendish was writing, saw the county hierarchy in disarray and only beginning to regain limited control in the provinces. Her own position as a wife whose husband endorsed her work indicates immediately the interrelationship of status and gender hierarchy: to suggest that one (gender) might benefit from reform is to point, inevitably, towards the instability of the other (status). These are the contexts which produced the ideologies of her texts: the very circumstances of social change and mobility in the 1650s which contributed to Cavendish becoming a playwright simultaneously threatened her position as an aristocrat.

It is possible to read back into her plays the circumstances of their production, and to see the insistence with which her texts designate the dirty, low, waste parts of society in relation to social mobility (Bridget Greasy, citizens' wives) as a product of irresolubly contradictory ideologies of gender and of class. Although at times, as in *The Convent of Pleasure*, Cavendish makes links between women of different status in terms of their relationship with men, it is also often the case that the assertion of stability of status and the fixed lowerness of the lower orders stands surety for the noble ladies' liberation from gender constraints and entry into the theatre of the world.

Thus the 1650s proved a period of innovation in women's relationships to the writing and publishing of plays, if not their performance. Indeed, the reception of women performers at the Restoration was overdetermined by the link between women and whores in a way that Protectorate production was not – as Thomas Jordan's apparently sympathetic articulation of the ideologies of female performance in his prologue and epilogue to *Othello* suggests. In the prologue he wrote:

> 'Tis possible a vertuous woman may
> Abhor all sorts of looseness and yet play;
> Play on the Stage, where all eyes are upon her,
> Shall we count that a crime *France* calls an honour . . .

The epilogue serves to reinforce the audience's sense that actresses are whores by, apparently, seeking to dispel it:

> And how d'ye like her, come what is 't ye drive at,
> She's the same thing in publick as in private;
> As far from being what you call a Whore,
> As *Desdemona* injur'd by the Moor?[50]

As a writer in exile and without hope of performance, Margaret Cavendish was not subject to the strictures against the theatre, or to the sexualised complexity of the reception of actresses. However, these very strictures against the stage provoked a reassessment of the nature of theatre around the question of opera, and this is the subject of chapter 5.

CHAPTER 5

Royal or reformed? The politics of court entertainment in translation and performance

The theory and practice of 'reformed' drama in the 1650s can be mapped in relation to both the contemporary political situations and the pre-war Caroline court. While Margaret Cavendish was writing and watching performances in exile, this story begins with an entertainment recorded as having been performed under the Commonwealth, before a visiting ambassador, and continues in the theorising about the place of reformed drama and opera which took place under the Protectorate.

Despite stylistic differences, in ideological terms masque and opera seem to have held comparable places in the theatrical debates of the 1650s, and in some cases the two words seem to cover similar material. For the purposes of this argument, which traces the interconnections of political circumstance and a genre, masque and opera function primarily as the locus of the debates about drama and theatre under the Protectorate. This chapter discusses the contextual and political implications of the genres and the way musical entertainment was part of the cultural and ideological disputes of the 1650s rather than the musical developments of the aria and recitative within the opera, or performance in masque, though in performance music would have played an important part in the drama, and would have complicated and elucidated the narrative.[1]

In 1653 the entertainment *Cupid and Death* was permitted, even sponsored, by the government. The government itself changed rapidly in 1653–4 when Cromwell dissolved the unpopular Rump and summoned a Nominated Assembly (better known as Barebones). This, in turn, was dissolved in December 1653, and by 16 December the Protector was ruling using the Instrument of Government. Famously, in September 1654 he spoke to a newly called assembly about the need for 'healing and settling'.[2]

Meanwhile, forms of theatrical activity continued. In 1653 Daniel Fleming recorded spending twopence on a play, and evidence that playing continued is provided by recorded moves against it in 1654 and raids on the still-functioning Red Bull in December of the same year.[3] Writing in 1656, the same year in which Davenant's opera began, the Spanish ambassador Giovanno Sagredo wrote a partial truth when he said that 'all conventicles and meetings are forbidden, and plays and parties in particular, from fear that under the guise of recreation they may be plotting something against the present rulers'.[4] Although this was true, it was not quite the only story. For even three years earlier parliament seems to have begun using entertainments to help to answer the question of how the new republic was to present itself. From the one theatrical production put on (possibly by the Committee of Council) in 1653 for the Portuguese ambassador, it is possible to trace the cultural changes that took place from the time of the Caroline court to the republic.[5]

CONTINUITY AND CRITICISM IN COURT ENTERTAINMENTS: 1634, 1643, 1653

Three texts, *The Triumph of Peace* (1634), *The Cruell Warre* (1643) and *Cupid and Death* (1653) provide an opportunity to explore the ideological position of court drama in the 1650s, and furnish further evidence about the relationship between pre- and post-war drama. The author of two of these texts, the masques *The Triumph of Peace* and *Cupid and Death*, was James Shirley, the Caroline dramatist, who lived on into the Civil Wars and continued to write. In some ways, Shirley's position as a dramatist is similar to that of Davenant (see chapter 7). Both knew and may have been helped by the powerful Bulstrode Whitelocke. In 1634 Shirley and Whitelocke both worked on *The Triumph of Peace*, and like Davenant they had both participated in what some (such as the author of *The Cruell Warre*) regarded as the worst excesses of courtly drama. It has even been suggested that Davenant ousted Shirley from his court position. Undoubtedly, Shirley wrote for the court but, as Martin Butler notes, such associations do not imply total personal identification with Charles's policies. Shirley's unperformed play *The Court Secret* (1642, published 1653), for example, is not emphatically pro-Stuart.[6]

The Triumph of Peace belongs to Shirley's period working for the Caroline court but it was first put on by the Inns of Court in 1634, when it was overseen to a large extent by Bulstrode Whitelocke, later lord chancellor under the Protectorate. Whitelocke took charge of the music (composed by Simon Ives and William Lawes, who had worked on other productions including *Britannia Triumphans*), and he was also involved in the organisation of both the antimasques and the procession.[7] *The Triumph of Peace* situates Shirley as a dramatist whose work was intimately involved with debates around the court, and (to an outsider) might appear to exemplify the virtues or vices of courtly drama. Nevertheless, Whitelocke's involvement in a masque ironically dedicated to the imprisoned William Prynne hints at the complexity of the religious and political cross-currents of the Caroline court, and also at the potential tensions between religion, politics and status.[8]

The masque was implicated in at least two debates – one between the king and the law about monopolies (addressed in an antimasque of projectors) and an equally complex debate on court theatricals. It may have been a response to Prynne's *Histrio-Mastix* which, in turn, may have been an attack on women's dancing in Walter Montagu's pastoral *The Shepherd's Paradise*.[9] Prynne suffered for his attack on the sports of the ruling powers: a year after his protest he was expelled from Lincoln's Inn, fined £5,000, mutilated and imprisoned. Although he was not released before the outbreak of war the case was not forgotten – as the spoof recantation of *Histrio-Mastix* of 1649 suggests.[10] Prynne's connection with *The Triumph of Peace* would be sufficient to make the masque memorable to a section of the public, but so would its lavish production.[11] *The Triumph of Peace* was *both* a 'triumph' – processing through the streets – and a masque. The structural use of a sequence of antimasques banished by Irene led Murray Lefkowitz to accuse it of lacking 'dramatic unity'.[12] However, it lived up to its name of 'triumph'. It was preceded by a huge procession through the streets: a public demonstration of power for the pleasure (and awe) of the bystanders.

The processional meant that the masque costumes were seen by more people than usual; and that the production involved a wider range of people than court festivities customarily did is indicated by the fact that the lord mayor arranged for the masque's second performance.[13] Martin Butler perceives *The Triumph of Peace* as successfully building a bridge between court and law, and he details the involvement of men who at other times opposed the crown.[14] Because of its dual status as triumph, this masque was unusual in having another audience – on the street – and its relationship to this audience was distinctly ambivalent. For instance, one detail recorded by Whitelocke was that for the procession even the beggars from the antimasque had to be mounted – 'but on the poorest, leanest jades that could be gotten out of the dirt carts or elsewhere'.[15] Overall, this production displayed a sort of conspicuous consumption calculated to gall critics of the court.

The published masque details the order and contents of the triumphal procession, giving descriptions of the elaborate costuming. More, it tells us something about the relationship between the procession and the inhabitants of the streets that it passed through. After the trumpeters who followed the antimasque figures came an actual military force:

The Marshal followed these, bravely mounted, attended with ten Horse and forty Foot, in coats and hose of scarlet trimmed with silver lace, white hats and feathers, their truncheons tipped with silver: these upon every occasion moving to and fro, to preserve the order of their march and restrain the rudeness of the people, that in such triumphs are wont to be insolent and tumultuary.

After these an hundred Gentlemen, gloriously furnished and gallantly mounted, riding two and two abreast, every Gentleman having many Pages, richly attired, and a Groom to attend him.[16]

In the middle of the 'triumphal' procession there was a genuine militia making sure that the separation between staged antimasque and riot was maintained, and preserving the safety of the aristocracy from the potentially antic disposition of the general populace. In the light of recent criticism of the court masque, seeing it as a peace-keeping force, this military presence to cow those outside the court seems ironic indeed and demonstrates the narrow bounds within which the symbolic discourse could operate. The procession might be seen in public, but the nature of the display itself was felt to be potentially disruptive: the masquers anticipated that what Martin Butler calls the 'plebeian audience' might not enter fully into the spirit of 'triumph'.[17] These spectators must have been in part the same as those for the lord mayors' shows: but this, a 'triumph', was a display of court wealth in front of them, not a show for them. They are offered the iconography of the masque without the hermeneutic provided by the narrative: in what sense can they be called an audience to the masque at all? All the bystanders could really see was a pageant signifying the richness and power of the court. Indeed, perhaps the pleasure of the procession was for those who processed in triumph, rather than for the onlookers. And the unity of the courtly symbolic system was protected from disruption by the presence of the military dressed in a strange mixture of riot gear and stage costume, capable equally of repelling overenthusiastic or angry observers.

The association between Whitelocke and Shirley in this court entertainment takes on new implications in 1643. The theatres were closed, Whitelocke was active in the new government and, just at this point, *The Tragedy of the Cruell Warre* (1643) was published.[18] The nature of *The Cruell Warre* indicates the increased drawing apart of the sides during 1643 and makes evident the socio-political significance which *The Triumph of Peace* had for contemporaries.[19] *The Cruell Warre* played on the implicit disjuncture of audiences and interests, underlining the differences between the message of the masque and what it presents as a 'reality'. *The Cruell Warre* follows the structure and even costuming of the masque quite closely, beginning with Confidence's arrival at a royalist camp and going on to parody the dance of the beggars. Other incidents are transformed to the detriment of royalists, as when Jollity and Laughter play at dice, 'where having spent their patrimony they returne to plunder, where with fire and sword they renew their stocks againe'.[20]

Presumably it is because of this close resemblance to the earlier text that Bulstrode Whitelocke himself has been suggested as the anonymous author of *The Cruell Warre*.[21] This is unlikely because *The Cruell Warre* does not seem to be sympathetic to the king, and during 1643 Whitelocke was heavily involved in peace talks with Charles I; he seems to have been among those genuinely keen to see them succeed. The publication of such a parody by him could only exacerbate bad relations and accelerate any drawing apart of king and parliament. It seems unlikely that Whitelocke would wish to offer the public a reminder of his involvement with *The Triumph of Peace*. Moreover, Whitelocke was actually involved in *regulating* scandalous print as a member of a committee to consider 'The Printing of Pamphlets of False News'.[22]

Whoever did write the parody was by 1643 intensely critical of the Caroline court as well as the royalist cause. As one commentator has put it, in taking the same form as *The Triumph of Peace*, *The Cruell Warre* is 'a piece of Royalist propaganda by a Royalist sympathiser . . . turned inside out to be used as a weapon against the Cavaliers themselves' – a comment which, problematically, insists on seeing *The Triumph of Peace* from a post-Civil War viewpoint, as 'royalist'.[23] The target of the parody is in part the perpetuation by *The Triumph of Peace* of the myths of the Stuart ruling class.[24] *The Cruell Warre* by its very existence bears witness to the puissance of Caroline self-mythologisations but also to the fragility of the symbolism of the court's theatrical expressions. The parody plays upon the apparent promises of the masque and what is now the case in England. The existence of *The Cruell Warre* suggests a particular political understanding of court culture, and its existence is evidence for a widespread apprehension, not simply a court knowledge, that the masque as a form was implicated in political debate and criticism, but also (by the 1640s) could be seen as having promulgated Caroline ideologies: *The Cruell Warre* can be seen as an outsider's commentary on the failure of law and monarchy to resolve the issues in that most seriously political of genres, the court masque. As well as 'exposing' as perfidious the symbolic language of the court, *The Cruell Warre* makes it obvious that by some in the 1640s, at least, the role of courtly entertainments was seen as putting state policy into an aesthetic and symbolic vocabulary. Although such masques might well be critical of the king, the parody pointedly offers an outsider's view, in which they are merely the symbolic language of kingly policy. Such parodic challenge to the verbal and visual rhetoric of court spectacle amounts to a deliberate demystification of the arts of monarchy – an example of a similar strategy of 'exposure' is the publication of the king's personal correspondence in *The King's Cabinet Opened*.[25]

The Cruell Warre's status as parody enables it to 'expose' *The Triumph of Peace*, as it were from the inside, to a large extent inhabiting the original text (though, paradoxically, it was in part able to do so because the earlier masque at least raised questions about Charles's policies on projectors and monopolists, and the status of rumour, thereby providing a format to be both used and subverted). The first stage of the original masque was a demonstration of power and wealth in a procession to court from Ely and Hatton houses, and the printed version of the masque gives a detailed description of the principal actors as they set off:

Fancy, in a suit of several-coloured feathers, hooded; a pair of bats' wings on his shoulders, riding alone as sole presenter of the Anti-masques.

After him rode Opinion and Confidence together; Opinion in an old fashioned doublet of blacke velvet, and trunk hose, a short cloak of the same with an antique cape, a black velvet cap pinched up, with a white fall, and a staff in his hand; Confidence in a slashed doublet parti-coloured, breeches suitable with points at knees, favours upon his breast and arm, and a broad-brimmed hat, tied up on one side, banded with a feather, a long lock of hair, trimmed with several-coloured ribbons; wide boots, and great spurs with bells for rowels. (p. 283)

The Cruell Warre reiterates such detailed description, suggesting that the parodist was working closely from the text. More signifi-cant imitation is the way the parody puts to work the antimasques from The Triumph of Peace. Within the Caroline masque the anti-masque presented those social dangers the government actually faced – in Triumph of Peace there is an antimasque of monopolists, a topical cause of anger – but the masque also plays on the status of the figures of Confidence, Opinion and Phansie as semi-alle-gorical figures and antimasque types. These serve as the main focus of the audience's contempt and laughter, thereby once again setting social comment at a distance.

The Cruell Warre exploits and inverts the masque's symbolism, and makes the ambiguous literal, in order to express the divisions within society rather than its unity. For example, the parody adapts the antimasque of the beggars' dance from The Triumph of Peace where a gentleman dancing alone is approached by two beggars and 'bestows his charity', but 'the Cripples upon his going off, throw away their legs and dance' (p. 291). The scene articulates the fears of the ruling class about the underclass: that they are com-mitted to begging, duplicitous and perfectly capable of working. However, the scene is rendered ambiguous by the commentary provided by Opinion and Phansie after the beggars have left:

OPINION: I am glad they are off, are these the effects of
    Peace?
  Corruption rather.
PHANSIE: O the beggars show
  The benefits of Peace.   (p. 291)

The 'effects of Peace' are that beggars (often ex-soldiers) fake disablement and make a living from begging rather than from work. How is the audience to construe Phansie's phrase the 'benefits of Peace'? Does the text suggest that too much ease, wealth, peace, breed corruption, or is the scene to be treated as carnival – a celebration, in its way, of peace? The placing of the beggars' dance within the antimasque allows the question to be raised without being resolved: Shirley's beggars are just one part in an episodic progression of antimasque incidents, and the two possible readings of the scene serve to cancel each other. But where *The Triumph of Peace* is ambiguous or ambivalent, *The Cruell Warre* is explicit, reworking this scene in a way which demonstrates both a social crisis and the ideological confusions of the earlier masque:

Last of all, came a Gentleman with Fiddlers, and a company of Beggars with him on their crooches, the minstrill plaid, and he danced which made the criples to throw away their legs and crooches to hear and see Mirth and Jollity in the Taverne with the grand Cavallier, which Opinion standing by and beholding spoke to Phansie, saying:

OPINION: I am sorry to see the effects of war and corruption.
PHANSIE: This beggars dance shewes what want we are likely to sustaine, when we part with all we have to helpe us; doe you not see how they be faine to limp and halt, though they are suffered to dance?
OPINION: Your interpretation makes me weary of beholding them, I pray you let us walke forth, whose heart cannot chuse but bleed to consider the bloud that hath been shed in this poor Kingdom, since Papists have been entrusted with Armes, which is contrary to Law, and the pollicy both of Queen Elizabeth's and King James his States. (p. 63)

The parody's recension of the original scene shows the sad plight of the people of England, crippled by Caroline excesses but nevertheless forced to dance to the royal tune – unless they continue the war. The commentary activates the suggestion latent in *The Triumph of Peace* that the poor lack incentive to work hard, but it blames war and cavalier attitudes. The cavaliers are seen as ruining the ordinary people, and the scene becomes evidence of Caroline cruelty as it fulfils the didactic potential that the corresponding scene in *The Triumph of Peace* refused or contradicted by the hints that it was the beggars' own choice. The pamphlet thus acts as an indictment of the myths of the Caroline court *and* as an indictment of the royal party in 1643.

So Shirley's masque and the implicit politics of the symbolism of court entertainment was remembered with great bitterness in the first year of the war. Nevertheless, ten years later, Shirley's masque *Cupid and Death* was performed before the Portuguese ambassador on 26 March 1653 (an alliance was signed in 1654).[26] After the outbreak of war Shirley seems to have returned from Sir John Ogilby's theatre in Dublin to become a schoolmaster, and it was during this time that he wrote *Cupid and Death*.[27] Possibly the masque was to be performed by the schoolboys that Shirley was teaching at the time, as was his *Contention of Ajax and Hercules* (1653): Shirley denied seeking a court performance, and how the entertainment migrated from the schoolroom to the 'court' on 26 March 1653 is not known.[28] But in order to find the script someone must have at least known of its existence or of earlier performances. This implies an instance of private or school performance, and that there was enough of a stage-culture for information to be passed on to those who arranged the performance.[29] And *Cupid and Death* may have been revived in 1659, further suggesting that it was known.[30] As we are told of the 'elegance' and 'curiosity' of the scenes and that the 'musical compositions' (undertaken by Luke Channen or Channell who later worked on Davenant's *Macbeth*) 'had in them great soul of harmony', it would appear that the rehearsals were not excessively rushed (p. 378). Therefore, when Shirley states that the staging was 'without any address or design of the Author', his denial may well be at least in part disingenuous: it seems likely that he would have known that his manuscript was being used. But the denial does alert us to the place of the masque in relation to the bans on public theatre – although court entertainment was not public it would be publicly known. Caught on the horns of this dilemma it is not surprising to find the published play presented as having been staged without the author's intent.

There are some qualities in *Cupid and Death* which make it suitable for a republican court. It is structured in a way both similar to and dissimilar from the court entertainments of the 1630s.[31] The piece departs from the usual masque structure in that it dramatises one of Aesop's fables rather than adapting mythology into an elaborate address to one single figure. Moreover, in adapting Aesop, *Cupid and Death* does imply overt political reference – as

B. A. Harris points out, the moral given to the tale by Ogilby specifically condemns Machiavels.[32]

In *Cupid and Death,* love (the ultimately mysterious binding power between prince and people so familiar from Stuart masques) forsakes courts. Some political connotations may reside in the fact that Death is an aristocrat and Despair would appear to be a wealthy commoner. The arrival of these two figures at an inn precipitates much alarm on the part of the Host and the Chamberlain. Later the Chamberlain exchanges their weapons during the night, and the plot revolves around this accidental exchange. It rebounds on the prankster when he is working as a travelling showman, leading his apes around a fair, and he is hit by an arrow which seems to belong to Death. As the result of the wound he is smitten by a ridiculous passion for his apes. When these are taken from him by a satyr he is desperate: 'What will become of me now? oh my Apes! / The darlings of my heart are ravish'd from me' (p. 395, lines 483–5). The chaos is eventually repaired by Mercury, who banishes Cupid from the courts of princes.

However, the significance of the performance of Shirley's masque in 1653 consists in its context as much as in the fable of the banishment of love from courts. As an entertainment staged under the Commonwealth, it is a vital part of the story of Civil War productions because his case suggests a continuing network of connections amongst the court (for whom Shirley worked during the 1630s) and the Commonwealth government circles. For instance, it was also in 1653 that the practice of the Inner Temple appointing a Master of the Revels was revived. And Whitelocke continued to enjoy masques, as he recorded during his embassy to Sweden. He records that women were used as actors – 'the men acting the men's parts and the women the women's' – and notes approvingly that the masque was intended 'to show the vanity and folly of all professions and worldly things; lively represented by the exact properties and mute actions, gentiely without the least offense or scandall'.[33] Whitelocke's love of theatre was tempered by the smallest gesture at reformation.

These three entertainments, one courtly, one anti-courtly and one performed at that paradoxical thing, a republican court, provide evidence of the complexity of the relationship between

Puritanism and theatre. Whitelocke's positions on drama and the existence of *The Cruell Warre* endorse David Norbrook's suggestion that although the argument for polarisation in the earlier Stuart period must break down, 'there were nevertheless tensions between courtly and religious allegiances'.[34] *The Triumph of Peace* sought to dissipate such tensions, and we note the centrality of the later disaffected Whitelocke in the court's arrangements. The failure of Caroline court culture to resolve social problems is made explicit in *The Cruell Warre*. Nevertheless, court entertainment resurfaced in the republican 'court' which seems to have used *Cupid and Death* as an attempt at national self-presentation, this time of the English republic to a foreign power.

Shirley's two masques are very different productions within the genre, reflecting the differing exigencies of a piece to be performed at a royal 'court' and a drama transferring from a school to a republican 'court'. The signal difference is between the relatively simple, linear, plot of *Cupid and Death* and the semi-ritualistic structure of *The Triumph of Peace* which is encoded for a court audience. The true readers of *The Triumph of Peace* must be those who saw and participated in this celebration of the halcyon court: the people watching the procession were not invited to make a complex reading of the show or to participate in the translation of politics into the resolutionary symbolism of masque.

In *The Cruell Warre* the tensions traceable in The *Triumph of Peace* during the 1630s become the divisions of the 1640s. In a sense, *The Cruell Warre* provides the 'tumultuary' reading of *The Triumph of Peace* that the military may have been present to forestall at the moment of performance. The masque and the parody offer versions of commentary on the possible divisions of society, and the politics of the relationship of the nation to political events. The banishment of love in the later *Cupid and Death* fits the piece aesthetically to performance at a republican court: the banishment of love from the court of princes puts the state on an entirely new footing and suggests the abandonment, forever, of the resolution of struggle between monarch and people through the mystification of state power embodied in love.

OPERA IN THEORY AND PRACTICE IN THE 1650s

If *Cupid and Death* illustrates the effects of changes in political circumstances on a genre inherited from the pre-war court, the introduction of a genre, opera, in the 1650s, shows dramatists making conscious attempts to deal with those circumstances. This in turn is linked to the re-establishment of something like a 'reformed' courtly context under the Protectorate. We are familiar with the moment when Charles II returned, renewing the imagery of kingly triumph – Joseph Beaumont wrote of this new triumph of peace, 'No Acclamations ever thundred from / More earnest Mouths; no Calm of Peace was e're / Welcom'd with such tempestuous Joys.'[35] But if the return of Charles II seemed to be a great turning-point, to contemporaries Oliver Cromwell's becoming Lord Protector had also been a startling change.

In some ways Cromwell's elevation to Lord Protector was a greater return to old ways of single rulers than even the return of Charles, though in other ways his status remained anomalous and undecipherable. Cromwell was neither a Venetian doge nor a king, and the symbolism of his government was ambiguous, resting somewhere between regal and republican rule. Although Cromwell refused the crown he adopted the trappings of royalty from the seal (1655), to the orb and sceptre (after the *Humble Petition and Advice*, 1657), and the running of an austere court.[36]

Poets as different as Edmund Waller and Andrew Marvell found it possible to celebrate the Protector as a single ruler if not quite a king.[37] Edmund Waller's *Panegyrick to My Lord Protector* (1655) conceptualises Cromwell's Protectorate as a restoration: 'Your drooping Country torn with Civill Hate, / Restored by you, is made a glorious State'; and he goes on to detail England's defence and trade by sea, picking up the naval and mercantile rhetoric of the Protectorate.[38] In the panegyric Waller reiterates the singleness of Cromwell after the republican government:

> When Fate, or Error had our Age mis-led,
> And o're these Nations such Confusion spread,
> The onely cure which could from Heav'n come down,
> Was so much Power and Clemency in one.
>   One, whose Extraction from an ancient line,
> Gives hope again that well-born Men may shine [39]

Although he has to relinquish the hinted rhyming of 'down' with 'crown', Waller's reiteration of 'one' endows Cromwell with quasi-monarchical singleness at the same time as he reinforces Cromwell's connection to the interests of an 'ancient line'. Warren Chernaik sees this poem as encouraging other royalists to engage with the Protectorate, and Waller justifies his own rhetorical engagement with the protector by Cromwell's greatness: 'Illustrious acts high Raptures do infuse, / And every Conqueror creates a muse.'[40] Certainly it sees Cromwell as he might hope to be seen, ruling 'with a strong, and yet a gentle hand'.[41] Waller chose to regard Cromwell as a glorious return to normality and quasi-monarchical culture, and indeed a London culture emerged which gradually mixed supporters of change and royalists. However, Cromwell also brought a drive to social reform – the theatres remained closed – and it is within this reforming context that the debate about opera began to form itself.

Opera arrived in England attended by contradictory explanations. Davenant had already planned to begin staging opera in 1639, but had been unable to do so; this postponement meant that opera was introduced at a vital moment in English cultural politics, the early 1650s. In discussing the merits of opera writers took two courses: they either associated it with the absent Stuart kings, or proposed it as a potentially reformed entertainment for the protector's capital. Characteristically, Richard Flecknoe did both. Opera (and courtly entertainment generally) was caught between the Stuart past and the present. But, as a new genre in England in the 1650s, opera had the potential to answer the moral slurs against pre-war theatre and become the new-minted and morally 'reformed' theatre of the 1650s. In this undertaking aesthetic and moral considerations were bound to political issues. The question, 'What is a commonwealth?' brought on its heels the question 'What is a morally beneficial drama?'

Continuities can be established between pre-war court entertainments and the operas of the 1650s, including resemblances between the masque and early English opera. Writers and other personnel involved in court entertainment before the war were amongst the practitioners of opera and entertainments after it – such as Shirley and Davenant. However, despite such echoes, ideological and contextual differences from pre-war drama are apparent in the theorisation of opera. In the simple gesture of calling a play an opera and structuring it as a series of entries, dramatists can be seen as attempting to redefine the nature of the work (as Jonson did with the publication of his *Works*, 1616, even though other 'works' had been published), and attempting to alter the assumptions of all those who might encounter it – audience and censor alike.

Although theorising about opera included ideas for performance, much Protectorate opera was not performed. The story of opera in the 1650s begins with James Howell's royalist translation of *The Nuptialls of Peleus and Thetis*, performed in Paris in 1654. Howell was the king's historiographer. His translation was followed by Richard Flecknoe's publication of *Ariadne Deserted by Theseus and Found and Courted by Bacchus* (1654), Flecknoe's play *Love's Dominion* and a further attempt at opera, *The Marriage of Oceanus and Brittania*, 'an Allegoricall Fiction' (1659). How did Howell come to translate an opera from the French? Claudio Monteverdi's first opera, *Orfeo*, had been performed at the Mantuan carnival season in 1607 and since then opera had been travelling from Italy to other parts of Europe.[42] In 1645, as England was locked in Civil War, Paris saw its first opera, *La Finta Pazza*, which Sacrati had written for the opening of the fourth opera-house in Venice.[43] Cavalli's *L'Egisto* arrived in Paris in February 1646, and in March 1647 Rossi's *Orfeo* was performed in Paris and an *abrégé* of the text was published.[44] It was the first opera designed specifically for production in Paris.[45] Although English people travelling in Italy had certainly seen opera, this fuller adoption of the form in Paris is important for English theatre, particularly because of the presence there of Henrietta Maria.[46] The rage for opera spread across Europe. In 1650 the first opera was performed at Brussels, in celebration of the wedding of Philip IV and repeated – in 1655 – for the benefit of the masque-loving ex-queen of Sweden, Christina, at whose court the theatre-going Bulstrode Whitelocke had been ambassador.[47]

Eugene Haun has argued that this European fashion had created a demand for opera in England, and that this generated the reprinting of several more or less musical works in the early 1650s.[48] His argument is difficult to support without evidence of performance. However, printed plays seem to have passed freely from printer to reader, even though they might have implications for the political debates of the period, whether from their medium, their message or the known beliefs of their author. Published opera went without comment, as with Howell's translation of Caprioli's *Le Nozze di Peleo e di Thetis* using the titles of 'ball' and 'masque'.

The opera celebrated the dispelling of disorder from France by the monarch, and is a celebration of the restoration of the king's

peace.[49] As such it was, even in translation, highly political material
– the translation was dedicated to the wife of the Marquess of
Dorchester, a royalist who had compounded for his lands. Howell
presents it as a new choice piece – he dates it 1 May 1654 and fore-
grounds its fashionable musical variety: 'so full of wit, and variety
of Musicall Airs, with other *Gentillesses*; I deemed it would be a
thing not unworthy of your Ladyships private entertainment'
(A1v). The short introduction ends on a note familiar from the
climax and conclusion of English court masques, the banishment
of Discord: 'Discord also would faine have been there, but that she
was ashamed to appeare upon the theatre, having been chased out
of *France*, and it had been to no purpose for her to disturb so joyfull
a meeting' (p. 1). The familiarity of the theme is counterbalanced
by the fact that the scene is not in the place assigned to it in the
English masque, particularly that of the later Caroline period
where Discord is often banished by the progress and process of the
masque's narrative.

Any masque-like movement from danger towards reconciliation
is pre-empted in *The Nuptialls of Peleus and Thetis* because the
ball/masque itself is constituted as a celebration. And so, because
of Howell's translation, opera came to England as the record of a
celebratory performance which eschewed even more completely
than the masque the dramatisation of conflict within the royal
state. The first speech, by Apollo (played by the king of France),
situates the coming dramatic action as taking place after a violent
but successfully resolved state crisis in a way which for an English
audience (particularly a royalist one) would dramatise the difference between England and France; it notes that 'glory' is prefer-
able to 'sport' against the background of civil conflict:

> That fierce destructive *Python* I did quell
> That ugly horrid *Serpent* hatch'd in Hell,
> Rebellion, which had poyson'd farre and nere
> Faire France I chac'd from off this Hemisphere.   (p. 1)

The early banishment of Discord means that in a more complete
way than *The Triumph of Peace* this masque is wholly celebratory.
And the sense of the piece being occasioned by political crisis
and its resolution is emphasised by the appearance of royal
actors. This underlines the feature (familiar to audiences of the

English masque) of there being some relationship between the actual, real-life performers and the dramatisation. After Apollo the muses speak, and Erato, played by Henrietta Maria's daughter, also known as Minette, tells of the ills suffered by princes – with clear reference to the princess's actual circumstances. It is easy to imagine the reaction of Cromwell's agent Thurloe, or other spies, if similar sentiments were to be delivered on an English stage:

> My stemm is more then of a mortall race;
> For to *great* Henrie's *grandchild* all give place:
>   My innocent and young aspect,
>   Inspires both pitty and respect;
>   And he who loudly would complain
>   Of *Princes* falls and *Peoples* raign,
>   Of angry stars, and destiny,
>   Let him but cast his eyes on me.   (p. 2)

Howell's translation, celebratory in tone and structure, underlined links between royalty, courts and opera. The emphasis on such connections is an indication of the place of opera in English debates over politics and aesthetics. The opera Howell translated was situated firmly in the tradition of courtly entertainment, and the fact that it had featured the English queen's daughter only serves to make very obvious the connection between this masque (or ball or opera) and court entertainments. Importantly, such words spoken by the ex-queen's daughter might have been enough to establish the character of opera at the French court for the English government. Indeed, in terms of the politics of translation, we do know that the theatrical happenings of the French court were monitored in England. For instance, the performance of *A King and no King* (with all that the title implies about both Cromwell and the exiled Stuart) including Henrietta Maria in 1654 drew comment among the English as well as the French, and the entertainments at Oxford during the 1640s had been reported in the press.[50]

What this example makes clear about the arrival of opera in England is that in the 1650s opera, as a genre, changes its meaning according to the political position in which it is implicated.[51] What Pêcheaux calls the 'ideological formations' in which the particular text is involved repeatedly refocus the politics of the genre.[52]

Thus, although Howell's translation evidently draws on the association between the court and the operatic genre, but opera was also justified from other ideological perspectives.

Howell's opera was associated with the Stuart court in France in a way that no opera produced in England was, but Richard Flecknoe (credited by historians of music with having written the first opera in English) also situates his first operatic piece in a royalist tradition. *Ariadne Deserted by Theseus and Found and Courted by Bacchus* (1654) – 'A Dramatick Piece Apted for Recitative Musick' – used a mixture of choral parts and arias. *Ariadne* was never performed and in comparison to Davenant's performed opera it is quite a slight piece.[53] But unlike Howell's work, with its wholesale importation of court values, *Ariadne* is self-conscious about its status as opera. Flecknoe describes taking a tour in Italy to escape the wars, and here he found opera 'exceedingly in vogue, and far advanced towards its perfection . . . I mean Recitative Musick, being a compound of Musick and Poetry together'.[54] Flecknoe saw the potential of such entertainment in both technical and ideological terms. He also provided a a polemical introduction in which he situated the genre explicitly in a courtly and historical context, as well as explaining its technical aspects. In the 'Preface declaring the excellency of recitative music', we encounter the association between royal entertainment and opera. Flecknoe takes the Italian tradition, projects it back into a royal, English or perhaps British context; and goes on to argue for the natural association between opera and royalty:

Tis many years since I proposed unto a Soveraign Prince the congruity, that as their Persons so their Musick should be elevated above the Vulgar; and made not only to delight the ear, but also their understandings; not patcht up with Songs of different subjects, but all of one piece, with design and plot, accommodated to their several dispositions, and ocasions (A3r–v)

Dryden was later to use a similar argument about the reflexive relation between the virtues of monarchs and the use of heroic verse drama to both describe and teach kingly deeds.[55] Flecknoe's polemic suggests, in its analysis of the politics of the hierarchical arrangement of dramatic genres, the questions faced by any dramatist seeking to perform opera in Commonwealth or Protectorate England. Flecknoe links opera to kings: 'Tis many years since I proposed unto a Soveraign Prince'. There is the suggestion that opera, being appropriately elevated and well-designed entertainment, is suitable for kings to listen to. There is perhaps also a suggestion of a hierarchy of understanding which is analogous to the notion of a hierarchy of sight-lines in the court performances, in which the king sat at the centre, unifying the whole spectacle in his own person because only from his, perspective could the scene be seen to be 'all of one piece'.[56] This keen sense of a socially significant hierarchy of genres and topics is reinforced by the verse of William Cavendish, Duke of Newcastle, which Flecknoe used to preface his *Relation of Ten Years Travels*, saying, 'Caesars should be thy Theme, on them to write . . .'[57] But Flecknoe's loyalist assertions are troubled by the oppositional status of monarchist discourse in the 1650s. What he says about the operatic genre is spoken not from a position of powerful centrality, but from the margins; his text addresses the relationship between opera and monarchy in a state where there is no monarch and in which many public spectacles are not tolerated. There is also a suggestion that opera is to be perceived in relation to other genres which are less fit to be performed before a governor and, by implication, not therefore fit to constitute or carry the meanings of that monarchical structure which (Flecknoe suggests) ought to be in power. In actually addressing the question of the suitability of genres to different ideologies and governments the passage suggests that it has been written from a position of displacement: it asserts opera as an adjunct of the rights of dethroned royalty. Flecknoe emphasises the monarchist structure of opera when he notes that it is not anarchically (and in the 'vulgar' or common fashion) 'patcht up with songs of different subjects'. In opera, he implies, not every subject is equally to the fore. Instead, there is proper hierarchy: low scenes and issues are subdued under the main theme as a country under a king or as the 'body' of the state under the king as 'head'. He offers a perception of opera as unitary, organic, 'all of one piece', like the organic metaphor of government and the parts as 'accommodated unto their several dispositions and ocasions'.

This passage delivers a commentary on the relationship between types of government and art, particularly that between the 'best' dramatic genres and the 'best' sorts of government. Opera is a return (for Flecknoe) to what is oldest and best: he goes on to seek to establish opera as intrinsically part of a classical-cum-ancient British tradition, and by association, monarchy: 'Nay, not only almost all the *Erudition* of those Times, but even the *Religion* too was delivered in *Musick*, witness the *Canticles* of *Moses*, the *Psalms* of *David*, the *Hymnes* of *Orpheus*, and finally the *Druads* songs, and the *Ballads* of the *British Bards*, &c.' (A4v). Musical performances are here given biblical, classical and druidic antecedents. Flecknoe suggests that the ancients 'told' important things using music and that the British priestly poets, the druids, continued the tradition. He explains:

Which Ballads (such was the Barbarism of insuing times) was in a manner the sole relict of this divine Science, untill *Claudio Montanendo* [sic] (in our Fathers days) principally, revived it, shall I say? or renewed it again by his admirable skill (like another *Prometheus*) conjoyning in one body again the scattered limbs of *Orpheus* (*Musick* and *Poetry*) (A4v–A5r)

In his rather desperate attempt to give opera a history as a British form Flecknoe is claiming that the British had been the custodians of the ancient traditions in which poetry and music were linked in performance. He presents himself as giving back to Britain her own invention, reinvented by the Italians.

The classical topic (Ariadne) suggests both the Italian influence and court entertainment, and the title *Ariadne* echoes one of Monteverdi's operas, *Arianna*, which was first performed in Mantua in 1608, but was revived in Venice in 1639.[58] Echoes are suggested by the fact that Monteverdi's opera was particularly famous for Ariadne's lament and Flecknoe's begins with one:

> ARIADNE: Ay me! and is he gon!
> And I left here alone!
> Ah *Theseus* stay -
> But see how he sails away   (p. 1)

This is followed by detailed directions, typical of Flecknoe's attention to the exact arrangements for staging his unperformed endeavours, but also indicating clearly that the piece was designed as opera: 'Here lively, and sprightly Musick is heard off, by degrees approaching the Place, and at last the Bacchanti, or fore-runners of *Bacchus* appear' (p. 7).

In *Love's Dominion* (1654) Flecknoe takes up a very different position on the politics of performance. Flecknoe's Protectorate play was dedicated to Cromwell's daughter Elizabeth Claypole, and might therefore be expected to address the questions of performance in the new state. Predictably, it ignores the links between monarchy and opera that the preface to Ariadne is so keen to establish, and concentrates instead on the possibility of performance. As Flecknoe wrote to Elizabeth Claypole:

never a more Innocenter thing appeared in court . . . For the rest, I dare not interest you in its more publique Representation, not knowing how the palat of the time may relish such Things yet, which, till it was disgusted with them, was formerly numbered among its chiefest Dainties.[59]

As we have seen, Flecknoe looked outside England for models of theatre functioning in what he perceived as a proper relation to society. In the light of this and his travels it seems likely that Flecknoe was aware of the debate taking place on the French theatre (sparked off by Corneille's *Cid*) and that he found some of the arguments about morality and the stage that were being put forward in France at least potentially applicable to the condition of the English stage. The French debate embraced the question of the moral implications and influence of theatrical representation.[60] Flecknoe writes in defence of the theatre in his introduction:

An academy of the choicest language, a Map of the best Manners and finally a mirror representing the actions of men (and therefore by a better title than that of *Plays*, called *Actions* by some, and Operas, or works, by others). (A4r)

This new stage that he envisages is, then, to be designed on the model of European drama. The purpose and teaching function of theatre is emphasised. Such new works are beneficial because, he explains, they operate by:

proposing the good for our example and imitation and the bad to deter us from it, and for the avoiding it. I cannot deny but aspersions (these latter times) have been cast upon it by the like of some who have written obscenely and scurrilously, and c. but instead of wiping them off, to break the glass was too rigid and severe. For my part I have endeavoured here the cleaning of it and the restoring of it to its former splendour. (A4r–v)

Flecknoe's metaphor of the mirror indicates the increasingly complex circumstances in which writers produced drama and opera during the 1640s and 1650s. However, the complexity lies in the positions which the argument had to negotiate (the fraught relationships between 'good' and 'bad' theatre, moral representation and the suppression of the stage) rather than in the theory he deployed in answer to them.

In order to produce an argument for reformed drama Flecknoe uses a crude model of drama as didactic, teaching the audience by showing noble actions. In contrast to Elizabethan attacks on the stage it ignores the possibility that the audience might through empathy come to favour villains; Flecknoe bypasses the more difficult aspects of the connection between audience and performance. The new plays, Flecknoe implies, are moral in a representational sense because they present (or re-enact) the 'best Manners' and (therefore) they move the audience to a better way of life. Producers of 'unreformed' drama are described by Flecknoe as having written on the mirror, overlaying its original fidelity to 'good' manners with 'scurrilous' writing. The suppression of the theatres has broken a 'mirror' which had been, potentially at least, morally and socially beneficial: for Flecknoe, here, the theatre reflects that part of society which is presented in it. If 'good' things are represented it becomes a tool with great potential for moral and social reform and can give an audience examples and instruction.

Flecknoe is arguing for the restoration of the stage in a morally reformed condition (something very close to what Davenant presented himself as doing in initiating opera). Of course, the government was not interested simply in the content of plays, but also in the kind of gathering a play might produce: a performance of drama might incite riot. Unlike Flecknoe, they seem to have grasped that however proper the political content of a play an actual production might turn that content on its head, and this as well as their fear of gatherings is suggested in their raids on illegal performances in the period leading up to the execution of the king.

Thus, Flecknoe both asserted the royal origin of opera as a genre in his preface to *Ariadne,* and addressed the question of what a moral representation might be under the Protectorate. What can these texts by Howell and Flecknoe tell us about the political and theatrical position of opera? It seems that *The Nuptials of Peleus and Thetis* and *Ariadne* can be seen as providing opera with its initial political and theatrical position in England under the Protectorate. Both plays have monarchical associations which are either evident within the text, in the case of Howell, or made explicit in the introduction, in the case of Flecknoe. Both are related to models from Europe: in Flecknoe's case this association would appear to be theoretical in part, and in the introduction to *Love's Dominion* he pursues the enquiry into what reformed drama might be. Howell supplies no polemic, but the association with courts and royalty is explicit in *Peleus and Thetis* as a translation of a masque performed at the French court. *Peleus and Thetis* and *Ariadne* provide positions for printed opera and entertainments which associate them with courts. The play, *Love's Dominion*, on the other hand, offers a polemic for a moral and improved stage. The crucial move from the first position to the second is found in the question of reformed drama as discussed in Flecknoe's dedication of *Love's Dominion*, proving that this could be adapted to the circumstances of the 1650s, as it was to be by Davenant.

Flecknoe's developing sympathies with the Protectorate, and his emerging sense of the potential of opera as reformed (rather than specifically royal) drama, can be traced in other dramatic and non-dramatic writings from the later 1650s. In 1659 Flecknoe published two further pieces, *The Idea of His Highness Oliver Late Protector and c* and another operatic piece, *The Marriage of Oceanus and Brittania* – 'an Allegorical Fiction really declaring Englands Riches, Glory and Puissance by Sea: To be Represented in Musick, Dances and Proper Scenes, All Invented, Written and Composed by Richard Flecknoe Esq.'. The prose memorial of Cromwell demonstrates the extent of Flecknoe's engagement with the new regime, and his comment that Cromwell is worthy of biography even though this is 'displeasing and ungrateful to the multitude', is illuminating.[61] So it is not surprising to find that in *The Marriage of Oceanus and Brittania* Flecknoe brought together his understanding of opera as a genre with a sense of the appropriate topics for a reformed drama. Flecknoe's insistence on the title-page that it was all – music, words, scenes – his own vision, suggests his sense of himself as creating new theatrical art from the old ways. The topic chosen echoes those of City entertainments and lord mayors' shows of the 1650s which Flecknoe may have seen. It fuses military themes with a celebration of England's wealth by trade and mobilises history to reinforce Cromwell's foreign policy by recalling the defeat of the Armada. The entries demonstrate the drunkenness of the Dutch and the defeat of the Spanish and French in sea

battles, with the patriotic naval scenes and colonial encounters
('Here the four parts of the World enter') punctuated by 'Castor
and Pollux in Grecian military habits' dancing on the ropes.[62] This
brings together the policies of the Protectorate with an opera
recast to become a relatively (though by no means wholly) popular
spectacle including rope-dancing and patriotic songs, 'inviting the
British Marriners and Souldiers to brave action by Sea'. One scene
includes the reception of news by a large crowd, and the general
public is shown rejoicing at a naval victory: it seems that the envisaged audience was not the wholly elite audience of the court
masque, and this is suggested by the ending which offers representatives of 'Nobility and Gentry', dancing with a 'Burgesse and
Citizen'. The entertainment culminates with the marriage in a
scene both reminiscent of the masque and indicative of the reformulated symbolics of the country in terms of trade (see also
chapter 7). Oceanus demonstrates the power of the marriage
when he invites 'swarthy Affrica, / Rich Asia and America' to pay
tribute at Brittania's wedding, dramatising the power of the
Protectorate in trade and war (p. 32). Flecknoe finally brought
together reformed drama and opera – just as the Protectorate
crumbled.

In the following chapter I look more closely at the purposes served
by such colonial fantasies in Protectorate theatre. At this point I
want to note the way in which by the end of the 1650s (sadly, but
characteristically, at the wrong moment for his own career)
Flecknoe had written and printed a piece which, while it treated
opera as a genre, also used it to fuse moral and political representation in nationalist spectacle. He had, in theory, arranged
opera in relation to contemporary national and aesthetic politics
to create a 'reformed' drama. Howell's translation, followed by
Flecknoe's shifting use of the idea of reformed theatre and opera,
make it clear that courtly entertainment in general and opera in
particular were implicated in political debates about aesthetics
and morality in the new nation.

CHAPTER 6

National identity, topic and genre in Davenant's Protectorate opera

Why, truly, your great enemy is the Spaniard. He is. He is a natural enemy, he is naturally so. He is naturally so, throughout, as I said before . . . And truly when I say that he is naturally throughout an enemy, an enmity is put into him by God.

Oliver Cromwell, Speech at the opening
of parliament, 17 September 1656[1]

Sir William Davenant was the only professional dramatist permitted to stage plays commercially and publicly in the entire period 1642–60. His Protectorate plays and operas came into existence at the border between government policy and commercial success (which was dependent upon the audience's pleasure). Therefore this chapter, in examining the circumstances of these performed plays, is a study in contradictions. It continues the work of chapter 5 in analysing the politics of opera as a genre, but extends its focus to discuss the politics of the kind of narrative which Davenant was staging, and to provide cultural and political contexts for his plays.

Prevailing critical assumptions about Davenant's theatre staged between 1656 and 1659 are based on the work of Harbage, and Nethercot's characterisation of Davenant's Protectorate drama as participating fairly completely in a 'royalist' ideology.[2] Even his most recent biographer, Mary Edmond, seems to see Davenant as a kind of royalist undercover agent attempting to restore the theatre.[3] Music historians, too, tend to see Davenant's opera solely in terms of the arrival of opera in England as an event in dramatic and musical history determined only by the ban on theatre, rather than as participating in more complex aesthetic and political issues of staging and performance.[4] However, Christopher Hill has opposed this view of Davenant as royalist drama in a partly accurate characterisation of the plays as 'propaganda'.[5]

2 *The Tears of the Indians*, by Bartolomé de las Casas translated by John Phillips,
frontispiece.

Davenant's musical entertainments performed at Rutland House and at the Cockpit between 1656 and 1659 mobilise old enemies – the Turks, the Spanish – as Islamic or European 'others', initially used to define contemporary 'Englishness'. It is therefore possible to trace changes in the way these operas attempt to legitimate the international ambitions of the English by presenting the audience with quasi-nationalist oppositions and juxtapositions – Englishness against otherness, Christian against pagan, Protestant against Catholic, European against non-European, English against Spanish.

In dramatising geographically distant though pertinent issues, Davenant does appear to avoid all obviously problematic political ground, including dangerous genres (such as tragedy) and domestic topics. Nevertheless, despite attempts to keep away from contentious issues and genres, his plays' involvement in political issues is inaugurated by their very attempt to avoid controversy. This aspect of the plays is particularly to the fore in those which dramatise English colonialist ambitions, *The Cruelty of the Spaniards in Peru* (proposed in 1655 but not performed until 1658) and *Sir Francis Drake*; but all the plays are important for the way they register a set of interwoven social affinities and cultural assumptions with the exigencies of Protectorate theatre and politics.

Two aspects of these operas in relation to the political and social transformations of the 1650s are especially significant.[6] First, the use of cultural difference as a field for analysing political power and, second, the politics of generic status in the presentation of 'operas' in the 1650s.

DAVENANT AND THE POLITICS OF PERFORMED OPERA

Davenant was on his way to Virginia in late spring 1650 when he was captured by the English in the Channel and imprisoned, for a time under threat of death. It seems that he struck a bargain with his imprisoners to produce theatre. That such an agreement was made is suggested also by the circumstances surrounding the production of the operas which followed his release; they were, increasingly, public theatre. Davenant was almost certainly aware of the published texts of Howell and Flecknoe, especially as he had first tried to stage opera in England as early as 1639.[7] It seems very likely that he took account of the reception which greeted opera

in Paris, but it is certain that he, like the other writers and trans-
lators of opera in the 1650s, used opera to affiliate his plays to the
Protectorate ethos of dramatic 'reformation'. Davenant's operas
were staged by a private individual but with government approval.

The texts were vetted by Thurloe, and Bulstrode Whitelocke
(who helped to organise *The Triumph of Peace*) also had some
involvement.[8] But despite government sponsorship, Davenant
operated in a legal and a discursive context determined by the
moves against the theatre in 1642 and subsequently. The fact that
the rhetoric of these strictures was partly moral, combined with
Cromwell's status as a moral and social reformer, provided the surviving and new dramatists with their cue to reply with offers of a
'reformed' stage.[9]

Davenant, like Shirley, had been a court dramatist and desig-
nated 'her Majesties servant' by Henrietta Maria. Indeed, the
female figures in his plays – such as Ianthe – may perhaps bear
traces of his admiration for her. In her service Davenant had been
noted as a writer of masques, including *Salmacida Spolia*, the last
Stuart masque.[10] To an extent this earlier career gave him the
visual and staging vocabulary that he used in Protectorate opera.
The spectacular scenery of court productions was part of
Davenant's understanding of the theatre from the start, and his
connection with Inigo Jones was followed by an association with
Jones's pupil John Webb, who designed the perspective scenery for
The Siege of Rhodes – an important link between the court masque
and the opera of the Protectorate.

Davenant's opera effected a transfer of techniques from court to
public stage, but ideologically the differences between masque
and opera were large. Although the masque might mediate
between king and people, it was tied to parameters of courtship
and produced by the need to mediate courtly relations. The
apology for the absence of court masques preceding *Britannia
Triumphans* (which took as part of its brief the justification of ship-
money) emphasises the 'natural' link between the masque and the
court: 'Princes of sweet and humane Natures have ever both
amongst the Ancients and Modernes in the best times, presented
spectacles, and personall representations, to recreate their Spirits
wasted in grave affairs of State, and for the entertainment of their
Nobilitie, Ladies and Courts.'[11] This elitist rhetoric is echoed in
Flecknoe's early disquisition on the 'naturally' monarchic proper-

ties of opera. But Davenant's Protectorate operas move from courtly conventions into a public and commercial context, and although Davenant's Protectorate dramas take several aspects from the masque – in terms of scenery, music, dance, singing (choric and aria), proscenium arches and women singing – they do not take over those things which specifically linked it with the Stuart court, such as the masque–antimasque structure which relied on a contrast between courtly participants and professional actors. Moreover, the operas of the 1650s also draw on the public acting traditions – using jugglers and varying kinds of entertainment. The discontinuities between the theatrical practices of masques and Davenant's Protectorate public theatre imply the differences between court entertainment performed in the presence of a monarch, and public entertainment sanctioned and even perhaps supported by a government which was, if not a republic, not a monarchy either. Form and structure in the operas was linked to story and available resources but it was also part of the way opera presented itself as 'reformed'.

Certainly the discontinuities were noted by contemporaries, as is indicated by Dryden's interpretation of reformed Protectorate representations:

It being forbidden in the Rebellious times to act Tragedies and Comedies, because they contained some matter of Scandal to those good people who could more easily dispossess their lawful Sovereign than endure a wanton jeast; and he was forc'd to turn his thoughts another way: and to introduce the examples of moral virtue writ in verse, and performed in Recitative Musique.[12]

Dryden's *post hoc* explanation of the novelty of Davenant's Protectorate theatre emphasises the ban on drama and presents Davenant's new 'operatic' practices as caused by political strictures. The changes in the plays were, as Dryden indicates, in both *what* was dramatised (the choice of a story), and *how* that dramatisation took place. The Protectorate audience itself existed in new circumstances which necessitated a radical break with the pre-war drama, especially the ideologies of courtly performances.

At the time, though, Davenant produced a theoretical and political defence which focussed on the government's ability to pacify the people, arguing that the people 'require continuall divertisements being otherwise naturally inclin'd to that Melancholy that breeds Sedition'. Davenant defended drama to Thurloe as divert-

ing the propensity of the populace to rebel and as able to educate
the people into supporting the interests of the state:

> If morall representations may be allow'd (being without obscenenesse,
> profaneness, and scandall) the first argument may consist of the
> Spaniards barbarous Conquests in the West Indes and of their several cru-
> elties there exercis'd upon the subjects of this Nation: of which some use
> may be made. And offers of this kind may evade that imputation of levity,
> since the People were in this way guided to assist their own interests by
> the Athenians and Romans.

The dramatist is replying to the ordinances against theatres
(such as that of 1648) on the ground available – that of the relationship between theatre and public morality – and it makes
explicit the close relationship between Davenant's theatre and the
government (in the shape of Thurloe and his agents). Indeed,
Davenant's analysis coincides with various arguments for reformed
theatre in the 1650s, by figures as diverse as Harrington, Jordan,
Flecknoe and the exiled Cavendishes, both William and Margaret
– and to an extent Milton in the 1640s.[13]

In organising the re-emergence of public drama, Davenant had
contact with Thurloe and with Bulstrode Whitelocke. Whitelocke
helped him in 1651, and after he was Protectorate ambassador to
Sweden. He seems to have acted as an informal protector for the
new opera. In 1652 Whitelocke inserted a full-length letter from
Davenant into his journal in the midst of pressing business; he did
so once more in September 1656, when Davenant was engaged in
the theatrical venture. Davenant appears to have cleared the forthcoming production with Whitelocke, writing:

> When I consider the nicety of the Times, I fear it may draw a curtain
> between your Lordship and our Opera; therefore I have presumed to
> send your Lordship, hot from the Press, what we mean to represent;
> making your Lordship my Supreme Judge, though I despair to have the
> Honour of inviting you to be a spectator.[14]

His bid for approval ends by invoking Whitelocke's 'antient relation to the Muses'.

Following these preparations, Davenant's first theatrical intervention in the debate about the reformed stage was performed.
The First Days Entertainment at Rutland House (staged on 23 May
1656) seems to have been the first piece of public theatre sanctioned by the Protectorate government, and as contemporary evidence suggests, it may have been in part an advertisement for what

was to follow.[15] It was not on the topic of the West Indies (probably because the expedition to Hispaniola in early 1655 had been a disaster) but instead addressed the question of performance. The formal aspects of the play, using songs, instrumental music and declamations, demonstrate the oblique generic relationship between these plays and pre-war genres, probably produced by the perceived crisis in that which it is permissible to articulate. Like a masque, the piece was called after the occasion of its production, but unlike a masque it was called after that only; the title tells us nothing about what is actually to be performed, only that it is to be '*by Declamations and Musick After the manner of the Ancients*' and the prologue describes it as 'Opera'.[16]

The drama itself continues the privileging of occasion over narrative found in the title, emphasising the morally beneficial effects of the stage upon spectators. It is careful to say nothing to offend the government, and because it consists in part of a debate between Aristophanes and Diogenes, on the topic of 'Publique Entertainments by Morall Representations', the play becomes very literally meta-theatrical – drama about the possibility of staging drama – in its attempt to answer allegations against the theatre on the moral ground set out for example in the 1642 and 1647 governmental attacks on plays. Part of the presentation as 'reformed' theatre involves claiming links between modern and classical drama. In the first part of the piece Aristophanes speaks in favour of public meetings for the making and appreciation of speeches (which sound very similar to *The First Days Entertainment* itself). There is also a defence of the 'Victor' – the protector – which caused Davenant some trouble after the Restoration. The second half consists of a debate between a Londoner and a Parisian on the relative merits of their cities and theatres. In some ways, particularly in terms of its strange form and consistently meta-dramatic quality, this piece is a more radical and innovative theatrical departure than the narrative pieces which were to follow it. It is structured as a debate which is also (in itself) a demonstration or exposition of the fact that reformed drama can exist.

The play represents, then, both theatrical revival and a visibly radical break with many pre-war conditions of the commercial theatre. Simultaneously, it shifts the modes of representation employed by public theatre perceptibly towards the kind found in the 'entries' of entertainments at the court of Charles I. This is evident in the way the title and its construction present it as an occasional piece, as well as in the lack of emphasis on narrative. That theatrical conditions changed during the 1640s and 1650s is indicated by the fact that Henrietta Maria rarely visited the theatre and Charles I never went, in marked contrast to the Restoration custom. Arguably, in this piece we see the change between the pre-war and Restoration stages in process. It could be said that *The First Days Entertainment* was the occasion of the theatrical conventions which, before the war, had been primarily associated with the court moving on to a stage that was 'public', in the sense that it was open to all.

This drama's staging innovations explicitly intervene in political and moral debates around theatre: *The First Days Entertainment* both exemplified and thematised the question of what a 'moral representation' might be. Davenant's pre-production discussions with Thurloe and Whitelocke indicate that the state had a close interest at least in the ideological, possibly theatrical, nature of the plays. Thus, Davenant's mid-century productions were from their inception associated with the movement for a morally reformed theatre, producing theatrical innovation in a context of close communication – even collaboration – with the government.

Moreover, the play's idea of a moral representation and the comparison of Paris and London demonstrate that the new theatre also saw itself in a European framework. While the arguments in *The First Days Entertainment* do not contain the elaborate analyses of the nature of theatrical representation contained in French texts like d'Aubignac's *Pratique du Théâtre*, those debates are likely to have influenced a dramatist present at Henrietta Maria's French court during the 1640s.[17]

The First Days Entertainment's emphasis on the potential orderliness of public entertainment in its shape and content strikes similar notes to the introductions of those other revived dramas of the 1650s, the lord mayors' shows. The play calls attention to its continuation of ancient custom in a way that occurs not only in Flecknoe (in the dedication to *Love's Dominion* rather than *Ariadne*) but also in the introduction to Edmund Gayton's contribution to the newly revived lord mayor's show of 1655.[18] Gayton's piece, addressed to the lord mayor, Alderman Dethicke, was produced for the first occasion that such pageants had been staged since the Civil War. Gayton, like Davenant and in the same year as *The First Days Entertainment,* wrote of performances as linking state and people, arguing that a show 'gaines at once Honour to the Magistrate and effects content to the People'.[19] The coincidence of Davenant's dramatic defence of theatre with similar justifications from both City poets and aspirant dramatists, suggests that under the Protectorate there was a tempering of the government's attitude to theatre, even an encouragment of certain kinds of 'reformed' shows.

Davenant's subsequent shows built on these changes in modes of public theatre, as indicated by the next production to be discussed, actually his third theatrical performance from the 1650s. *The Cruelty of the Spaniards in Peru,* first staged at the Cockpit during 1658 and simultaneously printed by Henry Herringman, was performed after *The First Days Entertainment* and the first part of *The Siege of Rhodes.* The play may have been intended for earlier performance but delayed by the Hispaniola expedition only to become viable again after the defeat of the Spanish at Santa Cruz in 1657. It was partly based on events recounted by the history of the Incas by Garcilasco de la Vega, a mestizo, born into the Quechuan language. His *Commentarios Reales* (1609) were translated into French in 1633 and the play derives both the general outline of its story and salient details – such as the civil war between the last two Incas and Inca prophecy of Spanish invaders – from this and mediating sources. De la Vega's anti-Spanish perspective made his text readily adaptable to Davenant's nationalistic polemic, and until the end of the play Davenant's text does echo de la Vega's sympathy for the plight of the historical Incas – broken under the combination of a prophecy foretelling the arrival of the Spanish, guns and forced conversions.[20]

The Cruelty of the Spaniards continues the work of *The First Days Entertainment* in changing theatrical codes, presenting itself as a new kind of drama in its formal aspects. Moreover, it registers contemporary concerns in its construction of Englishness through the representation of the native peoples of Peru and the Spanish. It yields information about the political position of opera in terms of what sort of narratives might be represented and how they might be staged. Clearly connected with Cromwell's ambitions, the first tableau reveals the play's significant absorption in contemporary ambition when 'a Lantchap of the West-*Indies*' is discovered. The 'argument' proceeds to the Spanish conquest of the Incan

Empire, and then 'discovers the cruelty of the Spaniards over the Indians, and over all Christians (excepting those of their own Nation)' and towards the conclusion 'it infers the Voyages of the English thither, and the amity of the Nations towards them' (A2v).

The Cruelty of the Spaniards episodically recounts the story of the arrival of the English in Peru, where they rescue the natives from the evil Spanish in accord with the Incan prophecy, interpreted by the Incas as fulfilled upon the arrival of the Spanish. The play draws on mythologisations of English conquest established around Drake, Raleigh and in the writings critical of Spanish conquest such as those of Bartolomé de las Casas (whose writings were popularised by Samuel Purchas).[21] Yet the resolution of the play takes place in the future, in the form of a fantasy of the reconquest of Spanish colonies by the English. So the play fuses mythologised past (the golden age of Elizabethan conquest) and the future (the age of reconquest in which the Incan prophecy of the arrival of the English will be fulfilled). The present, or moment of production, disappears as Elizabethan politics of nationhood and conquest merge into a fantasised future: the annexation of the euphoric values of Elizabethan Protestant conquest to an imagined future permit displacement of the present.

Like *The First Days Entertainment, The Cruelty of the Spaniards* demonstrates anxiety about its status as drama. Music and song are used as a semi-choric comment on tableaux and mimed actions, and interwoven with the action are a variety of tricks such as tumbling, juggling and acrobatics. The piece does not offer any obvious narrative links between the various 'entries' which are presented as singular, though sequential, episodes. The connotations of each tableau and mime would not be wholly obscure to the audience, but connection between the scenes and narrative does not inhere wholly in the spectacle.

The narrative, and thus much of the ideologically laden significance of the drama, consists not in what actually happened on stage, but in a libretto sold at the door and giving a very detailed description of what is witnessed on stage. The text provided, that is, a 'definitive' interpretation of events on stage (i.e. scenes, songs and acrobatics); it supplies a hermeneutic code, which links the visual and aural codes into a narrative and suggests an interpretation to the audience. The publication of the libretto can also be seen as an attempt to fix the dynamics of actual theatrical production in the single manifestation of the printed, published text which can be presented as standing for the performance. In the central role accorded to the libretto, this drama thus acknowledges the politicised nature of the Protectorate audience: Davenant also sent a copy of it to Bulstrode Whitelocke before the play was produced, seeking approval.

If the libretto was, in part, a signal of the play's good intentions, so was the topic dramatised. The tableaux register the colonial preoccupations of Protectorate foreign policy, reflecting Cromwell's campaign against Spain in presenting the story of the defeat of the Spanish in Peru as achieved by an alliance of the English and the native peoples. The natives of North and South America had been represented in English writing as both vicious and as noble savages.[22] Here they are initially presented as a semi-Edenic culture, into which the poisonous serpent of Spanish power has insinuated itself, a delineation of affairs in Peru which follows Elizabethan colonialist models and in doing so serves contemporary foreign policy.

Fulke Greville (for whom Davenant worked, and whose work is of considerable influence on him) described America in his *Life of Sidney* (published 1652) as the ultimate land of opportunity – for an overwhelmingly Protestant and English way of life:

To Martiall men he [Sidney] opened wide the door of sea and land, for fame and conquest. To the nobly ambitious the far stage of *America* to win honour in. To the Religious divines, besides a new Apostollicall calling of the last of heathen to the Christian faith, a large field of reducing poor Christians, mis-led by the Idolatry of *Rome* to their mother *Primitive* Church. To the ingeniously industrious variety of naturall richesses, for new mysteries, and manufactures to work upon. To the Merchant, with a simple people, a fertile and unexhausted earth. To the fortune-bound, liberty. To the curious, a fruitful womb of innovation. Generally the word gold was an attractive Adamant, to make men venture that which they have, in hope to grow rich by that which they have not.[23]

The New World was, clearly, a fantasy landscape, filled with possibility. As Roland Barthes puts it, the differential between the way of life there and the way of life in Europe was sufficient for the native peoples and their culture to become idealised, as they did for de las Casas on whose narrative and illustrations some parts of the text and visual tableaux of *The Cruelty of the Spaniards* are based.[24] This idealisation can be directly linked to material and national investments. Just as Greville, Davenant's mentor in his youth, associated the Americas with opportunity, wealth and the validation of masculinity, so de las Casas saw it as a paradise, an Eden spoilt by the exploitation of the noble natives. Davenant, like Greville, valorises the English and represents the natives as tractable, but he also produces a scapegoat – the serpent in this Eden is Spanish nationalism, Catholicism and colonial ambition.

The Spanish are represented as truly vile, and engaged in tortures similar to those which the natives themselves are sometimes seen as inflicting on Europeans. Vivid pictures of the cruelty of South Americans to each other are found in places such as *Purchas His Pilgrims*, where the Mexicans are contrasted with the Peruvians, and the Spaniards are the 'civilising' influence:

> they of Peru have surpassed the *Mexicans* in the slaughter and sacrifice of their Children . . . yet they of *Mexico* have exceeded them, yea all the Nations of the World, in the great number of men they have sacrificed and the horrible manner thereof . . . the men they did sacrifice were taken in the warres . . .
>
> . . .
>
> The *Spaniards* that saw these cruell Sacrifices, resolved with all their power to abolish so detestable and cursed butchering of men, and the rather, for that in one night they saw threescore or threescore and ten *Spaniards* sacrificed . . .[25]

Davenant's play replicates these circumstances, except that the torturers are the Spanish and the Peruvians the tortured. Thus Entry v gives us the Spanish as cannibals:

> A Dolefull Pavin is plai'd to prepare the change of the Scene, which represents a dark Prison at great distance; and farther to the view are discern'd Racks, and other Engines of torment, with which the Spaniards are tormenting the Natives and English Marriners, which may be suppos'd to be lately landed there to discover the Coast. Two Spaniards are likewise discover'd, sitting in their cloakes and appearing more solemn in Ruffs, with Rapiers and Daggers by their sides; the one turning a Spit, whilst the other is basting an *Indian* Prince, which is rosted at an artificiall fire. (p.19)

Needless to say, the English triumph sees the Spanish grovelling and the natives dancing in delight. But, equally predictably, once the natives are conquered and the Spanish removed the natives cease to be similar to their virtuous English conquerors, falling more readily into the position of the 'savage'. In this way the play sets up the co-ordinates of a colonial discourse which has three terms: the Christian conquerors, the pagan 'discovered', and the diabolic Spaniards. The status of the fantasised campaign is elevated to that of a crusade not against the Peruvians – whose country is a locus of desire, filled with possibility for the English – but against the Spanish. The colonial ambitions of England are justified in their treatment of the Spaniards and, particularly as the narrative is set in the future, there is no need to address the question of the political nature of the nation that will rule over the Peruvians.

The play's analysis of colonial ambition transforms the positions of the civilised and the barbaric through this addition of the Spaniards as a third term, a third nation. The political and theological status of each nation is not made explicit except in the broadest possible way: Roman Catholic Spaniards are defined against good Protestant English, but no question is raised about whether the good Protestants are monarchical or republican. Moreover, the disappearance of the present into the gap between past and future is one factor which enables the question of national authority to – conspicuously – disappear. It seems likely that such a use of narrative, both as a recapitulation of history and as a fantasy for the future, speaks to Cromwell's concern for colonial conquest in the regions traditionally fought over with Spain, and the dismal failure of the Hispaniola expedition of 1655 – an expedition which the play seems to have been intended to celebrate – accounts for the delay in performance until 1658. But the play entirely suppresses pressing contemporary questions, such as what the new nation might be or mean, under the new Protectoral constitution of 1657.

The context of *The Cruelty of the Spaniards* can be better understood when we realise that one of its two sources was directly supporting Cromwell's plans. In 1656 Milton's relative John Phillips translated Bartolomé de las Casas's earlier account of Spanish cruelty, *The Tears of the Indians*, and dedicated it to Cromwell. The play seems to use this text as well as de la Vega's *Commentaire*, taking from it the scene of the roasting of Indians. Phillips is voluble about the urgent need that the Peruvians have to be protected by the English, writing to Cromwell of 'the cry of Blood ceasing at the noise of Your great transactions, while You arm for their Revenge'.[26] The 'revenge' for which Phillips argues (and which coincides with Cromwell's interests) is acted out in Davenant's narrative of a glorious future crusade in the 'Sixt Song. Pursuing the Argument of that Prophecy, which foretells the subversion of the Spaniards by the English', ending with the 'grand Dance' including English soldiers in the contemporary uniform of the Protectorate. The scene emphasises the military prowess of the Protectorate and reinforces the righteousness of English ambition in general by dramatising contrasting attitudes of English and Spanish to the colonised Indians:

three *Indians* entering first, afterwards to them three *English* Souldiers, distinguisht by their Red-Coats, and to them a S*paniard*, who mingling in the measures with the rest, does in his gestures expresse pride and fullnesse towards the Indians, and payes a lowly homage to the English, who often salute him with their feet, which salutation he returns with a more lowly gravity. (p. 27)

The History of Sir Francis Drake, Davenant's other Protectorate play dramatising a story from an expansionist Elizabethan past, like *The Cruelty of the Spaniards*, uses nationalistic sources in mobilising myths of the past to validate the enterprises of the present. It was probably performed after *The Cruelty of the Spaniards* though the order is reversed in *A Playhouse to be Let* (1663). *The History of Sir Francis Drake* reuses well-known Elizabethan Drake material, revivifying Elizabethan history to reinforce Cromwell's policies. Philip Nichols introduces *Sir Francis Drake Revived* (1626, reprinted in 1652), the text on which Davenant's play is based, as calling upon 'this Dull or Effeminate age, to follow in his Noble Steps for Gold and Silver'.[27] Such a charge was readily redeployed as a way of imaging the republic's relationship to Charles's government, and in the Protectorate Davenant echoes Nichols in his appeal for an active foreign policy. Another piece of Drake material, *The World Encompassed* (1636), offered itself 'especially for the stirring up of Heroick Spirits, to benefit their Country'.[28] Such literature was periodically reprinted, and while it is of course possible that Davenant studied these books for his trip to Virginia, the narratives were also apparently woven into national consciousness and seem to have formed a part of the mythos of a Protestant Elizabethan echoed in Cromwell's foreign policy. He reiterated this policy in the 1656 inaugural speech to parliament (which forms the epigraph to this chapter), where he combined it with a call to action: 'Truly our business is to speak Things; the dispensations of God that are upon us do demand it.'[29] The colonialist representations of both *The Cruelty of the Spaniards* and *Francis Drake* reinforce Cromwell's foreign policy, call up memories of a heroic Protestant past, and avoid controversial domestic issues.

FROM OTHER TO HONOUR? RULE AND REPRESENTATION IN *THE SIEGE OF RHODES*

The dispensations of God may have suggested that an active military role was desirable for the new Protestant Protectorate, but militarism – especially crusading militarism – was expensive, and one of the most obvious 'threats' to Christendom, the Ottoman empire, was in an ambiguous trading relationship to Europe. Arguably, precisely this opposition of economic and ideological investment underlies the ambivalence found in the representation of the Turk in the most famous of Davenant's Protectorate performances, the two-part play or entertainment *The Siege of Rhodes*.[30]

The Siege of Rhodes shares with *The Cruelty of the Spaniards* a fascination with cultural difference, but the Turk was a very different 'other'. Perhaps it is this less direct involvement in a colonial project which precipitates a more complex and ambivalent representation of cultural difference than was given to the Spanish or the Indians. In the 'Preface to *Gondibert*', Davenant wrote of the Mahometan 'vaine pride of Empire', bearing out Walter Benjamin's later comment (on the German tragic drama) that for Europe 'the history of the Orient [was] where absolute imperial power was to be encountered'.[31] Yet in *The Siege of Rhodes* 1 and 2, we find this mythologisation gradually subverted and unravelled.

The performance and publication history of *The Siege of Rhodes* requires some explanation: contemporary political issues and theatre conditions changed hugely between its first performance and publication in 1656, its Restoration performance in 1661 and publication in 1663. The first part was entered in the Stationers' Register in 1656 and it is possible that the second part, entered in the Stationers' Register on 30 May 1659, was performed before the Restoration. A second quarto of the first part was printed in 1659 with a new place of staging. Thus, the first part of *The Siege of Rhodes* followed a few months after *The First Days Entertainment*, in 1656. It was published in that year and republished with *Francis Drake* in 1659. In 1661 both parts of *The Siege of Rhodes* were staged alternately at the Lisle's Tennis Court theatre, and in 1663 the revised version (and very different second part) were published. There is a printed text of part 1 from 1656 – a 'Representation by the Art of Prospective in Scenes' – and a text of the two parts with additions from 1663, after the performance which Pepys saw.[32] If the 1659 performance of the second part was substantially different from the 1661 performance recorded in the 1663 edition, and it seems possible that it was (particularly in view of the addition of the character of Roxolana to the 1661 performance), we have no record of it.

These performance issues are connected to musicological discussion about whether or not the two parts can be considered 'opera'. Once again, this depends on the use of the term 'opera'. The circumstances of the 1650s meant that it was unlikely to be called a 'play' (the Stationers' Register calls it a 'maske' but the title notes the presence of recitative) and the term 'Representation' suggests a claim to novelty and innovation as well as to a genre. Certainly, in contrast to *The First Days Entertainment*, its plotting and organisation are unlike that of the masque structure and imply the influence of opera as well as other traditions.[33] The first part is poised between the codes of public and private theatre; performed publicly it used Mrs Coleman to play the part of Ianthe – speaking, but veiled (1 *SR* 11.ii. 78).[34]

The representation of the Sultan in the 1656 play might have suggested analogies with Protectorate England to contemporaries. Parallels could be drawn with the way Cromwell's guards were referred to as 'janissaries', and he could also be seen as a despotic ruler ruled by the people. Both Cromwell and the Sultan had a standing army. Such analogies are present as hints in the text, but a reading which simply equated Cromwell with Solyman would be deaf to the play's complex representations of political power. The play works in relation to the political situation in several ways, re-using literary and political texts (reworking the political analysis suggested in Fulke Greville's writings into an almost Hobbesian analysis of the right to rule), and gesturing towards contemporary events.

By the time Davenant was writing, 'the Turk' had a long mythic history in England as an oppositional power threatening Christian virtues – as C. A. Patrides pointed out, the sultan was equated with Satan by Milton, amongst others, and figured as a scourge of

Christendom.[35] The 1656 play initially presents definite European values, in contrast to the Turkish 'other' whose fleet sailing towards them from Chios is 'but the forerunning Van / Of the prodigious Gross of Solyman' (1 *SR* i.ii.47–8). But later that scheme is questioned when the Turk comes to represent values similar to those of the Europeans. The initial image, of a European union defending an outpost against an enemy which traditionally pressed on the borders of the western world, threatening the end of Christendom itself, combined with the complication of this image in the action of both the plays, suggests the complex significance of the Turk in 1656.

Samuel Chew wrote that travellers returning from the East 'passed into English literature a picture of Islam as at once splendidly luxurious, admirable in its serenity, sombre in its cruelty and sensuality, and terrible in its strength'.[36] However, this is only part of the story. Turkey provided an 'other' against which Europe defined itself, but the status of this 'other' was consistently undermined by the close trading links between the various Christian countries and the Infidel. A double standard might be said to have existed, on one hand condemnation, on the other commerce.[37] Indeed, as Edward Said argues in his early work on orientalism, during the sixteenth and seventeenth centuries Turkey could be considered as notionally excluded from European organisation, but in fact participated in it.[38] Furthermore, Davenant's play draws on the fact that, although 'the Turk' is a recognisable enemy, as personified by the sultan, 'he' also presents a dangerous, uncanny *doppelgänger*, a representation of the West to itself in, for example, the detailed hierarchies and government which might be thought partially analogous to European monarchy in its most absolute aspects.

Said writes of western notions of the Orient, of 'Oriental despotism, Oriental splendour, cruelty, sensuality', making it much clearer than Chew that these are mythologisations. His argument centres around the development of the mythos of the Orient as an adjunct of the growth of trade in the eighteenth century, and particularly associates it with the trading companies. The play activates those discourses with which the East 'has helped to define Europe . . . as its contrasting image, idea, personality, experience', but also engages with the way actual contact with culturally different 'others' tends to disrupt mythic contrasts.[39] As in *The Cruelty of the Spaniards* battle is joined, but here it is situated on the edge of

Europe, at the very border with beyond. Instead of presenting two
European powers struggling for dominance in a landscape empty
of values (or of questionable values) as in Peru, it delineates a
complex struggle and even ultimately a sharing of values with a
near neighbour.

A combination of interest and antagonism can be found in
English attitudes to the Turk during the Civil War and
Protectorate, and *The Siege of Rhodes* bears out the dualism of the
West's sense of the Ottoman Empire. It can also be read against
specific historical shifts which, perhaps, permitted the sultan to be
presented as both a dangerous other and a humanisedly similar
subject. Significantly, English newspapers were interested in the
downfall of the notorious Ahmet I, Sultan Ibrahim, whose reign
during the 1640s was so ill-famed that no subsequent sultan was
named after him.[40] The 'extraordinary oppressions' which caused
him to be deposed were reported in England in the catastrophic
year 1649. The report provides quite startling analogues to the
English experience. The sultan, beset, appealed to the Mufti for
aid, but, 'he was forced to declare to the Grand Seigneur that the
Militia would not suffer Acmet Basha, the Grand Vizier, to enjoy
his place any longer'.[41]

The story of Ahmet I echoes English politics but it also shows the
famously united Turks as internally divided and therefore micro-
cosmically reinforces Said's argument that the idea of the 'Orient'
grew up after the period of the greatest Ottoman strength.
Davenant was writing of Turkey at a period when it no longer
posed such a threat to Europe as it had during the sixteenth and
parts of the seventeenth centuries; by the 1650s it was perceptibly
in a decline. Close economic intertwining had implications – in
1656 Cromwell had refused to help the Venetians against the
Turks because, as Christopher Hill puts it, 'too much English
capital in the Mediterranean was vulnerable to Turkish attack'.[42]
Nevertheless, a special factor in the position of the Ottoman
Empire in English eyes in the 1650s was its defeat by the fleet of
their Venetian allies at the mouth of the Dardanelles on 26 June
1656 – only months before *The Siege of Rhodes* was entered on the
Stationers' Register.[43] At the end of August 1656, the Venetian
representative Giavarina was finally granted an audience with
Cromwell. Giavarina reported the protector's response to the news
of the Turkish defeat: 'he added that now the strength of the Turks

was so attenuated it would be advisable for all Christian powers to join forces' – a suggestion which may indicate Cromwell's Protestant ambition, or his prudence in spending words but not arms. Either way, it is uncannily echoed in the situation of the first part of *The Siege of Rhodes*.[44]

These specific state interests were preceded by sources from the early and later seventeenth century which testify in a more general way to the interest of Europe in Turkey.[45] For example, *The Travellers Breviat*, excerpted from the work of the Spaniard Giovanni Botero, represents Turkey's restless expansionism, and Botero's work may have influenced Fulke Greville's *Treatie of Warres* which, as I suggest later, probably in turn influenced Davenant's treatment of war in *The Siege of Rhodes*.[46] *The Travellers Breviat* maintains a similar position to that delineated by Solyman in *The Siege of Rhodes*, asserting that the Turkish state is an expansionist war machine within which the sultan fuels the army by passing out parcels of conquered land to the army and the rest of the hierarchy, in return for arms, horses and provisions: 'The Turkes give their minds to nothing but warre, nor take care of anything else but provision of armour and weapons: courses fitter to destroy and waste, than to preserve and inrich provinces.' The *Breviat*, which went into many editions, also fostered the myth of Ottoman tyranny, asserting that Turkish 'government is merely tyrannicall: for the Great Turk is so absolute a Lord of all things contayned within the bounds of his dominions, that the inhabitants do count themselves his slaves not his subjects'.[47] On the other hand, Islam's religious unity is contrasted with schismatic Christendom.

The comfortable spectacle of the Turks in difficulties would certainly have provided a focus for a writer seeking to avoid the complex actualities of civil discord. It seems likely that as well as the regularly canvassed literary sources, the actual circumstances of Ottoman Turkey at the moment of the play's production, taken together with the nature of Protectorate foreign policy, economic links and the powerfully mythologised status of 'the Turk', also provided important stimuli to the representation of the Turk as different but yet familiar in the 1656 production of *The Siege of Rhodes*, part 1.[48]

The play narrates the siege of 1522, when the English were involved in garrisoning the island. It presents the audience with two rival armies fighting over the town. The Europeans – and especially English ('lions') – are represented in Rhodes, but the central conflict is between the Rhodian forces and the Turk. The Turk is initially represented as a powerful force, with his fleet moving towards Rhodes:

> ADMIRAL: Her shady wings to distant sight,
> Spread like the Curtains of the Night
> Each Squadron thicker and still darker grows;
> The Fleet like many floating Forrests shows.
>
> (1 *SR* I.i.11–14)

Thus, initially the Turk is represented as an 'other' – dark, plethoric, dangerous. However, the distinction between Turks and Rhodians cannot be fully maintained as the problems facing the two sets of rulers come to replicate each other and the attribution of virtue by nation becomes evidently ambiguous. Although the spirit of honour – valour – and manliness is exalted it cannot be placed firmly as a European virtue. The narrative turns on love and the conflict between love and honour. But the dynamic of the play invites us to identify Ianthe and the Sultan as those in mature possession of 'true' honour – presented as inhering in individual conduct, though that conduct has political implications. Honour is established as the primary value of Alphonso as soon as he arrives in Rhodes. Deciding to stay, despite danger, he says:

> Honour is colder Vertue set on fire:
> My Honour lost, her Love would soon decay:
> Here for my Tombe or Tryumph I will stay.
> My Sword against proud *Solyman* I draw,
> His cursed Prophet and His sensual Law.   (1 *SR* I.i.80–4)

Alphonso achieves military heroism, fending off the Turkish army, but the Sultan's generosity in taking Ianthe prisoner and then giving her a safe pass to him in Rhodes provokes a crisis in Alphonso. His jealousy disrupts the equation of virtue with Europe which the play seems initially to propose. Alphonso's certainty that honour is bound up with European values is shown to be mistaken in his own case as well as in that of the Sultan. Already in this speech from the first Entry he associates Solyman with sensuality, and Alphonso's crisis about the differentiation of the European and the Turk is posed by the play in the form of his unfounded jeal-

ousy. This is the main way in which the play presents the breakdown of distinctions between the Sultan and the Europeans, for
both audience and characters:

> ALPHONSO: Had Heav'n that Passe-port for our freedom
> sent
> It would have chose some better Instrument
> Then faithlesse *Solyman.*
> IANTHE: O Say not so!
> To strike and wound the vertue of your Foe
> Is cruelty, which war does not allow:
> Sure he has better words deserv'd from you.
> ALPHONSO: From me *Ianthe,* No;
> What he deserves from you, you best must know.

(1 SR iv.ii.27–35)

Definitions of honour, like the definitions of the Sultan as
enemy and 'other', turn out ambiguous and complicated. Honour,
as it is redefined, remains a principal value but is seen to be in the
possession of those characters who have a complex grasp of a difficult, even irresoluble, political reality – including, above all,
Ianthe whose virtue and wearing of armour make her into a kind
of *femme forte* by the end of the first play.[49] Thus, any national claim
to 'honour' is modified in relation to increasingly complex circumstances, and this modification turns on the changing status
and interrelationships of the Sultan, Ianthe, Alphonso.

The ambiguous nature of 'honour', a political virtue measured
in terms of self-government, is explored in the affective relationships of the central figures, on whom the audience's attention is
concentrated. In both plays Ianthe and Alphonso's success or
failure in producing honourable behaviour are bound up with
stereotypical versus sophisticated understandings of the Sultan.
The play's ambivalent reading of national stereotypes (in which
the audience must also have been implicated in terms of ideology
and popular mythology) is tied to an equally unravelling narrative
of love and honour: simple binary concepts of honour and nationhood are simultaneously undermined. As well as the problem of
where honour can be found in love relations, the play poses as
ambiguous the relationship between the Sultan's rule and aristocratic powerlessness in the face of popular demands. Thus the
1656 version, the first part, ends with the Sultan held off because
of Alphonso's heroism but this upbeat ending is qualified by his

jealousy over Ianthe which, although he recognises it, is not resolved in reconciliation, as his final words on the subject are, 'Draw all the Curtains and then lead her in; / Let me in darkness mourn away my sin' (1 *SR* v.iv.106–7).

Although the second part of the play only exists in the 1663 version, it is possible that it was performed before the Restoration, in 1659, as well as in the version seen by Pepys in 1661. In the second part of the play the Sultan and his people become a mirror-image of Rhodian questions about government as the Sultan and the Rhodian leaders confront the problem of negotiating a connection between rule and the people's will. The powerlessness of the Turkish absolute monarch at the hands of his people is echoed in the rebellion of the Rhodians against the continuation of battle. The dynamic of the play reinforces the differentiation of Solyman from the Turkish war-machine: he increasingly occupies a position which replicates the dilemmas of honour and love faced by the European protagonists. Conversely, the difficulties of the Sultan's absolutism are repeated in the conflicts amongst the people, Ianthe and the Grand Master of Rhodes.

In the second part of the play the Sultan speaks of the role of the absolutist ruler as emperor:

> SOLYMAN: Of spacious Empire, what can I enjoy?
>   Gaining at last but what I first Destroy.
>   Tis fatal (*Rhodes*) to thee,
>   And troublesome to me
>   That I was born to govern swarms
>   Of Vassals boldly bred to arms:
>   For whose accurs'd diversion, I must still
>   Provide new Towns to Sack, new Foes to Kill
>   Excuse that Pow'r, which by my Slaves is aw'd:
>   For I shall find my peace
>   Destroy'd at home, unless
>   I seek for them destructive Warr abroad . . .
>
> (2 *SR* ii.ii.52–64)

This simultaneously suggests the Sultan is an Eastern despot, and invites us to sympathise with him as a sole ruler facing the problem that the people inevitably determine a ruler's conduct. Even as he is distinguished from the Ottoman force his subjection to them is emphasised: despite the appearance of power, he is perpetually driven by the war-machine. In Rhodes Villerius has already made a very similar speech arguing that the will of the people cannot be resisted in times of crisis:

> Their strength they now will in our weakness find,
> Whom in their plenty we can sway,
> But in their wants must them obey,
> And wink when they the Cords of pow'r unbind.[50]

> (2 *SR* I.i.266–71)

The juxtaposition of these two quotations shows that the presentation of the Turkish state in *The Siege of Rhodes* cannot be in any simple way opposed to the European, or Christian, values provided by the force on Rhodes. The difference between the two populations would appear to be that the Rhodians are, in general, more tractable (or trickable) than the Turks, but each populace is represented as ultimately ungovernable except through a power which accepts and fulfils their wishes. The Turks do not rebel, as the Rhodians do, but then their leader epitomises rather than opposes them; the Sultan's project as absolute ruler is not to direct the people but to maintain peace 'at home', and his own position, by making war.

The uncontrollable force of the people is echoed in the Grand Master's acknowledgement of their will (2 *SR* I.i.263–71). When the people elect Ianthe as their ambassador to the Sultan, Villerius merely comments 'Who can resist, if they will have it so' (2 *SR* I.i.271). Neither the absolutist monarch nor the Rhodian militarised aristocracy are capable of overruling the desires of the people. The sole significant and recuperative difference between the Rhodians and the Turks is that the warlike disposition of the Turkish people forces the Sultan to acts of aggression whereas the Rhodian people demand peace; the question of who rules and how that rule is effected remains present. Villerius comments:

> *Ianthe* needs must go. Those who withstand
> The Tide of Flood, which is the Peoples will,
> Fall back when they would onward row:
> We strength and way presume by lying still.

> (2 *SR* I.ii.18–21)

In its clear indication that the ruling class must survive rebellion by floating with the tide this speech leaves Villerius in virtually the same position as the Sultan who will find peace destroyed at home unless he provides the people with wars abroad. The representation of government as overtaken by the will of the people is obviously suggestive of several political situations in England between 1642 and 1659. It also strikingly echoes a common topos also used in Fulke Greville's *Mustapha* (printed in 1609 and 1633), in which the character Rosten speaks of a swelling mob which 'as the *Waters* / That meet with banks of Snow, make Snow grow Water'.[51]

IMAGINING WAR: GREVILLE, HOBBES, DAVENANT

What was the genealogy of Davenant's Protectorate meditation on power relations? The influence of Hobbes is obvious, but other sources are less so. This brings me, finally, to some texts which Davenant here appears to be rereading in the light of the political circumstances and political theory of the Civil War. Fulke Greville's poem *A Treatie of Warres* apparently echoes Botero's *Breviat* in his opinion of Islamic addiction to war – 'Such the Religion is of Mahomet, / His doctrine, onely warre'.[52] It also seems to have influenced Davenant; certainly, both the *Treatie* and *The Siege of Rhodes* initially appear to be committed to a defence of national war (in Greville's case as a manifestation of God's revenge; *Treatie*, stanzas 33–6, 43) but then shift positions. Greville, presenting war as an effect of the fall (see stanzas 45–9), yet also presents a critique of the idea that war is necessary and inevitable. Each text implicitly questions the notion that a ruler's sanction justifies war, the assumption that colonial wars are ethical, and that any simplistic obedience is the duty of the people to the ruler. However, Davenant's text transforms Greville's Protestant pessimism into an analysis of government as solely expedient.

Davenant's play directs the audience's sympathy ambiguously by posing an increasing disjunction between Solyman's war against Rhodes versus the representation of the Sultan as highly moral in European terms. Just as the war in *The Siege of Rhodes* becomes increasingly hard to understand or justify (apparently posed finally as an effect of popular political discontent), *A Treatie of Warres* puts forward several possible but potentially contradictory analyses of the causes and nature of war, which can only be resolved by recourse to the will of God (stanza 50). An assumption that fallen humanity is violent and insurrectionist, needing restraint, is common to Greville and Davenant, as is an ambiguity about the political implications of that. Where Davenant's defence of drama concentrates on spectacle as social control, yet in *The Siege of Rhodes* presents the elite as endangered by but dependent on the people, Greville's is ambiguous about what constitutes 'good' 'authority':

> *Never did any Publicke misery*
> *Rise of itself*; Gods plagues still grounded are
> On common stains of our Humanity:
> > And to the flame, which ruineth Mankind,
> > Man gives the matter, or at least gives wind.
>
> Nor are these people carried into blood
> Onely, and still with giddy violent passion,
> But in our Nature, rightly understood,
> Rebellion lives, still striving to disfashion
> Order, Authority, Lawes, any good
> > That should restraine our liberty of pleasure,
> > Bound our designes, or give desire a measure . . .
>
> > (Stanzas 23–4)

This analysis of rebellion as at the core of the being of fallen man again links the individual (the root of rebellion in a fallen world) to all politics, honour and 'human nature'. As Norbrook suggests, Greville's work is ambivalent about the issues of Protestantism and courts, love and power, and this anxiety is re-articulated and changed in Davenant's *Siege of Rhodes*.[53] However, while Greville's play *Mustapha* seems to see all kings as tyrannical in that they inevitably deprive the people of their rights, *The Siege of Rhodes* invites empathy for the Sultan and suggests that neither the Turkish nor the Rhodian people are able to use power well.

The primacy of a theological schema in Greville's *Treatie* produces an ultimate return to and sanction of authority *per se*, whereas in Davenant's case the re-affirmation of 'love' has been partially removed from the political sphere into the private, even the domestic.[54] The resolutions allowed by love work only ambiguously in *The Siege of Rhodes*, against the background of a very full acknowledgement of the basis of government in power alone – an analysis which maps very evidently on to the central political concerns of the 1650s. The second *Siege of Rhodes* play, particularly, poses the interrelation of governor and people solely in terms of the pragmatic operations of power and in this sense, rather than in any politically challenging way (certainly it would be hard to read this analysis of rule as endorsing divine right royalism); *The Siege of Rhodes* manifests a radical uncertainty about the role of rulers, seeing them as ultimately almost powerless. Hobbes argued that a nation comes into being when the people 'confer all their power and strength upon one Man, or upon one Assembly of men, that may reduce all their Wills, by plurality of voices, unto one Will', and such power once conferred cannot be reclaimed.[55] However, Hobbes also argued that a citizen should support which-ever government was able to govern.

Seen from a Hobbesian perspective, *The Siege of Rhodes* hints that the ruling class, who have no remedies to offer, must be tem-porarily ruled by the voice of the people. This is reinforced by Villerius' concluding speech in the exchange which can be read as strongly reminiscent of Hobbes's analysis of power in the state. The play maintains a distinction between Rhodians and Turks only around war as conducted in the case of the Turks *by* the ruler but at the behest of the people, and in the case of the Rhodians as being stopped when the people take control. In this way the play offers difference which is then dissolved into familiarity, offers a drama of conquest which then turns into a drama of compromise, offers a dramatisation of a crusade which then turns upon itself to question the premises of rulership which set it up. In terms of the politics of England in 1656, 1659 and 1661, the *Siege of Rhodes* plays offer a commentary on politics and honour which could be read as suggesting the similarity of all forms of power (and there-fore, perhaps, leading towards engagement with the current power). This analysis of politics as a matter of power alone is extended in the second part, and appears to be only slightly obscured in the Restoration (1663) version of the two plays, where the introduction of the second woman's part serves to concentrate the play around more individualistic dilemmas of love.

As the only dramatist sanctioned by the Protectorate to put on public plays, Davenant needed to establish his drama as in some sense national, or nationalist, while also differentiated from the monarchist rather than 'reformed' opera written by dramatists not directly engaged with representing as respectable the present pol-itics of nationhood. His Protectorate drama demonstrates a need to validate the present and revise the past. The pressing need to establish the present as legitimate was almost impossible to fulfil through the tried method of recourse to validating mythologisations of history. Virtually any dramatisation of domestic history would inevitably raise the question of the nature of kingship, government, republic, Protectorate. Thus Davenant's opera and other pieces could have no recourse to the type of re-evaluations of history found (for example) in Shakespeare's history plays. From a dramatist's point of view, it is hard to see how the nation might in any way be presented to itself without the inevitable highlighting of sources of division. Davenant ignores domestic history, using the broader outlines of the relationship between Europe and states outside Europe against which his plays provide stories of English exploits abroad to produce entertainment acceptable to all shades of opinion on the question of domestic government. He both retreated from history altogether (as in *The First Days Entertainment*) and dramatised England's role in international affairs in which other participants in events could be characterised as 'other'.

Thus Davenant's Protectorate writing constitutes both a radical break with earlier theatrical practice and a continuity with that provided for the court: the impulse to validate the present is strong in *The Siege of Rhodes*, as it had been in court masques like *Salmacida Spolia*, produced in 1640 when it was still possible for the person of the king to act the part of the antidote to discord. Sixteen years later this had become impossible. The resemblances between court masques and the operas, detailed in this chapter, serve also to emphasise the radical discontinuities between the two. This links the equally problematic ideological positions of theatrical practice and the dramatisation of history. The present that Davenant's Protectorate plays sought to validate demanded not only a reversal of the political impulses which had driven his prewar drama, but also that he provide a theatrical practice acceptable to a government which, in many contexts, found theatre politically unacceptable.

History and theatrical practice were both visibly politicised; the connections between Davenant's productions and the specific ideological exigencies of the 1650s are evident. 'Opera' provided a solution of some sort to the theatrical problem, but that solution itself may have been complicated by the strong connection between that genre and courts. The dramatisation of conflict between nations provided a possibility for a mythologisation of the nation through the constitution of 'others', and therefore the thorny questions of domestic division could be avoided. However, in responding to political circumstances – even in avoiding particular topics – the plays differently illuminate the complexity of the relations of political discourses and dramatic and theatrical genres in the mid-1650s.

Genre, politics and place: the social body in the dramatic career of John Tatham

Louis XIV's pronouncement of 1655 – 'L'état, c'est moi' – could not have been made in England at the same moment. The contrast in circumstances and the effects on political thought are illuminating. Under the English republic a central question was who or what constituted the nation or body politic, and that question haunted the Protectorate.[1] My subject here, the dramatist John Tatham, was involved in the symbolisation of the state in different ways at different moments in his career, which spans the period of Civil War and Protectorate, running from 1640 to 1664. Official policy towards theatre was transformed several times in the twenty-four years of Tatham's career, from the banning of public performance to the renewal of the lord mayors' shows under the Protectorate and then to the new civic shows of the Restoration. The Restoration was simply the climax of the transformations which dominated his whole career.[2]

Tatham's texts indicate the way one writer at least experienced the necessity of rethinking the political imaginary imposed by the regicide and declaration of the republic. Tatham's 'personal' politics are not at stake, rather the way in which genres, political circumstances and the 'political imaginary' of the 1650s – what *could* be thought, envisaged, imagined, even prophesied in political terms – shaped the way his writing and shows articulated ideas of the social body. Accordingly this chapter examines the figuring of the body politic in Tatham's plays, including his problematic first play, *The Distracted State* (1651), his entertainments and lord mayors' shows.

EARLY NETWORKS AND CIVIC CONNECTIONS: 1640–1650

Tatham seems to have begun his career as a member of a group of writers who were seeking careers in theatre when war began. His first publication, *The Fancies Theater*, includes a short pastoral drama called *Love Crowns the End*, 'performed by schollers . . . in the County of Nottingham in the yeare 1632', around the time of the vogue for pastoral at court and after Jonson's masque at nearby Bolsover.[3] His peers greeted the volume enthusiastically – it appeared with a plethora of commendatory verses by younger writers.[4] There are verses by the playwrights Richard Brome and Thomas Nabbes, who also wrote verses for each other's volumes, as did C.G., another contributor.[5] Another associate, Thomas Rawlins, wrote *The Rebellion*, published in 1640 when, according to its commendatory verses (to which Tatham contributed), he was a young man.[6] Martin Butler identifies Tatham as a member of a group around the Red Bull including Richard Brome, Thomas Nabbes, Thomas Heywood, Thomas Rawlins, Nathaniel Richards and Thomas Jordan. [7]

Aspiration rather than intimacy, it seems, motivated Tatham's choice of Sir John Winter as dedicatee of *The Fancies Theater*. A court figure, Winter was involved in the scandals in the forest of Dean where the crown was attempting to extend its prerogative by depriving residents of commoners' rights. He had supported Charles in his personal rule, became master of requests to Henrietta Maria, and helped to collect money from other Roman Catholics for the Scottish war.[8] We can be sure that Tatham was not, except by aspiration, a court writer. His circle were young when the wars began; Thomas Jordan also wrote entertainments during the Protectorate (in 1657 he published *Fancy's Festivals: A Masque*, 'as it hath been privately presented') and continued to write civic shows after the Restoration.[9] However, only Jordan, Tatham (and Brome, in terms of publication) survived into the 1650s as writers of drama. Thus, the largely untheatrical 1640s had been the period of Tatham's literary maturation. He, too, was one to whom 'Civill War hath been a nursery'.[10] Tatham's next publication was a volume of verse, *Ostella* (1650), which contains some poems on pre-war theatre and confirms his association with this circle; it was not until 1651 that his first play was published, a puzzling political allegory called *The Distracted State*.

1651: ENIGMATIC ALLEGORY IN *THE DISTRACTED STATE*

Set in Sicily, *The Distracted State* is caught in a contradiction: it presents republican politics in some detail, yet does so under the twin signs of disaster and satire. Moreover, the play poses a critical and hermeneutic puzzle: although it evidently dramatises political crises, even its date of composition, remains problematic because of Tatham's claim to have written it, prophetically, in 1641. The title, assertion of earlier composition, and epigraph, all encourage us to read it in relationship to contemporary politics. But which particular state, precisely, are we to consider as ruined by rebellion? Are we to read it in relation to 1641 or 1651?

John M. Wallace argues strongly for a 1651 date of composition in order to make it a part of the controversy over the Oath of Engagement. Part of the attempt of the new state to ensure loyalty and to formalise its relationship to its subjects or citizens was the establishment in 1649 of an Oath of Engagement which promised loyalty 'to the Commonwealth of England as the same is now established, without a King or House of Lords', to be taken by members of parliament (and others). Although this specific debate was part of a more general discursive crisis in state language, loyalty and incorporation, it is indicative of the republic's crisis in political representation and self-conceptualisation.

A stronger argument for seeing the play primarily in relation to the Commonwealth rather than the outbreak of Civil War, however, is that although there is no conclusive evidence that the play was not begun in the early 1640s, the first audience would indeed have read the play on its publication in 1651 and in the light of the crises of loyalty and iconography precipitated by regicide and republic.

The peculiarities of the prefatory material are continued by the plot, which demands some detailed discussion. It combines tragic and satiric qualities in a generic and political complexity, as the play imagines situations that it has, apparently, no desire to sponsor.[11] The plot turns on the question of what it means when the ruler is not the divinely sanctioned king, leaving the field open for a range of republican and tyrannical possibilities. Formally it is a tragicomedy, though resolution and restoration come only in the final scene of the fifth act. The audience (not the characters) know the king is alive, so, like Thomas Middleton's *The Phoenix*, *The Distracted State* has a double structure, in that for many of the characters the action is tragic almost to the end of the play, while the audience is alerted to the possibility of a tragicomic structure when they discover that the king is alive at the beginning of the third act. Within this structure, the play explores the different kinds of government which emerge in the absence of a rightful ruler. And the rightful ruler is signified not by methods of rule but by the metaphysical guarantee of true royal lineage – blood – or what Louis Marin called the 'imaginary absolute of the monarch'.[12]

However, even as it invites us to detect topical references, the play evades offering conclusive answers. Its generic hybridity, its strangeness as a play and its ambivalent voicing of political theory suggest the marginal status of drama as a politicised genre in the 1650s.[13] Unlike Tatham's later texts this play lacked a production context. It seems only loosely tied to the institutions which produced culture and reproduced ideology, a marginality announced by the play's complex and readerly form.

The plot is roughly as follows. The opening establishes the deposed king as the rightful ruler but also suggests that (like Charles I) he was not a perfect king; the usurper, his brother Mazares, claims to have taken the throne because 'the Publike wrong' forced him to oppose the king. From this point, *The Distracted State* is organised around a series of usurpations which need to be seen in the light of the complex tragic/tragicomic structure of the play and the way it presents the various options available to a state without a 'true' king. They also raise questions about the nature of the body of the king and what (metaphysical?) qualities underwrite his rule.[14]

Mazares' reign is punctuated by asides on the relationship between kings and Machiavellian tyrants. Agathocles, a subject, opens the play with the words, 'Heaven where's thy Vengeance, / Canst thou endure this Mockery?' (i.i, p. 1), evidence of his loyalty to Evander. He attacks Mazares, the fraternal usurper; 'From you our rising Sun, we must expect / A Vertuall fervor. Obedience is my safety. / My wishes! trifles' (i.i, p. 1). Mazares, on the other hand, speaks the language of Machiavellian 'necessity', associated with justifications of the regicide. News that the 'late tyrant' has been killed and cast into a river makes 'true' monarchy the lost object of the play and precipitates an accumulation of usurpations in which figures such as Cleander, a 'Magazine of policy' (ii. i, p. 10), seek power.

The first act introduces Agathocles, a Sicilian, whose development we trace through the whole action and whose ethics (and fortunes) ultimately collapse. In *The Prince* Machiavelli uses the Sicilian tyrant Agathocles to discuss the two ways in which a prince may rise from a private station, either 'by some wicked and unlawfull meanes a man rises to the Principality; or when a private person by the favour of his fellow Citizens becomes Prince of his countrey'.[15] The familiarity of the name Agathocles from Machiavelli might lead a reader to anticipate his role as a usurper, but for most of the play he is loyal to the 'true' king, abandoning this position only gradually.

The scene switches abruptly, in Act III, to the banished – but living – king, Evander. At this point the reader (or audience) comes into possession of special generic knowledge: the king may well, tragicomically, return. Indeed, unframed by the anticipation of the return of Evander, the ensuing transformations of government would constitute a revolutionary's guidebook to the possibilities and pitfalls of Machiavellian government.

By the time the scene returns to Evander's subjects they are ruled by Archias. Power and rule are in an entirely arbitrary relation; in Act IV all exit leaving Antanter alone to comment aptly, 'These are fine turning times, I wonder when / 'Twill come to my turn to be King' (IV.i, p. 24).[16] At this climax of political possibility when, indeed, the choice of governments and governors seems wholly arbitrary, Agathocles and Epecides discuss the meaning of government:

> AGATHOCL.: How sweet and freely Rome enjoy'd her self,
>   'Till she submitted to the Power and
>   Pride of one man's Rule? Tell me
>   What good did ever
>   Kings bring unto our Country, what wee might not
>   Have purchas'd without 'em? Ills they have
>   Almost incredible: Our Coffers emptied,
>   To fill their Treasury, and maintain their Riot.
> EPEC: And wedded to perpetual Slavery.
>   For when one Tyrant falls another Rises
>   From his Corrupted loynes, that proves far worse
>   Perhaps than did the former, so that wee
>   Must never hope for better, but be Arm'd
>   With Patience to endure the worst.   (IV.i, p. 24)

Rome, of course, is paradigmatic of a state which changed from a republic to a monarchy, proposed by Agathocles as a degeneration. Agathocles describes kings as simply tyrants, selfishly consuming the resources of the country.

Thus, the play's progressive investigation of governments further and further from royal rule is traced in the path of Agathocles. Before the righteous rule of Evander is successfully reasserted he finally enters politics, having come to believe that 'all / Men Naturally have Ambition to / Make great their line, and families by succession' (v.i, p. 26). The last act contains a total of three usurpations – two actual and one attempted – before 'tragedy' becomes tragicomedy with the restitution of the kingdom to its 'rightful' ruler.

Although the didactic aspect of the play triumphs with the return of Evander, the build-up of usurpation after usurpation is the energising force of the play. The play's argument in favour of *de jure* kingship also fulfils the contrary purpose of alerting its audience to a great variety of political possibilities within a particular historical situation. Thus, arguably, republicanism in this play is analysed and imagined but 'as the thought of another', framed by the reader's knowledge of the tragicomic return of the king which provides a 'safe' framework.[17]

One way to reconcile the tragicomic structure created by the last-minute return of the king with the incipient tragic structure is to think of the play as a satire, parodying the bids for power of the early 1650s. It uses the satiric strategy Michael Seidel identifies as the prolonging of crisis 'at the very time that the action mocked and parodied would or could, in other circumstances, and in other literary modes, resolve it'. This describes neatly the relationship between the prolonged tragic structure and repeated disasters of the play. The tragicomic dénouement, which only happens in the very last scene, emphasises the way that 'usurpation that prevents restoration' functions as a satiric means of imagining crisis.[18] Yet the prolonging of usurpations is drawn out to emphasise the irresolubility of political agony.

The Distracted State's combination of conflicting elements and a probably knowing resistance to historicising criticism makes it, despite its apparent naïvety, difficult to 'read it off' against one historical context. It exceeds 'topical' categories in terms of an apparent refusal to allow closure in a single allegorical or topical interpretation. It is a clear instance in which the censoring conditions of its production, more particularly its complex response to those conditions, make interdictions on drama 'productive as well as prohibitive' of meaning.[19] It is also Tatham's only play which, ambivalently, explores the potentially exciting, potentially tragic, possibilities of the republic of the 1650s. Like the *Andronicus* plays of the late 1650s and early 1660s, *The Distracted State* dramatises not only the specific events of the present, but also the political possibilities and questions of kings, states, usurpers in the 1650s.[20] In a sense, for this play, the king constitutes the state but it also imagines the republican alternatives that were the actual context of its moment of production and the reality of its audience in 1651. Under a period of censorship of the theatre, Tatham produced a complex drama of the unresolved political issues of the period after 1649 but before the Protectorate; a drama which addresses in a generically complex way the issues of the needs of state in terms of government. It is hard to say whether such a detailed exploration of political issues and possibilities that were so alive for contemporaries might have been performed on the pre-war stage. Certainly, *The Distracted State* is evidence that the theatrical issues of the 1650s, including censorship, generated highly complicated responses.

1657: SENATORS OR SLAVES? TATHAM'S CIVIC SHOWS FOR THE NEW NATIONS OF THE 1650S AND 1660S

The rest of Tatham's career is bound up with the crises of government and the politics of London's streets. Just as the absence of regal control structured *The Distracted State* it shaped the rest of Tatham's writing career. The problematic relationship between the one divinely sanctioned kingly body and the necessity to rule the state explored in *The Distracted State* recur in the practical framework of the lord mayors' shows in which the 'headless' state of the 1650s must be given iconographic, poetic and visual life in such a way as to knit together a reconceptualised body politic. The London streets and political theory meet in the demands of Tatham's mid-century career as writer of civic/national pageants.

Tatham's next play, *The Scots Figgaries*, like *The Distracted State*, is one for which no stage history has yet been discovered. However, its topical anti-Scots animus may have brought Tatham some public attention (it was reprinted). The play turns the religious schisms of the 1640s into a London comedy in which the Scots infiltrators and perpetrators of false ideas – Folly, Billy, Jocky and Scarefoole – are ultimately defeated by the good magistrates Resolution and Surehold. Uphadyay is wrong to suggest that the satirical Scots dialect renders it unintelligible: like *The Distracted State* it is enigmatic, but clearly situated in London and anti-Scots.[21] *The Scots Figgaries* uses comedy to support London authorities, a clearer endorsement of particular power structures than offered in *The Distracted State*, and such valorising of London's magistrates is made literal in the next transformation in Tatham's career when he became a regular writer of City shows. Contrary to much critical opinion, Cromwell's Protectorate coincided with the resurgence and recasting of the lord mayors' shows in the City of London, after a gap between 1640 and 1655.[22] These civic shows are marked by the shifting relationships between national and civic government, played out in the use of City space, the modes of address adopted by the introductions to the pageants, and the printing and distribution of pamphlets to a wider audience: the shows began a month after Cromwell had appointed the mayor, John Dethicke, to investigate the print trade.[23]

From the voices of City MPs in 1641 to the anti-Rump mobs of early 1659, the City was attempting both officially and unofficially to play a central part in political change and to revive its own business status. Yet the City itself was no autonomous group – both Firth and Ashley emphasise the differences amongst aldermen and 'rich merchants' and Cromwell, himself no merchant, had difficult relations with the City.[24] The shows of this period must have worked not only to figure the new nation but to offer a more nuanced harmonisation of intra-City and mercantile politics.

Tatham wrote shows from 1657 to 1664. Writing the poetry which was spoken and, perhaps as significantly, printed in books to be distributed on the day and afterwards, Tatham was involved in mediating the relationship between the City and Westminster, and, during the Protectorate, in shaping the conception of a new, kingless, state in relation to the City. The shows indicate the changing position occupied by the City during the Protectorate and after, dramatising the interrelations of trade and politics. As one commentator put it, 'Trade is the life of a State, *Manufactures* are the very sinews of *Trade*, and *Money* is the soule of both', and as his use of the organic metaphor suggests, London was a vital link between government politics and trade.[25] The shows put on by the guilds were verbal, visual, spatial and, later, printed dramatisations of these relations. The spatial politics of London was traditionally articulated by the show in terms of the mayor's journey from the City to Westminster and back (often by water) and the Protectorate reconfigured the meanings of such a journey in terms of the relationship between mayor and national government, politics and mercantile interests.

Two kinds of show might take place in the City. The lord mayor would annually, on the day following St Simon and St Jude's day, go by barge or by horse along the Strand from the City (usually in this period from Three Cranes Wharf) to Westminster (or to the Tower if the monarch was away) where he would take the oath and then return by barge to the City. At this point there would be a procession, often to his house, accompanied by guild pageantry and shows, including drolls. During the 1620s and 1630s such shows were written by Anthony Munday and Thomas Middleton. The second type of show would involve a visit to the City by one in authority, often a monarch, and might take the form of a triumphal entry or the fulfilment of an invitation from the City to dine at the Guildhall. In both cases the ceremony had meanings specific to the City and its relations with the government.[26]

These civic rituals seem to have been deeply affected by the crises of the Civil War. In the years 1641–2, when London was undergoing an upheaval in the structure of its management in which City MPs were influential in parliament, and the management of the City itself was transformed into a pro-parliamentary structure, shows ceased. Later the attitude of City government to national government was sour, particularly after the apprentice invasions of the Commons in 1647. Withington notes that there was some splendour when a mayor of the Goldsmiths' Company took office, in 1643 and 1653, but between 1640 and 1655 shows ceased.[27] There were, however, some entries. The entry of a ruler into the City brings into play ideas of 'honour' slightly different from the lord mayor's show; the City is at pains to present itself in a favourable light to its ruler but also, on its home territory, to address the ruler as it would like that ruler to be. Cromwell visited the City on several occasions, and a speech survives which was given by the recorder in 1654 when he was entertained at the Guildhall. First, the recorder expatiated on the difficulties of rulers, emphasising their status as servants of the people:

Governors are like the heavenly bodies, much in veneration, but never in rest; and how can it otherwise be expected, when they are not made for themselves . . . but for the safety, and good of Mankind? As in the the Natural, so in the Civil world, Great things being ordained to serve the lesse; we see the Sun by its beames serving the eye of the meanest fly, as well as of the greatest Potentate. The Supremacy of *Salus Populi* was the conclusion of the twelve Tables . . . [28]

Such an address leaves no doubt that the City authority believed that a populist government existed, though it situates power in a secular ruler not in parliament. This was further emphasised with the assertion that 'they leave it to other Nations to salute their Rulers and Victorious Commanders with the names of *Caesares* and *Imperatores*, and after triumphs to erect for them their *arcus Triumphales*' (A3v). One might detect in all this a difficulty about how to address Cromwell, who was neither a monarch nor a mere minister. Nevertheless, such sentiments were, of course, radical departures from monarchist rhetoric, and the conclusion of the recorder's speech is notable for its characterisation of the role of the City as both hierarchised and collective:

This City seldome goes alone in publique Actions: it was anciently called by *Stephanides* the heart of the Nation; and if the heart be in a Politique consideration, as it is in the naturall, it will communicate life and spirits into the other members, by which meanes the whole body may unanimously contribute their desires and endeavours to oppose the common Enemy and after all our distractions [see the] Nation established upon the firm Basis of peace and righteousnesse . . . (A3v–A4r)

The ancient metaphor of the state as a body is used here to figure the role of the City as heart, mediating between different parts of the nation and renewing them. The recorder is not talking about a social body which could be seen as unanimous and homogeneous: in 1653 to 1654 the Protectorate was being established, and issues about taxation in 1653 had exacerbated poor relations between Cromwell and the City.[29]

Perhaps the speech's difficulty, even sharpness, about what the Protector was – ruler or only chief commander – sprang from the ambiguity of his symbolic, if not literal, place in 1653–4. Mervyn James writes of the social body that 'the persisting tensions between whole and differentiation meant that the process of incorporation into the social body needed to be continually reaffirmed, and the body continually recreated'.[30] The problem of the English Civil War and its aftermath had made visible the metaphors by which such recreation of the social body worked, such as that of the 'body politic'. The recorder addresses this epistemological crisis by an assertion of ancient metaphor underlined by ancient authority: but one can immediately imagine a royalist response to the deployment of the organic metaphor alongside *salus populi*, and after the regicide.

Although the Goldsmiths' records indicate that three barges were prepared for the mayor's journey in 1653, lord mayor's shows resumed after Cromwell became Lord Protector. It is possible that, just as with drama, the Protectorate inaugurated the possibility of a return to the old customs.[31] We know that Davenant's entertainments were permitted by Cromwell: did the Protector have an equally active hand in setting in train the shows? Some evidence is supplied by the prefaces to the first three pamphlets commemorating the shows which repeatedly link themselves with Roman civil government. The introduction to the first Protectorate show, Edmund Gayton's *Charity Triumphant* (for Dethicke, 1655) – like Davenant's *First Days Entertainment* – addresses the relationship between its generic status and politics:

My Lord
View the Roman State under which Government soever you please, whether in the beginnings, under many happy Kings, or in its change from Monarchy to Democracy, or in its little resurrection to Aristocracy . . . you shall alwaies find every Age, and sort of Govenours, adorning and exemplifying their several Authorities by Anniversary Shewes and Pomps to the People, who are naturally pleas'd with such Gleams and Irradiations of their Superiors, and gaines at once Honour to the Magistrate and effects content to the People.[32]

Gayton's appeal on behalf of shows combines populist and ethical grounds, suggesting that shows and spectacles are suitable to all forms of government. His other publications from the 1650s were satirical, and the rationale of shows furnished by the introduction might be ironic. This describes the 'metropolis' as mediating Commons and national government as the 'publike Banquet, whereunto you invite the Commons of the City'. Gayton sees the gap in the shows as 'extinguishing those *Civic Rights*, and suppressing the Genius of our Metropolis' and describes their renewal as 'this return of the City-Gallantry'. The 'Civic Rights' have a dual aspect and a dual public; the visual, 'Scenicall Contrivement and Pageant Bravery is but an *Ephemeral* or *Diurnall* birth and issue of one day', whereas the poetry lasts on and, 'by this Paperwork [gives] a procession to your Nobleness and Piety beyond the *Demeans* of *Cheapside*' (p. 5). Thus, like other drama of the 1650s the civic show is both theatre and print event; spectacle and print collude to register the centrality of the City and its trading relations – and implicitly its national political power. Gayton's poem glorifying the Mercers' Company continues this dual emphasis on the local, spatial celebration of the City and the claim to a wider audience and significance through print.

The records of the shows use the vocabulary of Roman entertainments to enhance the importance of the City and to suggest historical precedent. The pageant for Vyner in 1656, written by I.B., continues the Roman comparison, London 'being divided into Wards: and secondly, having Sherriffs instead of Consuls, and an assembly of Senators or Aldermen'.[33] He makes explicit the symbolic place of the City and the importance of spectacle in maintaining the City's claim to epitomise the nation as a whole:

It was a comely sight to see all the Companies striving to set forth and brighten the glory of the day. For what Infamy could there have been greater, then now to be morose, sullen, and niggardly, when all eares are listening for no news but those of Feasts and Triumphs . . . ? when all the Nation seems to be drawn together, and to be Epitomiz'd within the Walls of her Metropolis. (p. 9)

The record of this small pageant also suggests the potential of the performed shows to be interpreted by spectators in terms of civic and national politics. The procession began at the north-eastern edge of the City, Cripplegate Ground, with men 'exercising arms'. These men 'march'd in a military order' to the lord mayor's house and thence to 'three Crane wharf'. Here the party split in two with the red soldiers in one set of barges and those under the sign of green 'wafting to the other side of the water' before embarking on a water-fight all the way to Westminster, while a third body with 'Pikes and Musquets' produced 'Thundering Ecchoes' of their fight from Barnard's Castle. On arrival at Whitehall on the way to Westminster they 'saluted the Lord Protector and his Councell, with severall peales of shott, which the Lord Protector answered with signal testimonies of grace and courtesie' (B1v). Most significant, while the Lord Mayor was taking his oath the waterfight began again: both parties began a sharp incounter one with another, which continuing a short space, the green colours sounded a parley; which being accepted, both parties suddenly became friends (p. 11). The combined iconography of militarism and trade was used repeatedly in the shows of the 1650s. Nevertheless, the symbolism of green versus red, especially when combined with the military show emanating from Barnard's Castle, would remind spectators of the recent national wars.

The return procession, from Barnard's Castle to Cheapside and the Guildhall, shifted the emphasis to the relationship between the guild and the nation and City. It was marked by Mr Jerman's designs for pageants representing the Skinners' Company and emphasising the role of the City authorities in making order and preserving trade. The civic environment contained islands of strangeness, as we find in the 'Speech from off the Wildernesse at Soper-Lane End' whose 'wild' presence in the City served to underline the productive presence of trade:

> Order, saith *Plato*, is the Soul of things,
> And from that Fountain every good Art springs;
> Beasts become tame and usefull, Man would be,
> More fierce then they, did not Authority
> Awe his unruly Actions   (p. 14)

Like pre-war shows, Protectorate pageants exist as both ephemeral spectacle and as printed records. The show, and particularly the record, strove significantly to articulate a harmonious version of the sometimes vexed relations between national government, City authorities and merchant and trade interests in the guild. They were ritual moments, but of mediation not simply celebration. Thus, in 1657 in *Londons Triumph*, Tatham, too, made an attempt to provide an overall context for the presentation of civic pageants under the Protectorate government by referring to Rome:[34]

Erasmus, (speaking of the Romane Magistrates) saies, They were grave in their Conversation severe in their Judgement, and constant in their purpose. They were either Elected out of the Elder, Richer and Wiser sort, called *Patricci*, sometimes *Patroni* (as Patrons and Fathers assisting the Commonwealth in their Affairs). Or out of the Commonalty; the one called *Magistrates Plebii*, having relation in their addresses to the Patricii, as the Common Council may have to your Lordship. (A3r)

Although this draws on relatively typical terms for the valorisation of civic authority it is Tatham's only attempt in the Protectorate period to delineate overtly a new, national chain of authority into which the post-monarchical lord mayors' shows could fit. Tatham here describes a classical analogue for the lord mayor and relates the show to this ideal. The evidence suggests that the reformation of the civic shows in a post-monarchical era led to a reformulated iconography of civic pride which was not tied to the king as ruler but which still drew on the interwoven nature of 'people', 'nation', 'metropolis', 'trade', 'citizen' and 'merchant'. This absence of a chain of specifically regal authority linking the City to the nation in the iconography of the entertainment marks Tatham's shows of the 1650s, although in other ways they reiterate pre-war tropes. Spectacle and the disseminated pamphlets played different, though linked, parts in this reconceptualisation.

For example, the role of the City in generating trade and supporting the nation is central to the shows as in 1657 when a 'pilgrim' emphasises the wealth of the City and its international trade relations:

> Grand City; Thou Minerva, Nursery
> To Arms, Fames Garden Military.
> The Merchants Treasure, and their safety too,
> What parts in all the World but trade with you?
> Europe, wherein you seated are, doth fill
> Your lapp with choice varieties: the ill-
> Complexion'd Affrican unto your Breast
> Poures forth his Spicie Treasure; and the rest
> Crown you with Gold and Onix stones; Thus they
> (As once to Rome) now to you tribute pay.[35]

In a movement in some ways reminiscent of Davenant's (and Flecknoe's) use of colonial setting to resolve the crisis of nation, this show does not link up the idea of the colony and trade with the king as centre. Trade is here a civic virtue, continuing the theme of the great metropolis civic, classical, military and European.

The Clothworkers' show in 1658 again emphasises specifically civic, even Calvinist, virtues. It is presented by Industry and Honour to the new mayor, Sir John Ireton. Industry is dressed in grey citizen garb but this is overlaid with a mixture of citizen and guild iconography: 'clothed in Grey, on her head a Kirchief, in one hand she bears a Card or Shears, in the other a Scepter; on the top of which Scepter, is an open hand, and in the midst of it an Eye; and at the end of the Scepter, two small Wings'.[36] The code of honour in both these pageants emphasises *civic* virtue, operating without the iconography of royal power anterior to the City: the sceptre becomes appropriated to an entirely civic iconography. Honour, like Industry, becomes a civic virtue; 'a Man with a grave

Aspect, his Brows encircled with Palm, a chain of Gold about his Neck, and Bracelets of Gold about his Wrests; his Garments of Purple colour'd Sattin' (p. 11). Honour and Industry, allied to other virtues, symbolically conquer vice; and the purple, like the sceptre, is here liberated from a specifically monarchist system of value.

Thus, these pageants are intent on reconstructing the civic show as part of the symbolic reorganisation of the idea of the English Protectorate. They move decisively away from royalist tropes, but uncertainty about how to conceptualise the new order may be signalled in some features of the shows, for instance, the absence of what Sheila Williams calls 'private feud and the occasional heightening of feeling' in the writing as well as a significant attention to detail and hierarchy; it was I.B.'s show which first carried the order of the procession.[37] Their printed status seems to have been important.[38] However, as in Flecknoe's *Oceanus* the pageants of the Protectorate are attempting to find a celebratory language for the virtues of the new commonwealth and this involved an emphasis on both the revival of industry after the war and on England, epitomised in London, as a magnet acquiring resources from all over the world.

The desires of the City government and the power of the City and its shows in conceptualising the nation were dramatised in the political and civic wrangling around Tatham's last show before the Restoration. Preparations for Tatham's 1658 show, after Cromwell's death, are recorded only with an order for a barge and 'eight sufficient able men to carry the Master, the Warden and the rest of the gentlemen', but the records of preparations for the 1659 show indicate the government's fear of civic violence and their need to conciliate.[39] By September 1659 parliament and army were virtually incapable of co-ordinated action. This came to a crisis over a petition from John Lambert's regiment, found by the intemperate Arthur Haselrig and read to the House.[40] This precipitated an attempted parliamentary coup, and a successful counter-coup by the army. The MPs were expelled on 13 October and news of this reached General Monck in Scotland on 17 October. On 25 October the Council of State was to be formally replaced by the Committee of Safety, and Monck began moving down the country with his army. Lambert was sent to meet him, leaving behind a humiliated Fleetwood.

In the midst of these events the City, now apparently hostile to

the Rump, was attempting to prepare its show, and these preparations indicate the delicate balance of Fleetwood's control of
London in October 1659. On 13 October, the morning of the
coup and counter-coup by the army, when Lambert's soldiers sur-
rounded the House to prevent MPs entering, some MPs appealed
to the Common Council for aid, but they refused: parliament's
gates were locked once more. In the records of the 'Orders of the
Court of Assistants' for the same morning we find the court
decided to consult the lord mayor and aldermen 'whether it will
bee seasonable and Convenient for this Company to proceed in
their intended p^{r}pracon of Pagete and other Publique Showes in
Hand for the Lord Majors Day'.[41] On 18 October the wardens
reported that the aldermen 'would not prescribe the Company
what to doe therein', but 'In sume did seeme to give incouragment
to ye Compa proceedings in their intended Corse'.[42] So they went
ahead. The Council of Officers replaced the Council of State with
the Committee of Safety. On 18 October Fleetwood became com-
mander-in-chief and Lambert major-general. On 26 October the
Committee of Safety was officially formed and on 28 October they
decided to send a force to meet General Monck.

On 27 October – very close to the day of the show – the wardens
reported that other people besides themselves and the aldermen
were concerned about tumults:

This day Mr Wardens reported to the Co^{rt} that the Lord Majo^r had
acquainted then wth some intimacon from the Lord ffleetwood and
Councell of Officers to hand the Publiq Show on the Lord Majo^{rs} day forborne in regard of the pn^t [present] troubles and Conco^{r}se of People
occassioned thereby wch might bee of dangerous Consequence That
thereupon they had repaired to the Co^{rt} of Aldrn to Signifie the great
Charge already expended by the Company and the forwardnes of their
p^{r}paracons against the day and the expectacons of the people upon the
rumor of their intended triumphs and desired the further Advice and
Judgem^t of that Co^{rt} what would be fitt for this Company to do therein
That the Co^{ty} of Aldren had noiated a Select number of Aldren and wth
them Mr Wardens . . . had reco^{r}se to the Lord ffleetwood and Councell
that the Lord ffleetwood did seeme to disowne the privitie or knowledge
of any such intimacon and upon the reasons given to the Councell they
were left to their own libertie to proceed in their intended Co^{r}se of a
Show wth some Caution of Carefulnesse.[43]

Even though the company and City had themselves been consid-
ering abandoning the show they now resisted pressure from

Fleetwood to do so, on the grounds that it was too late to cancel. The large deputation from the City which led to Fleetwood's denial of his 'intimation' suggests strongly that the Committee of Safety preferred to back down and allow the show to go ahead, risking rioting and possibly worse, rather than have the City openly flout their instructions, which seems from this document the probable outcome of a prohibition so close to the show. This incident gives a remarkable, though ephemeral, insight into the political negotiations which took place around the symbolic celebration of the City customs and the City's repeated assumption of a pivotal role in politics through their proximity to the seat of government. Fleetwood's use of 'intimation' to the lord mayor may be a clue to the way the lord mayors' shows started again.

The City had changed greatly since the shows stopped in 1640. In the next few months it was to change radically again as Monck's soldiers, unwillingly, razed its defences. Paradoxically, one observer records this as the occasion of the *rapprochement* between the citizens and the army – problematic since the late 1640s – which facilitated the return of Charles II. Destroying the City's defences on parliament's orders, the soldiers:

did give obedience to their Orders, and beat down the Gates and Percullices; but in such a manner, and with such discourse, that the Citizens were scarce displeased with them. . . At *Newgate*, the Officer that commanded when the Gates broke in pieces, took some small parcels of Wood, and gave all his Soldiers for the Medals that the Parliament promised them.[44]

Words, spectacle and symbol again combine to reconfigure the place of the City in political life. The stage was set for Monck's dinner at the Guildhall and his insistence on a free parliament. Indeed, such events as the officer's ironic gesture and Fleetwood's loss of control may suggest a way in which Tatham's scurrilous political satire *The Rump* came to the stage in 1659. However, by the next year another revolution in government had taken place and Tatham was writing shows in a kingdom.

It is at this point that Tatham's old friend, Jordan, once again comes into view. They still knew each other: indeed, some evidence of the theatrical activity of 1659 suggests that the group from the 1630s remained in some contact. Jordan's insistently royalist writing contrasts with Tatham's pragmatic career since their first association before the Civil War. In his compilation of work produced during and after the Civil War, *Wit in a Wildernesse*, Jordan printed a poem to Tatham:

> The Sun hath twenty Summers strew'd the earth
> With flowers, since our Acquaintance first took birth
> It was a season when our Drums and Flutes
> Did give precedency to *Love* and *Lutes*:
> When men of Piety were so restrain'd,
> They durst not think a K. could be Arraign'd:
> Plays were in fashion too, they did not fear,
> To have their plots brought to the Theater . . .[45]

The final jibe at Hewison – 'great Colonels did use / To wear blew Frocks, and cobble Porters shoes' – might suggest 1659–60 as a date of composition. Unlike anything we have from Tatham, this volume enables us to trace Jordan's associations during the Protectorate when he seems to have had patrons amongst the conservative City merchants – such as William Christmas – and others living in Hackney.[46] These mercantile connections may have provided the context for *Fancy's Festivals*, 'Cupid His Coronation' and other performances; moreover, it might have been a formalisation of these connections that led to Jordan being employed to write for guild entertainments in the period between Monck's demolition of the City gates and the return of the king in May 1660. These events are recorded in Jordan's *A Royal Arbor of Loyal Poesie* (1660), which implicitly traces the transformation of the ideological, material and social conditions of theatre in the short space of 1659 to 1660. It includes a highly ambivalent poem allegedly spoken *to* Monck when he dined at 'Skinners-Hall' on Wednesday 4 April 1660:

> I have with wary eyes observ'd your steps,
> Your Stands, your Turns, your Pauses and your Leaps,
> And finde, however you may mask your brow,
> You are a States-man, and ambitious too:
> A right self-ended Person, for t'be known,
> Yours and the Publick Safety are all one;
> You are ambitious to be *good*, that feat
> Our Statesmen mist, for they were to be *greatest*:
> But yet (as *Solomon* made the choice which
> Commanded all) Wisdom will make you rich,
> And great, and glorious; and these shall last
> As long as time, and after time is past:
>   . . .

My Lord, I scorn to flatter, I'le be true t'ye,
All the good Deeds y'have done, are but your Duty.[47]

The 'turn' in the implication of 'ambitious' at 'ambitious to be *good*' is hardly convincing, particularly as good and great – or at least rich – are coincident. Indeed, the poem addresses the ambivalence of Monck's position with a sharpness absent in many other contemporary poems.

Nevertheless, on 9 April Jordan provided a more elaborate entertainment at Goldsmiths' Hall, using the rebellious 'Massianello, *Fisherman of Naples*' – as in *The Rebellion of Naples* – to thematise the 'rebellion' and Cromwell; Massianello claims, 'I was as great as wickedness could make me' (B4r). Rather than being the property of great houses and royalist closet performance this drama from the 1650s had a London mercantile context and patrons.

In the Skinners' Hall speech Jordan ends with a call for the return of the king and full royal symbolism: '''Tis yet but twilight, could we see the sun / . . . the work were done.' The return of the king reactivated a national symbolism in which civic authority is once more monarchically validated. At first, indeed, Charles II provided what Clifford Geertz calls the 'charisma' of a king by re-uniting 'a governing elite and a set of symbolic forms expressing the fact that it is in truth governing'.[48] The Restoration brought with it a new version of the recurrent difficulties of Tatham's career, in terms of the relation between genre, centre and audience. But at first Charles's return gave him a new vocabulary. The early pageants in 1660 employ a general address to the king on behalf of a loyal but sorry kingdom which is, simultaneously, celebrating the king's return. As Nicholas José suggests, the *moment* of the Restoration transformed Tatham's shows, providing Tatham's work with both the apparently unified audience that Rochester saw 'fencing' the king's route to London, and with a newly transparent royal iconography and the kind of closure made available by the presence of the king.[49] However, the pageants and entries of 1662 and 1663 present a more complicated picture of the post-Restoration relationship between City shows and the new order.

On 29 May 1660 Charles II went from the City to Whitehall in a procession which mingled City and court, the Dukes of York and Gloucester coming directly in front of the lord mayor (the most important last).[50] The new regime had symbolically united with the City which had been a significant force in Charles I's demise. On Thursday 5 July, Charles was entertained by *London's Glory: Represented by Time, Truth and Fame*, a 'triumph' which closely and probably consciously echoes the entries of the 1620s and 1630s.[51] Tatham describes himself as the 'humblest' of the mayor's servants, points out that he did the show in 1659 and commends the popular new mayor, Thomas Aleyn, on the issue of loyalty, saying, 'As your Loyalty hath been great, your Joy cannot be little' (A1v). The pageant addresses the issue of the Restoration. Time, for example, kneels and 'on his bended knee your Pardon Craves / Having been made a Property to Slaves' (p. 1). Tatham addresses the king in naturalised absolutist terms:

> TIME: Such is Vertual Fervour of your Beams,
>   That not Obliquely but directly Streams
>   Upon your Subjects; so the Glorious Sun
>   Gives growth to th'infant Plants he smiles upon.   (p. 1)

The insistence on clarity is of particular interest in relation to the anxiety about genre and audience in Tatham's later shows. The clear presence of Charles II acts as a momentary guarantee that meaning is anchored by a king's presence in the land. The meaning of Tatham's civic pageantry ceases to be obscure or oblique for the moment of the Restoration; the audience, apart from the king, is united for a moment in loyalty, abjection and thankfulness.

The use of Time and Truth as symbolic figures also echoes prewar pageants, but the unity between king and people invoked here seems to have had the ephemeral quality of collective euphoria. In the lord mayor's show of the same year, some months later, the political and ideological co-ordinates of the celebratory theatrical performance seem to have re-emerged as potentially problematic. Although the king functions to relate City to nation – indeed, the apparent identification of the City with the king, even the predominance of royal iconography, can be found in the title *The Royal Oake* – anxieties appear about the clarity and transmission of meaning. The printed record takes up an explanatory position. Annotations appear explaining the historical derivation and significance of various passages. Surprisingly, Tatham explains the phrase 'I Oceanus . . . *am come to Grace my Daughter, Silver* Thames, / *So much admir'd and lov'd by Royall* James' (p. 6), explaining that

King James was *'a great lover of this river'*. This superfluity of annotation is more than fashion: it is an attempt to fix detail and
meaning. The problems the text faces are strangely familiar from
the 1650s: how is it to mythologise the new king, and to whom is
this mythologisation to be presented. Such apparatus occurs in
other texts of the Civil War period which seek to stabilise and make
evident the 'true' meaning – in political terms – of the words and
situations. Examples are found in Christopher Wase's attentive
glossing of the Greek plays he translated, and Davenant's libretto
'explaining' *The Cruelty of the Spaniards in Peru*. The printed text is
being used to explain the show which, it seems, is perceived as
inadquate, or not sufficiently tied to accepted systems of meaning.

However, this is a post-Restoration text and might be expected
to echo the earlier *London's Glory* in a new-found ease of meaning
under Charles II. One marginal note would be slender evidence
of 'anxiety', but this introduction of printed marginalia is greatly
elaborated in *Aqua Triumphalis* (1662), when the City of London
entertains the newly married king and queen upon the river.
Tatham begins by apologising for the entertainment because of
the 'shortnesse of time allowed me, and the uncertainty of their
Majesties Arrivall' (p. 2).[52] The performance, which reiterates the
link between London and colonial trade, links 'Loyalty' to the
citizen and operates with full-blown monarchical symbolism. The
uncertainty appears to be about the audience of the piece. It is
neither certainly a citizens' celebration nor is it for the benefit of
the royal couple – an entertainment which would be closer, generically and therefore iconographically, to the masque. Thus at two
junctures the printed programme produces 'Explanations' of
what is happening – in case the show and the words are not
enough, in themselves, to make an interpretation possible. How
far are civic virtues contiguous with monarchical values and which
set of iconographic codes should be paramount?

One problem was that as a show the civic symbolism had
recourse to conceptions of the body politic which were archaic. As
Joanne Altieri notes, Tatham's shows use pre-war codes and
devices which seemed outdated in 1660. In the 1650s he had
adapted old-style shows to a moment when the nation could only
be ambiguously symbolised; the return of the monarch perhaps
exposed the stylistic compromises. The archaism is a sign of the
crisis in meaning in these entertainments (we remember that

court masques have lapsed). However, in referring back to the old
court poets in what was to be his last show, *London's Triumphs*
(1664), Tatham makes explicit 'the interconnection of business
and court' in close co-operation but using appropriately distinguished poetic modes:[53]

> We hope your Majesty will not suppose
> You're with your Johnson or your Inigoes;
> And though you make a court, y'are in the City,
> Whose vien is to be humble, though not witty.[54]

This is indeed a simplistic and abject expression of City–court relations, but it presents a clearly defined aesthetic and hierarchical
differentiation of City from court. The relations indicated here are
distinct from the implied unity of audience and understanding of
the earliest post-Restoration entertainments by Tatham, which we
have traced dissolving and fracturing quite rapidly after 1660. The
particularity of *civic* symbolism – appropriate to a City entertainment – is made explicit as is the relation of a *City* entertainment to
the king. This distinction attempts to clarify the status of the City
while confirming its links with the monarch. Drama was caught
once again in the irresoluble issues of the politics of genre and
audience.[55] The following year brought the plague, and the next
show was by Jordan, in 1671.

Tatham's pageants certainly appear uncertain of their royalist
symbolism when they are compared with a contrasting celebration
of Charles II's return memorialised in two editions, one lavishly
illustrated. The day before the coronation, on 22 August, Charles
II had been entertained in the City in an entertainment written by
John Ogilby whose records, augmented in 1662, included a
cartoon of the order of the procession and pictures of four triumphal arches.[56] It also had swathes of annotation identifying the
performance with classical spectacle, and with imperial iconography. Interestingly, two figures with popular antecedents found
their way into the symbolism. The first was a figure of rebellion as
a woman, familiar from anti-parliamentarian polemic. Secondly,
we find the popular image of the Rump on a painting over one of
the triumphal arches:

the King, mounted in calm Motion, Usurpation flying before him, a
Figure with many ill-favoured Heads, some bigger, some lesser, and one
particularly shooting out of his Shoulder, like Cromwell's; Another Head

upon his Rump, or Tayl; Two Harpies with a Crown, chased by an Angel; Hells Jaws opening. (p. 28)

Such an image does indeed seem like a cruel answer to the recorder's use of the idea of the social body in 1653. The prominence of an image of such extraordinary violence, in the very City which, in some ways, belonged to parliament in the early 1640s, implies a significant lapse of memory. It is indeed the king's show in the City, with the text by the king's poet. Tatham, who had been involved in formulating the City as a new Rome in the 1650s, was now preparing entertainments for a City which had, it seems, lost all memory of its own history as if, indeed, it had been a 'slave'.

There is supporting evidence for the argument that 1660, although it brought a moment of clarity in the relation of Tatham's dramatic representations to politics, also soon afterwards brought renewed ideological complications. This is found in Tatham's use of a genre that was to become dominant on the Restoration stage, his topical comedy *The Rump*, performed in 1659.[57] 'Loyalty' here is an assumed certainty between text and audience – in *The Rump* Tatham sees himself speaking for and to a momentarily self-elected 'loyal party'. Never before and never again could this body be so clearly identified. But the significance of this 'loyalty' is predicated on the absence from the nation of the king to whom this fealty is owed. The return of that king was likely, almost certain, but not yet a historical fact – anticipation, as José points out, lent the political moment the possibility of using the king as a national fantasy. Notably it was this play which that intricate comic plotter Aphra Behn borrowed for one of her own comedies rereading the last days of non-monarchical government.[58]

Tatham's ability to stage such drama was provided by the collapse of the government he was attacking. Performed at a moment when London was awash with political polemic and scurrilous attacks on the Rump, *The Rump* was produced under quite different circumstances from the fractured multiplicities of *The Distracted State*, and forms part of a large body of anti-Rump satire and polemic. It takes actual living figures as its dramatis personae – the names lightly disguised in 1659 but not at all in 1660 when it continued to be staged and was printed in a second edition. It dramatises the events in London leading up to the bonfires and roastings of the Rump just after Monck arrived in London on 11

February 1660. Something which links this play to the plays of Tatham's associates in the 1650s, such as *The Rebellion*, and which also connects it to his career as a maker of City entertainments is the way in which the play concentrates on London. The play does not offer an answer to the often-asked question of whether it is 'royalist' or 'republican,' and – as Tim Harris notes – any understanding of 1659 needs to take into account the many different expectations of the Restoration held by different sections of the populace. *The Rump* is set before the Restoration became a clear issue and manages to mobilise both the radical potential of City resistance and its conservative implications in the way that it represents the revolt and petitions of the apprentices – dramatic events which both have basis in historical events.[59] The apprentices cry out for a 'Free Parliament' and the end of the corrupt Committee of Safety. At the same time as the play exploits the radical potential of the City's anger it reinvokes the stabilising possibility of monarchy in the apprentices' shouts of 'Viva le roy' (IV.iii, p. 42).

1671: CODA

Tatham provides an example of the career of a playwright under the strictures against theatre from 1642 to 1660: pro-Caroline, pro-Stuart, pro-City, possibly Catholic, Tatham nevertheless worked under the Protectorate. He appears to have lacked the personal connections which helped Davenant. Some might say he was also without talent. However, his career demonstrates that ideas of Protectorate drama as essentially royalist cannot work, and gives an example of a sequence of texts in different genres reacting to changing political imperatives. *The Distracted State* indicates that generic doubleness and difficulty of allegorical interpretation are features of Civil War drama as well as the product of aesthetic sophistication (as they are more usually regarded). During the years in which he was working, both drama and pageants were caught up in rapidly changing imperatives and interdictions. The pageants were part of the Protectorate reconfiguring of a symbolic mediation of national government, merchant and City, a matrix within which the City was attempting to maintain a central place. The genres in which he was writing constantly raised issues about politics – usually, too, the changing politics of the regulation of drama. This seems to mark the printed texts that accompanied and substantiated the performances in their gaps, fractures, marginalia, footnotes.

A final irony is the fact that the 1663 lord mayor's show is licensed by Roger l'Estrange, inaugurating a whole new set of imperatives and repressions. In 1664, Tatham disappears and so do the lord mayors' shows, not to reappear until 1671 when the first of Jordan's Restoration shows, *London's Resurrection*, was performed. *London's Resurrection* incorporated 'drolls' first printed in 1661 and which seem very like the dialogues of the Civil War. And Jordan's drolls actually dramatise the Civil War – in *London's Resurrection*, 'A Country-man, A Citizen and *Sedition* an old Instrument of *Oliver's* Faction' talk politics. Though here, of course, Citizen and Country-man are free of the taint of sedition; the third figure, 'Oliver Faction', who corrupts idle apprentices with political stratagems, is very clearly an outsider to the symbolic systems aimed to incorporate court, country, City – at least for the duration of the show.[60]

CHAPTER 8

True and loyal? Politics and genre in Civil War and Protectorate tragicomedy

READING TRAGICOMEDY

Tragicomic genres from the 1650s can be seen as reworking Caroline models, and such generic familiarity has led critics to understand them as consisting dominantly of royalist plays by royalists. Tragicomedy was, indeed, like tragedy, invoked by contemporaries as a pattern for events: texts using the title or genre of tragicomedy play on that sense and work to reproduce feelings about it in their audience. Yet the tragicomedies of the 1650s present not solely what in Restoration tragicomedy Nancy Klein Maguire describes as an 'analysis of the psychic forces which impelled the mid-century generation of Royalists', though that is part of what they do. Nor, taken as a short period, do they demonstrate the 'generic evolution' Laura Brown discusses. Rather, the form in the 1650s offered writers a complex discursive space for debate within inevitably compromised royalisms against the unresolved context of the Commonwealth and Protectorate.[1]

In the 1650s tragicomedy (loosely defined) implied the text's use of a shape of crisis followed by a restoration, combined with self-conscious applicability to contemporary events leading to an interpretation of history through literary structures and vice versa.[2] As a genre, tragicomedy invites mixed responses from the spectator or reader.[3] However, to see such texts as solely symptomatic of a 'royalist' state of mind would naturalise the form to a problematic degree; it is as sophisticated and critical as the author and audience, certainly as complex as other dramatic genres from the 1650s. One observer commented, 'we seem to ore'act to some wel contrived Romance', and this felt applicability in the term and shape of tragicomedy is indicated by the way many of the popular political dramas call themselves tragicomedies, including *The*

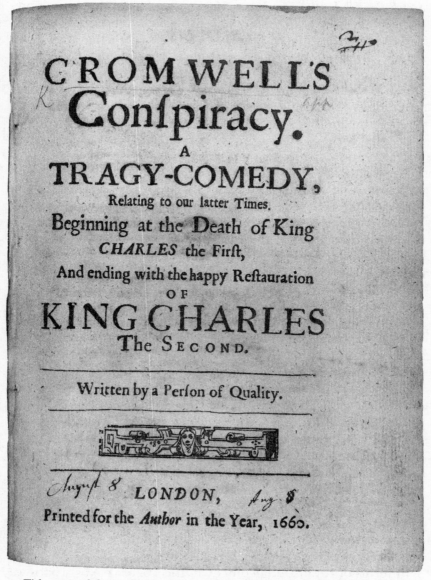

3 Title-page of *Cromwell's Conspiracy. A Tragy-Comedy* (August 1660), indicating the temporal resonances of the genre.

Scotch Politick Presbyter and *New-Market Fayre.*[4] That the term 'tragi-comedy' indicated both genre and continued reference to politics is shown by the title of Francis Osborne's *The True Tragicomedy Formerly Acted at Court* (c.1655) where 'tragicomedy' simultane-ously implies a political critique of contemporary events and genre.[5] Thus, tragicomedies from the 1650s blend idealised repre-sentations of kingship with acute judgements on contemporary politics; the 'loyal' reshaping of history into a tragicomic structure is coupled with a comic or ironic apprehension of contemporary politics – one which is, in Maguire's terms, 'pragmatic'.

Tragicomedies from the 1640s to the mid-1660s rework a famil-iar narrative of crisis to 'restoration', only these narratives are in a strikingly different relationship to actual time if produced in 1651, 1660 or 1665. With temporal and political changes came shifts in the way central issues were represented. These included: the rela-tionship between 'truth' and 'loyalty', the relationship (or lack of it) between 'power' and 'authority', and the linked use of time (especially the 'moment of restoration' – *the* tragicomic moment) and space, especially the catalytic space of pastoral.

The temporal and generic focus of tragicomedy on a moment of 'restoration' meant that it offered a certain amount of discursive and political freedom to work out the meanings of truth, loyalty, royalism and honour. Indeed tragicomedy, moulded around the idea of restoration and, therefore, with a time-frame which always reached towards that definitional instant, produced freedoms within its very constraints. The insistence on the restorative poten-tial of time permitted tragicomedy in the 1650s to become a space for negotiation within royalism and with other, more cynical, pol-itics. *Cromwell's Conspiracy. A Tragy-Comedy* (1660), rewriting *The Famous Tragedie of Charles I*, makes explicit the linking of tragicomic and historical–political time when its title-page refers to '*Cromwell's Conspiracy. A Tragy-Comedy*, Relating to our latter Times. Beginning at the Death of King Charles the First, And ending with the happy Restauration of King Charles the Second'.[6]

In terms of royalist tragicomedy in the 1640s, 1650s, 1660s we might ask how these plays both addressed contemporary events and presented themselves as honourable and loyal to the particu-lar imagined moment of resolution or restoration around which they shaped themselves. At each of the moments investigated here – the crisis after the king's capture and the 1650s; the late

Protectorate and Restoration, and, briefly, the period after the Restoration – obviously, royalists might have widely differing views of the nature and possibilities of government. More importantly, events such as the capture of the king, his death, the emergence of the Protectorate and the shock of the Restoration itself reshaped, whether violently or subtly, the views of contemporaries and the aspirations and fantasies of those using this genre. Indeed, produced at the deeply problematic moment of the 1650s, how royalist were they and in what terms?

TRAGICOMEDY, PASTORAL AND ROYALIST FANTASY 1647–1658

> *Morpheus* (thou Turn-key to all humane sence)
> Unlock my braine, that I may flie from hence,
> Out of this Cage of sleep, let me not lie
> And drown my senses in stupidity.
> My thoughts surprise my thoughts, I cannot rest,
> I have a *Civill Warre* within my brest . . .[7]

John Quarles's lyric is not unusual in responding to the closing events of the second Civil War (Charles's imprisonment and the regicide) as the beginning of a bad dream. But if the 'truth' – or immediate situation – of the 1650s was a bad dream then the 'loyalty' which imagined a restoration of Stuart power was also a projective fantasy. The extent to which the regicide dramatised the dissociation of political power from the king disturbed even supporters of the regicide. As earlier chapters argued, a new configuration of ethics and aesthetics was required to deal with this split and the tragicomedies and pastoral tragicomedies of the 1650s accordingly use the frames of pastoral, dream and enchantment ending with awakening and return.

Tragicomedy was particularly important to royalist writers after the king's capture, when the possibility of a return of the old ways began to recede. In a topical royalist tragicomedy after 1649, if the tragic event is the regicide then the tragicomic dénouement must involve a return of ousted monarchy, or an event which readers could see as standing for that. The actual return of the monarch seemed less and less likely during the 1650s when royalists might feel with Sir Edward Dering that the transformation of Caroline England into post-war England made the country 'the Stage /

Both of a Golden, and an Iron Age'.[8] The 'golden age' of monarchy seemed distant indeed.

With obvious resonances for an 'iron age', tragicomedy was self-consciously assumed as part of the late Civil War and post-regicidal aesthetic claims of the new, powerless, royalism. William Cartwright's pre-war tragicomedies were posthumously published as *Comedies, Tragicomedies, With Other Poems* (1651) with a frontispiece connecting Cartwright with 'right'. Its fifty-four commendatory verses demonstrate the claimed status of poetry, 'wit' as royal and loyal by those who regarded themselves as loyal followers of the Stuarts.[9] Cartwright's own status as a royalist hero was underwritten by the fact that he died of camp fever at Oxford in 1643 instead of living on into the compromises of the 1650s and 'his' volume, like the 1647 Beaumont and Fletcher folio, self-consciously shaped 'loyal' cultural politics in the 1650s. Cartwright's pre-war tragicomedies *The Royal Slave* and *The Lady Errant* indicate that tragicomedy, seen retrospectively as a Caroline and now 'loyal' royalist genre, played a part in expressing the mythic and symbolic aspects of post-Civil War royalist culture. In these circumstances tragicomedy inscribed both a continuation of loyalty and a pattern which suggested the possibility of restoration. As Edward Sherburne wrote in his commendatory verse to Cartwright's volume:

> How subject to new Tumults is this Age!
> With *War* lesse vex'd now than *Poetick Rage*!
> Were not State-Levellers enough! that yet
> We must be plagued with Levellers of Wit?
> *Delvers* in Poetry? That only skill
> To make Parnassus a St George's Hill.[10]

In transposing to poetry the lost battles of the Civil War and reworking the struggles of Levellers and Diggers as aesthetic battle the poem annexes Cartwright's plays to a defence of hierarchised society against new men, new ideas, and *salus populi* politics.[11] For Sherburne, the survival of 'wit' underwrites the moral superiority of aristocrats.

Assertions of loyalty, figured as future closure, could only be part of a response to the complex situation after the fall of the Stuarts. As Richard Tuck points out, English political theorists in the mid-seventeenth century sought a new, urgently needed, terminology as traditional political discourses no longer gave a sufficient account of political circumstances.[12] Like political discourse, tragi-comic plays and pastoral entertainments were attempting to artic-ulate questions of the relationship between power and right – actual circumstances versus what ought to be. In the late sixteenth century a theorist known only as T.B. formulated a distinction between power and authority, asserting that authority was 'a certain reverend impression in the minde of Subjectes . . . touch-ing the Prince's virtue and government', and power that 'without which no Prince can either defende his owne or take from others . . . Power or strengthe is attayned unto theis five wayes vis: *Money, Armes, Counsell, Frendes* and *Fortune.*' Although this text is much earlier, it puts succinctly the relationship between the 'present occasions' of 1650s tragicomedy (in which the king had no power) and the ideal kingly authority. The central issue for the tragi-comedies which deal with political issues in the 1640s and 1650s is the same as that for the political theorists – who can declare the person wielding supreme power to be a usurper, and, can a king have authority but no power?

Using this distinction, Tuck argues convincingly that a new kind of royalism emerged after the regicide in 1649: one which acknowledged the sharp distinction between authority and power. The 'loyal' status of the tragicomic genre can be seen to be qual-ified by the author's (and implicitly readers') understanding of this split. This was the case even before the regicide. Richard Fanshawe's translation of Guarini's *The Faithfull Shepherd* returns to the Caroline Arcadia, if not to address these issues surrounding the division of power and authority, then to find a way round them. It proposes a split between coercive power and authority that would become familiar in the 1650s: 'Man's freedom is Heav'ns gift, which doth not take / Us at our word when forced vows we make' (1.i, p. 69). Moreover, although it was published in 1648, it focusses on young Charles Stuart – not Charles I – in a fantasised reunion of power and authority, figured as marriage.

Fanshawe's translation of *Il Pastor Fido* (1647, 1648) uses pas-toral to figure the ethical valency of royalist political claims. It ends, 'True joy is a thing / That springs from Vertue after suffer-ing.'[13] Directed by hints from the text's dedication to the Prince of Wales, an English reader of the 1640s and 1650s would have read this as a moral on the story of the faithful shepherd, but also as a commentary on the state of England during the Civil War. Battista

Guarini's tragicomedy had been used before as a politicised commentary. Famously, readers of Fletcher's *The Faithful Shepherdess*
(1608) were admonished to 'remember, shepherds to be such as
the ancient poets, and modern, of understanding, have received
them: the owners of flocks and not Hirelings'.[14] Stuart pastoral
offered a critique, but it often (not always) did so within the preserve of the disguised and dancing court elite, as in Walter
Montagu's *The Shepherds Paradise*, designed specifically for aristocratic performance and consumption. This, too, found publication in the 1650s, printed in 1659 with a high royalist address to
the reader: 'such as are . . . qualified, may here read upon the
square; others will find themselves unconcern'd'. Thus, Arcadia
was a transformational locus for the resolution of court and
national problems. It was not – *pace* Laurence Lerner – simply
'about shepherds'.[15]

Fanshawe's introduction in 1648 proposed Guarini's pastoral as
a fantasy of royal restoration. Although Fanshawe's translation was
in part a product of the Caroline court's embracing attitude to
European culture in the 1630s, combined with the cult of love and
the sacralising of court ritual, it appeared in 1648 when Charles I
was powerless – and it already looks forward to the restoration –
not of Charles I, but his son:

Your Highnesse may have seen at *Paris* a Picture (it is in the Cabinet of
the *Great Chancellor* there) so admirably design'd that, presenting to the
common beholders a multitude of little faces (the Famous ancestors of
that Noble man); at the same time, to him that looks through a *Perspective*
(kept there for the purpose) there appears onely a single portrait in great
of the Chancellor himself; the Painter thereby intimating, that in him
alone are all his Progenitors; or perchance by a more subtile Philosophy
demonstrating, how the *Body Politick* is composed of many *naturall ones*;
and how each of these, intire in itself and consisting of head, eyes, hands
and the like is a head, an eye, or a hand in the other: as also, that mans
Privates cannot be preserved, if the *Publick* be destroyed, no more than
these little Pictures could remain in being, if the great one were defaced:
which great one likewise was first and chiefest in the painters designe,
and that for which all the rest were made.

Just so our Author (exposing to *ordinary view* an Enterlude of
Shepherds, their loves, and other little concernments, with the stroke of
a lighter pencill) presents through the perspective of the *Chorus*, another
and more suitable subject to his *Royall Spectators*. He shews to them the
image of a *gasping State* (once the most flourishing in the world): a *wild*

Boar (*the sword*) depopulating the *Country: the Pestilence* unpeopling the *Towns*: their Gods themselves in the mercilesse humane *Sacrifices* exacting bloody contribution from both . . . Yet in the *Catastrophe, the Boar* slain, the *Pestilence* . . . ceased . . . and all this miraculous change occasioned by the presaged Nuptials of two of Divine (that is Royall) extraction; meaning those at that time of the *Duke of Savoy* with the *Infanta of Spain*, from which fortunate conjunction hee prophesies a finall period to the troubles that had formerly distracted the state: *so much depends on the marriage of Princes* . . . Yet because it seems to me (beholding it *at the best light*) a *Landskip* of these Kingdomes (your *Royall Patrimony*). (A3v)

Thus the little world of shepherds stands for the whole of the great world, and, more specifically for England, Scotland and Ireland; and the reader is invited to understand the tragicomedy as a pastoral allegory of the Civil War in England and a prophecy of its happy resolution – in the marriage and restoration of Charles II. The dedication ends with the prospect of the prince's marriage as a palliative, 'uniting a miserably divided people in a publick joy: or by such other wayes and meanes as it may have pleased *the Divine Providence* to ordain for an *end of our woe*; I leave that to Providence to determine' (A3v–A4r).

This is evidently loyal, but it is a peculiar sort of royalism which has, as Graham Parry has noted, entirely erased the potential restoration of Charles I.[16] The necessary vagueness with which Guarini's tragicomedy allegorises the Civil War enables Fanshawe to suppress the disturbing elements of the situation in 1647–8, including the behaviour of Charles I. In his appeal to Charles *fils* Fanshawe seems to anticipate the political circumstances of the later 1640s and 1650s – essentially, defeat and to some extent accommodation to the new regimes – which underlie later royalist tragicomedies.

With regard to contemporary events, tragicomedy and pastoral tragicomedy used Arcadian and other settings to claim to be addressing political issues obliquely, or, as it were, within the 'enchanted' space of tragicomic discourse. Obviously pastoral forms imply different political agendas, but the dramatic pastorals of the 1640s and 1650s attempt to include the reader in critical commentary by acknowledging the tension in the idea of retirement from the political sphere as always already political. *The Shephearde's Oracle* (1644), a royalist pastoral by J. S., shows the banishment of Anarchus by Philarchus and Philortus, hinting that pastoral is a mode of social commentary: 'The sense of this Eclogue is covered with a vaile, but so thin that an easie eye may transpect it.'[17] This notification indicates that pastoral, in the very act of 'veiling' politics, instantiates itself as political discourse. Thus, the activity of reading is made political, here royalist: the reader here is positioned as royalist simply by having been able to 'transpect' the veil.

Entertainments intended for private performance used a similar veiled-but-visible formulation to exploit the politicised potential of pastoral during and after the Civil War. Sir William Denny's manuscript pastoral, *The Shepherds Holiday*, dated 1 June 1651, deploys a personified 'truth'. In part it seems to be a subversive echo of the parish world of Laudian enforcement of Charles's *Book of Sports* in its insistence on festivity.[18] The playlet appears to address the self-enclosed world of pastoral love and the textual 'key' provided turns out to unlock the thorny issues of married chastity versus virginity. Nevertheless, truth (Pega) is present in the play, described by the key as oracular: 'Pega shadows out Truth. As springs rise from underground so Truth, though from time to time in obscurity, at last appeareth as clear as those springs, flowing continually' (p. 68) Truth is implicated politically, and returning to the idea of the dream as a royalist troping of the republic, refers obliquely to a 'dark' present as well as the potential for a clear future. Moreover, truth is related to time by the Palmer who sets the pastoral, like Virgil's *Eclogues*, in an implicit relation to political disturbance: 'O giddy, stormy course of times, / That muffles truths of shepherds' rhymes!' (p. 75). Denny uses pastoral to make obscure reference to the present and the republic. Moreover, Denny's own career may reinforce the argument that pastoral is a genre suitable to those involved in politics: someone bearing the same name appears in the *Commons Journal* on 16 September 1643, as one who 'did publish a scandalous pamphlet', who is 'to be forthwith sent for, as a Delinquent, by the Serjeant at Armes for spreading and divulging a scandalous Pamphlet and Libel, to the Dishonour of both Houses of Parliament'. Denny's clerk, Thomas Hill, was also summoned to attend parliament.[19]

The 1650s saw the continual reworking of the oppositions of 'power' and 'authority', 'truth' and 'loyalty'. Pastoral offers a mode in which the royalists' paradox of the grim present in relation to their desired but unlikely future can be symbolically effaced by the transformation of political problems into those of

Arcadian love – as they are in Fanshawe's *Faithfull Shepherd*. It seems that during the 1650s it was fashionable to publish tragicomedies and pastoral adaptations, and that these – representing courts as mythic places, conflicts as resoluble, and monarchy as both desirable and restored – had a gestural status as 'royalist'. Killigrew, that royalist exile and maximiser *par excellence*, wrote tragicomedies – *The Pilgrim* (1645) and *Bellamira* (1652).[20] Other examples of royalist tragicomedies include Thomas Meriton's pastiche of pastoral sources *The Wandering Lover* (1658), remarkable for its borrowings from Sidney's *Arcadia*, and Thomas Forde's *Love's Labyrinth* (1660).[21] In the later 1650s Arcadia was a royalist analogy for England.

In part, tragicomedy imaginatively effects a desired reunion of 'truth' and 'loyalty' through the catalytic space of tragicomic pastoral. In drama, as Sukarta Chaudhuri has argued, pastoral brought with it its own implicit pattern in which 'characters escape from a corrupt or unhappy court into a pastoral or rural refuge. In this regenerative setting, they undergo a change in their nature and relationships; and finally, their problems resolved, they return to a new, revivified, courtly community.'[22] Even more pointedly than in earlier texts, tragicomedies from the 1650s drew on what Louis Montrose rightly identifies as the particular potential of pastoral to both obscure and clarify social relations and hierarchies in such a way as to 'include' the reader.[23] More specifically, in 1650s tragicomedy, this pastoral space provokes resolution because in it all laws are suspended, recast through pastoral's own dreamlike qualities which enable irresoluble political differences to be reconciled. Tragicomic pastoral can be considered as a disavowal in which the entry into pastoral allows resolution – in pastoral the audience's knowledge of the text and its context are held, as Freud spatialises it, 'side by side'.[24] Thus in the 1650s pastoral provides a space in which unanswerable questions from within the plot can be resolved, and in providing that resolution both invites and forestalls comparison with the world the reader inhabits.

The enchanted world of pastoral – already dreamlike because of pastoral's characteristic simultaneous denial and demystification of actual social relations – pointed out of the text towards the bad dream of the royalists' 1650s, but also towards the possible resolution of those ills. For instance, William Lower wrote a semi-tragicomic short pastoral called *The Enchanted Lovers* published at the

Hague in 1658, reprinted in a volume of three plays in 1661, which uses the metaphor of enchantment by sorcery to refer to Protectorate England.[25] The dramatis personae of *The Enchanted Lovers* uneasily combine the characteristics of plays set in Arcadia and in England: the hero, Thersander, is described as 'a Cavalier disguised in the habit of a Shepherd in love with Diana', who is 'a young lady disguised as a Sheapherdess' (p. 94). Of course, they do not recognise each other although they have already been lovers in Seville, where their happiness was spoilt when the tyrant Nearchus fell in love with Celia. In response, she took a sleeping potion which made her seem dead and Cleagenor (now Thersander) fled to Erithrea, an island governed by the semi-Circean enchantress Melissa. Here Celia (now Diana) has fled also. The revelation is further complicated by the fact that Melissa falls in love with Thersander/Cleagenor and punishes the lovers: she makes them appear to be dead and awake by turns. A fellow disguisee pleads for the restoration of love and liberty: 'render to this government again / The liberty to love, and to declare it' (v.iv. 143–4). The final descent of Diana makes clear that the pastoral tragicomedy is to be read as an allegory for the experience of loss and deprivation of exile and defeat; pastoral resolution is for the shepherds, not – yet – the cavaliers.

Thus, the pastoral space of disavowal in 1650s tragicomedy is tightly bound to a temporal structure also working towards the fixed point of 'restoration'. As Hayden White has suggested, the narrated present exists in terms of the production of a past in which the present is the future and a future in which the present is the past.[26] Royalist tragicomedy reshapes past and present in order to imagine a particular future. Tragicomedies of the 1650s, even more than most, invite the audience to imagine time twice, once as the narrated present of the 'dream' in relation to the extra-textual present, and again from the point of view of a future resolution.

Lois Potter rightly identifies one potential of the compensatory temporal organisation of royalist tragicomedy as allowing even loyal royalists to 'abdicate responsibility and leave matters in the hands of fate'.[27] However, as the evasion of contemporary circumstances by *The Faithful Shepherd* suggests, the ending of a tragicomedy could not wholly erase the complexity of actual political circumstances, nor compensate political change by producing a full closure in which circumstance and desire merge. Full closure was always undercut by the fact that in 'truth' restoration was unlikely throughout the 1650s. Tragicomedies represent the complexities of political struggle – including the excesses of kings (in, for example, *The Heroick Lover*) – but royalist tragicomedies structure a reader's thinking about political situations as a fantasy of restoration in which the play brings about a longed-for future state. Thus, tragicomic dénouements relate to the 1650s as prophecies fulfilled, enchantment defeated through pastoral encounters, deaths reversed. But the gap between representation and the actuality of the 1650s was part of the reading context of these plays. The untrue, even 'fraudulent', nature of the tragi-comic codes promising resolution (in representation) which has no likely parallel in actuality was always all too clear; the plays' re-enactment of scenes of defeat as scenes of triumph can to that extent be read as wish-fulfilment rather than as an incitement to political quietism.

Thus the writings of and about the 1640s and 1650s rework questions of the relationship between 'actual' and textual politics. A manuscript play, *The Female Rebellion*, uses Amazons (possibly reworking Massinger and Fletcher's *The Sea Voyage*, certainly sharply aware of pre-war tragicomedy) to explore political issues from the Civil War and Protectorate in a way which combines very serious political discussion and contemporary comment on 'cava-liers' as unheroic 'hectors'. The date of the tragicomedy is unknown, though it is probably by the lawyer Henry Birkhead who managed to survive much of the 1650s in All Souls while publish-ing royalist elegies. Harbage gives a date of 1659, though it might be a Restoration text.[28] It draws on Civil War and Protectorate slang and events such the Commissions of Array and refers to events memorialised in the pamphlet literature of the period, including the incident in which Charles I's correspondence was seized and opened. It also takes the debates about royal power from the Civil War period and genders them. Thus, in *The Female Rebellion*, Penthesilia and the others rebel against the authority of their Queen, provoking a discussion between the Queen and Penthesilia on the source of power in the state:

> QUEEN: Y'are then my Creatures; for I can, altho
>   I made ye not, by Law unmake ye; Thus
>   While we preserve your being, 'tis from Us.
> PENTH.: Sov'raigns that right first from us subjects gain'd,
>   Which we by our adherence still maintained.

QUEEN: From you? you never had Authority
　　　　To kill yourselves, less others, and could ye
　　　　That which you never had confer on me?　　　　(I.ii, p. 16)

Once again, as so often in the plays from 1640 to 1660, drama and political debate merge as Penthesilia and the Queen discuss popular versus divine right. Although the play is clear that the Queen's right to the throne is not enough to keep her on it, it ends with all threats to the throne re-harmonised in a masque; the Queen takes a consort to satisfy the army and – importantly – she enlarges her circle of counsellors. Thus in coming to a dramatic conclusion, it also alights on a plan for a political solution which includes monarchy and advice.

One of the conclusions we can draw from this, as from Fanshawe's interpretation of Guarini, is that these tragicomedies were self-conscious about the paradoxes in their repeated attempts to bring together historical and political events and the tragicomic genre. Throughout the 1650s the final act of the tragicomedy, the Restoration, necessarily remained in the imagined future. I would suggest that it is both the unsatisfactoriness of historical events, and the fact that the tragicomic resolution did not fit 'real' events, which might have caused writers to repeat the genre again and again, and I would tentatively suggest that Freud's theory of repetition offers a way to imagine a reader's pleasure in this repeated recapitulation. Freud writes of 'the constant recurrence of the same thing – the repetition of the same features or character-traits or vicissitudes, of the same crimes, or even the same names', and links it to a repetition of an unsatisfactorily resolved crisis.[29]

Tragicomedy allowed the audience or reader to repeat the events of recent history with a different conclusion. However, the very vocabulary it used, from pastoral to the discourse on usurpation, might be critical and was not necessarily framed by an assumed royalism. This comes to the fore in texts from the moment of the Restoration.

1659–1660: REPAIRING ROYALISM IN *THE HEROICK-LOVER,* *THE BANISH'D SHEPHEARDESS*

For 'royalists' the Restoration theoretically provided a reunion of 'power' and 'authority', brought the 'loyal' their due. In terms of the tragicomic genre we are tracing, it united history and desired future in a perfect present. But by 1659 things were more complicated than that. The moment of production of the tragicomedies from 1660–1 is, notionally, the very moment of restoration itself around which the texts are structured. Far from a celebratory immediacy in which historical and generic time melt gloriously together, these plays recapitulate events which began the conflict in the catastrophic moments of 1641–2 and reconsider the 'royalism' of the 1650s.

Dramatic texts which acknowledged and addressed the status quo were produced in the 1650s, such as *The Loyal Lovers* (discussed below) and the highly pragmatic comedy *The Hectors*.[30] *The Hectors*, particularly, engaged with events of the mid-1650s in a way that offers a vision of Protectorate society as capable of integration, political compromise and reinvigoration. A city comedy that refuses to traduce citizens, it takes as its butt the interrelationship between Dammees, or Hectors, and a group of card sharps who are ex-soldiers. This vein of pragmatic politics, accommodating critique of the earlier Stuarts, in part inhabits George Cartwright's rhymed *The Heroick Lover, or, the Infanta of Spain* (1661), a play which provides a resolution in the present (1660–1) but returns to the circumstances of the outbreak of the Civil War. It addresses questions about time and the production of tragicomic resolution in a way that may well emerge from the text having been written at different moments. It was finally published with a dedication to Charles II as 'a Poem, consisting more of fatal Truth, then flying Fancy: penn'd many years ago, but not published till now' (A3r).[31] The finishing touches seem to have been put to the play at the point of the Restoration, or in the first year after, when not only were Spain and France attempting to decide on the shape of the English state, but Charles seemed likely to marry a Spanish princess. Between August 1660 and May 1661 were taking place about a possible marriage to Catherine of Braganza, but in early 1661 the Spanish ambassador, was sufficiently unknowing to present Charles with a veritable 'litany of marriages'; it is hardly surprising that George Cartwright of Fulham thought that rescue by a Spanish match was a politically appropriate closure for his tragicomedy.[32]

The setting in Poland, a (Catholic) elective monarchy, ambiguously suggests both kingly power and participation in the choice of governors. *The Heroick Lover* combines two strands of plot. In one the Prince must give up his true love in order to marry the Spanish Infanta who arrives in the final act with fifty ships to help the King to reconquer his people. Interwoven with this is a play which reworks some of the events of 1641–2 including the impeachment of Strafford, citizens '*with a Petition*' 'to quit the Cardinal' (II. i, p. 11). Mediating between the two are two household servants who remain loyal to the King. The play opens with their even-handed assessment of the problems on the eve of the Civil War. Lycas speaks of the troubles of kings 'puzzled what to do', 'According to the Nature of the times, / Or else proceeding, from their proper crimes: / Requiring sometimes, more than is their due, / Or else refus'd, what them belongs unto'. Sotus follows this:

> The City's weary, and the Countrey too,
> And something shortly, murmure for to do.
> They will no longer have the King abus'd,
> Nor let themselves, so rigidly be us'd.
> But how to do't, they are not yet agreed,
> Out of the Court, such nettles for to weed.   (I.i, p. 2)

Two groups seek to influence the King, military moderates – 'I'le faithful be; be what he will' (II.i, p. 21) – and those grouped around the Cardinal – a figure who clearly stands for Laud – as a malign influence on the King. When the King is petitioned to abate taxes and to remove his evil counsellor (the Cardinal) he discusses the matter with the Cardinal, who is duly despotic:

> KING: What can we do against a multitude?
> CARDINAL: Do as you've done, use them extreamly rude.
> KING: But that will but provoke them more and more.
> CARDINAL: The way to keep them down's to keep them
>   poor.   (III.iii, p. 28)

At this point, harking back to Charles's personal rule, the play seems to be unsympathetic towards the King's counsellors and relatively understanding about the delicacy needed in negotiations between king and people. In its concentration on 1641–2 it offers a royalism relatively if not directly critical of the 'never to be forgotten Martyr', Charles, of his government. Indeed, the tragicomedy echoes political and parliamentary debates from the early 1640s, when Charles's ministers were described as intervening between king and people. As one parliamentary speaker put it, counsellors did not allow 'his Majesty to appear unto his people, in his own native Goodness, but they have eclipsed him by their interposition: although gross condense bodies may obscure and hide the Sun from shining out, yet is he still the same in his own splendour'.[33] In criticising counsel *The Heroick Lover* seems to produce a 'new' royalism in contrast to the court of Charles I.

Thus, the first part of the play concentrates on the issues of 1641 – advisors, taxation, flattering courtiers, the law and the people's misery, including circumstantial detail like the defence of London by the trained bands.

As the people break into open rebellion, trying the Admiral and dragging the Cardinal through the streets to prison (v.ii, p. 56), the King takes an increasingly hard line. In Act v he adamantly refuses to treat with the people – 'That Prince's not fit, a Scepter for to hold, / That will be by his Subjects, so controul'd' (v.v, p. 68).

However, the resolution of the tragicomedy is provided by the metamorphosis of 1642 into 1660 with the King reconquering the City and the Lord Mayor apprehending the stirrers up of rebellion to be beheaded (v.vi, p. 70). By the end of the play we have caught up with events of 1660 and the feelings of the play about rebellion seem to be influenced by the royalism of the Restoration. The King is transformed from someone who is misled by evil counsellors into the reconquering hero of 1660. The overlayering of 1642 and 1660 enable the immediate dissolution of sharp critique into celebration, and turns out to be a pattern of events favoured by post-Restoration tragicomedies. A further acknowlededgment of the compromises of 1660 is suggested in a poem published with the play which takes a swipe at Monck's own past:

> But Heav'n be prais'd, for this happy change,
> Though to frantique men, it seemeth strange.
> Well; do the rest, that we expect from thee,
> And second of this Kingdom shalt thou be:
>> Which will more honour be, unto thy name,
>> So for to live, then die with dirty fame. [34]

Thus, *The Heroick Lover* draws on both idealised and historical (or cynical) representations of contemporary politics. It puts historical events into a tragicomic pattern by running together the events of 1642 and those of 1660, and it avoids the presentation of a king who slips into having, as Charles Stuart and his court abroad did, mere authority and no power. The temporal over-layering, though possibly produced by two moments of writing, also indicates the uncertainty of how the moment of Restoration can actually be dealt with now it is within real as well as ideal time; the complex temporal structure of the play permits critique to blend into celebration by eclipsing the compromises intervening between the rule of king and prince.

Tragicomedies by another playwright also writing in the 1650s, Cosmo Manuche, also interprets the 1650s from the perspective of the moment of restoration, and his text from this moment is also marked by a complex use of tragicomic time. Manuche may have worked for both the Stuarts (possibly as a soldier) and Cromwell – Thurloe paid him for services, apparently spying, in 1656.[35] Certainly he was part of the household of James Compton, the Earl of Northampton, who also wrote plays and translations which remain in manuscript – some on Civil War topics. Some of Manuche's plays remain in manuscript and others were pub-lished.[36] They may have been performed in Islington, just outside London.[37] Like George Cartwright and the anonymous author of *The Female Rebellion,* Manuche was aware that kings and courts are far from ideal. Of his Protectorate or early Restoration plays *The Just General* echoes many of the pre-war tragicomic structures: love and pastoral convene to enable the resolution of the problems of court and courtiers. More incisive are *The Loyal Lovers* and a manuscript pastoral tragicomedy, *The Banish'd Shepheardess.*[38] In *The Loyal Lovers* and later in *The Banish'd Shepheardess* the ideal and the material or cynical aspects of Protectorate tragicomedy are brought together in ways which enable them to comment on each other.

In *The Loyal Lovers,* set during the Commonwealth, love causes the conversion of the father of Letitia from being a 'committee-man' to loyalty to the crown. The politics of love in *The Loyal Lovers* involves the reunification of the family through the daughter's mar-riage to a loyal cavalier. The play deals with political issues in a way which, at least initially, is comic rather than idealised. The scene is contemporary – 'Amsterdam' – and the issues revolve around topical and stereotypical representations of contemporary issues in London itself. Indeed, the play opens with the loyal royalist waiting for his confederates and buying a newsbook, an incident indicating the use of quotidian politics.

The later manuscript play from 1660, just possibly 1659, *The Banish'd Shepheardess*, seems at first to contrast with *The Loyal Lovers* in its use of pastoral but this play also points cynically to the inevitability that even Charles II's supporters must, by 1660, be tainted by engagement with Cromwell because of their own need to survive. The play is set after the death of Cromwell, and covers the events leading up to the Restoration. It is sharply aware of the paradoxes involved in the emerging loyalty of the moment of Charles's Restoration. Structured as if the whole play were acts four and five of a tragicomedy, several plots run alongside one another.[39] In Thessalia the banished queen, Corilliana, and her son Charilaus have their courts and wait, as did Charles II and Sir Edward Hyde in the Spanish Netherlands and Henrietta Maria in France.[40] Thessalia stands for France, and is the setting for Henrietta Maria's court in exile. The plot includes Arcadian scenes at court (the England from which everyone is banished is, as ever, Arcadia) and comic intrigue in which cavaliers, desperate for money, rob the servants of English officials who were preparing to flee the demise of the Protectorate and republic. While this might seem like a wholly royalist subject – and the play is at pains to abuse the dead Cromwell, referring to him as Pluto's 'new come favourite' (ii.i, p. 373) – it is also critical of the pre-war government. Thus, the prologue points towards the pre-war luxury of some subjects:

> Part, of Arcadia's flock; Sated: with Ease,
> And plenty, surfitts. Whils't the Rank desease,
> Rooted in Rebbells: bloud, To that height springs,
> That Their: proud heads: strikes at the Heads of Kings.

(p. 352)

This passage, suggesting that the causes of the war lay in the divisions of the 1630s, opens the play, and situates it in relation to the events which have led to Charles's exile. This prologue again reminds us – and more importantly its first, Restoration, audience of readers or spectators – of the contingent aspects of royalism in that it makes no attempt to exonerate the pre-war government: the suggestion that only part of the flock were kept luxuriously reminds us, once again, that even supporters of the king might

have opposed pre-war royal policy. The play itself opens with a dialogue in which the pragmatism of professional sailors is articulated
by Rock-shun: 'O. You are merry Sr. I serv'd Them: as many did. /
Layed by my Conscience, and tooke Their mony.' (I.i). Later in the
play, as it becomes increasingly obvious that Charilaus will be
recalled, he receives a letter, which

> . . . tells strange tailes: of some,
> Wee: have beene kind to,
> And, I could wish, Their innocency,
> Could protect Them: and cleare them:
> Of those scandalls, I, have no will to credit.   (IV.i, p. 408)

Thus, although Charilaus is presented as a pastoral monarch, easy
and familiar with servants and an able huntsman, rebellion is not
read by the play as something simple: royalism at the Restoration
sat uneasily next to the necessary adaptations that Charles II's subjects had made during the 1650s, of which Engagement was only
the most obvious. For once, we see pastoral encountering the way
in which the fantasy of restoration could map only problematically
on to any actual social and political present. Alongside the intelli-
gence that Charilaus receives suggesting that some who seemed
loyal may have been involved with the Protectorate government,
there is the trickery of Lysander. Lysander personifies the royalist
paradox, being described in the dramatis personae as one of the
'Loyall; Subjects to Charilaus: And Souldiers: of fortune' (p. 353)
– as the play knows, the two coexist precariously. Ultimately, this
is resolved, as Lysander's loyalty to the king is made clear in the
final act where one of Corilliana/Henrietta Maria's ladies in
waiting disguises herself as a goddess to punish the penitent servants of the collapsing English government. Until this point
Lysander has been involved in intrigues and deceits including
cowardice. Once more, as in *The Hectors*, Cowley's *Cutter of Coleman
Street* and *The Female Rebellion*, the cavalier army is characterised as
unreliable and self-interested; royalism is no indication of good
conduct.

The Banish'd Shepheardess presents the situation in 1659 as
fraught, with few clear boundaries between 'loyal' and 'disloyal'.
As I have shown, the play suggests causes for this in both past and
present. The exiled king and queen are placed in an isolated pastoral exile, interrupted by letters and later messengers from

England/Arcadia as the restoration of the king approaches. The moment of pastoral alienation and waiting for resolution – as found in *The Just General* – extends to fill the whole play yet, despite the Arcadian names, the part of the play in which Lysander and the rebel rogues appear seems close to a civic comedy such as Manuche's own *The Loyal Lovers* or *The Hectors*. These pragmatic details increasingly bear in on the melancholy solitude of the court's – enforced – pastoral retreat.

The final moments of *The Banish'd Shepheardess* offer not only a return but a promise for the future, as the maid Artesia notes:

> . . . Leave Them: to Their punishments,
> Whilst wee: resting in an assurance
> That ours is past. begin our Comicall prologue:
> With Their: Tragicall Epilogue. (III, p. 400)

The ideal future, familiar from 1650s tragicomedy, is here brought forward: delight is imminent though not, significantly, immediate. This is the way in which the text figures the comedic part of the tragicomic genre as falling into place. It is in terms of future promise that Charles II's restoration appeared, to monarchists (at the very point of the Restoration, as *The Banish'd Shepheardess* makes clear, most people seemed to be monarchists) to be a story with a happy ending. *The Banish'd Shepheardess* recognises this potential of the Restoration, but also recognises the fragility of a government which was, as Paul Seaward describes it, 'protected by little more than the popular enthusiasm the Restoration had generated'.[41]

If, as contemporaries kept asserting, the moment of the King's return seemed to surpass theatrical transformation in its glorious improbability, it was also problematic.[42] As Nancy Klein Maguire notes, in the production of an imaginary future the 'martyrdom' of Charles I is a key moment invoked though not shown in most Protectorate tragicomedies.[43] As Artesia's looking to the future suggests, the Restoration brought about another reordering of the events on the tragicomic sequence implicit in the death of Charles and the restoration of his son; for example, in *Cromwell's Conspiracy*, rewriting *The Famous Tragedie of Charles I*, Charles I dies in Act II, scene iv – neither beginning nor tragic end. The same play has Monck describing himself equivocally: 'I am as yet a stranger to my self, / Much more unto the City.' Thus, for the plays

published or written early in the 1660s the problematic issue to
deal with were that the necessity of living under the Protectorate
had produced an honourable gestural loyalty irremediably compromised by true circumstances. Around the handling or avoid-
ance of these questions the different political views of this moment
mark tragicomic drama.

TRUTH, TIME, AUTHORITY? REWRITING LOYALTY IN THE 1660s

To recap, if tragicomedy sat uneasily against the 'true' political
situation of the 1650s, the moment of the Restoration seemed to
correlate, at last, with the resolution of a tragicomic drama yet – as
The Heroick Lover and *The Banish'd Shepheardess* indicate – it introduced the problem of dealing with the past (and the present) in a
new way. The process of looking back began.

Francis Kirkman, who was involved in drama throughout the
Protectorate, lost no time in suiting comic drolls to newly festive
seasons. He also went into the bookselling trade. He reiterates the
resemblance between fact and fiction which had been a common-
place of English self-conceptualisation during the Civil War and
Protectorate.

> I have several *Manuscripts* of this nature, written by worthy Authors, and
> I account it much pity that they should now lie dormant and buried in
> oblivion, since ingenuity is so likely to be encouraged, by reason of the
> happy Restauration of our liberties. We have had the private Stage for
> some years clouded, and under a tyrannical command, though the
> publick Stage of *England* has produc'd many monstrous villains, some of
> which have deservedly made their *exit*. I believe future Ages will not credit
> the transactions of our late Times to be other than a *Play*, or a *Romance.*
> I am sure in most Romantick Plays there hath been more probability than
> in our true (though sad) Stories.[44]

Kirkman's chatty style enables us to see him working through the
complicated political situation which led to plays being desirable
again, and using a dramatic metaphor to do so. It only gradually
becomes clear that by 'Romantick Plays' he means tragicomedy,
with its improbable situations and reversals. He has tragicomedies
written in the past and the past itself seems like a tragicomedy. But,
unlike the plays of the 1650s, Kirkman is able to formulate events
of the last twenty years as expressed aptly by a dramatic genre –

though exceeding even such plays in their transformations and reversals.

As the rest of this study indicates, arguments that theatre sprang anew and began addressing political concerns for the first time at the Restoration are inadequate and misguided. Indeed, the dramatic genres of the 1640s and 1650s appear reworked in the comedies of dangerous, commercial, London life: precisely the issues of truth, loyalty and necessity become the central plots of Restoration comedy. For example, *The Presbyterian Lash* (1661) called itself a tragicomedy and continued the ironic, directly political, use of the term found throughout the 1650s.[45] Plays like *Cutter of Coleman Street* negotiate the new meaning of land and marriage after the Civil War sequestrations and other losses, by tracing the material circumstances of 'loyal' cavaliers and their seamy financial dealings. Where *Cutter of Coleman Street* points to the shifts of cavaliers, John Wilson's *The Cheats* recasts cavalier humiliation at the hands of committees into a comic mode. A sequence of plays troped Cromwell as a usurper – as in *The Usurper* (Edward Howard, 1664) and *Andronicus Comnenius* (1662) John Wilson's tragedy.[46]

After the moment of the Restoration, the temporal structure of tragicomedy, focussed around the Restoration as the restoration and making good of narrative lack, changed again as the future of diegetic time in the narrative of the Restoration became the past, looked back on from the present of actual time. Thus, the moment of the Restoration continued to provide tragicomic resolution in the new dramas of the 1660s. They also rework pastoral elements and the split between 'true' politics and the rejuvenation of courts. However, as Charles's reign became a reality and problems emerged about the succession, Catholicism, toleration, the moment of the Restoration came to be invoked with nostalgia, as a moment of national unity. It is appropriate, then, to conclude by looking briefly at the way two tragicomedies of the 1660s interpreted the 1650s.

As E. J. Burns notes, early Restoration comedies both rework the events now seen as constituting an 'interregnum' and use pastoral, setting the pastoral scene as the park, the Mall, the garden, the public pleasure ground.[47] Two plays set in the 1650s and Restoration, using park and garden as a kind of pastoral in a (loosely) tragicomic pattern, are Etherege's *The Comical Revenge* (first performed 1664) and Sir Charles Sedley's *The Mulberry*

Garden (1668). Both combine the dilemmas of love and honour with a plot of city intrigue. As a recent editor notes, *The Comical Revenge* draws on codes of comedy found in civic comedies of the 1620s and 1630s.[48] But what can also be emphasised is that such comic strategies were continued in the drolls, pamphlet drama and journalistic prose satires of the Civil War. The play is set in Protectorate and post-Protectorate London (the mention of Hewson at III.v, suggests the late 1650s).[49]

In *The Comical Revenge* control of the social spaces of park, garden, pleasure ground, confers control of the outcome of the scene. The quasi-pastoral spaces indicate a split in the play between the idealised courtship of royalist lovers and comic plots. Indeed the 'revenge' is that Sir Frederick Frolick makes Sir Nicholas Cully marry Frolick's ex-mistress, telling him to 'carry her into the country, come; your neighbours' wives will visit her, and vow she's a virtuous well-bred lady' (v.v.118–20). Much, in the play, hangs on the ability to interpret and take control of public space and to fulfil codes of honour – his cowardice confirms that Sir Nicholas Cully is, as Sir Frederick describes him:

... one whom Oliver, for the transcendent knavery and disloyalty of his father, has dishonoured with knighthood; a fellow as poor in experience as in parts, and one that has a vainglorious humour to gain a reputation amongst the gentry, by feigning good nature, and an affection to the king and his party. (I.ii.178–84)

The royalist Sir Frederick is the only figure able to move between the world of City dealings and the heroic plot. Like Lysander in *The Banish'd Shepheardess*, he is paradoxically in control of his destiny (though living by his wits). The play is split in two: the heroic – 'loyal' – lovers' plot is set against the – 'true' – satire of the supporters of the Rump. The 'high' lovers walk only in the private garden (whereas the widow also longs to go to the park). Moreover, this section of the play follows a tragicomic structure in which Colonel Bruce almost dies in a duel for Graciana before renouncing her with honour in favour of her sister Aurelia. While in the 1650s pastoral was a place to realise the conflicts of the Civil War, it is redeployed as the site of amorous intrigue and the site through which moral and political supremacy is established. Finally, the play is striking in the way it mobilises the Protectorate itself as a period of relative freedom.

The tragicomic schema of another split tragicomedy/comedy, *The Mulberry Garden*, is able to work because it was written and performed after the Restoration; this allows the multiple conflicts of the Civil War and Commonwealth to be compressed into the familiar opposition of 'roundheads' and 'cavaliers'. Sedley sets the play at the moment when General Monck has arrived in London, after his arrival and during his conference with the Rump and following that; the final scene of the play includes the offstage voices of the people celebrating the downfall of the Rump. This means that several aspects of the Commonwealth and Protectorate are simplified or suppressed: even the events of 1659 are only present insofar as they act as the hinge-points of the tragicomic genre. Once again, as in *The Heroick Lover* and *The Comical Revenge*, history serves the play by being restructured as tragicomedy with the divisions of the 1640s and 1650s compressed into a moment, and Sir Samuel Forecast is a 'roundhead', Eugenio a 'cavalier'. Simultaneously the tragicomedy (and the play's account of history) ends at the moment when the Restoration (at least in the play's terms) becomes inevitable.

The tragicomic plot exists in verse and turns on Eugenio's love for Althea, the daughter of Sir Samuel Forecast. Forecast opposes Althea's match with Eugenio, explaining that cavaliers are financially unstable – 'He had an Estate, 'Tis now sequester'd, he dare not show his Head . . . I should be sorry to see any Child of mine soliciting her Husband's Composition at a Committee' (II.i.28–34). Finally Eugenio emerges from hiding and rushes to speak with Althea, disguised as a Rump soldier. Their verse interview is interrupted by soldiers (as well as Althea's suitor Horatio), there is a fight (Horatio fights on Eugenio's side), and both Eugenio and Sir Samuel Forecast are taken to the Tower, Eugenio as a royalist and Forecast for hiding him. This is the low point of the tragic plot, and it is the entry of historic events into the drama that bring about the happy dénouement. As the terrified Forecast is about to be dragged to prison the cavalier Wildish enters:

WILDISH: Come, bear up, Sir, if there come a turn you'l be a great man.
FORECAST: I shall be hang'd on that side, and to speak my own Conscience, I have deserv'd it.
WILDISH: No, to lye in Prison for concealing Cavaliers, will be great merit; and let me tell you as a friend, there's like to be a turn suddenly, 'tis thought the General will declare like an honest man, I say

> no more; therefore carry yourself moderately, this accident may
> chance to do you good service, if you have the grace to make the
> right use on't. (IV.ii.190–200)

This hints to the audience that the triumph of Eugenio's love
will coincide with the Restoration and the end of the play, and the
visit paid by Forecast's royalist brother Sir John Everyoung to the
Tower confirms this, suggesting that Monck – notably a more
successfully recuperated figure than for George Cartwright or
Cromwell's Conspiracy – 'has today to some persons of quality
declared for the king' (v.iii.33). And the final act of the play sees
the release of Forecast, but the triumph of the tragicomic structure
is in the cries of the people on stage echoing the cries of the Rump-
burning citizens of London:

> EUGENIO: I hear the people's joyful cries,
>   Like conquering Troops o're flying Enemies;
>   They seem to teach us in a ruder way
>   The Honour due to this all-healing day.   (v.v.194–7)

Eugenio interprets the cries for us and facilitates the play's closure
as royalist. Thus, *The Mulberry Garden* is a dramatic document of
winner's history. The tragicomic structure of the 1650s is transformed using the 1650s as the time and London as the place, and
the tragicomic structure worked out at a distance from the conflicts and the fact that it did not in any way fit the historical 'facts'
which, as I have argued, influenced the genre in the 1650s. The
1650s are here represented as a time of the exuberant coexistence
of different ideologies of gender and power, but the tragicomic
plot exists in verse at a distance from the plots of city comedy. *The
Mulberry Garden* designates the 1650s both as a period of oppression and of sexual and social excitement and flux. As the title suggests, and as Burns indicates, London's gardens feature as a social,
hierarchical and ethical melting pot invoked in nostalgia – exciting, but also recuperated in the moment of the Restoration. Later
comedies rework the 1650s and the moment of the Restoration –
notably Aphra Behn's *The Rover I* and *II* and her *The Roundheads*,
which uses Tatham's 1659 comedy, *The Rump*. But as Charles's
reign progressed the moment of the Restoration inevitably
seemed less and less like the magical restoration of royalty, as
monarchical rule became visibly embroiled in political machina-
tions.

TRAGICOMEDY: RESTORATION VERSUS RESTORATION, TRUTH VERSUS LOYALTY

The relationships of tragicomic genre and pastoral language to dramatic discourse in the period 1640 to 1660 indicate that, as Annabel Patterson concludes (writing more specifically about Virgil's *Eclogues*), pastoral was used to provide an analysis of the conflicts of civil war, often in conjunction with tragicomedy. Tragicomedy and pastoral offered a compensatory structuring of the relationship between narrative time and historical time.[50] Questions of the government's legitimacy and rule, authority and power were repeatedly renegotiated in tragicomedy, but their use as closure in dramatic texts bore little resemblance to the political and social status quo of the 1640s and 1650s. Tragicomedy could recapitulate, but not resolve, political problems and, perhaps because of the way it constantly recast present events as about to be resolved, it became a central genre in royalist writing of the 1650s.

Protectorate tragicomedies repeat the loss of the 'true' ruler, his recovery and restoration, following banishment, pastoral retreat, and return. But as I have demonstrated, these plays are not usually uncomplicated celebrations of unproblematic 'royalist' ideals; their retelling of the loss of rule and the restoration of right with might is also in part inevitably a reworking and repeating of scenes of defeat (and of moral mistakes) as transformed by fantasy into scenes of victory. Pastoral and tragicomedy became registered as public languages in which political opinion was formed and disseminated by the press – as Annabel Patterson says of pastoral, so tragicomedy also was a literary–political language.[51] It was significant as a dramatic genre operating at the intersection of literature and politics, combining commentary on the political situation and a fantasy of the return of good government. Tragicomedies wove together 'truth' and 'loyalty' in an uneasy generic mixture held together into the 1660s by the strange turn of history whereby what seemed like a loyal fantasy came true with the Restoration – only to become reworked as a nostalgia for imagined social unity as the moment of closure in Restoration tragicomedies.

Coda

The Civil War produced a crisis in representation of which drama was the most extreme example and for which the debates on theatre were the crucible. Therefore, the critical orthodoxy – that the period of 1642 to 1660 is a gap in the staging, printing, political and social history of drama – invites re-evaluation.

The pamphlet plays and playlets, opera, shows, tragicomedies and plays discussed here indicate that dramatic and theatrical genres were not simply suppressed by the closures of the theatres in the 1640s. Rather, written and published drama (and such theatrical production as existed) was repeatedly and diversely affected and even transformed by the various situations of the Civil Wars, republic and Protectorate. It is also inadequate to see the drama produced as monolithically 'royalist'; people writing from a wide range of polemical positions used dramatic genres. The ban of 1642, and subsequent bans, produced circumstances in which dramatic texts had complex involvements in political debates and are often highly self-conscious about such involvement. The bans on theatre combined with relatively easy access to print meant that printed drama was a highly charged and politicised sector of printed literary–political debate. Moreover, the particular politicised circumstances of drama seem to have facilitated the use of dramatic texts as modes of persuasion (as in *The Famous Tragedie of Charles I* and *The Arraignment of Superstition*). Such plays appealed to widely differing readerships, using a range of literary–political languages. And as Francis Kirkham's 1661 playlist indicates, contemporaries did regard these plays from the 1640s and 1650s as part of the printed repertoire of dramatic texts. Kirkham's catalogue listed plays including *Marcus Tullius Cicero, Love Crowns the End, The Siege of Rhodes*, amongst performed and unperformed pre-war plays.

The 1640s and 1650s produced a diversity of genres in response to the changed circumstances of theatre and drama. But what happened to these genres at the Restoration? In 1660 Tatham wrote a preface to *London's Glory* performed before Charles II. Tatham claimed 1660 as 'the 12th Year of His Majestie most happy Reign', and such rewriting in the light of Stuart victory was typical of the reformulation of Civil War dramatic genres at the Restoration. Obviously, Charles II opened new theatres. These theatres, endowed but commercial, were to exist at the border between Whitehall and City, and in them the struggles of national, international and metropolitan politics were to be played out. However, like the closure of the theatres in 1642, the reopening of the theatres is an event which requires nuanced interpretation.

As the reworking of the Civil War in the plays of the period suggests, what happened in the post-Restoration theatre was shaped not solely by the dusted-off codes of Caroline theatre, but also by the theatrical legacy of Interregnum drama. Although the Restoration theatre was in no sense republican or regicidal, it was marked by the knowledge of political possibilities produced in the Civil War and Protectorate, and this knowledge is present generically, self-consciously and in terms of plots, in Restoration plays. The issues change, of course, but we can only keep our understanding of the Restoration theatre as 'national' and moulded by monarchy if we see it as also conditioned, in part, by the events which *deposed* the earlier Stuarts.

The last two chapters gave some indication of what happened to Civil War genres in the changing metropolitan and theatrical contexts of the Restoration. Some plays, like Davenant's, were staged in the new theatres. The civic shows changed, stopped, and were reconstituted. Restoration tragicomedies invoked the moment of Stuart return. Inevitably, too, the ways in which issues and genres from the 1640s and 1650s were presented was determined by the reconstruction of the Stuart monarchy. The representation of the Commonwealth period was transformed over the next thirty years and the compromised culture of a winner's history reshaped the cultural material produced in the 1640s and 1650s; the genres and topics we have examined were re-articulated in a theatre riven by different political factions and driven by new kinds of theatrical pleasure. The process whereby the Civil War was remembered in the Restoration was, as I suggested in the chapter on tragicomedy, one of simplification and selective forgetting.

But the Restoration theatre is not the only place we could look for the reordering of the genres of the 1640s and 1650s. For some writers, like Milton, the Restoration shaped history as tragedy. *Samson Agonistes*, published in 1671, reworks questions about the nature of reformed drama familiar from the 1650s.[1] Although Samson ends his life by pulling down 'a spacious Theater' where he is displayed to his enemies, the tragedy demonstrates a complex understanding of the politics and ethics of theatrical representation, and the peritexts of the classically structured 'dramatic poem' raise questions about the nature of dramatic genres and their relation to a vision of commonwealth. In 1641 Milton had written of the need for 'publique sports, and festival pastimes', 'the procurement of wise and artfull recitations' to be held 'in Theaters, porches, or what other place, or way may win most upon the people to receive at once both recreation, and instruction'.[2] Almost thirty years later, *Samson Agonistes* carefully argues for 'tragedy, as it was anciently composed' as the 'most profitable of all other poems', and a genre which interprets history:

Philosophers and other gravest Writers, as *Cicero, Plutarch* and others, frequently cite out of Tragic Poets, both to adorn and illustrate their discourse. The Apostle *Paul* himself thought it not unworthy to insert a verse of *Euripides* into the Text of Holy Scripture, I *Cor.* 15.33; and *Pareus*, commenting on the *Revelation*, divides the whole Book as a Tragedy, into Acts distinguished each by a Chorus of Heavenly Harpings and Song between.[3]

Such a defence of dramatic genre is familiar from the context of the 1650s. Traditionally read in terms of a retreat into interiority, and more recently in terms of the problematic nature of Samson's agency and his responsibility in relation to Dalila and the doubly 'theatrical' ending, *Samson Agonistes* is also innovative and self-reflexive in a way which implicitly takes up the debates about genre, moral representation and the politics of an audience's engagement with a play.[4] Indeed, the play's complicated self-reflexivity has caused one critic to describe it as 'an imitation of the emotional experience of attending to a tragedy'.[5] In *Samson Agonistes* the debates on reforming the theatre issue in a play which meditates on the nature of the genre.

The publication of *Samson Agonistes* suggests that the arguments surrounding representation and aesthetics generated in the Civil War did not disappear. Whilst Restoration theatre took up political–aesthetic debates about dialogue and drama, they were also rearticulated in adjacent genres. Transformed and with new political connotations, the debates about radicalism, aesthetics and politics and their representation can be found, for example, in later politically charged closet tragedy. We might include Byron's *Cain*, Shelley's 'Hellas' and *Prometheus Unbound.* In 1820 Shelley compares Prometheus, 'eyeless in hate', to Satan. He finds Prometheus 'exempt from the taints of ambition, envy, revenge, and a desire for personal aggrandisement, which in the Hero of *Paradise Lost* interfere with the interest'; his Prometheus exists not in an epic but in the more flexible rearticulation of the 'Greek tragic writers' through the self-reflexive potential of a verse dialogue or tragedy. And as he says, 'the sacred Milton was, let it ever be remembered, a republican and a bold enquirer into morals and religion'.[6] As Shelley knew, some of the genres he used for his own enquiries had their genealogies in the ideas and genres of the English Civil Wars.

Notes

PREFACE

1 Contrast the methodology adapted by Dale Randall, *Winter Fruit: English Drama 1642–1660* (University of Kentucky Press, 1995).

INTRODUCTION: HOW THE DRAMA DISAPPEARED

1 'Order for Stage-plays to Cease', *Acts and Ordinances of the Interregnum 1642–1660*, ed. C. H. Firth and R. S. Rait (London: HMSO, 1911), I, 26–7.
2 Exceptions include Lois Potter, ed., *The Revels History of Drama in English* (London: Methuen, 1981); Margot Heinemann, *Puritanism and Theatre* (Cambridge University Press, 1980); Martin Butler, *Theatre and Crisis 1632–1642* (Cambridge University Press, 1984). See also Dale Randall, *Winter Fruit: English Drama 1642–1660* (University of Kentucky Press, 1995), pp. 28–41.
3 Thomas Postlewait, 'Periodisation in Theatre History', *Theatre Journal*, 40, no. 3 (1988), 299–318.
4 Alfred Harbage, *Cavalier Drama: An Historical and Critical Supplement to the Study of the Elizabethan and Restoration Stage* (Oxford: Modern Language Association and Oxford University Press, 1936), p. 2.
5 See also the slightly different reading of the circumstances of the closing of the theatres given by Butler, *Theatre and Crisis*, pp. 246–7.
6 *Journals of the House of Commons*, v, 335b. See also Leslie Hotson, *The Commonwealth and Restoration Stage* (1928; rpt New York: Russell and Russell, 1962), p. 27.
7 See the opening chapters of Anthony Fletcher, *The Outbreak of the English Civil War* (London: Edward Arnold, 1981); Robin Clifton, 'The Popular Fear of Catholics During the English Revolution', *PP*, no. 52 (August 1971), 23–55; Christopher Hill, 'The English Revolution and Patriotism', in Raphael Samuel, ed., *Patriotism: The Making and Unmaking of British National Identity* (London: Routledge, 1989), I, 159–68; Peter Lake, 'Anti-Popery: the Structure of a Prejudice', in Richard Cust and Ann Hughes, eds., *Conflict in Early Stuart England* (Harlow: Longman, 1989), pp. 72–106.

8 Fletcher, *Outbreak*, pp. 184–5, 261, 409–10.

9 Hotson, *Commonwealth*, pp. 3–4. He quotes *A Second Discovery By the Northern Scout* (1642).

10 Butler, *Theatre and Crisis*, pp. 228–50, 289–91. Richard Overton, *New Lambeth Fayre* (1642); (attributed), *Canterbury his Change of Diet* (1641); (attributed), *The Bishop's Potion*. Another anti-episcopal playlet from 1641–2 is *A Rent in the Lawne Sleeves* (1641). There were also anti-Catholic playlets (e.g. *The Friers Last Farewell, A Disputation Between the Devil and the Pope* (1642)) and attacks on sectaries (e.g. *A Tale in a Tub* (1642)). The Overton canon is notoriously difficult to establish.

11 Hotson, *Commonwealth*, p. 4.

12 *Ibid.*; Mary Edmond, *Rare Sir William Davenant* (Manchester University Press, 1987), p. 78.

13 Butler, *Theatre and Crisis*, p. 1. The composition of the audience for so-called public and private London theatres remains a moot point and becomes even more difficult to assess after the closure of the theatres. On pre-war playgoing see Butler, *Theatre and Crisis*, pp. 293–306.

14 See also Valerie Pearl, *London and the Outbreak of Puritan Revolution* (Oxford University Press, 1961), pp. 237–9.

15 Henry Parker, *Observations Upon Some of His Majesties Late Answers and Expresses* (London, 1642) in William Haller, ed., *Tracts on Liberty in the Puritan Revolution* (New York: Columbia University Press, 1934), II, 165–213.

16 David Underdown, *Revel, Riot and Rebellion: Popular Politics and Culture in England 1603–1660* (Oxford University Press, 1985).

17 George Wither, *Mercurius Rusticus* (1642) quoted in Hotson, *Commonwealth*, p. 9. See also Henry Glapthorne, 'White-hall', in *White-Hall A Poem Written 1642 with Elegies on The Right Honourable Francis Earl of Bedford and Henry Earle of Manchester, Lord Privy Seale* (London, 1643); Hotson, *Commonwealth*, p. 14; *Perfect Occurrences* (9–16 May 1645).

18 *The Weekly Account* (4 Oct. 1643); *CSP Domestic*, 1641–3, p. 564; *Mercurius Verdicus*, E.279 (1), (19–26 Apr. 1645).

19 Hotson, *Commonwealth*, pp.29–30

20 *Ibid.*, p. 27.

21 *Journals of the House of Commons*, v, 439, cited Hotson, *Commonwealth*, pp. 28–31, 34–6, 76. An ordinance was passed on 9 February 1648 and printed on 11 February. See Firth and Rait, *Acts and Ordinances*, I, 1070.

22 *Journals of the House of Commons*, v, 612a, 648a. In September plays were still being performed. See Hotson, *Commonwealth*, pp. 37–8; *Perfect Occurrences* (1–8 Sept. 1648).

23 Hotson, *Commonwealth*, pp. 39–42, 42–4. For the famous raid see *Kingdom's Weekly Intelligencer* (2–9 Jan. 1649); *Perfect Occurrences* (29

Dec.–5 Jan. 1648–9). On raids in January 1650 see Hotson, *Commonwealth*, pp. 46–7 and *Mercurius Pragmaticus* (22–9 Jan. 1650); *The Man in the Moon* (23–31 Jan. 1650).

24 *Mr William Prynne His Defence of Stage-Plays, or a Recantation of a former Book of his called Histrio-Mastix* (London, 1649). See also William Prynne, *Histrio-Mastix* (London, 1633). Other contemporary defences of playing included the reprinting of Thomas Heywood, *The Actors Vindication* (1612; rpt 1658); *The Stage Players Complaint*, (1641); *The Actors Remonstrance* (Jan. 1643).

25 Hotson, *Commonwealth*, p. 42.

26 Reproduced in C. H. Firth, *NQ*, 8, series 5, 464; Hotson, *Commonwealth*, pp. 41–2. On the likely moment see Blair Worden, *The Rump Parliament* (Cambridge University Press, 1974) p. 218.

27 David Bevington, *Tudor Drama and Politics* (Cambridge, Mass.: Harvard University Press, 1968), pp. 24–6, 295–9.

28 Patrick Collinson, *The Religion of Protestants* (Oxford University Press, 1982), pp. 10–12, 141–88. See Collinson's critique of Michael Walzer's claims for Protestant radicalism in *The Revolution of the Saints* (London: Weidenfeld and Nicolson, 1966), p. 179.

29 Collinson, *Religion of Protestants*, p. 178.

30 Underdown, *Revel*, pp. 9–72.

31 Kevin Sharpe and Peter Lake, eds., *Culture and Politics in Early Stuart England* (Basingstoke: Macmillan, 1994), p. 1.

32 For the assumption that the Civil War had deep-rooted causes see e.g. Christopher Hill, *The World Turned Upside Down* (1972; rpt Harmondsworth: Penguin, 1978), *Intellectual Origins of the English Revolution* (1980; rpt Oxford University Press, 1985) and A. L. Morton, *The World of the Ranters* (London: Lawrence and Wishart, 1970). This assumption is shared by the non-Marxist liberal left tradition e.g. Lawrence Stone, *The Causes of the English Revolution 1529–1642* (London: Routledge and Kegan Paul, 1972), traces the causes of the Civil War back to Tudor political and religious policy (pp. 72–106). For an example of revisionist critique in action see e.g. John Adamson, 'Protesters at the Establishment: Radical Responses in England from 1645 to 1775', *TLS*, 7 June 1991, pp. 5–6.

33 J. C. D. Clark, *Revolution and Rebellion: State and Society in England in the Seventeenth and Eighteenth Centuries* (Cambridge University Press, 1986), p. 4.

34 J. C. Davis, *Fear, Myth and History* (Cambridge University Press, 1986), pp. 1–16.

35 See John Morrill, *The Revolt of the Provinces* (1976; rpt London: Longman, 1980), p. 13.

36 David Norbrook, 'Life and Death of Renaissance Man', *Raritan*, 8, no. 4, (Spring 1989) 89–110, p.100.

37 Cust and Hughes, *Conflict*, pp. 17, 26.

38 Kevin Sharpe, *Criticism and Compliment* (Cambridge University Press, 1987). Sharpe suggests that courtly culture is not sycophantic (pp. 8–22), but 'courtly modes' were critical without 'any suspicion of disloyalty' (p. 293). More recently he has argued for recognition of the 'connections and parallels between "low" and "high" cultural levels'. Sharpe and Lake, Introduction, *Culture and Politics*, p. 10.

39 Fletcher, *Outbreak*, pp. 110–11, 130, 171–5. On crowds see Paul Slack, ed., *Rebellion, Popular Protest and Social Order in Early Modern England* (Cambridge University Press, 1984); and Tim Harris, *London Crowds in the Reign of Charles II* (Cambridge University Press, 1987), pp. 5–11.

40 See Butler, *Theatre and Crisis*, pp. 55–83, 84–99, 181–250.

41 Johann Sommerville, *Politics and Ideology in England 1603–1640* (Harlow: Longman, 1986), pp. 1–5. See also Gordon J. Schochet, *Patriarchalism in Political Thought* (Oxford: Basil Blackwell, 1975).

42 Timothy Lang, *The Victorians and the Stuart Heritage* (Cambridge University Press, 1995), pp. xi–xii.

43 For example, R. Malcolm Smuts, *Court Culture and the Origins of a Royalist Tradition in Early Stuart England* (Philadelphia: University of Pennsylvania Press, 1987), pp. 285–92.

44 James Wright, *Historia Histrionica: An Account of the English Stage* (London, 1699) p. 7.

45 Hotson, *Commonwealth*, pp. 17, 34, 38, 40, 46, 49; 3–58.

46 *Ibid.*, p. 3.

47 J. F. Danby, *The Poets on Fortune's Hill* (London: Faber, 1952), pp. 19, 156–7, 160–1.

48 Butler traces the model of 'decadence', challenging the view which sees the suppression of drama as inevitable, noting that no evidence suggests that contemporaries regarded it this way. Butler, *Theatre and Crisis*, pp. 1, 7–19.

49 See Potter, *Revels*, p. 263.

50 David Norbrook, *Poetry and Politics in the Renaissance* (London: Routledge and Kegan Paul, 1984), p. 2. For the debates on literary value and the canon see Robert Von Hallberg, ed., *Canons* (Chicago and London: University of Chicago Press, 1984), esp. Barbara Herrnstein Smith, 'Contingencies of Value', pp. 5–40.

51 Harbage, *Cavalier*, pp. 7, 21–5.

52 *Ibid.*, p. 1.

53 Montague Summers, *The Playhouse of Pepys* (London: Kegan Paul, 1935), p. 1.

54 Dale Randall, *Winter Fruit*, pp. 16, 370.

55 G. Blakemore Evans, *Elizabethan–Jacobean Drama* (London: A. and C. Black, 1987), p. 3.

56 Stephen Gosson, *The Schoole of Abuse* (London, 1579); Phillip Stubbes, *The Anatomie of Abuses* (London, 1583). See also the group of texts regularly read by critics of Renaissance drama, running from John

Northbrooke, *A Treatise wherein Dicing, Dancing, Vain Plaies or Enterludes with other idle pastimes . . . are reprooved* (London, 1579) to William Prynne *Histrio-Mastix, The Players Scourge* (London, 1633). See Barish, *The Antitheatrical Prejudice* (Berkeley and London: University of California Press, 1981) p. 83.

57 William Van Lennep, ed., *The London Stage 1660–1800* (Carbondale Illinois: Southern Illinois University Press, 1965), I, xxi. See also Laura Brown, *English Dramatic Form 1660–1760* (New Haven and London: Yale University Press, 1981), p. xi.

58 Michel Foucault's writings on power and society have been influential in the construction of the dominant new historicist paradigms which interpret plays as cultural rituals enacting the movements of power. Also influential have been the interest in ritual, power and performance in the work of the anthropologists Clifford Geertz and Victor Turner but these seem to have been taken up, as it were, through a Foucauldian model of power. See Stephen Greenblatt in *Renaissance Self-Fashioning From More to Shakespeare* (Chicago and London: University of Chicago Press, 1980). See Clifford Geertz, *Local Knowledge* (New York: Basic, 1983), esp. 'Centers, Kings and Charisma: Reflections on the Symbolics of Power', pp. 121–46; Hildred Geertz and Clifford Geertz, *Kinship in Bali* (Chicago and London: Chicago University Press, 1975); Victor Turner, *The Anthropology of Performance* (New York: PAJ Publications, 1986), and *Process, Performance and Pilgrimage* (New Delhi: Concept, 1979). On new historicism see David Norbrook, 'Life and Death', pp. 89–110.

59 For instance, Stephen Greenblatt, 'The Improvisation of Power', in *Renaissance Self-Fashioning*, pp. 222–54.

60 Jonathan Goldberg, *James I and the Politics of Literature* (Stanford University Press, forthcoming), p. xi.

61 One example is Leonard Tennenhouse's beguilingly vague analysis of the closure of the theatres. He writes, 'Indeed, when the argument concerning access to aristocratic power came to an end, Renaissance theater came to an end.' Tennenhouse has restricted the role of theatre to an enactment of state concerns and kingly power, and therefore his argument is troubled (and potentially contradicted) by the theatrical developments of 1642 and after. Perhaps this is why he follows Summers, Harbage and others in seeing the demise of theatre as inevitable once those who opposed the monarchy took control, though he is marginally more sympathetic to what he calls the 'voices' against the stage. Leonard Tennenhouse, *Power on Display: The Politics of Shakespearean Genres* (New York and London: Methuen, 1986), p. 186.

62 Norbrook, 'Life and Death', p. 107.

63 *Ibid.*, p. 90.

64 See Catherine Gallagher, 'Marxism and the New Historicism', in *The*

New Historicism, ed. H. Aram Veeser (London: Routledge, 1989), pp. 37–48; James Holstun, 'Ranting at the New Historicism', *ELR* 19, no. 2 (1989), 189–225; Annabel Patterson, 'The Very Name of the Game: Theories of Order and Disorder', in *Literature and the English Civil War*, ed. Thomas Healy and Jonathan Sawday (Cambridge University Press, 1990), pp. 21–37. For the different claims of cultural materialists see Jonathan Dollimore, *Political Shakespeare: New Essays in Cultural Materialism*, ed. Jonathan Dollimore and Alan Sinfield (Manchester University Press, 1985), p. 15.

65 Christopher Hill, *Milton and the English Revolution* (1977; rpt London: Faber and Faber, 1979), p. 65. Hill's ideas on censorship were unequivocal: 'before 1641, and after 1660, there was a strict censorship. In the intervening years of freedom, a printing press was a relatively cheap and portable piece of equipment', *The World Turned Upside Down*, p. 17. Hill was followed by Margot Heinemann, *Puritanism and Theatre: Thomas Middleton and Opposition Drama under The Early Stuarts* (Cambridge University Press, 1980), pp. 18–22, 26–31, 36–47. See also Nigel Smith, *A Collection of Ranter Writings* (London: Junction Books, 1983), p. 8. However, the work of Hill and Heinemann lacked both detail and, to an extent, theorisation of what censorship might be or mean. These have been the twin directions of recent research; see on the one hand Janet Clare, *'Art made Tongue-tied by Authority': Elizabethan and Jacobean Dramatic Censorship* (Manchester University Press, 1990), and in terms of how censorship might be considered or affect writing practice, Annabel Patterson, *Censorship and Interpretation: The Conditions of Writing and Reading in Early Modern England* (Berkeley: University of California Press, 1987).

66 See Hill's analysis of self-censorship before 1640: *Milton*, e.g. p. 66. See also Kevin Sharpe's critique, *Criticism and Compliment*, pp. 36–8. Sharpe's critique is pertinent, but even so he does not take account of the changes from 1640 to 1642.

67 John Milton, *Areopagitica* (1643) in *The Works of John Milton*, ed. Frank Allen Patterson (New York: Columbia University Press), IV, 293–354.

68 On encryption see Patterson, *Censorship*; Lois Potter, *Secret Rites and Secret Writing* (Cambridge University Press, 1989).

69 Lucasta Miller, '"The Shattered Violl": Print and Textuality in the 1640s', in *Literature and Censorship*, ed. Nigel Smith (Cambridge: D. S. Brewer, 1993) pp. 25–38, p. 38. See also Richard Burt, *Licensed by Authority: Ben Jonson and the Discourses of Censorship* (Ithaca and London: Cornell University Press, 1993), pp. 1–25, 150–68; and '(Un)censoring in Detail: Thomas Middleton, Fetishism, and the Regulation of Dramatic Discourse', forthcoming in Gary Taylor, ed., *Thomas Middleton and Early Modern Textual Criticism* (Oxford University Press).

70 David Trotter, *The Poetry of Abraham Cowley* (London: Macmillan, 1979), p. 2.

71 See Conrad Russell, *The Crisis of Parliaments: English History 1509–1660* (1971; rpt Oxford University Press, 1982), pp. 361–3. On 'the popular', Antonio Gramsci, *The Cultural Writings*, trans. William Boelhower, ed. David Forgacs and Geoffrey Nowell-Smith (London: Lawrence and Wishart, 1985), p. 195; Stuart Hall, 'Notes on Deconstructing "the Popular"', in *People's History and Socialist Theory*, ed. Raphael Samuel (London: Routledge and Kegan Paul, 1981). See chapter 1.

72 Nigel Smith, *Literature and Revolution in England 1640–1660* (New Haven and London: Yale University Press, 1994) p. 71. Phillip Stubbes, *The Anatomie of Abuses*, ed. William B. D. D. Turnbull (1585; rpt London: W. Pickering, 1836), pp. 160–8, 214.

1 NEW NEWS FOR A NEW WORLD?

1 John Eliot, *Ortho-Epia Gallica* (1593), quoted D. C. Collins, *Battle of Nieuport*, Shakespeare Association Facsimiles no. 9, p. vi.

2 18 Nov. 1640, *The Diary of John Rous*, ed. Mary Anne Everett (Camden Society, no. 66, 1656) p. 109; William Walwyn, *The Power of Love*, in William Haller and Geoffrey Davis, eds. *The Leveller Tracts 1647–1653* (New York: Columbia University Press, 1944).

3 *The Knyvett Letters (1620–1644)*, ed. Bertram Scholfield (London: Constable, 1949) pp. 42–3.

4 Contrasting visions of the relationship of political agency to censorship, ideology and subjectivity are given by Richard Burt, see e.g. *Licensed by Authority*; David Norbrook, '*Areopagitica*, Censorship and the Early Modern Public Sphere', in Richard Burt, ed., *The Administration of Aesthetics* (Minneapolis and London: University of Minnesota Press, 1994), pp. 3–33, I borrow language here from p. 12. Contrast Dale Randall, *Winter Fruit*, p. 53.

5 Christopher Hill, 'Censorship and English Literature', *Collected Essays* (Brighton: Harvester, 1985) I, 32–71; Annabel Patterson, *Censorship and Interpretation*; Sheila Lambert, 'The Printers and the Government', in Robin Myers and Michael Harris, eds., *Aspects of Printing* (Oxford University Press, 1978), pp. 1–29.

6 See for example J. C. Davis, *Fear, Myth*, for a discussion of the use of pamphlet evidence.

7 Mikhail Bakhtin, 'The Problem of Speech Genres', in *Speech Genres and Other Late Essays*, trans. and ed. Caryl Emerson and Michael Holquist (Austin: University of Texas Press, 1986), pp. 60–65.

8 *Ibid.*, p. 66; 'From the Prehistory of Novelistic Discourse', in *The Dialogic Imagination*, ed. Michael Holquist, trans. Caryl Emerson and Michael Holquist (Austin: University of Texas Press, 1981), pp. 41–83, esp. pp. 44–5.

David Underdown rightly brings a more questioning approach to popular culture, particularly with regard to the issue of 'radical' potential in popular culture *per se, Revel,* p. 208. The debate over popular culture and historical methodology can be seen as taking three distinct and established trends. One can be seen as Foucauldian historical analysis including *The History of Sexuality,* 1, trans. Robert Hurley (London: Allen Lane, 1979). This concentrates on negotiations of power in social relations. Then there is the cultural history of work and popular ceremony including especially Robert Darnton, *The Great Cat Massacre* (London: Allen Lane, 1984). Thirdly, there has been British social history including particularly the work of Keith Wrightson, *English Society 1580–1680* (London: Hutchinson, 1982), and Lawrence Stone, *The Family, Sex and Marriage* (London: Weidenfeld and Nicolson, 1977).

During the 1980s the debate on what 'popular culture' might be and its relationship to political agency and radicalism became more self-reflexive. Stuart Clark attacks French history and its use of the term 'popular culture' in 'French Historians and Early Modern Popular Culture', *PP*, no. 100 (1983), 62–100; Dominick La Capra, 'Is Everyone a Mentalité Case? Transference and the "Culture" Concept', *History and Criticism* (Ithaca and London: Cornell University Press, 1985), pp. 71–94, esp. pp. 76–81, 88–92. Recently the assumption that popular culture is in some obvious way subversive or radical *per se* has been usefully questioned by Tim Harris, *London Crowds*. In alliance with the significant analyses of print culture by Roger Chartier and particularly his term 'appropriation', this new sense of the politically diverse, contradictory and problematic nature of the 'popular' has opened up the possibility of a nuanced investigation of the relationship between politics, print culture and the category of the popular, though Chartier himself appears to be reluctant to consider different readings and reading circumstances as political. As these opening chapters indicate, popular politics are by no means necessarily 'radical' politics but responses which may subvert or evade a dominant ideology in a number of ways. See Roger Chartier, ed., *The Culture of Print,* trans. Lydia G. Cochrane (Cambridge: Polity Press, 1989). See also Peter Burke's influential article, 'Popular Culture in Seventeenth-Century London', (1977), expanded and reprinted in *Popular Culture in Seventeenth-Century England,* ed. Barry Reay (Beckenham: Croom Helm, 1985).

9 Virginia Cox, *The Renaissance Dialogue* (Cambridge University Press, 1992), pp. 2, 26–30.
10 Peter Burke, 'The Renaissance Dialogue', *Renaissance Studies,* 3, no. 1, 1–12, pp. 2–3.
11 Linda Levy-Peck, *Court Patronage and Corruption in Early Stuart England* (Routledge: London, 1990), pp. 3, 1–5, 9–10.
12 John Pym, *The Declaration of John Pym, Esquire, upon the Whole Matter of*

the *Charge of High Treason against Thomas Earl of Strafford* (12 Apr.)
1641, p. 10. Quoted Linda Levy-Peck, *Court Patronage*, p. 204.

13 Kevin Sharpe, *The Personal Rule of Charles I* (New Haven and London:
Yale University Press, 1992), pp. 644–54 esp. p. 654; A. B. Worden,
'Literature and Political Censorship in Early Modern England', in A.
C. Duke and C. Tamse, eds., *Too Mighty to Be Free* (Zutphen: De
Walburg Pers, 1987), pp. 45–62.

14 Michael Frearson, 'The Distribution and Readership of London
Corantos in the 1620s', in Robin Myers and Michael Harris, eds.
Serials and their Readers 1620–1914 (Delaware: Oak Knoll Press,
1993), pp. 1–25.

15 Richard Cust, 'News and Politics in Early Seventeenth-Century
England', *PP*, no. 112 (August 1986), pp. 64, 60.

16 See also Edward Arber, ed., *Transcripts of the Register of the Company of
Stationers of London* (London: privately printed, 1875–94), IV,
528–30.

17 Cust, 'News', p. 64. Contrast Kevin Sharpe's account of dramatists as
perhaps experiencing 'a certain paranoia', *Personal Rule*, pp. 690–1.

18 Cust, 'News', p. 66.

19 *Ibid.*, pp. 78–9.

20 *The Journal of Sir Simon D'Ewes* (New Haven: Yale University Press,
1842), ed. Wilson Havelock Coates, pp. 191–2. See also Potter, *Secret
Rites*, pp. 3–7.

21 Donald F. McKenzie, *The London Book Trade in the Later Seventeenth
Century* (Syndics of Cambridge University Library, 1976), pp. 2–3.

22 Richard Overton, *New Lambeth Fayre*, E.138 (26), (1642), A2r–v, B4v.
One of the pamphlets actually signed by Overton. See also *Lambeth
Fayre* (1641).

23 Thomas Rogers, *Leicesters Ghost* (1605, rpt 1641). Ed. William B.
Franklin, Jr (University of Chicago Press, 1972); *The Organs Funerall*
(1642), E.141 (6).

24 *A Discourse or Dialogue Between . . . Lord Generall Militia and . . . the
Commission of Array*, E.240 (28), (1642), pp. 4–6. See also *A Dialogue
or Discourse Betwixt Two Old Acquaintance of Contrary Opinions* (1647).
Fletcher, *Outbreak*, pp. 244–6, 260–1, 322–4.

25 See e.g. Hezekiah Woodward, *A Briefe Dialogue Between a Creditor and a
Prisoner*, E.713 (5), (August 1653); *A Dialogue Arguing that Arch-
Bishops, Bishops etc., are to be Cut Off by Law of God*, E.34 (10), (1644).

26 See also Pearl, *Puritan Revolution*, pp. 238–40; Fletcher, *Outbreak*, p.
336.

27 I am grateful to Dr Julie Sanders for this point.

28 McKenzie, *The London Book Trade*, p. 10.

29 *The Wishing Common-wealthsman: Or a Dialogue betwixt Cautious a
Country Man and Wish-well a Citizen*, E.114 (11), (London, August
1642). Subsequent references in text.

30 Stuart Hall, 'Notes on Deconstructing the Popular', in Raphael Samuel, ed., *People's History*, pp. 227–40.

31 *The Wicked Resolution of the Cavaliers*, E.127 (42), (1642); *Times Changeling, Arraigned For Inconstancy at the Barre of Opportunity*, E.91 (31), (1643).

32 Underdown, *Revel*, p. 216.

33 *The Soudiers Language or a Discourse Between Two Soldiers*, E.10 (10) (1644). Collected by Thomason 26 Sept. 1644.

34 Hirst, *Authority and Conflict: England and 1603–1658* (London: Edward Arnold, 1986) pp. 250–1.

35 *The Reformed Malignants*, E.250 (6), (1643).

36 *Ibid.*, p. 4.

37 *The Arraignment of Superstition*, E.136 (31), (1641). The *Journal of William Dowsing* (London, 1786) suggests the impact of iconoclasm on parish life.

38 Elizabeth Skerpan, *The Rhetoric of Politics in the English Revolution 1642–1660* (Columbia and London: University of Missouri Press, 1992), pp. 64, 73, 77, 79.

39 Martin Butler, 'A Case Study in Caroline Political Theatre: Brathwaite's *Mercurius Britannicus* (1641)', *The Historical Journal*, 27, no. 4 (1984), 947–53. He argues that the play may have been performed at Paris (pp. 950–1). See also W. J. Adams, Jr, 'Richard Brathwaite's *Mercurius Britannicus*', *Modern Language Notes*, no. 26 (1911), 233–5.

40 James Harrington, *Oceana, The Political Works of James Harrington*, ed. J. G. A. Pocock (Cambridge University Press, 1977), p. 268. On public debate see pp. 100–6, 116.

41 James Harrington, *Valerius and Publicola* (1659) in Pocock, *The Political Works of James Harrington*, p. 783.

42 Margaret Spufford, *Small Books and Pleasant Histories* (Cambridge University Press, 1981), p. 7, quotes Bunyan, *Sighs From Hell* (1666?) (2nd edn) pp. 147–8.

43 Thomas Hobbes, *Behemoth, or the Long Parliament*, in *Collected Works of Thomas Hobbes*, ed. William Molesworth (London: Routledge/ Thoemmes Press, 1843; rpt 1994), VI, 375.

44 See, for example, Jean E. Howard, *The Stage and Social Struggle in Early Modern England* (London and New York, 1994), pp. 22–73. Jonas Barish, *The Antitheatrical Prejudice*, indicates the well-known Puritan attacks on theatre.

45 Jürgen Habermas, *The Structural Transformation of the Public Sphere*, trans. Thomas Burger (Cambridge: Polity Press, 1989) pp. 27, 29–30, 38–42; Butler, *Theatre and Crisis*, p. 233.

46 *Catalogue of the Thomason Tracts* (London: Longman, 1908), vol. I, pt 1, p. xi.

47 *Ibid.*, vol. I, pt 1, p. xxi.

48 Laurence Prince, *A New Dialogue Between Dick of Kent and Wat the Welchman*, E.228 (1), (London, 1654), A2v. For an analysis of rural literacy see Margaret Spufford, *Contrasting Communities: English Villages in the Sixteenth and Seventeenth Centuries* (Cambridge University Press, 1974), pp. 171–218.

49 Anthony Cotton, 'London Newsbooks in the Civil War: Their Political Attitudes and Sources of Information', Diss. Oxford University, 1971, p. 14; McKenzie cites a pamphlet of 1651 which had a print run of 1,000. *The London Book Trade*, p. 29.

50 Chartier, 'Texts, Printings, Readings', in *The New Cultural History*, ed. Lynn Hunt (Berkeley: University of California Press, 1989), pp. 154–75, p. 156.

51 Norbrook, '*Areopagitica*' in Burt, ed. *Aesthetics*, p. 24.

52 Natalie Zemon Davis, 'Printing and the People', in *Society and Culture in Early Modern France* (Cambridge: Polity Press, 1987) p. 19.

53 There is general agreement that literacy expanded during 1500 to 1700, though historians have used very different methodologies to arrive at their conclusions. Peter Clark's small sample of towns in Kent indicates that these towns 'saw a major growth in book ownership in the period 1560–1640 affecting not only prosperous *potentoires* but also in some measure the respectable society'. See 'The Ownership of Books in England 1560–1640: the Example of Some Kentish Townsfolk', in *Schooling and Society: Studies in the History of Education*, ed. Lawrence Stone (Baltimore and London: Johns Hopkins University Press, 1976), pp. 95–111. One might object that the sample is small and local and that the research stops short, on the verge of the major upheaval of the century, suggesting a trend which might or might not continue during the 1640s. Other historians use different measures including matriculation records of social background as in Lawrence Stone, 'Literacy and Education in England, 1640–1690', *PP*, no. 42 (1969), 69–139. Studies of literacy are beset by problems about how to determine the ability to write (is the ability to sign an adequate guide?) and about the relationship between the different skills of writing and reading. On the methodology of studies of literacy see R. Scholfield, 'The Measurement of Literacy in Pre-Industrial England', in *Literacy in Traditional Societies*, ed. Jack Goody (Cambridge University Press, 1968), pp. 310–25. The most recent study of literacy in seventeenth-century England is David Cressy, *Literacy and the Social Order: Reading and Writing in Tudor and Stuart England* (Cambridge University Press, 1980). Cressy uses the Protestation Oath of 1641 (returns 1642), the Vow and Covenant (1643) and the Solemn League and Covenant (1644). He writes, 'London parishes were always the first to subscribe . . . Mass involvement in public affairs was becoming habitual, and it was not confined to the metropolis', pp. 69–70. The

Protestation returns of 1642 and the Solemn League and Covenant (1644) provide statistics for those who could sign their name and suggest that London had a high rate of literacy – David Cressy gives the figure of 33 per cent to 39 per cent illiteracy in London in 1641–4, a figure much lower than any part of the country surveyed. See Spufford, *Small Books*, p. 22; Stone, 'Literacy and Education', pp. 110–11, 120–1; Cressy, *Literacy and the Social Order*, pp. 62–103.

In the light of these figures Stone's earlier emphasis on 'the widespread public participation in intellectual debate on every front' seems reasonable (Lawrence Stone, 'The Educational Revolution in England 1560–1640', *PP*, no. 28 (1964), 41–80). Moreover, pamphlet dialogues and playlets are well adapted for reading out loud, a practice which, as the historian of the book, Roger Chartier, persuasively argues, continued in public and private well into the eighteenth century, and which would ensure circulation beyond the literate alone. Roger Chartier, 'Texts, Printings, Readings', p. 159.

54 Cotton, 'London Newsbooks', p. 13. For the June 1643 ordinance against printing see Joseph Frank, *The Beginnings of the English Newspaper* (Cambridge, Mass.: Harvard University Press, 1961) p. 32. See also, Margaret Spufford, *Small Books*, pp. xviii, 19–21; Stone, 'The Educational Revolution', pp. 41–80, esp. pp. 43–7. There is also an Interregnum pamphlet dialogue on the topic of schooling: *A Discourse in Derision of a Teaching in Free-Schools*, E.53 (7), (1644).

55 *Mercurius Melancholicus*, E.410 (12) (2–9 Oct. 1647). Hotson, *Commonwealth*, pp. 26–7.

56 *Journals of the House of Commons*, Hotson, *Commonwealth*, p. 38.

57 McKenzie, *The British Book Trade 1641–1714: A Chronology and Calendar of Documents* (London: British Library, 1976); John Milton, *Areopagitica*, in *Works*, IV, 353. See also Conrad Russell, *The Crisis of Parliaments*, p. 369; Hirst, *Authority and Conflict*, p. 280.

58 Underdown, *Revel*, p. 208.

59 Hirst, *Authority and Conflict*, p. 250–1.

60 Henry Marten, 'Opinions offered', Brotherton ML 78:10. In Marten's papers there is also a manuscript dialogue – on polygamy.

2 'WITH THE AGREEMENT OF THE PEOPLE IN THEIR HANDS': TRANSFORMATIONS OF 'RADICAL' DRAMA IN THE 1640S

1 Compare Randall, *Winter Fruit*, p. 65.

2 Margaret Jacobs and James Jacobs, eds., *The Origins of Anglo-American Radicalism* (London: Allen and Unwin, 1984), p. 1; Conal Condren, *The Language of Politics in Seventeenth-Century England* (Basingstoke: Macmillan, 1994).

3 Ann Hughes, *The Causes of the English Civil War* (Basingstoke: Macmillan, 1990), p. 1.

4 A. L. Morton, *A People's History of England* (London: Gollancz, 1938), p. 250; (second edn, London: Lawrence and Wishart, 1948).

5 Richard Overton (attributed), *Vox Borealis or The Northern Discovery*, 'Printed by Margery Mar-Prelat in Thwackcoat Lane', (1641). One of the Marprelate Tracts very likely to be by Overton. See Don M. Wolfe, 'Unsigned Pamphlets of Richard Overton', *Huntington Library Quarterly*, 21, no. 2 (1958), 167–201. Wolfe's willingness to attribute pamphlets on stylistic grounds is sometimes problematic because of the parodic and intertextual nature of 1640s pamphleteering. See also Nigel Smith, 'Richard Overton's Marpriest Tracts: Towards a History of Leveller Style', in *The Literature of Controversy: Polemical Satire from Milton to Junius*, ed. Thomas Corns (London: Frank Cass, 1987), pp. 39–66, esp. pp. 43–4.

6 On the early pamphlets see Butler, *Theatre and Crisis*, pp. 238–42; Heinemann, *Puritanism and Theatre*, pp. 237–57.

7 Richard Overton (attributed), *The Arraignment of Mr Persecution* (1645), 'By Younge Martin Marpriest, Son to old Martin the Metropolitaine', 'Printed by Martin Claw-Clergie . . . to be sold at his shop in Toleration Street, at the Sign of the Subjects Liberty, right opposite to the Persecuting Courts'. Subsequent references in text.

8 Henry Parker, *Observations*, in William Haller, ed., *Tracts on Liberty in the Puritan Revolution*, vol. II; subsequent references in text.

9 *Martin's Echo*, E.290 (2), (June 1645). Non-dramatic follow-up railing against those who 'free us from Episcopall Persecution, to devour us with Presbyterian cruelty', p. 2. See also, *The Agreement of the People* (Oct., 1647); *Petition to the House of Commons* (1648).

10 John Lilburne, *The Legall Fundamental Liberties* (1649). See Don M. Wolfe, *Leveller Manifestoes of the Puritan Revolution* (New York: Thomas Nelson, 1944); William Haller and Geoffrey Davis, eds., *The Leveller Tracts 1647–1653* (New York: Columbia University Press, 1944).

11 William Walwyn, monologue, *A Prediction of Master Edwards His Conversion; A Parable or Consultation of Physicians Upon Master Edwards; Truth's Victory Over Tyrants and Tyranny*, E.579 (12), (1649), p. 4. See also Pauline Gregg, *Free-Born John* (London: Dent, 1961; rpt 1986), p. 295. On Lilburne's writing see also Joan Webber, *The Eloquent 'I': Self and Style in Seventeenth-Century Prose* (Madison and London: University of Wisconsin Press, 1968), p. 6.

12 On Presbyterianism in London government and the Commons, see for example Gregg, *Free-Born John*, pp. 147–52, 170–94. See also P. W. Thomas, *Sir John Berkenhead 1617–1679* (Oxford: Clarendon Press, 1969), pp. 121, 127–31.

13 Marchmont Nedham (Mercurius Pragmaticus) (attributed), *The Levellers Levell'd* (1647), ed. Philip C. Dust, *AEB*, 4, nos. 3 and 4 (com-

bined), (1980), 182–240. See p. 199. Subsequent references in text. *Hampton Court Conspiracy*, E.416 (15), (London, Nov. 1647).

14 Marchmont Nedham, *The Case of the Commonwealth of England Stated* (1650); Joseph Frank, *Cromwell's Press Agent: A Critical Biography of Marchmont Nedham* (Lanham: University Press of America, 1980), pp. 73–90.

15 *The Scotch Politike Presbyter. A Tragi-Comedie* (1647); *A New Bull-Bayting* (1649). Subsequent references in text.

16 *New-Market Fayre* I and II (June 1649, 16 July 1649), ed. Paul Werstine in *AEB*, 6, nos. 2 and 4 (1982), 71–103, 209–39. Attributed to Overton by Don M. Wolfe, 'Unsigned Pamphlets', using stylistic evidence. For representations of the wives of army grandees, see also John Tatham, *The Rump* (1659); *Cromwell's Conspiracie* (1660).

17 Paul Werstine attributes *New-Market Fayre* to John Crouch on the evidence of the dedicatory poem which addresses him as 'the Man in the Moone'. Werstine does not note connections additional to or other than royalist ones, such as the setting-on of the Man in the Moon's dog by the character of Overton in *A New Bull-Bayting*. Werstine says that the plays have hitherto been considered anonymous and is apparently unaware of Don M. Wolfe's attribution of *New-Market Fayre* to Overton. Although Wolfe too seems to attribute the play on slender evidence his comment is apposite: 'Though at first glance, because Charles is mentioned as a martyr, the tracts may appear to be royalist in origin, the . . . two sympathetic references to *The Agreement of the People* in Part II eliminate the possibility of royalist authorship' (Don M. Wolfe 'Unsigned Pamphlets', pp. 197–8). However, one could alter his phrase to 'simply royalist authorship', and his comment does not address the problem of how contemporaries conceptualised their own political positions. The question of authorship remains unresolved, but this in itself is evidence of the political and rhetorical complexity of these satires.

18 Lois Potter, *Secret Rites*, pp. 35–6.

19 *Ibid.*

20 Richard Baxter, *Reliquiae Baxterianae*, ed. Matthew Sylvester (London, 1696), p. 53. See also Gregg, *Free-Born John*, pp. 156–7; A. S. P. Woodhouse, *Puritanism and Liberty* (1938; rpt London: Dent, 1986), p. 23.

21 See J. C. Davis, *Fear, Myth*, pp. 108–9.

22 *Grand Plutoe's Progresse*, E.405 (16), (Sept. 1647). See *Journal of the House of Commons*, V, 246.a. Quoted in Hotson, *Commonwealth*, p. 24.

23 Samuel Sheppard, *The Second Part of the Committee Man Curried*, E.401 (40), (1647).

24 J. C. Davis, *Fear, Myth*, p. 143. See also Hyder E. Rollins, 'Samuel Sheppard and His Praise of Poets', *SP*, 24, no. 1 (1927), 509–56. See pp. 523–9.

25 Robert Ashton, 'From Cavalier to Roundhead Tyranny', in *Reactions*

to the English Civil War, ed. John Morrill (London: Macmillan, 1982), pp. 185–207. Hirst, *Authority and Conflict*, p. 283.

26 Anthony Ascham, *A Discourse Wherein is Examined What is Particularly Lawful During the Confusion and Revolution in Government* (London, 1648); John Goodwin, *Right and Might Well Met* (London, 1648).

27 *Stop Your Noses, or England at Her Easement, Evacuating those Clods at Westminster* (London, 1648).

28 Richard Overton, *The Bayting of the Great Bull of Bashan* (1649). Written by Overton in the Tower.

29 *An Honest Discourse Between Three Neighbours, touching the Present Government in these Three Nations*, E.840 (10), (1655). See also *Free-Born John*, Gregg, pp. 340–5. Hill, *World Turned Upside Down*, p. 240.

30 *The Picture of a New Courtier Drawn in a Conference between Mr Timeserver and Mr Plainheart*, (E.875 (7), (London 1656). Subsequent references in text.

31 Henry Neville (attributed), *Shuffling, Cutting and Dealing in a Game at Pickquet*, E.983 (9), (London, 1659). Similar sentiments were expressed by Marchmont Nedham, *Interest Will Not Lie* (1659).

32 Jonathan Dollimore, *Radical Tragedy: Religion, Ideology and Power in the Drama of Shakespeare and His Contemporaries* (Brighton: Harvester, 1984) pp. 3–4.

33 Leonard Tennenhouse, *Power on Display*, p. 186.

34 Jonathan Dollimore, *Radical Tragedy*, pp. 3–5.

35 Harold Love, 'State Affairs on the Restoration Stage 1660–1675', *Restoration and Eighteenth-Century Theatre Research*, no. 14 (May 1975), 1–22.

3 ROYALIST VERSUS REPUBLICAN ETHICS AND AESTHETICS
THE FAMOUS TRAGEDIE OF CHARLES I AND *THE TRAGEDY OF THE FAMOUS ORATOR MARCUS TULLIUS CICERO*

1 See Steven N. Zwicker's discussion of *Eikon Basilike* and *Eikonoklastes*, *Lines of Authority* (Ithaca and London: Cornell University Press, 1993) pp. 37–47.

2 *The Famous Tragedie of Charles I* (1649); *The Tragedy of the Famous Orator, Marcus Tullius Cicero* (1651). Subsequent references in text. See also the discussion of *The Famous Tragedie*, Nigel Smith, *Literature and Revolution*, pp. 81–4; compare Randall, *Winter Fruit*, pp. 103–11.

3 See Gregg, *Free-Born John*, pp. 263–5, on the illegality of Capel's trial.

4 P. W. Thomas, *Berkenhead*, suggests that 'when, as frequently happened, [royalist writers] were caught their work was taken over by other writers', pp. 150–1. Joseph Frank, *Beginnings*, pp. 174–5, 193–7.

5 Nigel Smith proposes Samuel Sheppard as author, *Literature and Revolution*, pp. 81–6.

6 Because of the parodic and intertextual nature of Civil War journal-

ism, attribution must be tentative. Techniques of satirical polemic included the imitation of styles and reworking of genres as well as fake attribution.

7 Joseph Frank, *Marchmont Nedham*, pp. 56–63. Marchmont Nedham, *Digitus Dei* (London, 1649); Marchmont Nedham, *A Most Pithy Exhortation* (London, 1649).

8 Joseph Frank, *Marchmont Nedham*, pp. 64–74. Marchmont Nedham, *The Case of the Commonwealth Stated* (London, 1650).

9 Potter, *Secret Rites*, p. 101; Nancy Klein Maguire, *Regicide and Restoration* (Cambridge University Press, 1992), pp. 5–6.

10 Smuts, *Court Culture*, pp. 246–7, see also pp. 269–73.

11 On the manufacture of myth see Christian Jouhaud, 'Printing the Event: From La Rochelle to Paris', in *The Culture of Print*, trans. Lydia G. Cochrane, ed. Roger Chartier (Cambridge: Polity Press, 1989), pp. 290–335.

12 Although the siege of Colchester is now understood as an afterpiece to the defeat of the royalist army, to contemporaries it assumed symbolic proportions. See: *A Great and Bloudy Fight*, E.456 (11), (Aug. 1648); *Colchesters Tears*, E.455 (16), (13 July 1648); *The Colchester Spie*, E.458 (4), (11 Aug. 1648); *Mercurius Anglicanus*, E.576 (22), (31 Aug., 1648); *The Moderate Intelligencer*, E.461 (22), (24–31 Aug., 1648); *The Moderate*, E.461 (16), (22–9 Aug., 1648); *Another Bloudy Fight*, E.456 (26) (21 Aug., 1648); *Another Great Fight*, E.457 (15) (Aug., 1648); *A True . . . Relation . . . Sent in a Letter*, E.461 (24), (Aug., 1648); *A Letter From Sir Marmaduke Langdale*, E.457 (20), (Aug., 1648); *A True and Perfect Relation*, E.462 (16), (6 Sept., 1648); *Colchester Surrendered*, E.461 (15), (Aug., 1648); *Articles For the Surrender*, E.461 (18), (29 Aug. 1648). Lisle had already appeared in *Cola's Furie* and was known for fleeing the battle of Poulmounty, Ireland, in 1643.

13 *Sir Charles Lucas His Last Speech*, E.462 (20), (1648); Lionel Gatford, *England's Complaint*, E.461 (27), (31 Aug. 1648); *The Triumph of Loyalty*, E.463 (3), (29 Aug. 1648); *The Cruell Tragedy . . . of Hamar and Shechem*, E.462 (30), (Aug. 1648).

14 John Milton, Sonnet xv, 'On the Lord General Fairfax at the Siege of Colchester', *The Works*, I, Pt 1, 64.

15 Johann Sommerville, 'Oliver Cromwell and English Political Thought', in *Cromwell and the English Revolution*, ed. John Morrill (Harlow: Longman, 1990), pp. 234–58. John Milton, *Tenure of Kings and Magistrates*, in *Works*, V, 1–59. Subsequent references in text.

16 Edward Chayney, *The Grand Tour and the Great Rebellion* (Geneva: Slatkine, 1985), pp. 56–7.

17 Mary Douglas, *Purity and Danger: An Analysis of the Concepts of Pollution and Taboo* (1966; rpt London: Routledge and Kegan Paul, 1985), pp. 3, 99–100.

18 P. W. Thomas, *Berkenhead*, p. 151.

19 *Craftie Cromwell* (London, 1648). Thomason's copy dated February 1648.

20 Potter, *Revels*, p. 287.

21 See David Norbrook, 'Macbeth and the Politics of Historiography', in *The Politics of Discourse*, ed. Kevin Sharpe and Stephen Zwicker (Berkeley and Los Angeles: University of California Press, 1987), pp. 78–116.

21 See Victoria Kahn, *Machiavellian Rhetoric: From the Counter-Reformation to Milton* (New Jersey: Princeton University Press, 1994), pp. 3–10, 130–2. Kahn pinpoints the problematic way in which the reception of Machiavelli's texts has been divided into the 'Machiavel' and the prudential rhetorician of classical republicanism, arguing that the two are held in tension in seventeenth-century reading of Machiavelli and that tension is the source, for them, of Machiavellian rhetoric as a meta-discourse.

22 Andrew Marvell, 'An Horatian Ode upon Cromwell's Return From Ireland', *The Complete Poems*, ed. Elizabeth Story Donno (1972; rpt Harmondsworth: Penguin, 1979), pp. 55–8 175–6. Johann Sommerville, 'Oliver Cromwell', pp. 234–58.

23 A. B. Worden, 'Classical Republicanism and the Puritan Revolution', in Hugh Lloyd-Jones *et al.*, eds., *History and Imagination* (London: Duckworth, 1981), p. 183; Markku Peltonen, *Classical Humanism in English Political Thought* (Helsinki, 1992), esp. pp. 240–69.

24 Zera S. Fink, *The Classical Republicans: An Essay in the Recovery of a Pattern of Thought in Seventeenth-Century England* (Evanston, Ill.: Northwestern University Press, 1945), e.g. pp. 10–27; David Norbrook, 'Macbeth', pp. 81, 84, 91–2. See J. G. A. Pocock, *The Machiavellian Moment: Florentine Political Thought and the Atlantic Republican Tradition* (Princeton University Press, 1975).

25 George Buchanan, *Tyranicall Government Anatomized: A Discourse Concerning Evil Counsellors* (London, 1643).

26 Annabel Patterson, 'Pastoral versus Georgic', in *Renaissance Genres*, ed. Barbara Lewalski (Cambridge, Mass.: Harvard University Press, 1986), p. 259; Graham Parry, 'A Troubled Arcadia', in *Literature and the English Civil War*, ed. Healy and Sawday, pp. 38–55. See also, Patterson, *Pastoral and Ideology: Virgil to Valéry* (Oxford: Clarendon Press, 1988).

27 *Augustus, or an Essay of those Measures and Counsels, Whereby the Commonwealth of Rome was Altered and Reduced into a Monarchy* (London, 1632). Subsequent references in text.

28 Worden, 'Classical Republicanism', pp. 182–200.

29 Jonathan Scott, *Algernon Sidney and the English Republic, 1623–1677* (Cambridge University Press, 1988) p. 15.

30 See Nigel Smith, 'Popular Republicanism in the 1650s: John Streater's "Heroick Mechanicks"', in David Armitage *et al.*, eds.,

Milton and Classical Republicanism (Cambridge University Press, 1995) pp. 137–55.

31 *The Life and Records of John Milton,* ed. J. Milton French (New Brunswick: Rutgers University Press, 1950), II, 310–11, quoted Joad Raymond, *Making the News* (Gloucester: Windrush Press, 1994), p. 335.

32 A. B. Worden, *The Rump Parliament, 1648–1653* (Cambridge University Press, 1974) p. 238.

33 *Ibid.*, pp. 195, 252.

34 Paul Bunyan Anderson, 'George Wither and the "Regalia"', *Philological Quarterly,* 14 (Oct. 1935), 366–8.

35 For a discussion of political process and the Franchise, see Derek Hirst, *The Representative of the People? Voters and Voting in England Under the Early Stuarts* (Cambridge University Press, 1975), pp. 18–23, 44.

36 Thomas Hobbes, *Leviathan,* ed. C. B. Macpherson (1651; rpt Harmondsworth: Penguin, 1981), 'Of Commonwealth', Pt II, chapter 21, p. 267. Richard Tuck, *Philosophy and Government 1572–1651* (Cambridge University Press, 1993), pp. 346–7.

37 James Harrington, *Commonwealth of Oceanea,* in *Political Works of James Harrington,* J. G. A. Pocock (ed.), (Cambridge University Press, 1977), p. 162.

38 Marcus Tullius Cicero, 'Defence of Milo', quoted by Robert N. Wilkin, 'Cicero and the Law of Nature', in *The Origins of the Natural Law Tradition,* ed. Arthur L. Harding (Dallas: Southern Methodist University Press, 1954), pp. 23–4.

39 Potter, *Revels,* p. 295.

40 Quoted in D. R. S. Bailey, *Cicero* (London: Duckworth, 1971), p. 176. See also pp. 276–7; *Livy in The Suasoriae of Seneca the Elder,* trans. William A. Edward (Cambridge University Press, 1928).

41 T. R., *Cicero's Prince: The Reasons and Counsels for Settlement and Good Government of a Kingdom Collected out of Cicero's Works* (London, 1668), A2v.

42 Edward Dacres, trans., *Nicholas Machiavel's Prince* (London, 1640; rpt Menston: Scolar Press, 1969). Ronald Hutton, *The Restoration: A Political and Religious History of England and Wales, 1658–1667* (Oxford University Press, 1985), pp. 189–90, 285–6.

43 Christopher Wase, *Cicero Against Catiline in IV Invective Orations* (London, 1671). Subsequent references in text. See also, Christopher Wase, *The Electra of Sophocles* (1649).

44 John Milton, *Tenure of Kings and Magistrates,* in *Works,* v, 1–59.

45 Smith, *Literature and Revolution,* p. 17.

46 *HMC,* de l'Isle, VI, 400, letter from Sidney's brother (17 June 1656). Quoted in Jonathan Scott, *Algernon Sidney and the English Revolution,* pp. 114–15.

INTERCHAPTER. 'THE LIFE OF ACTION': PLAYING, ACTION
AND DISCOURSE ON PERFORMANCE IN THE 1640S

1 *Mercurius Pragmaticus*, Sept. 21–8, 1647; quoted Hotson, *Commonwealth*, p.15.
2 William Prynne, *Histrio-Mastix* (London, 1633), sig. *2v.
3 See Alice Rayner, *To Act, To Do, To Perform: Drama and the Phenomenology of Action* (Ann Arbor: University of Michigan Press, 1994) p. 15.
4 Judith Butler, *Gender Trouble: Feminism and the Subversion of Identity* (London: Routledge, 1990) pp. 144–5.
5 Folger MS.X.d.600, quoted by Nigel Smith, *Literature and Revolution*, p. 172.
6 After the order of 17 July which included rope-dancing in the list of forbidden activities, John Warner, lord mayor of London, attempted to put down the puppet plays at Bartholomew Fair. See 'The Dagonizing of Bartholomew Fair', in Hyder E. Rollins, 'A Contribution to the History of the English Commonwealth Drama', *SP*, no. 18 (1921), 280–3.
7 Butler, *Theatre and Crisis*, pp. 240–7.
8 Louis B. Wright, 'The Reading of Plays During the Puritan Revolution', *Huntington Library Bulletin*, no. 6 (Nov. 1934), 73–112.
9 Adam Fox, 'Popular Verses and Their Readership in the Early Seventeenth Century', in *The Practice and Representation of Reading in England*, ed. James Raven, Helen Small, Naomi Tadmor (Cambridge University Press, 1995), pp. 125–37, p. 133.
10 Alex Helm, *The English Mummers' Play* (Woodbridge: D. S. Brewer, 1981) p. 7. See also Sandra Billington, *Mock Kings in Medieval Society and Renaissance Drama* (Oxford University Press, 1991).
11 See Hotson, *Commonwealth*, pp. 45–9.
12 *The Arraignment, Conviction and Imprisonment of Christmas*, E.315 (12), (1646); Hotson, *Commonwealth*, p. 124.
13 James Wright, *Historia Histrionica*, p. 12. Hotson records evidence of playing around Christmas 1648 – playing began again on 1 January when the ordinance of 16 July 1647 expired and in December and January 1649 measures were once again taken against the stage. Hotson, *Commonwealth*, pp. 26–7, 46–7.
14 *A Bartholomew Fairing*, E.565 (6), (Aug. 1649).
15 Laurence Prince, *A New Dialogue Between Dick of Kent and Wat the Welchman*, E.487 (4), (1654).
16 *A New Fiction or, As Wee Were*, E.1088 (3), (London, April 1661). Thanks to David Bond for generously bringing this text to my attention.
17 E.g. *Mercurius Poeticus*, 'St George and the Dragon Anglice', 669.f.23 (66), (Feb., 1659); *St George For England*, C.40.m.11, (1659).
18 Alex Helm, 'In comes I, St George', *Folklore*, no. 76 (Summer 1965), 18–137, p. 121. E. K. Chambers, *The English Folk-Play* (Oxford:

Clarendon Press, 1933), pp. 183–4. Margaret Spufford, *Small Books*, p. 253.

19 *Perfect Occurrences*, E.260 (37), (9–16 May) 1645.

4 GENDER AND STATUS IN DRAMATIC DISCOURSE MARGARET CAVENDISH, DUCHESS OF NEWCASTLE

1 Margaret Cavendish, *Playes* (London, 1662), A15r. Subsequent references in text. The Duke of Newcastle also theorised about the restoration of the theatre, writing to Charles Stuart advocating the restoration of public and more 'popular' theatres and festivities. See S. Arthur Strong, *A Catalogue of Letters . . . Exhibited in the Library at Welbeck* (London: John Murray, 1903), pp. 226–7. See also Douglas Grant, *Margaret the First* (London: Rupert Hart-Davies, 1957), pp. 149–50; Timothy Raylor, *The Seventeenth Century*, 9, no. 2 (1995).

2 Caroline Neely, 'Constructing the Subject: Feminist Practice and the New Renaissance Discourses', *ELR*, 18, no. 1 (Winter 1988), 4–22, esp. p. 5. On the category 'woman' see Denise Riley, *'Am I that name?': Feminism and the Category of Women in History* (Basingstoke: Macmillan, 1988), pp. 1, 10–11.

3 See Sophie Tomlinson, '"She that Plays the King": Henrietta Maria and the Threat of the Actress in Caroline Culture', in Gordon MacMullan and Jonathan Hope, eds., *The Politics of Tragicomedy* (London: Routledge, 1991); Elizabeth Howe, *The First English Actresses* (Cambridge University Press, 1992), pp. 19–26; *Renaissance Drama by Women: Texts and Documents*, ed. S. P. Cerasano and Marion Wynne-Davies (London: Routledge, 1996).

4 Obviously, the satirical frame of this makes the tone of specific remarks hard to gauge, and it is responding directly to Prynne (*Histrio-Mastix*, p. 214), but this seems to be a serious suggestion. *Mr William Prynne his Defence of Stage Plays* (London, 1649; privately printed, 1922), p. 7.

5 *Playes* (1662), A2r. Grant, *Margaret*, p. 161.

6 Thomas Killigrew, e.g. *Thomaso, or, The Wanderer* and *Bellamira* and his *Comedies and Tragedies* (London, 1664).

7 See Catherine Gallagher 'Embracing the Absolute: The Politics of the Female Subject in Seventeenth-Century England', *Genders*, no. 1 (Spring 1988), 24–39.

8 Samuel Pepys, *The Diary of Samuel Pepys*, ed. R. C. Latham and W. Matthews (London: G. Bell and Sons, 1974), VIII, 242–4. Grant, *Margaret*, pp. 15–19.

9 *The Letters of Dorothy Osborne*, ed. G. C. Smith (Oxford: Clarendon Press, 1928), pp. 37, 41; *The Diary of John Evelyn*, ed. E. S. de Beer, (Oxford University Press, 1955), III, 481.

10 Letter from Charles North to his father, 13 April 1667. Bodley MS. North c.4. fol 146. Thanks to Professor Robert Jordan.

11 See for example Kathleen Jones, *A Glorious Fame: The Life of Margaret Cavendish Duchess of Newcastle* (London: Bloomsbury, 1988).

12 Natalie Zemon Davis, '"Women's History" in Transition: The European Case', *Feminist Studies*, nos. 3/4 (Winter 1975/6), 90, quoted in Joan Kelly, 'The Social Relations of the Sexes', in *Women, History and Theory* (Chicago and London: University of Chicago Press, 1984), p. 9.

13 See Clifford Leech, 'Private Performances and Amateur Theatricals (Excluding the Academic Stage) from 1580 to 1660. With an Edition of Raguaillo d'Oceano, 1640', Diss. University of London, 1935, pp. 363–6.

14 Richard Luckett, 'Music', in *The Diary of Samuel Pepys*, x, 258–82, 263.

15 'The Concealed Fansyes', ed. Nathan Comfort Starr in *PMLA*, no. 156 (1931), 802–38. 'A Pastorall', MS see Bodl. Rawlinson poet. 16. fol. 49, 50 for the sisters' dedications of the 'Pastorall' to their father. Elizabeth Brackley writes of Newcastle's 'judgements of pure wit', fols. 50. Subsequent references in text.

16 Sandra A. Burner, *James Shirley: A Study of Literary Coteries and Patronage in Seventeenth-Century England* (New York and London: University Press of America, 1988), pp. 146–7.

17 *HMC: Twelfth Report*, Appendix, Pt VII: The Manuscripts of S. H. Le Fleming (London, 1890), pp. 20–1

18 *Cupid's Banishment*, ed. C. E. McGee, *Renaissance Drama*, no. 19 (1988), 226–64. See also Suzanne Gossett, '"Man-maid begone!" Women in Masques', *ELR*, 18, no. 1 (Winter 1988), 96–113; Eric Walter White, *A History of English Opera* (London: John Lehmann, 1951), p. 41.

19 'Christmas Entertainment' MS. Bodl. Rawlinson D 1361 fols. 306–28. I am once again grateful to David Bond. The later date is suggested when Amyntas invites Obligia and Sapientia to go to the Duke's theatre (fol. 315v).

20 See, for example, Cavendish's *The Blazing World* (London, 1668).

21 *Playes* (1662), A3r–B1v. Cavendish's introductions contain a number of defences of her writing.

22 Elaine Hobby's incisive suggestion that the scenes are for the reader to 'act out' points towards the questions of the subject positions in the reading of plays. See Elaine Hobby, *Virtue of Necessity* (London: Virago, 1988) pp. 110–11.

23 Denise Riley, '*Am I That Name?*', p. 25. See *The Female Academy* (*Playes*, 1662), pp. 652–79.

24 *Poems, or Several Fancies* (London, 1668), frontispiece.

25 See Sigmund Freud's classic account of the multiple and unspecified position of the fantasist in '"A Child is Being Beaten": A Contribution

to the Study of the Origins of Sexual Perversions', *Works*, ed. James Strachey (London: Hogarth Press, 1955), XVII, 175–204.

26 *Poems*, p. 131.

27 Margaret Cavendish, *Sociable Letters* (London, 1664), pp. 406–7. Subsequent references in text. Thanks to Sophie Tomlinson for discussing this with me and see her '"My Brain the Stage": Margaret Cavendish and the Fantasy of Female Performance', eds. Clare Brandt and Diane Purkiss, *Women, Texts and Histories 1575–1760* (London: Routledge, 1992) pp. 134–63.

28 See Kate Lilley, ed., 'The Contract', in *The Description of a New World Called the Blazing World* (London: William Pickering, 1992).

29 Lisa Jardine, *Still Harping on Daughters: Women and Drama in the Age of Shakespeare* (Brighton: Harvester, 1983), p. 31; Laura Levine, 'Men in Women's Clothing: Anti-Theatricality and Effeminization from 1579 to 1642', *Criticism* 28, no. 2 (1986), 121–43; Phyllis Rackin, 'Androgyny, Mimesis, and the Marriage of the Boy Heroine on the English Renaissance Stage', *PMLA*, no. 102 (1987), 29–41; Kathleen McLuskie, 'The Act, the Role, and the Actor: Boy Actresses on the Elizabethan Stage', *NTQ*, 3, no. 10 (1987), 120–30.

30 Kathleen McLuskie, 'The Act, the Role', p. 124.

31 Ann Rosalind Jones, 'Nets and Bridles: Early Modern Conduct Books and Sixteenth-Century Women's Lyrics', in Nancy Armstrong and Leonard Tennenhouse, eds., *The Ideology of Conduct: Essays in Literature and the History of Sexuality* (London: Methuen, 1987), pp. 39–72, 44.

32 Sherry B. Ortner, 'Gender and Sexuality in Hierarchical Societies: the Case of Polynesia and Some Comparative Implications', in Sherry Ortner and Harriet Whitehead, eds., *Sexual Meanings: The Cultural Construction of Gender and Sexuality* (Cambridge University Press, 1981), p. 359.

33 This tends to dehistoricise the problems, aims and conditions of early modern cultural production. See Germaine Greer *et al.* eds., *Kissing the Rod* (London: Virago, 1988), p. 1; for an analysis of this tendency see Diane Purkiss, 'Material Girls: The Seventeenth-Century Woman Debate', *Women, Texts*, ed., Brandt and Purkiss, pp. 69–133.

34 Margaret Ezell, *The Patriarch's Wife: Literary Evidence and the History of the Family* (Chapel Hill and London: University of North Carolina Press, 1987), pp. 2–4.

35 Brian Manning, *The English People and the English Revolution* (London: Heinemann, 1976), p. 229.

36 Edward Hyde, Earl of Clarendon, *The History of the Great Rebellion*, ed. W. D. Macray (Oxford: Clarendon Press, 1888), III, 381.

37 Ann Rosalind Jones, *The Currency of Eros: Women's Love Lyric in Europe 1540–1620* (Bloomington and Indianapolis: Indiana University Press, 1990), pp. 1–4; 'Surprising Fame: Renaissance Gender

Ideologies and Women's Lyric', in Nancy K. Miller, ed., *The Poetics of Gender* (New York: Columbia University Press, 1986), pp. 74–96, 80.

38 Margaret Cavendish, *The Worlds Olio* (London, 1655), p. 41.

39 Elizabeth Poole, *An Alarum of Warre*, E.555 (23), (1648), pp. 5–6. See S. D. Amussen, 'Gender, Family and the Social Order 1560–1725', in Anthony Fletcher and John Stevenson, eds., *Order and Disorder in Early Modern England* (Cambridge University Press, 1985), p. 199.

40 Catherine Gallagher, 'Embracing the Absolute', pp. 24–33.

41 *The Worlds Olio*, p. 48.

42 Margaret Cavendish, *Bell in Campo*, in *Playes* (London, 1662).

43 Thanks to Sophie Tomlinson for this suggestion.

44 Jones, *Glorious Fame*, p. 90.

45 *The Matrimonial Trouble*, in *Playes* (London, 1662), I.ii, p. 424. See also *The Convent of Pleasure*, in *Playes, Never Before Printed* (London, 1668), III.vi.

46 Mendelson, *The Mental World of Stuart Women: Three Studies* (Brighton: Harvester, 1987), p. 5.

47 Margaret Cavendish, *The Presence*, in *Playes, Never Before Printed* (London, 1668).

48 Peter Stallybrass, 'Patriarchal Territories: The Body in Enclosed', in Margaret W. Ferguson, Maureen Quilligan, Nancy J. Vickers, eds., *Rewriting the Renaissance* (University of Chicago Press, 1986), p. 134.

49 S. D. Amussen, 'Gender, Family and the Social Order', p. 216; Anthony Fletcher, *Reform in the Provinces: The Government of Stuart England* (New Haven: Yale University Press, 1986), p. 357.

50 Thomas Jordan, *A Royal Arbor of Loyal Poesie* (London, 1660), pp. 21–3.

5 ROYAL OR REFORMED? THE POLITICS OF COURT
ENTERTAINMENT IN TRANSLATION AND PERFORMANCE

1 G. Reinhard Pauley, *Music and the Theatre* (Englewood Cliffs: Prentice Hall, 1970), pp. 66–9. Curtis Alexander Price, *Henry Purcell and the London Stage* (Cambridge University Press, 1983) compares English and European operatic traditions.

2 *Writings and Speeches of Oliver Cromwell*, ed. Wilbur Cortez Abbott (Cambridge, Mass.: Harvard University Press, 1937–47), III, 434–43, 454.

3 Hotson, *Commonwealth*, pp. 54–6; *The Faithfull Scout* (24 Feb.–3 Mar., 1654); *Kingdom's Weekly Intelligencer*, E.821 (13), (26 Dec.–2 Jan., 1654); Daniel Fleming, *HMC : Twelfth Report*, Appendix, Pt VII, p. 22.

4 Giovanno Sagredo, *CSP Venetian*, p. 165 and pp. 138, 312.

5 I cannot yet trace records of who paid for *Cupid and Death*, and who commissioned it. PRO S.P.89,4, 132, 134, do refer to the visit of the Portuguese ambassador. Music from a 1659 performance exists, BL

MS. Add. 17,799, and is recorded by the Consorte of Musicke with Anthony Rooley (DHM, 1995), Add. 05472 77428 2. See Clifford Leech, 'Private Performances and Amateur Theatricals', p. 202.

6 *The Court Secret*, in *Six New Plays* (London, 1653).

7 Murray Lefkowitz, *William Lawes* (London: Routledge and Kegan Paul, 1960), p. 205.

8 James Shirley, *The Bird in a Cage* (London, 1633). As Clifford Leech notes, this dedication was 'ironic'. See Clifford Leech, ed., *The Triumph of Peace*, in *A Book of Masques* (Cambridge University Press, 1967), p. 278.

9 Walter Montagu, *The Shepherd's Paradise* (1659); William Prynne, *Histrio-Mastix*.

10 *William Prynne His Defence of Stage Playes*.

11 Lefkowitz, *Lawes*, p. 211.

12 *Ibid.*, p. 213.

13 See Clifford Leech, *A Book of Masques*, p. 306; also, Walter Greg, 'The Triumph of Peace: A Bibliographer's Nightmare', *The Library*, 5, series 1 (Sept. 1946), 113–26.

14 Martin Butler, 'Politics and the Masque: *The Triumph of Peace*', in *The Seventeenth Century*, 2, no. 2 (1987), 117–41.

15 *A Book of Masques*, p. 206.

16 *The Triumph of Peace*, in *A Book of Masques*, p. 284. Subsequent references in text.

17 For a reading of the masque as a peace-keeping influence see Kevin Sharpe, *Criticism and Compliment*, pp. 260–4. On the audience in the street see Martin Butler, 'Politics and the Masque', pp. 127, 136. The street audience was only in part an audience; indeed, the way the parade was designed to pass in front of them before reaching its destination made their presence, for the masquers, part of the spectacle.

18 The debate on *The Cruell Warre* may be found in the following articles: Jean Fuzier, 'English Political Dialogues 1641–1651: A Suggestion for Research with a Critical Edition of *The Tragedy of the Cruell Warre* (1643)', *CE*, no. 14 (Oct. 1978), 49–68. See also, Jean Jacquot, 'Une parodie du *Triumph of Peace*, masque de James Shirley: note sur l'édition par J. Fuzier, de *The Tragedy of the Cruell Warre*', *CE*, no. 15 (Apr. 1979), 77–80.

19 For a summary of activities in 1643 see Derek Hirst, *Authority and Conflict*, pp. 234–41.

20 *The Cruell Warre*, *CE*, no. 14, A3r. Subsequent references in text.

21 George Bas, 'More About the Anonymous *Tragedy of the Cruell Warre* and James Shirley's *Triumph of Peace*', *CE*, no. 17 (Apr. 1980), 43–57, p. 53. Bas suggests Bulstrode Whitelocke as a possible author, p. 53.

22 Ruth Spalding, *The Improbable Puritan: A Life of Bulstrode Whitelocke* (London: Faber and Faber, 1975), p. 100.

23 See Bas, 'More About the Anonymous *Tragedy of the Cruell Warre*', pp. 4–6.
24 See Hirst, *Authority and Conflict*, p. 237.
25 *The King's Cabinet Opened* (1645).
26 James Shirley, *Cupid and Death*, ed. B. A. Harris, in *A Book Of Masques*, pp. 371–405. See also John Ogilby, *The Fables of Aesop Paraphras'd in Verse and adorned with Sculpture* (London, 1651). The illustrations which may well have influenced Cupid and Death are opposite p. 41, ' Of an Aegyptian King and his Apes'. That both Davenant and Shirley wrote prefatory verses to this volume, in Davenant's case from the Tower, provides another link in the web of connections between Davenant, Shirley and the government. See also, *The Contention of Ajax and Hercules* (London, 1653) and Edward Dent, *Foundations of English Opera* (Cambridge University Press, 1928), p. 54. He claims that this was also performed during the Commonwealth.
27 Allan H. Stevenson, 'James Shirley and the Actors at the First Irish Theatre', *MP*, 40, no. 2 (1942), 147–60; 'Shirley's Years in Ireland', *Review of English Studies*, no. 20 (1944), 19–28; Marvin Morillo, 'Shirley's "Preferment" and the Court of Charles ', *Studies in English Literature 1500–1900*, no. 1 (1960), 101–17.
28 *Cupid and Death*, p. 337. Subsequent references in text. See also Eric Walter White, *A History of English Opera*, p. 60.
29 Wayne H. Phelps, 'Cosmo Manuche, Royalist Playwright of the Commonwealth', *English Language Notes*, 16, no. 3 (1979), 207–11.
30 R. G. Howarth, *TLS*, 15 Nov. 1934.
31 Compare Dent, *Opera*, p. 85. He emphasises the resemblance between *Cupid and Death* and the masque form.
32 B. A. Harris, *Cupid and Death*, p. 403; Annabel Patterson, *Fables of Power* (Durham, N.C.: Duke University Press, 1991).
33 Bulstrode Whitelocke recorded the masques and entertainments of Queen Christina of Sweden which he attended. See *Journal of the Swedish Embassy in the years 1653 and 1654* (London, 1772), I, 304–5, 437–8 (dancing), 420, 431 (music); II, 52–3 (masque). The timing of Whitelocke's departure for Sweden would appear to preclude his direct involvement in *Cupid and Death*, though his continued interest in entertainment is attested by his reports from the Swedish court. He even took the preacher Ingelo to Sweden with him, Ingelo having been previously thrown out of his living in Bristol for 'his Flaunting apparell' and for 'his being given so much to Musick not only at his owne house, but at houses of entertainment out of Towne'. See 'Records of a Church in Bristol 1640–1687', in *Bristol Record Society Publications*, no. 27, (1974), 102. I am grateful to Dr Jonathan Barry for bringing this document to my attention. The continued involvement of Whitelocke in theatre before and after the war signals to us once more that there were real conflicts, but not ones amenable to simplistic analysis as cavalier versus Puritan. On the appointment of

the Master of the Revels at the Inner Temple in the 1650s, see Nethercot, *Davenant*, p. 299.

34 David Norbrook, 'The Masque of Truth: Court Entertainments and International Protestant Politics in the Early Stuart Period', *The Seventeenth Century*, 1, no. 2 (1986), 82–110. See p. 100.

35 *The Complete Poems of Joseph Beaumont*, ed. Alexander B. Grosart (Edinburgh University Press, 1880), 11, 146. Nicholas José, *Ideas of the Restoration in English Literature, 1660–1700* (London: Macmillan, 1984), pp. 2–6.

36 Derek Hirst, 'The Lord Protector, 1653–1658', in ed., John Morrill, *Cromwell*, pp. 119–48.

37 See Warren Chernaik, *The Poetry of Limitation: A Study of Edmund Waller* (New Haven and London: Yale University Press, 1968), pp. 156–7.

38 Edmund Waller, *A Panegyrick To My Lord Protector* (London, 1655), p. 3.

39 *Ibid.*, p. 6.

40 Chernaik, *Poetry of Limitation*, pp. 154–5; *Panegyrick*, p. 8.

41 *Panegyrick*, p. 3.

42 James Howell, *The Nuptialls of Peleus and Thetis: Consisting of a Mask and a Comedy, or the Great Royall Ball* (London: Henry Herringman, 1654). Trans. from Caprioli. See Alfred Loewenburg, *Annals of Opera 1597–1940*, second rev. edn (Geneva: Societas Bibliographica, 1955), column 31. Howell probably also wrote the dialogue, *A Discourse or Parley Continued Between Patricus and Peregrine Touching the Civill Wars of England and Ireland*, E.61 (140), (1643). See Denis Arnold, *Monteverdi* (1963; rpt London: J. M. Dent and Sons, 1975), p. 17. *Nuptialls* was collected by Thomason in May 1654. Earlier in May Howell had published a royalist elegy on the Duke of Dorset in *Ah, Ha, Tumulus, Thalamus*, E.228 (1), (1654).

43 Loewenburg, *Annals*, column 120. Loewenburg notes a letter from the singer Antonio Melani to his protector Prince Mattais de Medici indicating that an unknown opera was performed at the Palais Royal in February or March 1645. See column 20.

44 *Ibid.*, column 23.

45 *Ibid.*, column 25.

46 *Ibid.*, column 24. John Evelyn saw Rovetta's *Ercole in Lida* at the Venice carnival in 1645.

47 Loewenburg, *Annals*, column 27, Zamponi's *Ulisse all' Isola di Circe*.

48 Eugene Haun, *Hark What Harmony* (New York: Columbia University Press, 1961). Haun misses the 1650s Interregnum performance contexts for *Fancy's Festivals*. Leech, 'Private Performances', pp. 202–8, argues convincingly the idea that specifically this kind of entertainment – drolls/masques, not emplotted but of discrete episodes – was fashionable during the Protectorate. See Louis B. Wright, ' Reading of Plays'.

49 See Philip Knachel, *England and the Fronde* (New York: Cornell

University Press, 1967). A French *ballet du cour* was actually performed in London in 1660 celebrating the English peace as boding better relations between France and Spain: *La Balet de la Paix* (London, 1660).

50 Annabel Patterson, 'The Very Name of the Game', in Healy and Sawday, eds., *Literature and the English Civil War*, p. 21.

51 Michel Pêcheaux, *Language, Semantics, Ideology*, trans. Harbans Nagpal (London: Macmillan, 1982), p. 111.

52 *Ibid.*

53 Haun is unqualified in his support for *Ariadne, Hark*, p. 48.

54 Richard Flecknoe, *Ariadne Deserted by Theseus and Found and Courted by Bacchus* (London, 1654), 'A Dramatick Piece Apted for Recitative Music'. Subsequent references in text.

55 John Dryden, 'Of Heroique Playes', in *The Works of John Dryden*, ed. H. T. Swedenberg, Jr, George R. Guffey, Alan Roper (Berkeley and Los Angeles: University of California Press, 1956–79), XI.

56 See Stephen Orgel, *The Illusion of Power: Political Theater in the English Renaissance* (Berkeley: University of California Press, 1975), pp. 9–20.

57 William Cavendish, Duke of Newcastle, in a prefatory poem to Richard Flecknoe's *A Relation of Ten Years Travels* (London, 1654), A4r.

58 Other operas by Monteverdi were performed in 1641. See Arnold, *Monteverdi*, pp. 18–22, 46–8.

59 Richard Flecknoe, *Loves Dominion* (London, 1654), 'A dramatique Piece, Full of Excellent Moralitie'.

60 On literary travel in the 1640s and 1650s see Edward Chayney, *The Grand Tour*. On Flecknoe, pp. 344–9.

61 Richard Flecknoe, *The Idea of His Highness Oliver Late Protector and c* (London, 1659).

62 Richard Flecknoe, *The Marriage of Oceanus and Brittania* (1659), p. 21. Subsequent references in text.

6 NATIONAL IDENTITY, TOPIC AND GENRE IN DAVENANT'S PROTECTORATE OPERA

1 Oliver Cromwell, speech at the opening of parliament (17 Sept. 1656), *Writings and Speeches of Oliver Cromwell*, IV, 261. As early as summer 1654 Thomas Gage had told Cromwell that the Spanish colonies in the West Indies, even Central America, were ripe for reconquest. See S. R. Gardiner, *History of the Commonwealth and Protectorate* (London: Longmans, Green, 1894–1901), III, 346. Thomas Gage's *The English–American his Travail by Sea and Land: or, a new Survey of the West Indias* (London, 1648) was dedicated to Thomas Fairfax and encouraged an attempted reconquest of the West Indies. The dedication attacked the Spanish (A4r) and argued that the attempt was not as difficult as might be imagined (A3v). The book was reissued in 1655.

2 Lois Potter's study in *The Revels History* must be excepted from this criticism. The source of the many other writers who take Davenant as unproblematically 'royalist' lies in the pioneering scholarly work on Interregnum drama from the 1930s. See Alfred Harbage, *Sir William Davenant Poet Venturer 1606–1668* (University of Philadelphia Press), pp. 123–6, 130. See Arthur H. Nethercot, *Sir William Davenant* (University of Chicago Press, 1938); Alfred Harbage, *Cavalier Drama*. Followed by Patrick Joseph Canavan, 'A Study of English Drama as a Reflection of Stuart Politics', Diss. University of Southern California, 1950; Mary-Joe Purcell, 'Political–Historical Bearings in Original Interregnum Drama 1649–1660', Diss. University of Missouri, 1959; John William Bernet, 'Toward the Restoration Heroic Play: The Evolution of Davenant's Serious Drama', Diss. Stanford University, 1969. More recently see Mary Edmond, *Rare Sir William Davenant*, pp. 122–3, 130–3.

3 *Ibid.*, p. 122.

4 Eric Walter White, *A History of English Opera*, pp. 29–30.

5 Christopher Hill, *God's Englishman: Oliver Cromwell and the English Revolution* (Harmondsworth: Penguin, 1972), p. 190.

6 Pêcheaux, *Language, Semantics*, p. 111.

7 Edmond, *Rare Sir William Davenant*, pp. 75–6. Davenant was in the Tower 1650–2, reimprisoned for debt, and finally released in 1654.

8 *Ibid.*, p. 122. On Thurloe see Nethercot, *Sir William Davenant*, pp. 295–6, 322, 331; Hotson, *Commonwealth*, p. 150; *State Papers of John Thurloe*, VIII, 544. *CSP Domestic*, 1655–6, p. 396.

9 The ordinance of 11 February 1647/8 speaks of plays in terms of morality and social control as 'condemned by ancient Heathens and much less to be tolerated among Professors of the Christian Religion', and 'the occasion of many and sundry great vices and disorders'. Charles Firth and S. Rait eds., *Acts and Ordinances*, I, 1070–1. See also Hyder E. Rollins, 'The Commonwealth Drama: Miscellaneous Notes', *SP*, no. 18 (1921), 267–333; 'A Contribution to the History of The Commonwealth Drama', *SP*, no. 20 (1923), 52–69; Hotson, *Commonwealth*, pp. 46–51, 118.

10 *Salmacida Spolia* (London, 1640) was presented by the king and queen on 21 January 1640 and demonstrates the banishment of Discord by the 'secret power' of the king (B1r). See Martin Butler's account (challenging that of Stephen Orgel in *The Illusion of Power*): 'Politics and the Masque: Salmacida Spolia', in *Literature and the English Civil War*, ed. Healy and Sawday, pp. 59–74. See also R. Malcolm Smuts, 'The Political Failure of Stuart Cultural Patronage', in *Patronage in the Renaissance*, ed. Guy Fitch Lytle and Stephen Orgel (New Jersey: Princeton University Press, 1981), pp. 165–206.

Davenant's masques used elaborate and significant scenery. *Britannia Triumphans* (1638), for example, was described as 'By Inigo Jones, Surveyor of His Majesties workes, and William Davenant her

Majesties servant'. Davenant's first collaboration with Jones, *The Temple of Love* (London, 1635), used a proscenium arch and scenery of the kind Davenant uses in *The Cruelty of the Spaniards in Peru.* However, Dent notes that, unlike operatic music, the musical accompaniment to this masque serves no dramatic function (*Foundations*, p. 40).

See also Roy Strong, *Splendour at Court: Renaissance Spectacle and the Theatre of Power* (London: Weidenfeld and Nicolson, 1973); *The Court Masque*, ed. David Lindley (Manchester University Press, 1984); John Peacock, *The Stage Designs of Inigo Jones* (Cambridge University Press, 1995), pp. 2–3.

11 *Britannia Triumphans* presented at court on Twelfth Night 1638 (London, 1638) A2r. See Philip Bordinat and Sophia Blaydes, *Sir William Davenant* (Boston: G. K. Hall, 1981).

12 John Dryden, 'Of Heroique Plays', p. 9.

13 Plans and analyses of the potential for a reformed theatre existed throughout the period of closure from the projects of Milton (1641–3) – see *Reasons of Church Government* (1641), p. 40, Marten and Flecknoe and Harrington in the later 1650s, as well as the royalist exiles including the Duke of Newcastle. The mixture of control and education can be found in a range of contemporary discourses. Even Balthazar Gerbier offered a programme 'to cause publicke Gratis Lectures to be read' (A2r). The 'lecture' mentions music and dancing with biblical justification (pp. 15, 17) and rehearses the educational properties of entertainment in a way which was to become increasingly familiar during the 1650s. See *A Publique Lecture On all the Languages, Arts, Sciences, and Noble Exercises, which are taught in Sr Balthazar Gerbiers Academy* (London, 1650); C. H. Firth, 'Sir William Davenant and the Revival of Drama During the Protectorate', *EHR* (April, 1903), 103–20; James R. Jacob and Timothy Raylor, 'Opera and Obedience: Thomas Hobbes and *A Proposition for Advancement of Moralitie* by Sir William Davenant', *The Seventeenth Century* 6, no. 2 (Autumn 1991), 205–50, 212.

14 Bulstrode Whitelocke, *Memorials of English Affairs* (London, 1732), p. 650; Harbage, *Davenant*, p. 124. While in the Tower (see n. 7 above), Davenant wrote parts of *Gondibert* and commendatory verses for Ogilby's *Aesop's Fables* (see chapter 5). See *The Diary of Bulstrode Whitelocke 1605–1675*, ed. Ruth Spalding (Oxford University Press, 1990), pp. 449, 526–7. Whitelocke may not have been the only member of the new regime to help Davenant; he wrote thanking Henry Marten after his release from prison in 1652; *HMC*, XXXI, p. 389, Marten manuscripts in Brotherton Library, Leeds. See also John Aubrey, *Brief Lives*, ed. Oliver Lawson Dick (1949; rpt Harmondsworth: Penguin, 1962), pp. 178–9.

15 Edmond, *Rare Sir William Davenant*, p. 124.

16 William Davenant, *The First Days Entertainment at Rutland House: By Declamations and Musick After the manner of the Ancients* (London, 1657). Performed 23 May 1656, A4r. See *How Daphne Pays His Debts* (1656); Edmond, *Rare Sir William Davenant*, p. 122–3. Critical suggestion that *The Siege of Rhodes* had no links with the masque form can be qualified by reference to the other dramatic pieces he staged – particularly *The First Days Entertainment*. Hëdbáck, p. lxviii.

17 Davenant took up residence in Paris in 1646. The French debates on theatre included the issue of moral instruction in theatrical representation. See Henry Phillips, *The Theatre and its Critics in Seventeenth-Century France* (Oxford University Press, 1981), pp. 17–36; J. Chapelain, *Opuscules critiques*, ed. Alfred C. Hunter (Paris: E. Droz, 1936), pp. 124–5; Fr H. Abbé d'Aubignac, *Pratique du théâtre*, ed. P. Martino (Paris: Alger, 1927), pp. 318–19 (cited by Phillips, pp. 26–7); Henry Lancaster, *A History of French Dramatic Literature in the Seventeenth Century* (Baltimore: Johns Hopkins University Press, 1929–42), Pt 2, I, 9–14, 130–45.

18 Flecknoe, *Love's Dominion*, A2v.

19 Edmund Gayton, *Charity Triumphant, or the Virgin-Shew*, acted 29 October 1655 (London, 1655), p. 3.

20 *The Cruelty of the Spaniards in Peru* (London, 1658). Performed by July 1658. See also the exchange on the making ready of a new playhouse, *HMC: Twelfth Report*, Pt VII.

See Garcilasco de la Vega, *Le Commentaire Royal, ou L'Histoire des Yncas, Roys du Peru* (1609; trans. Paris, 1633). There is an English translation in 1688 and a twentieth-century translation by Harold V. Livermore, *Royal Commentaries of the Incas: A General History of Peru* (Austin and London: University of Texas Press, 1966). This text forms the basis of the first three entries of *The Cruelty of the Spaniards* but Davenant could have found all he needed in Samuel Purchas, *Purchas His Pilgrimes*, Pt IV, pp. 1454–82. The prophecy of the arrival of the Spanish appears in the death testament of Huaina Cápac: 'Many years ago it was revealed to us by our father the Sun that after twelve of his sons had reigned, a new race would come, unknown in these parts, and would again subdue all our kingdoms and many others to their empire. I suspect that these must be those we have heard of off our coasts' (I, Bk 9, p. 577). For the 'discord between the two brothers, the last Inca kings' (see II, 723). See John Grier Varner, *El Inca: The Life and Times of Garcilasco de la Vega* (London and Austin: University of Texas Press, 1968); Janet Clare, 'Davenant's *Cruelty of the Spaniards in Peru* – masque for the Protectorate?' (Paper given at conference on 'Politics and Patronage', Reading, 1992).

21 See S. R. Gardiner, *History of the Commonwealth and Protectorate*, III, 350–70, 383. On uses of Drake, Raleigh and de las Casas in promoting the New World see Loren E. Pennington, 'The Amerindian in

English Promotional Literature 1575–1625', in K. R. Andrews, N. P. Canny and P. E. H. Hair, ed., *The Westward Enterprises* (Detroit: Wayne State University Press, 1979), p. 183.

22 See Hill, *God's Englishman*, pp. 149–55. In Davenant's *History of Sir Francis Drake* (London, 1659), the native peoples are represented as both noble and base at different points in the plot. See also Peter Hulme, *Colonial Encounters: Europe and the Native Caribbean, 1492–1797* (London: Methuen, 1986).

23 Fulke Greville, *Life of Sidney* (London, 1652), pp. 132–3.

24 Roland Barthes, *Mythologies*, trans. Annette Lavers (1957; Collins: London, 1973), pp. 165–6. Bartolomé de las Casas, *The Tears of the Indians*, trans. John Phillips (London, 1656). First published as *Brevissima Relacioón de la Dedstruyción de las Indias* (1551).

25 *Purchas His Pilgrims* (London, 1625), Bk 5, pt III, p. 1037; p. 1039.

26 De las Casas, *The Tears*, A3v. For an account of the doomed Hispaniola expedition see Gardiner, *Commonwealth and Protectorate*, III, 344–68.

27 Philip Nichols, *Sir Francis Drake Revived* (London, 1621) reprinted 1626, 1652. Quotation from title-page of 1626 edition. Notably, these texts were already in a nostalgic relation to Elizabethanism when they were published at the end of the reign of James I and the beginning of the reign of Charles I, so their recycling in the 1650s drew on structures of nostalgia already present in English culture ready to be given a new coloration.

28 *The World Encompassed* (London, 1636).

29 Abbott, ed., *Writings of Cromwell*, IV, 260.

30 T*he Siege of Rhodes* was performed after the Restoration, rather than functioning as part of *A Playhouse to be Let* in 1663 as did *Francis Drake* and *The Cruelty of the Spaniards*.

31 William Davenant, 'Preface to *Gondibert*', *Gondibert: An Heroick Poem*, ed. David F. Gladish (Oxford University Press, 1971), p. 10. On empire as restless, pp. 30–1. See also Walter Benjamin, *The Origin of German Tragic Drama* (London: New Left Books, 1977), pp. 69–72.

32 William Davenant, *The Siege of Rhodes*, ed. Ann-Marie Hedbäck. Hedbäck gives a composite text of the 1656 edition of part one and the 1663 edition of both. The play exists in four texts: 1656, 1659, 1663, 1670, and the first part was entered on the Stationers' Register on 27 August 1656. See Hëdbáck, pp. xiv–xxiv; Sophia B. Blaydes and Philip Bordinat, *Sir William Davenant 1629–1985: An Annotated Bibliography* (London: Garland Publishing, 1986), pp. 33–5.

Dent argues that the play as written was cut for the 1656 performance, asserting that the duet at the end of Entry IV makes no sense without the scene including Roxolana, present in the later edition. However, the clear argument against this is that Alphonso is already jealous in Entry IV.ii. 34–67 which is present in the early text. See Dent, *Foundations*, pp. 65–6. For a model of the Rutland House stage see Richard Southern, *Changeable Scenery* (London: Faber and Faber, 1952), figs. 10–15.

33 See Dent, *Foundations*, and counter-arguments as put by Hëdbáck p. lxviii. The status of *The Siege of Rhodes* as 'opera' is disputed, but given Davenant's interest in opera as early as 1639 Dent is probably wrong to conclude that Davenant's *sole* reason for calling it 'opera' was to get around the theatre laws.

34 Rosamund Gilder, 'Enter Ianthe Veil'd', *Theatre Arts Monthly*, no. 1, (1927), 29–38. W. J. Lawrence assesses Aubrey's casual claim that 2 *SR* was performed before the Restoration in *The Elizabethan Playhouse*, second series, (Stratford-upon-Avon: Shakespeare Head Press, 1913), pp. 136–7. From Aubrey's evidence it is not possible to be certain either way; *Brief Lives*, p. 88.

35 C. A. Patrides, 'The Judgements of God', in *Premises and Motifs in Renaissance Thought and Literature* (Princeton University Press, 1982), pp. 137–51; esp. p. 150.

36 Samuel Chew, *The Crescent and the Rose: Islam and England during the Renaissance* (New York: Oxford University Press, 1937), pp. 102–4.

37 Hill points out that English merchants paid to maintain an ambassador in Constantinople throughout the 1630s. *God's Englishman*, p. 159.

38 Edward Said, *Orientalism* (London: Routledge and Kegan Paul, 1978), pp. 1–2, 73–5. See also, Christine Woodhead, '"The Present Terrour of the World"? Contemporary Views of the Ottoman Empire c.1600', in *History* 72, no. 234, (Feb. 1987), 20–41.

39 Said, *Orientalism*, pp. 1–2.

40 Woodhead, '"Present Terrour"', pp. 20–4, 36–7.

41 *A True Relation of What Passed in Constantinople* (London: 1649).

42 Hill, *God's Englishman*, pp. 158–9.

43 Stanford Shaw, *The History of the Ottoman Empire and Modern Turkey* (Cambridge University Press, 1976), I, 200. An additional factor may have been Admiral Blake's successful bombardment of Porto Farina, near Tunis, April 1655, in which some of the sultan's ships may have been damaged. See S. R. Gardiner, *History of the Commonwealth and Protectorate*, III, 382–3.

44 Abbott, ed., *Writings of Cromwell*, IV, 243.

45 The most obvious instance in English is Richard Knolles, *The General Historie of the Turkes* (London, 1603). Hedbäck, ed., *The Siege of Rhodes*, pp. xlii–xliii. There were also plays using the Turk – forty-seven between 1558 and 1642 according to Louis Wann, 'The Oriental in Elizabethan Drama', *MP*, no. 12 (1914/15), 423–47. This literature is significant both as Davenant's potential reading and as part of the circulation of opinions about the Turk with which his plays engaged, not specifically as sources.

46 Giovanni Botero, *The Travellers Breviat*, trans. Robert Johnson

(London, 1601), p. 40. Abbreviated from *Delle Relationi universali di Giovanni Botero*, widely published and translated. Fulke Greville, *The Writings of Fulke Greville*, ed. Joan Rees (London: Athlone Press, 1973), p. 165. On Greville's complex and ambivalent attitude to monarchy, which often found expression in the posing of a possibility of rebellion only to withdraw it, see David Norbrook, *Poetry and Politics in the Renaissance*, pp. 157–74.

47 *Breviat*, pp. 41, 43.

48 See Hĕdbáck, ed., *The Siege of Rhodes*, pp. xxxi–lxiii.

49 Ian McLean, *Women Triumphant: Feminism in French Literature 1610–1652* (Oxford: Clarendon Press, 1977), pp. 64–87. See also the parody in George Villiers, Duke of Buckingham, *The Rehearsal*, ed. D. J. Crane (University of Durham Publications, 1976), I.i.165–80.

50 Compare *Mustapha*, v.iii.7–8, in *Poems and Dramas of Fulke Greville*, ed. Geoffry Bullough (Edinburgh and London: Oliver and Boyd, 1939), II. I have used Bullough's edition for comparisons, also consulting the 1609 edition of *Mustapha* in which most of Act v is missing and the edition in Greville's posthumous *Certaine Learned and Elegant Works* (London, 1633).

51 Compare *Mustapha*, v.iii.25–31; *Treatie of Warres*, ed. G. Bullough, *Poems*, I.214–30. See also the *Treatise of Monarchy* in *The Remains of Sir Fulke Greville, Lord Brooke; Being Poems of Monarchy and Religion* (London, 1670) which we have to assume was not seen by Davenant as it was only published long after Greville's death. However, it is an extended meditation on rule and monarchy which continues the preoccupations found elsewhere in Greville's writings and, like *A Treatie of Warres* and *Mustapha*, compares the Christian and Islamic Ottoman worlds.

Dilemmas of love and honour occur in Fulke Greville's *Mustapha* where both Camena and Achmat suffer tortures of conscience over decisions which cannot be resolved without suffering. In both cases the problem is the fundamentally poor communication between the ruled and the ruler (exemplified in the Sultan's lack of direct communication with his son, who his new wife plans to have killed) and the dilemmas faced by families divided by state power struggles. See *Mustapha*, II.i.51–70; II.iii. Moreover, In Greville's *Mustapha* there are several passages which parallel the issue of the people's power found in *The Siege of Rhodes*, though as David Norbrook points out (*Poetry and Politics in the Renaissance*, p. 159) the argument for the people's liberty is checked and order restored. The play's ultimate support for authority, voiced by Achmat, does not make it any less serious in its consideration of power and rule: and a reading of the play in terms of subversion and containment would be blind to the serious meditation on power and its implications in terms of rule – the power of the monarch is contingent, fragile and the only bulwark against chaos rather than a mysterious unifying force. See IV.iii.17–18, when Rosten says, 'Achmat! The mysteries of Empire are dissolved. / Furie hath made the People know their forces.' See also, chorus primus, lines 42–3. As well as containing characters who put the argument about right and power explicitly, primarily Achmat who moves towards rebellion and then retreats, much of *Mustapha* provides an indirect commentary on the nature of monarchical power. See I.i.1–5; II.i.69–77 (Achmat); II.ii.36–46, 106–17; chorus secundus 105–20, 200–10; III.i.40–50; IV.iv.40–55; V.ii.1–7; V.iii.59–122. This final passage is a long speech by Achmat in which he changes from being an advocate of the liberty of the people to become a defender of monarchy and order. Compare 2 *SR*, II.ii.52–64.

52 Greville, *A Treatie of Warres* in *Poems and Dramas*, II, stanzas 17, 64–5 in which he contrasts the warlike Turks with the divided Christians. Subsequent references in text.

53 Norbrook, *Poetry and Politics in the Renaissance*, pp. 157–74, esp pp.158–9.

54 Hobbes, *Leviathan*, pp. 226–8.

55 *Ibid.*, p. 227.

7 GENRE, POLITICS AND PLACE: THE SOCIAL BODY IN THE DRAMATIC CAREER OF JOHN TATHAM

1 Louis Marin, *Portrait of the King* (Minneapolis: University of Minnesota Press, 1988), p. 9.

2 Compare Paula R. Backscheider, *Spectacular Politics: Theatrical Power and Mass Culture in Early Modern England* (Baltimore and London: Johns Hopkins University Press, 1993) pp. 1–2.

3 *The Fancies Theater* (London, 1640).

4 See Sukarta Chaudhuri, *Renaissance Pastoral and its Developments* (Oxford University Press, 1989), p. 375.

5 Richard Brome's political position in the late 1630s and early 1640s has been disputed by Martin Butler and Kevin Sharpe. It seems to me most likely that Brome and his associates were operating with close City connections on the eve of the Civil War; the rest of my argument will bear this out. Before he disappears from records in 1641, Thomas Nabbes was writing plays for the audiences of both court and public theatres. See Butler, *Theatre and Crisis*, pp. 214–20, Sharpe, *Criticism and Compliment*, pp. 29–35.

6 Thomas Rawlins published *The Rebellion* (London, 1640), emerging after the Restoration to run Charles II's mint. Lesley Anne Upadhyay suggests that *The Distracted State* might have been written 'soon after Thomas Rawlins' *The Rebellion*' and Tatham may have known the play. Her evidence for this (that in Rawlins's play as in *The Distracted State* a physician administers poison) is suggestive rather than adequate as

proof ('Two Political Comedies of the Restoration: An Annotated Old-Spelling Edition, with Critical and Historical Introduction of John Tatham's *The Rump* and Aphra Behn's Adaptation, *The Roundheads*' (Diss. University of London, 1974), pp. 12–14).

7 A table of 'Dedications and commendatory verses in published popular literature 1637–41' includes Tatham as a playwright on the strength of *Love Crowns the End*, performed at a school and printed in *The Fancie's Theatre*. See Butler, *Theatre and Crisis*, pp. 185–6.

8 See David Underdown, *Revel*, pp. 108–10; Robin Clifton, 'The Popular Fear of Catholics', M. R. Smuts on Henrietta Maria's court, 'The Puritan Followers of Henrietta Maria in the 1630s', (2 *EHR*, 153, no. 366 (1978), 26–46.

9 Thomas Jordan survived throughout the 1640s and 1650s producing entertainments and provided Restoration civic shows, *Fancy's Festivals* (1657); 'Cupid His Coronation' Bodl. MS. Rawlinson B.165 fols. 107–13. See Van Lennep, ed., *The London Stage 1660–1800*, I, 200, 212, 223 etc., John Tatham, *Ostella: or the Faction of Love and Beauty Reconciled* (London, 1650). Gardiner, *History*, II, 116. John Tatham, *The Distracted State: A Tragedy* (London, 1651), 'Written in the Yeer, 1641'.

10 J. R., *Distracted State*, A3r.

11 John M. Wallace, 'The Date of John Tatham's *The Distracted State*', *Bulletin of the New York Public Library*, no. 64 (1970), 29–40.

12 Louis Marin, *Portrait*, p. 7.

13 Tatham even describes his play as 'distractions' in the dedication to John Sedley, Baronet (apparently the father of the dramatist Sir Charles Sedley, and who seems to have died around 1639).

14 In Bourdieu's terms, the play explores power as the 'innumerable operations of credit by which agents confer on a person . . . the very powers that they recognise in him'. Pierre Bourdieu, 'Symbolic Power and the Political Field', in *Language and Symbolic Power*, ed., John B. Thompson, trans. Gino Raymond and Matthew Adamson (Cambridge: Polity Press, 1991), p. 192.

15 Nicholas Machiavelli, *Nicholas Machiavel's Prince*, pp. 61–2.

There was a later tradition in which Agathocles (from Machiavelli's *Prince*) is analogous to Cromwell. Reginald Perrinchief published *The Syracusan Tyrant* – 'the Life of Agathocles with some Reflexions on the practices of modern usurpers' (1661), opening his book with a broad hint at Cromwell: 'Our Age hath had too fresh an Experience of this: for the methods of tyranny have been acted with so much industry, and continued with so great success among us.' Here the typological connection between past and present is clear, as it is once more in 1683 when the figure of Agathocles is revived in a poem based on Perrinchief. The author says of the Agathocles figure, tho it may be the parallel is not exactly drawn, I suppose there will need no key to decipher him'. Reginald Perrinchief, *The Syracusan Tyrant or, The Life of Agathocles with Some Reflexions on the Practices of Modern Usurpers* (London, 1661), A5v.

16 A further reminder of topical implications appears when we see a mob which supports Archias, recalling, perhaps, the apprentice riots of the late 1640s (III, p. 16). Contrast the 'mobs' in Tatham's *The Rump* (1659) and in Thomas Rawlins's *The Rebellion*.

17 See Stephen Greenblatt, 'Invisible Bullets', in *Shakespearean Negotiations* (Berkeley: University of California Press, 1980), pp. 21–65.

18 Michael Seidel, 'Crisis Rhetoric and Satiric Power', *NLH*, 20, no. 1 (Autumn 1988), 165–86 esp. pp. 166, 167.

19 Burt, '(Un)censoring in Detail', pp. 3, 9.

20 See *Andronicus, or Impieties Long Success* (London, 1661). On usurpers, see also Leonard Willan, *Orgula, or the Fatal Error* (London, 1658).

21 Uphadyay, 'Two Political Comedies', p. 15.

22 For example David M. Bergeron, *English Civic Pageantry 1558–1642* (London: Edward Arnold, 1971), dates the last pre-Restoration pageant 1639: pp. 217, 241. Randall discusses shows with drolls; *Winter Fruit*, pp. 140–56.

23 *CSP Domestic*, 1655–6. See also Kris Collins, 'Merchants, Moors, and the Politics of Pageantry', unpublished MPhil, Oxford University, 1995.

24 Maurice Ashley, *Financial and Commercial Policy Under the Cromwellian Protectorate* (London: 1934; rpt Frank Cass, 1962) pp. 4–6.

25 John Battie, *The Merchants Remonstrance* (revised edn 1648, p. 1).

26 Mervyn James, 'Ritual, Drama and Social Body in the Late Medieval English Town', *PP*, no. 98 (Feb. 1983), 3–29.

27 Robert Withington, *English Pageantry: An Historical Outline* (1926; rpt New York: Benjamin Blom, 1963), I, 43.

28 *Mr. Recorders Speech to the Lord Protector upon Wednesday the eighth of Febr. 1653 being the day of his Highnesse Entertainment in London* (London, 1654). Subsequent references in text.

29 Ashley notes Ludlow's *Memoirs*, i, 383, on Cromwell's unfriendly reception by the City when he dined there in 1654; *Financial and Commercial Policy*, p. 3; see also S. R. Gardiner, *History*, II, 308–9.

30 Mervyn James, 'Ritual', p. 8.

31 Withington, *English Pageantry*, II, 43

32 Edmund Gayton, *Charity Triumphant*, p. 3.

33 I. B., attributed (without evidence) to John Bulteel. I. B. may even be the J. B. discussed below, *London's Triumph* (London, 1656), A4v. Subsequent references in text.

34 John Tatham, *Londons Triumph* (London, 1657).

35 *Ibid.*, B 2r–B2v. Compare the civic iconography of Flecknoe's *Oceanus*.

36 John Tatham, *Londons Tryumph* (London, 1658), p. 6.

37 Sheila Williams, 'The Lord Mayor's Show in Tudor and Stuart Times', *Guildhall Miscellany*, no. 10, (Sept. 1959), n.p.

38 *The Citie's New Poets Mock Show*, 669.f.22 (48), (1659). The initials J. B. appear on commendatory verses to Richard Brome's *A Jovial Crew* and to Thomas Jordan's *Poetical Varieties* (edn 1637); these may indicate that 'J. B.' was one of the Tatham–Jordan circle.

39 Guildhall MS 17.100. A contract between the ironmongers and the watermen, 1658.

40 See the sequence of events in Ronald Hutton, *The Restoration: A Political and Religious History of England and Wales 1658–1667* (Oxford University Press, 1985), pp. 64–74.

41 Sheila Williams, 'The Lord Mayor's Shows From Peele to Settle', Diss. University of London, 1957. Appendix 2, 'Grocers' Wardens of the Bachelors' accounts,' quoting Grocers' Hall MSS. 775/777, p. 477. Williams, p. 122–3.

42 Grocers' Hall MSS. 775/777, p. 477. Williams, p. 123.

43 Grocers' Hall MSS. 775/777, p. 479. See Williams, pp. 123–4.

44 Thomas Gumble, *The Life of General Monck* (London, 1671), p. 241.

45 'To his faithful ingenuous friend and old acquaintence John Tatham, Gent', in *Wit in a Wilderness of Promiscuous Poesie*, n.p., n.d., possibly 1665.

46 'An Epithalamium, on the noble Nuptials of Mr Will. Christmas Merchant, and Mrs Elizabeth Christmas', *Wit*; Robert Brenner, *Merchants and Revolution: Commercial Change, Political Conflict, and London Overseas Traders, 1550–1653* (Cambridge University Press, 1993), pp. 81, 383; Brenner identifies Christmas as a Merchant Adventurer of 'conservative'-cum-'royalist' sympathies.

47 *A Royal Arbor of Loyal Poesie* (London, 1660), B1v. Subsequent references in text. See also *A Speech at Vintner's Hall* (London, 1660).

48 Clifford Geertz, 'Centers, Kings and Charisma: Reflections on the Symbolics of Power', in *Local Knowledge* (New York: Basic Books, 1983), pp. 121–46.

49 José, *Ideas of the Restoration*, p. 124.

50 Guildhall MS. 11,928.

51 John Tatham, *London's Glory: Represented by Time, Truth and Fame* (London, 1660). Subsequent references in text. This show was seen by Evelyn and Pepys. See *The Diary of John Evelyn*, III, 259; *The Diary of Samuel Pepys*, I, 277.

52 John Tatham, *Aqua Triumphalis* (London, 1662). Reference in text.

53 Joanne Altieri notes that after the Restoration Tatham continues to allegorise the connection between court and City. Joanne Altieri, *The Theatre of Praise: The Panegyric Tradition in Seventeenth-Century English Drama* (Newark: University of Delaware Press, 1986), pp. 91–5.

54 John Tatham, *London's Triumphs* (London, 1664), p. 7.

55 Records exist: Jarman was paid £30, Tatham £12. Guildhall MS. 15.869, fol. 36v.

56 John Ogilby, *The Entertainment of His Most Excellent Majestie Charles II in His Passage through the City of London to His Coronation* (1661; 2nd edn, London, 1662). The first edition was less elaborate. Subsequent references in text.

57 Van Lennep, *London Stage*, 1, 11. See also Upadhyay, 'Two Political Comedies', pp. 34–6; *The Dramatic Works of John Tatham*, ed. J. Maidment and J. Logan (London: H. Sotheran, 1879), p. 196.

58 Aphra Behn, *The Roundheads; or the Good Old Cause* (London, 1682). See also Nicholas José, *Ideas of the Restoration*.

59 Tim Harris, *London Crowds*, p. 61.

60 *London's Resurrection* (London, 1671), pp. 11–14; a droll from this show was first printed in *Merry Drollery* (London, 1661) pp. 171–5.

8 TRUE AND LOYAL? POLITICS AND GENRE IN CIVIL WAR AND PROTECTORATE TRAGICOMEDY

1 Nancy Klein Maguire, *Regicide and Restoration*, p. 5, Laura Brown, *English Dramatic Form*, p. xi; Mildmay Fane is a good example of such compromised and conflicted royalism: against ship-money, a Commissioner of Array for Charles I, a compounder and a pastoral poet and playwright. See Fane, *Otia Sacra* (London, 1648); *Raguallo d'Oceano and Candy Restored, 1641*, ed. Clifford Leech (Louvain, 1938); Patterson, *Pastoral and Ideology*, p. 162.

2 On the renaming of plays as tragicomedies in the 1650s see Lois Potter, '"True Tragicomedies" of the Cvil War and Commonwealth', in *Renaissance Tragicomedy*, ed. Nancy Maguire (London: AMS Press, 1987), pp. 196–217, esp. pp. 197–8.

3 The most obvious analogy as a mixed genre is the production of mixed emotions by film melodrama.

4 Lois Potter, '"True Tragicomedies"', p. 196. On contemporary uses of pastoral, rather than tragicomedy, in relation to the Civil War, see Graham Parry, 'A Troubled Arcadia', in Healy and Sawday, *Literature and the English Civil War*, eds., pp. 38–58. Following Maguire and Potter closely, Randall surveys tragicomedy, *Winter Fruit*, pp. 337–67.

5 Francis Osborne, *The True Tragicomedy Formerly Acted at Court*, ed. Lois Potter with John Pitcher (New York and London: Garland, 1983). See pp. xxxii–xxxv. See also Francis Osborne, *Political Reflections Upon the Government of the Turkes* (London, 1656), e.g. p. 127.

6 *Cromwell's Conspiracy. A Tragy-Comedy* (London, 1660) E.1038 (2).

7 John Quarles, *Regale Lectum Miseriae* (London, 1649), A5r.

8 Sir Edward Dering, 'On the Incomparable Poems of Mr William Cartwright', in William Cartwright, *Comedies, Tragicomedies, With Other Poems*, ed. Humphry Moseley (London, 1651), n.p.

9 See William Cartwright, *Comedies, Tragicomedies, With Other Poems* (London, 1651).

10 Edward Sherburne, 'On the publication of the Posthume Poems of M. William Cartwright', *Comedies, Tragicomedies*, n.p.

11 Although the great period of Leveller publication was over by 1651, Lilburne remained prolific. See Gregg, *Freeborn John*, pp. 402–4.

12 Richard Tuck, 'Power and Authority in Seventeenth-Century England', *The Historical Journal*, 17, no. 1 (1974), 43–61. He quotes T.B. in 'Observations politicall and civill,' BL Add. MS. 27320 fols. 23, 24 (p. 44).

13 Richard Tuck, 'Power and Authority', p. 53; Battista Guarini, *The Faithfull Shepherd*, trans. Richard Fanshawe, 1647, ed. J. H. Whitfield (Edinburgh University Press, 1976), p. 411. See also *The Faithfull Shepherd* (1648), which contains the dedication and preface to the Prince of Wales. Subsequent references in text, to this edition.

14 *The Faithful Shepherdess* (London, 1608), p. 14.

15 Walter Montagu, *The Shepherds Paradise*, A3v; Laurence Lerner, *Uses of Nostalgia* (London: Chatto and Windus, 1972), p. 39.

16 See Graham Parry, 'A Troubled Arcadia', p. 45.

17 J. S., *The Shephearde's Oracle*, E.52 (2), (?Oxford, 1644), A1v. Sometimes attributed to James Shirley.

18 William Denny, *The Shepherds Holiday*, in *Inedited Poetical Miscellanies 1584–1700*, ed. Henry Huth (London: Chiswick Press, 1870), pp. 61–116. Subsequent references in text. See Harbage, *Cavalier Drama*, p. 217. The critical potential of pastoral in the shifting circumstances is currently much debated. See Annabel Patterson, *Pastoral and Ideology*. On Laudian revels see Leah Marcus, *The Politics of Mirth* (Chicago and London: University of Chicago Press, 1986), p. 17; 'Pastimes Without a Court' analyses the use of rustic imagery in poetry after its courtly focus has been transformed by civil war. For a qualification of royalism and an emphasis on the need to see pastoral in the 1620s as involved in the discourses of civic humanism and the construction and literalisation of community, see Michelle O'Callahan, 'Writing the Country and Spenserian Pastoral', forthcoming; '"Talking Politics": Tyranny, Parliament and Christopher Brooke's *The Ghost of Richard the Third* (1614)', forthcoming, *Historical Journal* (1997).

19 McKenzie, *The British Book Trade*, p. 6. *Commons Journal*, ii. 769, 16 Sept. 1643.

20 Thomas Killigrew, *Comedies and Tragedies* (London, 1664). See also Alfred Harbage, *Thomas Killigrew: Cavalier Dramatist* (University of Philadelphia Press, 1930).

21 Thomas Meriton, *The Wandering Lover* (London, 1658), 'Being Acted severall times privately at sundry places'; Thomas Forde, *Love's Labyrinth* (London, 1660). Reworks Robert Greene's *Arcadia*.

22 Chaudhuri, *Renaissance Pastoral*, p. 252.

23 Louis Montrose, 'Of Gentlemen and Shepherds: The Politics of Elizabethan Pastoral Form', *ELH*, 50, no. 3 (Fall 1983), 415–59.

24 Obviously, Freud used the term 'disavowal' to refer to fetishism and to a psychic structure leading to psychosis; here I am using it to refer to a reading structure in which contradictory knowledge is allowed to coexist. J. Laplanche, J. B. Pontalis, *The Language of Psychoanalysis* (London: Karnac Books and the Institute of Psycho-analysis, 1988), pp. 118–121.

25 William Lower, *The Enchanted Lovers*, in *The Dramatic Works and Translations of William Lower*, ed. William Bryon Gates (The Hague, 1658; rpt University of Philadelphia Press, 1932). Subsequent references in text.

26 'Actually, however, human beings can will backward as well as forward in time; willing backward occurs when we rearrange accounts of events in the past that have been emplotted in a given way, in order to endow them with a different meaning or to draw from the new emplotment reasons for acting differently in the future from the way we have become accustomed to acting in our present.' Hayden White, 'Getting out of History', *The Content of the Form*, (forthcoming), p. 150

27 Potter, '"True Tragicomedies"', p. 214.

28 *The Female Rebellion: A Tragicomedy*, ed. Alexander Smith (Glasgow, n.p., 1872). Manuscript in the Hunterian Museum, Glasgow. Subsequent references in text. In correspondence with the Hunterian, Joan Pittock-Wesson considers the autograph of the play to be MS. Tanner 466 in the Bodleian, and that the copy at the Hunterian may have been made by his sister after his death. Opinion on the date of composition varies from the 1650s to the latter part of the reign of Charles II. The play's clear grip on precise circumstances and language of the 1650s and the allusion to the closure of the theatres in the epilogue have permitted inclusion here.

29 Freud on repetion: *Beyond the Pleasure Principle*, in *Works*, XVIII, 35–6.

30 *The Hectors, or the False Challenge* (London, 1656).

31 George Cartwright, *The Heroick Lover, or, the Infanta of Spain* (London, 1661). Harbage's Annals gives the dates of composition as 1645–55. A reference to the breaking down of the City gates suggests that it was at least altered after Monck came to London in 1659 (see v.vi, p. 68–70). However, this does not invalidate Cartwright's claim to have written the play earlier. A plot summary is given by Randall, *Winter Fruit*, pp. 363–6.

32 Keith Feiling, *British Foreign Policy 1660–1672* (London: Frank Cass, 1968), pp. 2–3, 37–9. Inhabiting the national narrative there may also be references to Charles's mistress, Barbara Villiers.

33 Sir Benjamin Rudeyard, speech to the Commons, Nov. 1640. See John Rushworth, *Historical Collections* (London, 1720), III, 1351–2.

34 'To My Lord General Monck, Upon his opportune coming into England', *The Heroick Lover*, p. 77.

35 *CSP Domestic*, 1655–6, p. 348.

36 Wayne H. Phelps, 'Cosmo Manuche, Royalist Playwright', pp. 207–212.

37 At the household of James Compton. See Hilton Kelliher, 'A Hitherto Unrecognised Cavalier Dramatist: James Compton, third Earl of Northampton', *British Library Journal*, 6, no. 2 (1980), 158–87. After early opposition to ship-money Compton served in Charles I's army, stayed in England during the 1650s and wrote plays.

38 Cosmo Manuche, *The Loyal Lovers* (London, 1652); *The Just General* (London, 1652); *The Banish'd Shepherdess*, ed. P. J. Canavan, in 'A Study of English Drama', pp. 351–444.

39 See F. H. Ristine, *English Tragicomedy* (New York: Columbia University Press, 1910), p. xii.

40 Subsequent references to Canavan's edition in text. The dating of the play is suggested by the dates of the events it deals with from Cromwell's death to what may be a reference to the Act of Oblivion. It seems unlikely to have been written long after the Restoration, as there are no scenes set in England demonstrating the ecstatic welcome of the king and Henrietta Maria which suggests, perhaps, that the play was written at the moment when the king was invited back. It could, of course, have been written later and simply have missed out all post-Restoration events. Hutton, *Restoration*, pp. 3–5. See also Maguire, *Regicide*, pp. 44–46.

41 Paul Seaward, *The Cavalier Parliament and the Reconstruction of the Old Regime, 1661–1667* (Cambridge University Press, 1989), p. 11.

42 See José, *Ideas of the Restoration*, pp. 1–5.

43 *Cromwell's Conspiracie*, collected by Thomason in August 1660, incorporating a scene with '*K. Charles as on the Scaffold, Dr. Juxon andc with men in vizards*' (II.iv, p.7); the execution turns out to be merely the first instance in the malpractices of Cromwell's regime. Maguire, *Regicide*, pp. 34–42.

44 Francis Kirkman, 'The Stationer to the Reader', in John Webster and William Rowley, *The Thracian Wonder* (London, 1660), A2r.

45 Francis Kirkman (attributed), *The Presbyterian Lash* (London, 1661).

46 José, *Ideas of the Restoration*, pp. 126–8; John Wilson, *Andronicus Comnenius* (London, 1664); Edward Howard, *The Usurper*, acted 1664.

47 E. J. Burns, 'Park and Playhouse: Restoration Comedy and the Pastoral Fiction', Diss. Oxford University, 1981, Abstract, and pp. x, 4.

48 *The Comical Revenge*, in *The Plays of Sir George Etherege*, ed. Michael Cordner (Cambridge University Press, 1982); Abraham Cowley, *Cutter of Coleman Street* (1663), in *The English Writings of Abraham Cowley*, ed. A.R. Waller (Cambridge University Press, 1905), vol. II; Sir Charles Sedley, *The Mulberry Garden* (1668), in *The Poetical And Dramatic Works of Sir Charles Sedley*, ed. V. de Sola Pinto (London: Constable, 1928). For recent debate on Restoration tragicomedy see

Laura Brown, *Dramatic Form*; J. Douglas Canfield, 'The Ideology of Restoration Tragicomedy', *ELH*, no. 51 (1983), 440–64; Nancy Klein Maguire, 'The "Whole Truth" of Restoration Tragicomedy', in *Renaissance Tragicomedy*, ed. Nancy Klein Maguire.
49 Cordner, *Plays of Etherege*, p. 3.
50 Annabel Patterson, *Pastoral and Ideology*, p. 133. Brian Manning, *The English People and the English Revolution*, pp. 183–92.
51 *Pastoral and Ideology*, p. 134.

CODA

1 *Samson Agonistes* in *The Works of John Milton* vol. 1, pt 2, pp. 330–99. It is notoriously difficult to date the composition of *Samson Agonistes*. Many scholars date it between 1667 and publication in 1671, though some critics have argued for composition in 1640–1, 1647–53, 1660–1. See Mary Ann Radzinowicz, *Toward 'Samson Agonistes'* (New Jersey: Princeton University Press, 1978), pp. 387–407.
2 John Milton, *The Reason of Church Government* (London, 1641), p. 40. On the iconoclasm of *Samson Agonistes* see David Loewenstein, '"Casting down imaginations": Milton as Iconoclast', in Christopher Kendrick, ed., *Critical Essays on John Milton* (New York: G. K. Hall, 1995), pp. 115–30, esp. p. 123.
3 'Of that Sort of Dramatic Poem Which is Called Tragedy', *Samson Agonistes*, p. 331. On classical drama as 'exemplary to a Nation', see also *Reason of Church Government* (1642), pp. 37–9. Pareus saw Revelation as 'after the manner of a *Drammatical Representation*' (c2v), and his Civil War translator Arnold understands his commentary as setting 'downe with the finger of God, the certaine event and issue of the whole warre'. See David Pareus, *A Commentary on the Divine Revelation of the Apostle and Evangelist John*, trans. Elias Arnold (Amsterdam, 1644), *2r. I am very grateful to Jonathan Rogers for pointing this out to me.
4 See John Guillory, 'The Father's House: *Samson Agonistes* in its Historical Moment', in Mary Nyquist and Margaret W. Ferguson, eds., *Re-membering Milton: New Essays on the Texts and Traditions* (London: Methuen, 1988), pp. 148–76.
5 William Flesch, 'Reading, Seeing, and Acting in *Samson Agonistes*', in Kendrick, ed., *Critical Essays*, pp. 131–46, p. 139.
6 Percy Bysshe Shelley, *Prometheus Unbound*.

Select bibliography

REFERENCE

Arber, Edward, ed. *Transcripts of the Register of the Company of Stationers of London.* 5 vols. London, privately printed, 1875–1894.

Firth, C. H. and R. S. Rait. *Acts and Ordinances of the Interregnum 1642–1660.* 3 vols. London: HMSO, 1911.

Harbage, Alfred, ed. *Annals of English Drama 975–1700*, 3rd edn rev. Samuel Schoenbaum and Sylvia Stoler Wagonheim. 1964; rpt London: Routledge, 1989.

Lennep, William Van, ed. *The London Stage 1660–1800.* Carbondale, Illinois: Southern Illinois University Press, 1965, I.

Journals of the House of Commons, 1641–1660.

Public Record Office. *Calendar of State Papers Domestic Series*, 1641–1661.

Public Record Office. *Calendar of State Papers Venetian*, 1653–1656.

MANUSCRIPTS

Bodley MS. North c.4.

MS. Bodl. Rawlinson poet. 16.

Brotherton ML 78:10

Guildhall MS. 17.100.

Guildhall MS. 11.928.

Guildhall MS. 15.869.

Commonwealth Exchequer Papers, PRO/S.P.28,354.

Auditor's Books, PRO/E.404, 157.

State Papers Portugal, PRO/S.P.4, 89,132, 134.

PRIMARY SOURCES: PRINTED

Where place of publication is not given it is assumed to be London.

The Actors Remonstrance. 1643.

The Agreement of the People. 1647. In *Leveller Manifestoes of the Puritan Revolution.* Ed. Don M. Wolfe. New York: Columbia University Press, 1944.

Andronicus, or Impieties Long Success. London, 1661.

Another Bloudy Fight at Colchester. 1648.

The Arraignment, Conviction and Imprisonment of Christmas. 1646.

The Arraignment of Superstition or a Discourse Between a Protestant, a Glasier and a Separatist. 1641.

Articles For the Surrender of Colchester. 1648.

Ascham, Anthony. *A Discourse Wherein is Examined What is Particularly Lawful During the Confusion and Revolution of Government.* London, 1648.

Aubrey, John. *Brief Lives.* Ed. Oliver Lawson Dick. 1950; rpt Harmondsworth: Penguin, 1949 repr. 1962.

B., I. (attributed to John Bulteel). *London's Triumph.* London, 1656.

B., O. *A Dialogue or Discourse Betwixt Two Old Acquaintence of Contrary Opinions.* 1647.

B. T. *The Rebellion of Naples.* London, 1649.

La Balet de la Paix. London, 1660.

A Bartholomew Fairing. 1649.

Battie, John. *The Merchants Remonstrance,* Rev. edn, 1648.

Baxter, Richard. *Reliquiae Baxterianae.* Ed. Matthew Sylvester. London, 1696.

Beaumont, Francis and John Fletcher. *Comedies and Tragedies.* London, 1647.

Philaster or Love Lies a-Bleeding. 1609. Ed. Andrew Gurr. London: Methuen, 1969.

Beaumont, Joseph. *The Complete Poems of Joseph Beaumont.* 2 vols. Ed. Alexander B. Grosart. Edinburgh: Edinburgh University Press, 1880, vol. II.

Behn, Aphra. *The Roundheads; or the Good Old Cause.* Ed. Montague Summers, *The Works of Aphra Behn.* 6 vols. 1682; rpt London, William Heinemann, 1915, vol. I.

The Rover I and II. Ed. Montague Summers. *The Works of Aphra Behn,* vol. I.

The Bishops Potion. 1641. Attrib. Richard Overton.

The Bloody Court, or the Fatall Tribunall. 1649.

The Bloody Game of Cards. London, 1643.

Botero, Giovanni. *The Travellers Breviat.* Trans. Robert Johnson. London, 1601.

Brackley, Elizabeth and Jane Cavendish. *The Concealed Fansyses.* Ed. Nathan Comfort Starr. *PMLA,* no. 46 (1931), 802–38.

Brathwaite, Richard. *Mercurius Britannicus, or the English Intelligencer: a Tragi-Comedy at Paris.* 1641.

A Brief Dialogue Between a Zelotopit one of the Daughters of a Zealous Roundhead, and Superstition, a Holy Fryer, newly come out of France. 1642.

Brome, Richard. *The Antipodes.* Ed. Ann Haaker. 1640. London: Edward Arnold, 1967.

A Jovial Crew. Ed. Ann Haaker. 1652; rpt London: Edward Arnold, 1968.

Brothers of the Blade Answerable to the Sisters of the Scabbard. 1641.

Buchanan, George. *Tyranicall Government Anatomized: A Discourse Concerning Evil Counsellors.* London, 1643.

Burkhead, Henry. *Colas Fury or Lirendas Miserie.* Kilkenny, 1646.

Carmina Colloquia. 1659.

Cartwright, George. *The Heroick Lover, or, the Infanta of Spain.* London, 1661.

Cartwright, Sir William. *Comedies, Tragicomedies, With other Poems.* London, 1651.

The Cavaliers Catachisme. 1643.

The Cavaliers Jubilee, or Long Look'd for Come at Last: viz. The Generall Pardon. 1652.

Cavendish, Margaret, Duchess of Newcastle. *Playes.* London, 1662
   Playes, Never Before Printed. London, 1668.
   A Description of a New World Called The Blazing World. London, 1668.
   Poems, or Several Fancies. London, 1668.
   Sociable Letters. London, 1664.
   The Worlds Olio. London, 1655.

Chapelain, Jean. *Opuscules critiques.* Ed. Alfred C. Hunter. Paris: E. Droz, 1936.

The Citie's New Poets Mock Show. 1659.

The Colchester Spie. 1648.

Colchester Surrendered to the Lord Generall. 1648.

Colchesters Tears. 1648.

Conference Between O. Cromwell and Hugh Peters in St James's Park. London, 1660.

Corneille, Pierre. *The Cid.* Trans. John Cairncross. 1637; Harmondsworth: Penguin, 1975.

The Country-mans Care and the Citizens Feare. 1641.

The Court Career. London, 1659.

Cowley, Abraham. *Cutter of Coleman Street.* In *The English Writings of Abraham Cowley.* 2 vols. Ed. A. R. Waller. Cambridge University Press, 1905 vol. II.

Craftie Cromwell: or Oliver Ordering our New State. London, 1648.

Craftie Cromwell: or Oliver in His Glory as King. London, 1648.

Cromwell, Oliver. *Writings and Speeches of Oliver Cromwell.* 4 vols. Ed. Wilbur Cortez Abbot. Cambridge, Mass.: Harvard University Press, 1937–47.

Cromwell's Conspiracy. A Tragy-Comedy. 1660.

Crouch, Humphrey. *The Lady Pecunia's Journey Unto Hell.* 1654.

The Cruell Warre (1643). Ed. Jean Fuzier. In *Cahiers Elizabethan's*, no. 14 (October 1978), 49–68.

The Cuckoo's Nest at Westminster. London, 1648.

Cupid's Banishment. Ed. C. E. McGee. *Renaissance Drama*, no. 19 (1988), 226–64.

d'Aubignac, Fr. Abbé. *Pratique du theatre.* Ed. P. Martino. Paris: Alger, 1927.

Davenant, Sir William. *Britannia Triumphans.* London, 1638.

The Cruelty of the Spaniards in Peru. London, 1658.

The First Days Entertainment at Rutland House: By Declamations and Musick After the Manner of the Ancients. London, 1657.

The History of Sir Francis Drake. London, 1659.

A Playhouse to be Let. London, 1663.

'Preface to *Gondibert*', *Gondibert: An Heroick Poem.* Ed. David F. Gladish. Oxford University Press, 1971.

Salmacida Spolia. London, 1640.

The Siege of Rhodes. Ed. Ann-Marie Hëdbáck. Uppsala: Acta Universitatis Upsaliensis, Studia Anglistica Upsaliensia 14, 1973.

The Temple of Love. London, 1635.

Works of Sir William Davenant. London, 1673.

De las Casas, Bartolomé. *The Tears of the Indians.* 1551. Trans. John Phillips London, 1656.

De la Vega, Garcilasco. *Le Commentaire Royal, ou L'Histoire des Yncas, Roys du Peru.* 1609. Trans. Paris, 1633.

Royal Commentaries of the Incas: A General History of Peru. 2 vols. Trans. Harold V. Livermore. Austin and London: University of Austin Press, 1966.

A Declaration of the Lords and Commons Assembled in Parliament: For the Suppressing of all Tumultuous Assemblies, Under Pretence of Framing and Presenting Petitions to Parliament. London, 1648.

Denny, William. *The Shepherds Holiday.* In *Inedited Poetical Miscellanies 1584–1700.* Ed. Henry Huth. London: Chiswick Press, 1870, pp. 61–116.

A Description of the Passage of Thomas Late Earle of Strafford, over the River of Styx. London, 1641. Attrib. Richard Overton.

The Devill and the Parliament: or, the Parliament and the Devil A Contestation Between them for the Precedencie. London, 1648.

A Dialogue Arguing that Arch-Bishops, Bishops etc., are to be cut off by Law of God. 1644.

Dialogue Between an Excise Man and Death. 1659.

A Dialogue Between Mistris Macquerella, a Suburb Bawd, Mrs Scoloendra, a Noted Curtezan, and Mr Pimpinello an Usher and c. 1650.

A Dialogue Between Sacke and Six. 1641.

A Dialogue Betwixt the Ghosts of Charles I and Oliver the Late Usurping Protector. 1659.

A Dialogue Betwixt a Horse of Warre and a Mill-Horse. 1644.

A Dialogue or Discourse Betwixt Two Old Acquaintence of Contrary Opinions. 1647.

266 *Select bibliography*

Digges, Dudley. *An Answer to a Printed Book*. Oxford, 1642.

A Discourse in Derision of a Teaching in Free-Schools. 1644.

A Discourse or Dialogue Between The Two Now Potent Enemies: Lord Generall Militia and His Illegal Opposite the Commission of Array. 1642.

The Discourse and Sad Complaints Betwixt the French-man and the Irish-man. 1646

A Discreet and Judicious Discourse Between Wisdom and Pietie. n.p, 1642.

The Disease of the House, or the State Mountebanck Administering Physick to a Sick Parliament. London, 1649.

A Disputation Between the Devil and the Pope. 1642.

The Dolefull Lamentation of Cheapside Cross. 1641.

The Downefall of Temporizing Poets. London, 1641.

Drake, Sir Francis. *The World Encompassed*. London, 1636, rpt 1652.

Dryden, John. 'Of Heroique Plays'. In *The Works of John Dryden*. oo vols. Ed. T. Swedenberg Jr, George R. Guffey, Alan Roper. Berkeley and Los Angeles: University of California Press, 1956–79, vol. XI.

The Earle of Straffords Ghost 1644.

Etherege, George. *The Comical Revenge, or, Love in a Tub*. In *The Plays of Sir George Etherege*. Ed. Michael Cordner. Cambridge University Press, 1982.

Evelyn, John. *The Diary of John Evelyn*. 6 vols. Ed. E. S. de Beer. Oxford University Press, 1955.

The Famous Tragedie of Charles I. 1649.

The Famous Tragedy of the Life and Death of Mistress Rump. 1660.

Fane, Mildmay. *Otia Sacra*. London, 1648.

Raguallo d'Oceano and Candy Restored, 1641. Ed. Clifford Leech. Louvain: 1938.

Fanshawe, Richard, trans. *The Faithfull Shepherd*. Battista Guarini. 1647; rpt Edinburgh University Press, 1976. Ed. J. H. Whitfield.

trans. *The Faithfull Shepherd*. London, 1648.

trans. *To Love Only For Loves Sake*. London, 1654.

The Female Rebellion: A Tragicomedy. Ed. Alexander Smith. Glasgow: n.p., 1872.

Filmer, Sir Robert. *The Anarchy of a Limited or Mixed Monarchy*. 1648.

The Necessity of the Absolute Power of all Kings and Especially the King of England. London, 1648.

Patriarcha and Other Political Works of Sir Robert Filmer. Ed. Peter Laslett. Oxford: Basil Blackwell, 1949.

Patriarcha and Other Works. Ed. Johann Sommerville. Cambridge University Press, 1991.

Flecknoe, Richard. *Ariadne Deserted by Theseus and Found and Courted by Bacchus*. London, 1654.

The Idea of His Highness Oliver Late Protector and c. London, 1659.

Loves Dominion. London, 1654.

The Marriage of Oceanus and Brittania. 1659.

A Relation of Ten Years Travels. London, 1654.

Fletcher, John. *The Faithful Shepherdess.* London, 1608.
Fletcher, John and Philip Massinger *Sir John van Olden Barnavelt.* Ed. T. H. Howard-Hill. London: Malone Society, 1980.
Forde, Thomas. *Love's Labyrinth.* London, 1660.
The Friers Last Farewell. 1642.
Fuller, Thomas. *Andronicus, or, An Unfortunate Politican.* 1646.
Gage, Thomas. *The English–American his Travail by Sea and Land: or, a new Survey of the West Indias.* London, 1648.
Gatford, Lionel. *England's Complaint.* 1648.
Gayton, Edmund. *Charity Triumphant or the Virgin-Shew.* 1655.
Chartae Scriptae or a New Game at Cards. 1645.
Gerbier, Balthazar. *A Publique Lecture On all the Languages, Arts, Sciences, and Noble Excercises, which are taught in Sr Balthazar Gerbiers Academy.* London, 1650.
Gillespie, George. *A Late Dialogue Betwixt a Civilian and a Divine, Concerning the Present Condition of the Church of England.* 1644.
Glapthorne, Henry. *White-Hall A Poem Written 1642 with Elegies on The Right Honourable Francis Earl of Bedford and Henry Earle of Manchester, Lord Privy Seale.* London, 1643.
Goodwin, John. *Right and Might Well Met.* London, 1648.
Gosson, Stephen. *The Schoole of Abuse.* London, 1579.
Grand Plutoes Remonstrance. 1642.
A Great and Bloudy Fight at Colchester. 1648.
Greville, Fulke, Lord Brooke. *Certaine Learned and Elegant Workes.* London, 1633.
Life of Sidney. London, 1652.
Mustapha. London, 1609.
Poems and Dramas of Fulke Greville. 2 vols. Ed. Geoffrey Bullough. Edinburgh and London: Oliver and Boyd, 1939.
The Remaines of Sir Fulke Greville, Lord Brooke; Being Poems of Monarchy and Religion. London, 1670.
The Writings of Fulke Greville. Ed. Joan Rees. London: Athlone Press, 1973.
Haller, William, ed. *Tracts on Liberty in the Puritan Revolution.* 3 vols. New York: Columbia University Press, 1934.
Haller, William and Geoffrey Davis, eds. *The Leveller Tracts 1647–1653.* 3 vols. New York: Columbia University Press, 1944.
The Hampton Court Conspiracy. London, 1647.
The Political Works of James Harrington. Ed. J. G. A. Pocock, Cambridge University Press, 1977.
The Hectors, or the False Challenge. London, 1656.
Hells Higher Court of Justice. London, 1661
Hells Trienniall Parliament Summoned Five Yeers Since by King Lucifer. 1647.
Herbert, Thomas. *Newes Newly Discovered.* 1641.
Herle, Charles. *An Answer to Doctor Ferne's Reply, Entitled Conscience Satisfied.* London, 1643.

Hey Hoe For a Husband; or the Parliament of Maids. London, 1647.

Heylyn, Peter, attrib. *Augustus, or an Essay of those Measures and Counsels Whereby the Commonwealth of Rome was Altered and Reduced into a Monarchy.* London, 1632.

Heywood, Thomas. *The Actors Vindication.* 1612; rpt 1658.

If You Know Not Me, You Know Nobody. London, 1605.

HMC: Twelfth Report, Appendix, Part VII: The Manuscripts of S. H. Le Fleming Esq., London, 1890.

Hobbes, Thomas. *The Collected Works of Thomas Hobbes.* 12 vols. Ed. William Molesworth. London: Routledge/Thoemmes Press, 1843, rpt 1994.

Leviathan; or the Matter, Forme and Power of a Commonwealth Ecclesiastical and Civill. Ed. Crawford Burroughs Macpherson. 1651; rpt Harmondsworth: Penguin, 1981.

An Honest Discourse Between Three Neighbours, touching the Present Government in these Three Nations. 1655.

How Daphne Pays His Debts. 1656.

Howard, Sir Robert. *The Committee.* London, 1662.

Howell, James. *Ah, Ha, Tumulus, Thalamus.* 1654.

(attrib.) *A Discourse or Parley Continued Between Patricus and Peregrine Touching the Civill Wars of England and Ireland.* 1643.

Dodonas Grove, or the Voccall Forest. London, 1640.

(attrib.) *Englands Teares for the Present Warres.* 1644.

trans. *The Nuptialls of Peleus and Thetis: Consisting of a Mask and a Comedy, or the Great Royall Ball.* London, 1654.

(attrib.) *The Vision or a Dialog Between the Soule and the Bodie.* 1652.

The Humble Petition of Divers Well-Affected Persons of the Cities of London, Westminster, the Borough of Southwark, Hamlets and Parts Adjacent. 1649.

The Humble Petition of Divers Well Affected Women. London, 1649.

The Humble Petition of Many Thousands of Wives and Matrons of the City of London. London, 1643.

Hyde, Edward, Earl of Clarendon. *The History of the Great Rebellion.* 6 vols. Ed. W. D. Macray. Oxford: Clarendon Press, 1888.

I Marry Sir, Heere is Newes Indeed, Being the Copie of a Letter which the Devil Sent to the Pope of Rome. London, 1642.

John Presbyter Not Dead. 1647.

Jonson, Ben. *The Alchemist.* Ed H. T. Mares. London: Methuen, 1971.

Bartholomew Fair. Ed. D.Duncan. Edinburgh: Oliver and Boyd, 1972.

Works of Ben Jonson. 11 vols. Ed. C. H. Herford, E. Herford and Percy Simpson. Oxford: Clarendon Press, 1925–52.

Jordan, Thomas. *Fancy's Festivals: A Masque.* London, 1657.

London's Resurrection. London, 1671.

Poetical Varieties. London, 1637

A Royal Arbor of Loyal Poesie. London, 1660.

Rules to know a Royall King from a Disloyall Subject. London, 1642.

A Speech at Vintner's Hall. London, 1660.

The Kentish Fair. Ed. William Charles Woodson. 1648; rpt *AEB*, no. 8 (1984), 3–15.

Killigrew, Thomas. *Comedies and Tragedies.* London, 1664.

The Kingdomes Monster Uncloaked from Heaven. 1643.

Kingdom's Weekly Intelligencer.

The Kings Cabinet Opened. London, 1645.

Kirkman, Francis (attrib.) *The Presbyterian Lash.* London, 1661.

   'The Stationer to the Reader'. In John Webster and William Rowley. *The Thracian Wonder.* London, 1660.

   A True, Perfect and Exact Catalogue of All the Comedies, Tragedies, Tragi-Comedies, Pastorals, Masques and Interludes that Were Ever Yet Printed and Published Till this Present Year 1661. London, 1661.

Knolles, Richard. *The General Historie of the Turkes.* London, 1603.

The Last News in London, or a Discourse Between a Citizen and a Countrey Gentleman as they did Ride Between London and Ludlow. 1642.

The Last Will and Testament of Charing Cross. London, 1646.

Last Will and Testament of Sir James Independent. London, 1647.

A Letter From Sir Marmaduke Langdale to Sir Charles Lucas: With a Hopefull Assurance of Speedy Relief to Colchester. 1648.

Lilburne, John. *Englands New Chaines Discovered.* 1649.

   The Legall Fundamental Liberties. 1649.

The Lofty Bishop, the Lazy Brownist, and the Loyall Author. 1640.

Londons Joyfull Gratulation. 1643. Attrib. Thomas Jordan.

London's Metamorphosis, or, a Dialogue Between London and Amsterdam. 1647.

Lower, William. *The Enchanted Lovers.* The Hague, 1658. In *The Dramatic Works and Translations of William Lower.* Ed. William Bryon Gates. University of Philadelphia Press, 1932.

Machiavelli, Nicholas. *Nicholas Machiavel's Prince.* Trans. Edward Dacres. 1640; rpt Menston: Scolar Press, 1969.

The Maids Petition. London, 1647.

The Malignants Conventicle. 1643.

The Man in the Moon. 23–31 Jan. 1650.

Manuche, Cosmo. *The Banish'd Shepherdess.* In 'A Study of English Drama', by P. J. Canavan, pp. 351–444.

   The Loyal Lovers: a Tragicomedy. London, 1652.

   The Just General: A Tragicomedy. London, 1652.

Marvell, Andrew. *The Complete Poems of Andrew Marvell.* Ed. Elizabeth Story Donno. 1972; rpt Harmondsworth: Penguin, 1979.

Massinger, Philip. *A New Way to Pay Old Debts.* Ed. T. W. Craik. 1633; rpt London: Ernest Benn, 1964.

   Believe As Ye List. Ed. C. J. Sisson. Oxford: Malone Society, 1927.

May, Thomas. *The Tragedy of Antigone, the Theban Princess.* London, 1631.

   The Tragedie of Cleopatra. London, 1639. Rpt 1654.

   The Tragedie of Julia Aggripina. London, 1639. Rpt 1654.

Mercurius Honestus or Newes from Westminster. 1648.

Mercurius Melancholicus. Ding Dong, or Sir Pitifull Parliament on his Death Bed. London, 1648.
Mercurius Poeticus. St George and the Dragon Anglice. 1659.
Mercurius Verdicus. 19–26 April 1645.
Meriton, Thomas. *The Wandering Lover*. London, 1658.
A Messenger from the Dead: Conference Between Henry the 8 and Charles the First. 1658.
Middleton, Thomas. *A Game at Chess*. Ed. J. W. Harper. 1625; rpt London: Ernest Benn, 1966.
    A Mad World My Masters. Ed. Standish Henning. 1608; rpt London: Edward Arnold, 1965.
    The Phoenix. 1607; rpt *The Works of Thomas Middleton*. 8 vols. Ed. A. H. Bullen. London: John C. Nimmo, 1885, I.
Milton, John. *The Works of John Milton*. 18 vols. Ed. Frank Allen Patterson. New York: Columbia University Press.
Mr William Prynn His Defence of Stage-Plays, or a Recantation of a former Book of his called Histrio-Mastix. London, 1649.
Mistris Parliament Brought to Bed. Ed. Lois Potter. *AEB*, NS 1, no. 3 (1987), 1–129.
Mistris Parliament Her Gossiping. Ed. Lois Potter. *AEB*, NS 1, no. 3 (1987) 144–157.
Mistris Parliament Her Invitation. Ed. Lois Potter. *AEB*, NS 1, no. 3 (1987) 158–170.
Mistris Parliament Presented in Her Bed. Ed. Lois Potter. *AEB*, NS 1, no. 3 (1987) 130–143.
The Moderate. 22–9 Aug. 1648.
The Moderate Intelligencer. 24–31 Aug. 1648.
Montagu, Walter. *The Shepherds Paradise*. London, 1659.
More, Thomas. *Utopia*. 1516; trans. 1551; rpt London: Dent, 1951.
Nedham, Marchmont. *The Case of the Commonwealth of England Stated*. London, 1650.
    The Case of the Kingdom Stated. London, 1647.
    Digitus Dei: or, God's Justice Upon Treachery and Treason; Exemplified in the Life and Death of the late James Duke of Hamilton. London, 1649.
    A Most Pithy Exhortation Delivered in an Eloquent Oration to the Watry Generation Aboard their Admirall at Graves-end. By the Right Reverend, Mr Hugh Peters, Doctor of the Chair for the Famous University of Whitehall, and Chaplain in ordinary to the High and Mighty K. Oliver, the first of that name, as it was took verbatim in short hand (when he delivered it). London, 1649.
    A Plea For the King and Kingdome. 1648.
Nedham, Marchmont, ed. *Mercurius Pragmaticus*. Sept. 1647–Dec. 1648.
    (attrib.) as Mercurius Pragmaticus. *The Levellers Levell'd*. Ed. Philip C. Dust. 1647; rpt *AEB*, 4, nos. 3 and 4 (1980), 182–240.
    (attrib.) *Loyalty Speakes Truth: Or, a Conference of the Grand Mercuries, Pragmaticus, Melancholicus, Elenctius*. 1648.
Neville, Henry. (attrib.) *An Exact Diurnal of the Parliament of Ladies*. 1647.

(attrib.) *The Ladies a Second Time Assembled.* 1647.

(attrib.) *News From the New Exchange or the Commonwealth of Ladies.* 1650

(attrib.) *Shuffling, Cutting and Dealing in a Game at Pickquet: Being Acted From the Year 1653 to 1658. By O.P. and others.* 1659.

A New Conference Between the Ghosts of King Charles and Oliver Cromwell. London, 1659.

A New Fiction, or As Wee Were. 1661.

A New Marriage Between Mr King and Mrs Parliament. 1648.

Newes From Rome, or A Relation of the Pope and His Patentees Pilgrimage into Hell. 1641.

Newes, True Newes, Laudable Newes, Citie Newes, Countrey Newes, 1642.

Nichols, Philip. *Sir Francis Drake Revived.* London, 1621.

Nick Froth and Rule-rost. 1641

No-Body His Complaint, and Doctour Some-Body. 1652.

Ogilby, John. *The Fables of Aesop Paraphras'd in Verse.* London 1651.

The Entertainment of His Most Excellent Majestie Charles II in his Passage through the City of London to his Coronation. 2nd edn, London 1662.

The Old Proverb, As Good to Be a Knave as Amongst Knaves. 1646.

The Organ's Funerall. London, 1642.

Osborne, Dorothy. *The Letters of Dorothy Osborne.* Ed. G. C. Smith. Oxford: Clarendon Press, 1928.

Osborne, Francis. *Political Reflections Upon the Government of the Turkes.* London, 1656.

The True Tragicomedy Formerly Acted at Court. Ed. Lois Potter with John Pitcher. New York and London: Garland, 1983.

Overton, Richard. (attrib.) *The Arraignment of Mr Persecution.* 1645.

Articles of High Treason Exhibited Against Cheap-side Crosse. 1642. Signed.

(attrib.) *The Bayting of the Great Bull of Bashan.* July 1649.

(attrib.) *Canterbury his Change of Diet.* 1641

(attrib.) *Lambeth Fayre.* 1641.

(attrib.) *Last Will and Testament of John Presbyter.* London, 1647.

(attrib.) *Martin's Echo.* 1645.

(attrib.) *A New Bull-Bayting.* Aug. 1649.

New Lambeth Fayre. 1642. Signed.

A Tragi-Comedy Called New-Market Fayre I and II. Ed. Paul Werstine. 1649; rpt *AEB*, 6, nos. 2 and 4 (1982), 71–103, 209–239. Attrib. Richard Overton and John Crouch.

(attrib.) *A Pack of Patentees.* 1641.

(attrib.) *A Rent in the Lawne Sleeves.* 1641.

Vox Borealis or the Northern Discoverie. 1641.

(attrib.) *Westminster Fayre.* 1647.

Pareus, David. *A Commentary on the Divine Revelation of the Apostle and Evangelist John.* Trans. Elias Arnold. Amsterdam, 1644.

Parker, Henry. *Observations Upon Some of His Majesties Late Answers and Expresses.* 1642. Ed. William Haller. *Tracts on Liberty,* vol. 11.

Jus Populi. London, 1644.

Peacham, Henry. *A Dialogue Between the Cross in Cheap and Charing Cross.* 1641.

Peck, Francis. *New Memoirs of the Life and Political Works of Mr John Milton.* London, 1740.

Pepys, Samuel. *The Diary of Samuel Pepys.* 11 vols. Ed. R. C. Latham and W. Matthews. London: G. Bell and Sons, 1974.

Perfect Occurrences. 9–16 May 1645; 1–8 Sept. 1648; 29 Dec.–5 Jan. 1648–9.

Perrinchief, Reginald. *The Syracusan Tyrant or, The Life of Agathocles with Some Reflexions on the Practices of Modern Usurpers.* London, 1661.

The Picture of a New Courtier Drawn in a Conference between Mr Timeserver and Mr Plainheart. London, 1656.

The Poets Knavery Discovered. 1642

The Poets Recantation. 1642.

Poole, Elizabeth. *An Alarum of Warre.* 1648.

Prince, Laurence. *A New Dialogue Between Dick of Kent and Wat the Welchman.* 1654.

A Private Conference Between Mr L. Robinson and Mr T. Scott Occasioned by the Publishing His Majesties Letters and Declaration. London, 1660.

Prynne, William. *Histrio-Mastix, The Players Scourge.* London, 1633.

Purchas, Samuel. *Purchas His Pilgrims.* London, 1625.

R., T. *Cicero's Prince: The Reasons and Counsels for Settlement and Good Government of a Kingdom Collected out of Cicero's Works.* London, 1668.

Rawlins, Thomas. *The Rebellion.* London, 1640.

Mr Recorders Speech to the Lord Protector upon Wednesday the eighth of Febr. 1653 being the day of his Highnesse Entertainment in London. London, 1654.

'Records of a Church in Bristol 1640–1687'. In *Bristol Record Society's Publications,* 27 (1974).

The Reformed Malignants. 1643.

The Remarkable Funerall of Cheapside Crosse in London. 1642.

The Resolution of the Women of London to the Parliament. London, 1642.

Revolutionary Prose of the English Civil War. Ed. Howard Erskine-Hill and Graham Storey. Cambridge University Press, 1983.

Richards, Nathaniel. *Tragedy of Messallina.* London, 1640.

Rogers, Thomas. *Leicesters Ghost.* 1605, rpt 1641. Ed. William B. Franklin Jr. University of Chicago Press, 1972.

Rushworth, John. *Historical Collections.* 10 vols. London, 1720.

S., J. *An Excellent Comedy Called the Prince of Priggs Revels.* London, 1651.

S., J. *A Pleasant Conference Between A Popish Recusant and A Protestant.* 1642.

Sadler, Anthony. *Inquisitio Anglicana: or the Disguise discovered.* London, 1654.

The Subjects Joy for the Kings Restoration. London, 1660.

Sadler, John. *Masquerade du Ciel.* London, 1640.

The Rights of the Kingdom. London, 1649.

Shelley, Percy Bysshe. *The Complete Poetical Works.* Ed. Thomas Hutchinson. London: Oxford University Press, 1952.

St George For England. 1659.

The Scotch Politike Presbyter. A Tragi-Comedie. 1647.

A Second Discovery By the Northern Scout. 1642.

Sedley, Sir Charles. *The Poetical And Dramatic Works of Sir Charles Sedley.* 2 vols. Ed. V. de Sola Pinto. London: Constable, 1928.

Shakespeare, William. *Measure For Measure.* Ed. J. W. Lever. 1623; rpt London: Methuen, 1965.

    Complete Works. Ed. Peter Alexander. London and Glasgow: Collins, 1957.

Sheppard, Samuel. *Animadversions Upon John Lilburnes Last Two Books, the One Intitled London's Liberty in Chaines Discovered, the other Anatomy of the Lords Cruelty.* 1646.

    The Committee-Man Curried. London, 1647

    The Famer Fam'd. London, 1646.

    The Joviall Crew or, the Devill Turn'd Ranter. London, 1651.

    The Second Part of the Committee Man Curried. 1647.

    The Times Displayed in Six Sestyads. London, 1646.

    The Yeare of Jubilee; or, England's Releasment. London, 1646.

Sherburne, Edward, trans. *Medea: a Tragedy Englished by E.S.* London, 1648.

Shirley, James. *The Contention of Ajax and Hercules.* London, 1653.

    '*Cupid and Death:* A Masque'. Ed. B. A. Harris. In *A Book Of Masques.* Cambridge University Press: 1967.

    The Dramatic Works and Poems. 6 vols. Ed. William Gifford. London: John Murray, 1833, vol. v.

    Six New Plays. London, 1653.

    The Triumph of Peace. Ed. Clifford Leech. In *A Book of Masques.* Cambridge University Press, 1967.

Sir Charles Lucas His Last Speech At the Place of Execution Where he Was Shot to Death. London, 1648.

The Souldiers Language or a Discourse Between Two Souldiers. 1644.

The Soundheads Description of a Roundhead. 1642.

Spelman, John. *A View of a Printed Book.* Oxford, 1642.

A Spirit Moving in the Women-Preachers. London, 1646.

The Spirituall Courts Epitomised in a Dialogue. London, 1641.

The Stage Players Complaint. 1641.

Stop Your Noses, or England at Her Easement, Evacuating those Clods at Westminster. London, 1648.

Stubbes, Phillip. *The Anatomie of Abuses.* Ed. William B. D. D. Turnbull, 1585; rpt London: W. Pickering, 1836.

Suckling, Sir John. *The Poems, Plays and Other Remains of Sir John Suckling.* 2 vols. Ed. W. Carew Hazlitt. 1892; rpt New York: Books For Libraries Press, 1969.

Tatham, John. *Aqua Triumphalis*. London, 1662.
    The Distracted State: a Tragedy. London, 1651.
    The Dramatic Works of John Tatham. Ed. J. Maidment and J. Logan. London: H. Sotheran, 1879.
    The Fancies Theater. London, 1640.
    London's Glory: Represented by Time, Truth and Fame. London, 1660.
    (attrib.) *Knavery in All Trades*. London, 1664.
    Londons Triumph. London, 1657.
    Londons Tryumph. London, 1658.
    Londons Tryumph. London, 1661.
    Londons Tryumphs Celebrated. London, 1663.
    Londons Triumphs. London, 1664.
    Neptunes Address. London, 1661.
    Ostella; Or The Faction of Love and Beauty Reconciled. London, 1650.
    The Rump, or the Mirrour of the Late Times. London, 1659.
    The Scots Figgaries. London, 1652.
Taylor, John. *A Tale in a Tub*. London, 1641.
    A Pedlar and a Romish Priest. 1641.
Thurloe, John. *A Collection of State Papers*. 7 vols. Ed. Thomas Birch. London, 1742.
Times Alteration, or a Dialogue Between My Lord Finch and Secretary Windebanke. London, 1641.
Times Changeling, Arraigned For Inconstancy at the Barre of Opportunity. London, 1643.
Tom Nash His Ghost. York and London, 1642.
The Tragedy of the Cruell Warre. In 'English Political Dialogues 1641–1651: A Suggestion for Research with a Critical Edition of *The Tragedy of the Cruell Warre* (1643)'. Ed. Jean Fuzier. *CE*, no. 14 (Oct. 1978), 49–68.
The Tragedy of the Famous Orator, Marcus Tullius Cicero. 1651.
A True and Exact Relation Sent in a Letter From an Officer in the Army to a Member of the House of Commons. 1648.
A True and Perfect Relation of the Condition of these Noblemen and Gentlemen in Colchester and of their Reason in Yielding Up the Said Town to the Lord Fairfax. 1648.
A True Relation of What Passed in Constantinople. London, 1649.
The Triumph of Beautie, As it was Performed by Some Young Gentlemen, for whom it was Intended, at a Private Recreation. 1646.
The Triumph of Loyalty: or the Happinesse of a Suffering Subject. 1648.
Two Knaves For a Penny. 1647.
Villiers, George, Duke of Buckingham. *The Rehearsal*. Ed. D. J. Crane. University Of Durham Publications, 1976.
A Vindication of Cheapside Crosse. Oxford, 1643.
Waller, Edmund. *A Panegyrick To My Lord Protector*. London, 1655.
Walwyn, William. *The Power of Love*. In *Leveller Tracts* ed. William Haller and Geoffrey Davis.

A Prediction of Master Edwards His Conversion. 1646.

(attrib.) *Truth's Victory Over Tyrants and Tyranny.* 1649.

Wase, Christopher. *Cicero Against Catiline in IV Invective Orations.* London, 1671.

The *Electra of Sophocles, presented to Her Highness the Lady Elizabeth, with an Epilogue Shewing the Parallel in Two Poems the Return and the Restauration.* 1649.

The Weekly Account. 4 Oct. 1643.

Westminster Fayre. 1647. Attrib. Richard Overton.

Wharton, Sir George. *Grand Pluto's Progresse.* London, 1647.

The Whirligigge Turning. 1647.

Whitelocke, Bulstrode. *The Diary of Bulstrode Whitelocke 1605–1675.* Ed. Ruth Spalding. Oxford University Press, 1990.

Journal of the Swedish Ambassy in the Years 1653 and 1654. 2 vols. London, 1772.

Memorials of English Affairs. London, 1732.

The Wicked Resolution of the Cavaliers. London, 1642.

Willan, Leonard. *Orgula, or the Fatal Error.* London, 1658.

Williams, Richard. *Peace, and No Peace. Or, A Pleasant Dialogue Between Philoeiremus, A Protestant, A Lover or Peace: Philo Polemus, A Separatist, An Incendiary of War.* 1643.

Wilson, John. *The Cheats.* London, 1663.

The Wishing Common-wealthe Man: Or a Dialogue betwixt Cautious a Country Man and Wish-well a Citizen. London, 1642.

A Wonderfull Plot or Mystery of State. 1647.

Woodhouse, A. S. P., ed. *Puritanism and Liberty: Being the Army Debates (1647–1649) From the Clarke Manuscripts.* 1938; rpt London: Dent, 1986.

Woodward, Hezekiah, *A Briefe Dialogue Between a Creditor and a Prisoner.* 1653.

Wright, James. *Historia Histrionica.* London, 1699.

SECONDARY SOURCES

Adams, W. J. 'Richard Brathwaite's *Mercurius Britannicus*'. *Modern Language Notes,* no. 26 (1911), 233–5.

Adamson, John. 'Protesters at the Establishment: Radical Responses in England from 1645 to 1775'. *TLS,* 7 June 1991, 5–6.

Altieri, Joanne. *The Theatre of Praise: The Panegyric Tradition in Seventeenth-Century English Drama.* Newark: University of Delaware Press, 1986.

Amussen, S. D. 'Gender, Family and the Social Order 1560–1725'. In *Order and Disorder in Early Modern England.* Ed. Anthony Fletcher and John Stevenson. Cambridge University Press, 1985.

Andrews, K. R., N. P. Canny and P. E. H. Hair. *The Westward Enterprise.* Detroit: Wayne State University Press, 1979.

Arnold, Dennis. *Monteverdi.* London: J. M. Dent, 1963.

Ashley, Maurice. *Financial and Commercial Policy Under the Cromwellian Protectorate.* 1934 London: rpt Frank Cass, 1962.

Ashton, Robert. 'From Cavalier to Roundhead Tyranny'. In *Reactions to the English Civil War.* Ed. John Morrill. London: Macmillan, 1982.

Backscheider, Paula R. *Spectacular Politics: Theatrical Power and Mass Culture in Early Modern England.* Baltimore and London: Johns Hopkins University Press, 1993.

Bailey, D. R. S. *Cicero.* London: Duckworth, 1971.

Bakhtin, Mikhail. *The Dialogic Imagination.* Ed Michael Holquist, trans. Caryl Emerson and Michael Holquist. Austin: University of Texas Press, 1981.

  'The Problem of Speech Genres'. In *Speech Genres and Other Late Essays.* Trans. and ed. Caryl Emerson and Michael Holquist. Austin: University of Texas Press, 1986.

Rabelais and His World. Trans. Hélène Iswolsky. 1965; rpt Bloomington: Indiana University Press, 1984.

Barber, Sarah. 'Irish Undercurrents to the Politics of April 1653'. *Historical Research,* vol. 65 (1992), 315–35.

Barish, Jonas. *The Antitheatrical Prejudice.* Berkeley and London: University of California Press, 1981.

Barthes, Roland. *Mythologies.* Trans. Annette Lavers, 1957; London: Collins, 1973.

Bas, George. 'More About the Anonymous Tragedy of the Cruell Warre and James Shirley's *Triumph of Peace'. Cahiers Elisabethains,* no. 17 (April 1980), 43–57.

Benjamin, Walter. *The Origin of German Tragic Drama.* Trans. John Osborne. London: New Left Books, 1977.

Bernet, John William. 'Toward the Restoration Heroic Play: The Evolution of Davenant's Serious Drama'. Diss. Stanford University, 1969.

Bevington, David. *Tudor Drama and Politics.* Cambridge, Mass.: Harvard University Press, 1968.

Blaydes, Sophia B., and Philip Bordinat. *Sir William Davenant 1629–1985: An Annotated Bibliography.* London: Garland Publishing, 1986.

Bordinat Phillp, and Sophia B. Blaydes. *Sir William Davenant.* Boston: G. K. Hall, 1981.

Bourdieu, Pierre. *Language and Symbolic Power.* Ed. John B. Thompson, trans. Gino Raymond and Matthew Adamson. Cambridge: Polity Press, 1991.

Boyce, Benjamin. 'News From Hell'. *PMLA,* 58, no. 2 (1943), 402–37.

Brenner, Robert. *Merchants and Revolution: Commercial Change, Political Conflict, and London Overseas Traders, 1550–1653.* Cambridge University Press, 1993.

Brown, Laura. *English Dramatic Form 1660–1760: An Essay in Generic History.* New Haven and London: Yale University Press, 1981.

Burke, Peter. 'Popular Culture in Seventeenth-Century London'. 1977, rpt in *Popular Culture in Seventeenth-Century England.* Ed. Barry Reay. Beckenham: Croom Helm, 1985.

Burner, Sandra A. *James Shirley: A Study of Literary Coteries and Patronage in Seventeenth-Century England.* New York and London: University Press of America, 1988.

Burt, Richard, ed. *The Administration of Aesthetics.* Minneapolis and London: University of Minnesota Press, 1994.

Butler, John. *A Biography of Richard Cromwell, 1626–1712, the Second Protector.* Lampeter: Edwin Mellen, 1994.

Butler, Martin. 'A Case Study in Caroline Political Theatre: Brathwaite's *Mercurius Britannicus* (1641)'. *The Historical Journal,* no. 27 (1984), 947–53.

'Entertaining the Palatine Prince'. *ELR,* 13, no. 3 (1983), 319–44.

'Politics and the Masque: Salmacida Spolia'. In *Literature and the English Civil War.* Ed. Thomas Healy and Jonathan Sawday. Cambridge University Press, 1990, pp. 59–74.

'Politics and the Masque: *The Triumph of Peace'. The Seventeenth Century,* 2, no. 2 (1987), 117–41.

Theatre and Crisis 1632–1642. Cambridge University Press, 1984.

Canavan, Patrick Joseph. 'A Study of English Drama as a Reflection of Stuart Politics'. Diss. University of Southern California, 1950.

Canfield, J. Douglas. 'The Ideology of Restoration Tragicomedy'. *ELH,* no. 51 (1983), 440–64.

Capp, Bernard. *The World of John Taylor the Water-Poet.* Oxford: Clarendon Press, 1994.

Cerasano, S. P., and Marion Wynne-Davies. *Renaissance Drama by Women: Texts and Documents.* London: Routledge, 1996.

Chambers, E. K. *The English Folk-Play.* Oxford: Clarendon Press, 1933.

Chartier, Roger, ed. *The Culture of Print: Power and the Uses of Print in Early Modern Europe.* Trans. Lydia G. Cochrane. Cambridge: Polity Press, 1989.

Chartier, Roger. 'Texts, Printing, Readings'. In *The New Cultural History.* Ed. Lynn Hunt. Berkeley: University of California Press, 1989.

Chaudhuri, Sukarta. *Renaissance Pastoral and its Developments.* Oxford University Press, 1989.

Chayney, Edward. *The Grand Tour and the Great Rebellion.* Geneva: Slatkine, 1985.

Chernaik, Warren. *The Poetry of Limitation: A Study of Edmund Waller.* New Haven and London: Yale University Press, 1968.

Chew, Samuel. *The Crescent and the Rose: Islam and England During the Renaissance.* New York: Oxford University Press, 1937.

Clare, Janet. *'Art Made Tongue-Tied by Authority': Elizabethan and Jacobean Dramatic Censorship.* Manchester University Press, 1990.

'Davenant's *Cruelty of the Spaniards in Peru* – Masque for the Protectorate?' Paper given at conference on 'Politics and Patronage', Reading, 1992.

Clark, J. C. D. *Revolution and Rebellion: State and Society in England in the Seventeenth and Eighteenth Centuries.* Cambridge University Press, 1986.

Clark, Peter. 'The Ownership of Books in England 1560–1640: The Example of Some Kentish Townsfolk'. In *Schooling and Society: Studies in the History of Education.* Ed. Lawrence Stone. Baltimore and London: Johns Hopkins University Press, 1976, pp. 95–111.

Clark, Stuart. 'French Historians and Early Modern Popular Culture'. *PP*, no. 100 (August 1983), 62–100.

Clifton, Robin. 'The Popular Fear of Catholics During the English Revolution'. *PP*, no. 52 (August 1971), 23–55.

Cogswell, Thomas. *The Blessed Revolution: English Politics and the Coming of War, 1621–1624.* Cambridge University Press, 1989.

Collins, Kris. 'Merchants, Moors, and the Politics of Pageantry'. Unpublished MPhil, Oxford University, 1995.

Collinson, Patrick. *The Religion of Protestants.* Oxford University Press, 1982.

Condren, Conal. *The Language of Politics in Seventeenth-Century England.* Basingstoke: Macmillan, 1994.

Coole, Diana H. *Women in Political Theory.* Brighton: Harvester, 1988.

Cotton, Anthony. 'London Newsbooks in the Civil War: Their Political Attitudes and Sources of Information'. Diss. Oxford University, 1971.

Coughlan, Patricia. '"Enter Revenge": Henry Burkhead and Cola's Furie', *Theatre Research International,* 15, no. 1 (1989), 1–17.

Cox, Virginia. *The Renaissance Dialogue.* Cambridge University Press, 1992.

Cressy, David. *Literacy and the Social Order: Reading and Writing in Tudor and Stuart England.* Cambridge University Press, 1980.

Cust, Richard. 'News and Politics in Early Seventeenth-Century England'. *PP*, no. 112 (August 1986) 60–91.

Cust, Richard, and Ann Hughes, eds. *Conflict in Early Stuart England.* Harlow: Longman, 1989.

Danby, J. F. *The Poets on Fortune's Hill.* London: Faber, 1952.

Darnton, Robert. *The Great Cat Massacre.* London: Allen Lane, 1984.

Davis, Natalie Zemon. *Society and Culture in Early Modern France.* Cambridge: Polity Press, 1987.

Davis, J. C. *Fear, Myth and History.* Cambridge University Press, 1986.

Davison, Dennis. *Restoration Comedies.* Oxford University Press, 1970.

Dent, Edward. *Foundations of English Opera.* Cambridge University Press, 1928.

Dollimore, Jonathan. *Radical Tragedy: Religion, Ideology and Power in the Drama of Shakespeare and His Contemporaries.* Brighton: Harvester, 1984.

Dollimore, Jonathan, and Alan Sinfield, eds. *Political Shakespeare: New Essays in Cultural Materialism.* Manchester University Press, 1985.

Douglas, Mary. *Purity and Danger: An Analysis of the Concepts of Pollution and Taboo.* 1966; rpt London: Routledge and Kegan Paul, 1985.

Duke, A. C., and C. Tamse, eds. *Too Mighty to Be Free.* Zutphen: De Walberg, 1987.

Edmond, Mary. *Rare Sir William Davenant.* Manchester University Press, 1987.

Edward, William A., trans. *The Suasoriae of Seneca the Elder.* Cambridge University Press, 1928.

Evans, G. Blakemore. *Elizabethan–Jacobean Drama.* London: A. and C. Black, 1987.

Ezell, Margaret. *The Patriarch's Wife: Literary Evidence and the History of the Family.* Chapel Hill and London: University of North Carolina Press, 1987.

Fink, Zera S. *The Classical Republicans: An Essay in the Recovery of a Pattern of Thought in Seventeenth-Century England.* Evanston: Northwestern University Press, 1945.

Firth, C. H. 'Sir William Davenant and the Revival of Drama During the Protectorate'. *EHR* (April 1903), 103–20.

Fletcher, Anthony. *The Outbreak of the English Civil War.* London: Edward Arnold, 1981.

Reform in the Provinces: The Government of Stuart England. New Haven: Yale University Press, 1986.

Fox, Adam. 'Popular Verses and Their Readership in the Early Seventeenth Century'. In *The Practice and Representation of Reading in England.* Ed. James Raven, Helen Small, Naomi Tadmore. Cambridge University Press, 1995.

Foucault, Michel. *The History of Sexuality.* 4 vols. Trans. Robert Hurley. London: Allen Lane, 1979, vol. 1.

Frank, Joseph. *The Beginnings of the English Newspaper.* Cambridge, Mass.: Harvard University Press, 1961.

Cromwell's Press Agent: A Critical Biography of Marchmont Nedham. Lanham: University Press of America, 1980.

Freud, Sigmund. *The Standard Edition of the Complete Psychological Works.* 23 vols. Ed. James Strachey. London: Hogarth Press, 1953–68.

Gallagher, Catherine. 'Embracing the Absolute: The Politics of the Female Subject in Seventeenth-Century England'. *Genders,* no. 1 (Spring 1988) 24–39.

Gardiner, S. R. *History of the Commonwealth and Protectorate.* 3 vols. London: Longmans, Green, 1894–1901.

Geertz, Clifford. *Local Knowledge.* New York: Basic Books, 1983.

Geertz, Hildred, and Clifford Geertz. *Kinship in Bali.* Chicago and London: Chicago University Press, 1975.

Gilder, Rosamund. 'Enter Ianthe Veil'd'. *Theatre Arts Monthly,* no. 1 (1927), 29–38.

Goldberg, Jonathan. *James I and the Politics of Literature,* Stanford University Press.

Goody, Jack, ed. *Literacy in Traditional Societies.* Cambridge University Press, 1968.

Gossett, Suzanne. '"Man-maid begone!" Women in Masques'. *ELR,* 18, no. 1 (Winter 1988), 96–113.

Gramsci, Antonio. *The Cultural Writings.* Trans. William Boelhower, ed. David Forgacs and Geoffrey Nowell-Smith. London: Lawrence and Wishart, 1985.

Grant, Douglas. *Margaret the First.* London: Rupert Hart-Davies, 1957.

Greg, Walter. '*The Triumph of Peace.* A Bibliographer's Nightmare'. *The Library,* ser. 5, no. 1 (September 1946), 113–26.

Greenblatt, Stephen. *Learning to Curse.* London: Routledge, 1990.
Renaissance Self-Fashioning From More to Shakespeare. Chicago and London: University of Chicago Press, 1980.
Shakespearean Negotiations. University of California Press, 1988.

Greer, Germaine, Susan Hastings, Jeslyn Medoff, Melinda Sansome, eds. *Kissing the Rod: An Anthology of Seventeenth-Century Women's Verse.* London: Virago, 1988.

Guillory, John. 'The Father's House: *Samson Agonistes* in its Historical Moment'. In *Re-membering Milton: New Essays on the Texts and Traditions.* Ed. Mary Nyquist and Margaret W. Ferguson. London: Methuen, 1988.

Habermas, Jürgen. *The Structural Transformation of the Public Sphere.* Trans. Thomas Burger. Cambridge: Polity Press, 1989.

Hall, Stuart. 'Notes on Deconstructing "the Popular"'. In *People's History and Socialist Theory.* Ed. Raphael Samuel. London: Routledge and Kegan Paul, 1981.

Hallberg, Robert Von, ed. *Canons.* Chicago and London: University of Chicago Press, 1984.

Harbage, Alfred. *Cavalier Drama: An Historical and Critical Supplement to the Study of the Elizabethan and Restoration Stage.* Oxford: Modern Language Association and Oxford University Press, 1936.
Thomas Killigrew: Cavalier Dramatist. University of Philadelphia Press, 1930.
Sir William Davenant Poet Venturer 1606–1668. University of Philadelphia Press, 1935.

Harris, Tim. *London Crowds in the Reign of Charles II.* Cambridge University Press, 1987.
'The Problem of "Popular Political Culture" in Seventeenth-Century London'. *History of European Ideas,* 10, no. 1 (1989), 43–58.

Haun, Eugene. *Hark What Harmony*. New York: Columbia University Press, 1961.

Healy, Thomas, and Jonathan Sawday, eds. *Literature and the English Civil War*. Cambridge University Press, 1990.

Heinemann, Margot. *Puritanism and Theatre: Thomas Middleton and Opposition Drama under the Early Stuarts*. Cambridge University Press, 1980.

Helm, Alex. 'In comes I, St George'. *Folklore*, no. 76 (Summer 1965), 18–137.

Hertz, Neil. 'Medusa's Head: Male Hysteria under Political Pressure'. *Representations*, 1, no. 4 (Fall 1983), 27–55.

Hill, Christopher. 'The English Revolution and Patriotism'. In *Patriotism: The Making and Unmaking of British National Identity*. 3 vols. Ed. Raphael Samuel. London: Routledge, 1989, vol I.

God's Englishman: Oliver Cromwell and the English Revolution. Harmondsworth: Penguin, 1972.

The Intellectual Origins of the English Revolution. Oxford: Clarendon Press, 1980.

Milton and the English Revolution. 1977; rpt London: Faber and Faber, 1979.

The World Turned Upside Down. 1972; rpt Harmondsworth: Penguin, 1978.

Hirst, Derek. *Authority and Conflict: England 1603–1658*. London: Edward Arnold, 1986.

'The Lord Protector, 1653–1658'. In *Cromwell and the English Revolution*. Ed. John Morrill. Harlow: Longman, 1990, pp. 119–48.

The Representatives of the People? Voters and Voting in England Under the Early Stuarts. Cambridge University Press, 1975.

Hobby, Elaine. *Virtue of Necessity: English Women's Writing 1649–88*. London: Virago, 1988.

Holstun, James. 'Ranting at the New Historicism'. *ELR*, 19, no. 2 (1989), 189–225.

Hotson, Leslie. *The Commonwealth and Restoration Stage*. 1928; rpt New York: Russell and Russell, 1962.

Hulme, Peter. *Colonial Encounters: Europe and the Native Caribbean, 1492–1797*. London: Methuen, 1986.

Hume, Robert D. *The Development of English Drama in the Later Seventeenth Century*. Oxford: Clarendon Press, 1976.

Hutton, Ronald. *The Restoration: A Political and Religious History of England and Wales 1658–1667*. Oxford University Press, 1985.

Irigaray, Luce. *This Sex Which is Not One*. Trans. Catherine Porter with Carolyn Burke. 1977; rpt New York: Cornell 1985.

Jacob, James R., and Timothy Raylor. 'Opera and Obedience: Thomas Hobbes and "A Proposition for Advancement of Moralitie" by Sir William Davenant'. *The Seventeenth Century*, 6, no. 2 (Autumn 1991), 205–50.

Jacob, James, and Margaret Jacobs, eds. *The Origins of Anglo-American Radicalism*. London: Allen and Unwin, 1984.

Jacquot, Jean. 'Une parodie du *Triumph of Peace*, masque de James Shirley: note sur l'édition par J. Fuzier, de *The Tragedy of the Cruell Warre'*. *Cahiers Elisabethains*, no. 15 (April 1979), 77–80

Jardine, Lisa. *Still Harping on Daughters: Women and Drama in the Age of Shakespeare*. Brighton: Harvester, 1983.

Jones, Ann Rosalind. *The Currency of Eros: Women's Love Lyric in Europe, 1540–1620*. Bloomington and Indianapolis: Indiana University Press, 1990.

'Nets and Bridles: Early Modern Conduct Books and Sixteenth-Century Women's Lyrics'. In *The Ideology of Conduct: Essays in Literature and the History of Sexuality*. Ed. Nancy Armstrong and Leonard Tennenhouse. London: Methuen, 1987, pp. 39–72.

'Surprising Fame: Renaissance Gender Ideologies and Women's Lyric'. In *The Poetics of Gender*. Ed. Nancy K. Miller. New York: Columbia University Press, 1986, pp. 74–96.

Jones, Kathleen. *A Glorious Fame: The Life of Margaret Cavendish Duchess of Newcastle*. London: Bloomsbury, 1988.

José, Nicholas. *Ideas of the Restoration in English Literature, 1660–1700*. London: Macmillan, 1984.

Jouhaud, Christian. 'Printing the Event: From La Rochelle to Paris'. In *The Culture of Print: Power and the Uses of Print in Early Modern Europe*. Ed. Roger Chartier, pp. 290–335.

Kahn, Victoria. *Machiavellian Rhetoric: From the Counter-Reformation to Milton*. New Jersey: Princeton University Press, 1994.

Kantorowicz, Ernst H. *The King's Two Bodies: A Study in Mediaeval Political Theology*. New Jersey: Princeton University Press, 1957.

Kelliher, Hilton. 'A Hitherto Unrecognised Cavalier Dramatist: James Compton, Third Earl of Northampton'. *British Library Journal*, 6, no. 2 (1980), 158–87.

Kelly, Joan. 'The Social Relations of the Sexes'. In *Women, History and Theory*. Chicago and London: University of Chicago Press, 1984.

Knachel, Philip. *England and the Fronde*. New York: Cornell University Press, 1967.

La Capra, Dominick. 'Is Everyone a Mentalité Case? Transference and the "Culture" Concept'. In *History and Criticism*. Ithaca and London: Cornell University Press, 1985.

Lakoff, George, and Mark Johnson. *Metaphors We Live By*. Chicago and London: University of Chicago Press, 1980.

Lakoff, George. *Women, Fire and Dangerous Things: What Categories Reveal About the Mind*. Chicago and London: Chicago University Press, 1987.

Lambert, Sheila. 'The Printers and the Government, 1604–1637'. In *Aspects of Printing From 1600*. Ed. R. Myers and M. Harris. Oxford University Press, 1978, pp. 1–29.

Lancaster, Henry. *A History of French Dramatic Literature in the Seventeenth Century.* 9 vols. Baltimore: Johns Hopkins University Press, 1929–42.

Lang, Timothy. *The Victorians and the Stuart Heritage.* Cambridge University Press, 1995.

Lawrence, W. J. *The Elizabethan Playhouse.* Second series, Stratford-upon-Avon: Shakespeare Head Press, 1913.

Leech, Clifford. 'Private Performances and Amateur Theatricals (Excluding the Academic Stage) From 1580 to 1660. With an Edition of "Raguaillo d'Oceano", 1640'. Diss. University of London, 1935.

Lefkowitz, Murray. *William Lawes.* London: Routledge and Kegan Paul, 1960.

Lerner, Laurence. *Uses of Nostalgia.* London: Chatto and Windus, 1972.

Levine, Laura. 'Men in Women's Clothing: Anti-Theatricality and Effeminization from 1579 to 1642'. *Criticism,* 28, no. 2 (Spring 1986), 121–43.

Levy-Peck, Linda. *Court Patronage and Corruption in Early Stuart England.* London: Routledge, 1990.

Lindley, David, ed. *The Court Masque.* Manchester University Press, 1984.

Loewenburg, Alfred. *Annals of Opera 1597–1940,* 2nd rev. edn. Geneva: Societas Bibliographica, 1955.

Loewenstein, David. '"Casting down imaginations": Milton as Iconoclast'. In *Critical Essays on John Milton.* Ed. Christopher Kendrick. New York: G. K. Hall, 1995.

Love, Harold. 'State Affairs on the Restoration Stage 1660–1675'. *Restoration and Eighteenth-Century Theatre Research,* no. 14 (May 1975), 1–22.

Lytle, Guy Fitch, and Stephen Orgel, eds. *Patronage in the Renaissance.* Princeton University Press, 1981.

McKenzie, Donald F. *The British Book Trade 1641–1714: A Chronology and Calendar of Documents.* London: British Library, 1976.

The London Book Trade in the Later Seventeenth Century. Syndics of Cambridge University Library, 1976.

McLean, Ian. *Women Triumphant: Feminism in French Literature 1610–1652.* Oxford: Clarendon Press, 1977.

McLuskie, Kathleen. 'The Act, the Role, and the Actor: Boy Actresses on the Elizabethan Stage'. *NTQ,* 3, no. 10 (1987), 120–30.

Maguire, Nancy Klein. *Regicide and Restoration.* Cambridge University Press, 1992.

'The "Whole Truth" of Restoration Tragicomedy'. In *Renaissance Tragicomedy.* Ed. Nancy Klein Maguire. London: AMS Press, 1987.

Manning, Brian. *The English People and the English Revolution.* London: Heinemann, 1976.

Marcus, Leah. *The Politics of Mirth.* Chicago and London: University of Chicago Press, 1986.

Marin, Louis. *Portrait of the King.* Minneapolis: University of Minnesota Press, 1988.

Mendelson, Sara Heller. *The Mental World of Stuart Women: Three Studies.* Brighton: Harvester, 1987.

Miller, Lucasta. 'The Shattered Violl: Print and Textuality in the 1640s'. In *Literature and Censorship: Essays and Studies 1993.* Ed. Nigel Smith. Cambridge: D. S. Brewer, 1993.

Montrose, Louis. 'Of Gentlemen and Shepherds: The Politics of Elizabethan Pastoral Form'. *ELH,* 50, no. 3 (Fall 1983), 415–59.

Moretti, Franco. *Signs Taken For Wonders: Essays in the Sociology of Literary Forms.* 1983; rpt London: Verso, 1988.

Morrill, John. *The Revolt of the Provinces: Conservatives and Radicals in the English Civil War.* 1976; rpt London: Longman, 1980.

Morillo, Marvin. 'Shirley's "Preferment" and the Court of Charles I'. *Studies in English Literature 1500–1900,* no. 1 (1960), 101–17.

Morton, A. L. *The World of the Ranters.* London: Lawrence and Wishart, 1970.

Neely, Caroline. 'Constructing the Subject: Feminist Practice and the New Renaissance Discourses'. *ELR,* 18, no. 1 (Winter 1988), 4–22.

Nethercot, A. H. *Sir William Davenant.* University of Chicago Press, 1938.

Norbrook, David. 'Life and Death of Renaissance Man'. *Raritan,* 8, no. 4 (Spring 1989) pp. 89–110.

'Macbeth and the Politics of Historiography'. In *The Politics of Discourse.* Ed. Kevin Sharpe and Stephen Zwicker. Berkeley and Los Angeles: University of California Press, 1987, pp. 78–116.

'The Masque of Truth: Court Entertainments and International Protestant Politics in the Early Stuart Period'. *The Seventeenth Century,* 1, no. 2 (1987), 81–110.

Poetry and Politics in the Renaissance. London: Routledge and Kegan Paul, 1984.

Orgel, Stephen. *The Illusion of Power: Political Theater in the English Renaissance.* Berkeley: University of California Press, 1975.

Ortner, Sherry B. 'Gender and Sexuality in Hierarchical Societies: The Case of Polynesia and Some Comparative Implications'. In *Sexual Meanings: The Cultural Construction of Gender and Sexuality.* Ed. Sherry B. Ortner and Harriet Whitehead. Cambridge University Press, 1981.

Park, Katherine and Lorraine J. Daston. 'Unnatural Conceptions: The Study of Monsters in France and England'. *PP,* no. 92 (1981), 20–54.

Parry, Graham. 'A Troubled Arcadia'. In *Literature and the English Civil War.* Ed. Thomas Healy and Jonathan Sawday. Cambridge University Press, 1990, pp. 38–55.

Patrides, C. A. *Premises and Motifs in Renaissance Thought and Literature.* Princeton University Press, 1982.

Patterson, Annabel. *Censorship and Interpretation: The Conditions of Writing and Reading in Early Modern England.* Berkeley: University of California Press, 1987.

Fables of Power: Aesopian Writings and History. Durham, NC: Duke University Press, 1991.

'Pastoral Versus Georgic'. In *Renaissance Genres.* Ed. Barbara Lewalski. Cambridge, Mass.: Harvard University Press, 1986.

Pastoral and Ideology: Virgil to Valéry. Oxford: Clarendon Press, 1988.

'The Very Name of the Game: Theories of Order and Disorder'. In *Literature and the English Civil War.* Ed. Thomas Healy and Jonathan Sawday. Cambridge University Press, 1990.

Pearl, Valerie. *London and the Outbreak of Puritan Revolution.* Oxford University Press, 1961.

Pearson, Jacqueline. *The Prostituted Muse: Images of Women and Women Dramatists 1642–1737.* Brighton: Harvester, 1988.

Pêcheaux, Michel. *Language, Semantics, Ideology.* Trans. Harbans Nagpal. London: Macmillan, 1982.

Phelps, Wayne H. 'Cosmo Manuche, Royalist Playwright of the Commonwealth'. *English Language Notes,* 16, no. 3 (1979), 207–11.

Phillips, Henry. *The Theatre and its Critics in Seventeenth-Century France.* Oxford University Press, 1981.

Pocock, J. G. A. *The Machiavellian Moment: Florentine Political Thought and the Atlantic Republican Tradition.* Princeton University Press, 1975.

Postlewait, Thomas. 'Periodisation in Theatre History'. *Theatre Journal,* 40, no. 3. (1988), 299–318.

Potter, Lois, ed. *The Revels History of Drama in English.* London: Methuen, 1981.

Secret Rites and Secret Writing. Cambridge University Press, 1989.

'"True Tragicomedies" of the Civil War and Commonwealth'. In *Renaissance Tragicomedy.* Ed. Nancy Maguire. London: AMS Press, 1987, pp. 196–217.

Price, Curtis Alexander. *Henry Purcell and the London Stage.* Cambridge University Press, 1983.

Purcell, Mary Joe. 'Political–Historical Bearings in Original Interregnum Drama 1649–1660'. Diss. University of Missouri, 1959.

Raab, Felix. *The English Face of Machiavelli.* London: Routledge and Kegan Paul, 1964.

Rackin, Phyllis. 'Androgyny, Mimesis, and the Marriage of the Boy Heroine on the English Renaissance Stage'. *PMLA,* no. 102 (1987), 29–41.

Radzinowicz, Mary Ann. *Toward 'Samson Agonistes'.* New Jersey: Princeton University Press, 1978.

Randall, Dale. *Winter Fruit: English Drama 1642–1660.* University Press of Kentucky, 1995.

Raymond, Joad. *Making the News: An Anthology of the Newsbooks of Revolutionary England.* Gloucestershire: Windrush Press, 1993.

Rayner, Alice. *To Act, To Do, To Perform: Drama and the Phenomenology of Action* (Ann Arbor: University of Michigan Press, 1994).

Riley, Denise. *'Am I That Name?': Feminism and the Category of Women in History.* Basingstoke: Macmillan, 1988.

Ristine, F. H. *English Tragicomedy.* New York: Columbia University Press, 1910.

Rollins, Hyder E. 'The Commonwealth Drama: Miscellaneous Notes'. *SP*, no. 20 (1923), 52–69.

' A Contribution to the History of the English Commonwealth Drama'. *SP*, no. 18 (July 1921), 267–333.

'Samuel Sheppard and His Praise of Poets'. *SP*, 24, no. 1 (1927), 509–56.

Rubin, Gayle. 'The Traffic in Women: Notes on the "Political Economy" of Sex'. In *Towards an Anthropology of Women.* Ed. Rayna B. Reiter New York: Monthly Review Press, 1975.

Russell, Conrad. *The Crisis of Parliaments: English History 1509–1660.* 1971; rpt Oxford University Press, 1982.

Said, Edward. *Orientalism.* London: Routledge and Kegan Paul, 1978.

Samuel, Raphael, ed. *People's History and Socialist Theory.* London: Routledge, 1981.

Schochet, Gordon J. *Patriarchalism in Political Thought.* Oxford: Basil Blackwell, 1975.

Seaward, Paul. *The Cavalier Parliament and the Reconstruction of the Old Regime, 1661–1667.* Cambridge University Press, 1989.

Seidel, Michael. 'Crisis Rhetoric and Satiric Power'. *NLH*, 20, no. 1 (Autumn 1988), 165–86.

Sharpe, Kevin. *Criticism and Compliment.* Cambridge University Press, 1987.

The Personal Rule Of Charles I, New Haven and London: Yale University Press, 1992.

Sharpe, Kevin, and Lake, Peter. *Culture and Politics in Early Stuart England.* Basingstoke: Macmillan, 1994.

Shaw, Stanford. *The History of the Ottoman Empire and Modern Turkey.* 2 vols. Cambridge University Press, 1976.

Skerpan, Elizabeth. *The Rhetoric of Politics in the English Revolution 1642–1660.* Columbia: University of Missouri Press, 1992.

Slack, Paul, ed., *Rebellion, Popular Protest and Social Order in Early Modern England.* Cambridge University Press, 1984.

Smith, Nigel. *A Collection of Ranter Writings.* London: Junction Books, 1983.

Literature and Revolution in England 1640–1660. New Haven and London: Yale University Press, 1994.

'Popular Republicanism in the 1650s: John Streater's "heroick Mechanicks"'. In *Milton and Classical Republicanism.* ed. David Armitage *et al.* Cambridge University Press, 1995, pp. 137–55.

'Richard Overton's Marpriest Tracts: Towards a History of Leveller Style'. In *The Literature of Controversy: Polemical Satire From Milton to Junius*. Ed. Thomas Corns. London: Frank Cass, 1987.

Smuts, R. Malcolm. *Court Culture and the Origins of a Royalist Tradition in Early Stuart England*. Philadelphia: University of Pennsylvannia Press, 1987.

'The Political Failure of Stuart Cultural Patronage'. In *Patronage in the Renaissance*. Ed. Guy Fitch Lytle and Stephen Orgel. New Jersey: Princeton University Press, 1981, pp. 165–206.

'The Puritan Followers of Henrietta Maria in the 1630s'. *EHR*, 153, no. 366 (1978), 26–46.

Sommerville, Johann. 'Oliver Cromwell and English Political Thought'. In *Cromwell and the English Revolution*. Ed. John Morrill. Harlow: Longman, 1990, pp. 234–258.

Politics and Ideology in England 1603–1640. Harlow: Longman, 1986.

Southern, Richard. *Changeable Scenery*. London: Faber and Faber, 1952.

Spalding, Ruth. *The Improbable Puritan: A Life of Bulstrode Whitelocke*. London: Faber and Faber, 1975, p. 100.

Spink, Ian. *English Song Dowland to Purcell*. 1974; rpt New York: Taplinger, 1986.

Spufford, Margaret. *Contrasting Communities: English Villages in the Sixteenth and Seventeenth Centuries*. Cambridge University Press, 1974.

Small Books and Pleasant Histories. Cambridge University Press, 1981.

Stallybrass, Peter, and Allon White. *The Politics and Poetics of Transgression*. London: Methuen, 1986.

Stevenson, Allan H. 'James Shirley and the Actors at the First Irish Theatre'. *MP*, 40, no. 2 (1942), 147–60.

'Shirley's Years in Ireland'. *Review of English Studies*, 20 (1944), 19–28.

Stone, Lawrence. *The Causes of the English Revolution 1529–1642*. London: Routledge and Kegan Paul, 1972.

The Crisis of the Aristocracy, 1558–1641. Oxford: Clarendon Press, 1965.

'The Educational Revolution in England 1560–1640'. *PP*, no. 28 (July 1964), 41–80.

The Family, Sex and Marriage. London: Weidenfeld and Nicolson, 1977.

'Literacy and Education in England, 1640–1690'. *PP*, no. 42 (1969), 69–139.

Uncertain Unions and Broken Lives. Oxford University Press, 1995.

Strong, S. Arthur. *A Catalogue of Letters and Other Historical Documents Exhibited in the Library at Welbeck*. London: John Murray, 1903.

Strong, Roy. *Splendour at Court: Renaissance Spectacle and the Theatre of Power*. London: Weidenfeld and Nicolson, 1973.

Summers, Montague. *The Playhouse of Pepys*. London: Kegan Paul, 1935.

Tennenhouse, Leonard. *Power on Display: The Politics of Shakesperean Genres*. New York and London: Methuen, 1986.

Thomas, Keith. 'The Puritans and Adultery: The Act of 1650 re-considered'. In *Puritans and Revolutionaries: Essays in Seventeenth Century History Presented to Christopher Hill.* Ed. Donald H. Pennington and Keith Thomas. Oxford University Press, 1978, pp. 257–82.

Thompson, E. N. S., *The Controversy Between the Puritans and the Stage.* New Haven: Yale University Press, 1899.

Trotter, David. *The Poetry of Abraham Cowley.* London: Macmillan, 1979.

Tuck, Richard. 'Power and Authority in Seventeenth-Century England'. *The Historical Journal,* 17, no. 1 (1974), 43–61.

Turner, Victor *The Anthropology of Performance.* New York: PAJ Publications, 1986.

   Process, Performance and Pilgrimage. New Delhi: Concept, 1979.

Underdown, David. *Revel, Riot and Rebellion: Popular Politics and Culture in England 1603–1660.* Oxford University Press, 1985.

Upadhyay, Lesley Anne. 'Two Political Comedies of the Restoration: An Annotated Old-Spelling Edition, with Critical and Historical Introduction, of John Tatham's *The Rump* and Aphra Behn's Adaptation, *The Roundheads*'. Diss. University of London, 1974.

Varner, John Grier. *El Inca: The Life and Times of Garcilasco de la Vega.* London and Austin: University of Texas Press, 1968.

Veeser, H. Aram, ed. *The New Historicism.* London: Routledge, 1989.

Wallace, John M. 'The Date of John Tatham's *The Distracted State*'. *Bulletin of the New York Public Library,* no. 64 (1970), 29–40.

Walzer, Michael. *The Revolution of the Saints.* London: Weidenfeld and Nicolson, 1966.

Wann, Louis. 'The Oriental in Elizabethan Drama'. *MP,* 12, no. 3 (1914/15), 423–47.

Webber, Joan. *The Eloquent 'I'; Self and Style in Seventeenth-Century Prose.* Madison and London: University of Wisconsin Press, 1968.

White, Eric Walter. *A History of English Opera.* London: John Lehmann, 1951.

Wilkin, Robert N. 'Cicero and the Law of Nature'. In *The Origins of the Natural Law Tradition.* Ed. Arthur L. Harding. Dallas: Southern Methodist University Press, 1954.

Williams, Sheila. 'The Lord Mayor's Show in Tudor and Stuart Times'. *Guildhall Miscellany,* no. 10 (Sept. 1959), n.p.

   'The Lord Mayor's Shows From Peele to Settle'. Diss. University of London, 1957.

Wilson, John Harold. *A Preface to Restoration Drama.* Cambridge, Mass.: Harvard University Press, 1968.

Wiseman, Susan. '"Adam, the Father of all Flesh", Porno-Political Rhetoric and Political Theory in and After the English Civil War'. *Prose Studies,* 14, no. 3 (Dec. 1991), 134–57.

Wolfe, Don M. *Leveller Manifestoes of the Puritan Revolution.* New York: Thomas Nelson, 1944.

'Unsigned Pamphlets of Richard Overton'. *Huntington Library Quarterly*, 21, no. 2 (1958), 167–201.

Woodhead, Christine. 'The Present Terrour of the World? Contemporary Views of the Ottoman Empire c.1600'. *History*, 72, no. 234 (Feb. 1987).

Worden, A. B.. 'Classical Republicanism and the Puritan Revolution'. In *History and Imagination: Essays in Honour of H. R. Trevor-Roper*. Ed. Hugh Lloyd-Jones, Valerie Pearl and Blair Worden. London: Duckworth, 1981.

'Literature and Political Censorship in Early Modern England'. In *Too Mighty to Be Free*. Ed. A. C. Duke and C. Tamse.

Wright, Louis B. 'The Reading of Plays During the Puritan Revolution'. *Huntington Library Bulletin*, no. 6 (Nov. 1934), 73–112.

Wrightson, Keith. *English Society 1580–1680*. London: Hutchinson, 1982.

Zagorin, Perez. *A History of Political Thought in the English Revolution*. London: Routledge and Kegan Paul, 1954.

Zwicker, Stephen. *Lines of Authority*. Ithaca: Cornell University Press, 1993.

Index